Anatomy of a Trial

Second Edition

11/22/19
To Scott
From
Best Wishes
Looking Forward
To Seeing You again Soon

Anatomy of a Trial

A HANDBOOK FOR YOUNG LAWYERS

Second Edition

AMERICAN BAR ASSOCIATION
Section of Litigation

PAUL MARK SANDLER

With commentary from Judges Marvin E. Aspen, Marvin J. Garbis,
Paul W. Grimm, Mark A. Drummond, and W. Michel Pierson

Cover design by Monica Alejo/ABA Publishing.

The materials contained herein represent the opinions of the authors and/or the editors, and should not be construed to be the views or opinions of the law firms or companies with whom such persons are in partnership with, associated with, or employed by, nor of the American Bar Association or the Section of Litigation unless adopted pursuant to the bylaws of the Association.

Nothing contained in this book is to be considered as the rendering of legal advice for specific cases, and readers are responsible for obtaining such advice from their own legal counsel. This book is intended for educational and informational purposes only.

Printed in the United States of America.

18 17 16 15 14 5 4 3 2 1

Library of Congress Cataloging-in-Publication Data
Sandler, Paul Mark, author.
  Anatomy of a trial : a handbook for young lawyers / By Paul Mark Sandler. -- Second edition.
    p. cm.
  Includes index.
  ISBN 978-1-62722-453-6 (alk. paper)
  1. Trial practice--United States. I. Title.
  KF8915.S24 2014
  347.73'75--dc23
                                        2014006826

Discounts are available for books ordered in bulk. Special consideration is given to state bars, CLE programs, and other bar-related organizations. Inquire at Book Publishing, ABA Publishing, American Bar Association, 321 N. Clark Street, Chicago, Illinois 60654-7598.

www.ShopABA.org

Contents

FOREWORD

This is an indispensable volume for every aspiring trial lawyer—and a valuable addition to the library of every experienced practitioner, as well.

Paul Sandler is a highly accomplished, nationally known trial lawyer. Focusing on the records of three of his actual trials—one criminal, two civil (one jury, one nonjury)—he dissects the proceedings, punctuating sophisticated insight and analysis with generous amounts of transcript. The text is enriched by the thoughtful commentary of five distinguished trial judges.

"A trial is more than a matter of presenting a series of individual fact questions in arid fashion to a jury. The jury properly weighs fact questions in the context of a coherent picture of the way the world works."[1] This book teaches how to draw that picture—from opening statement through final argument—and how to do so in the most compelling way.

Every trial lawyer knows that evidence at trial "has force beyond any linear scheme of reasoning, and as its pieces come together a narrative gains momentum, with power not only to support conclusions but to sustain the willingness of jurors to draw the inferences, whatever they may be, necessary to reach an honest verdict."[2] In this volume, Paul thoroughly and cogently discusses the effective organization, preparation and presentation of evidence, both testimonial and tangible.

This book also focuses on a critical feature of virtually every contemporary trial—expert testimony. "'[A] certain patina attaches to an expert's testimony unlike any other witness; this is 'science,' a professional's judgment, the jury may think, and give more credence to the testimony than

---

1. *In re Diet Drugs Prods. Liab. Litig.*, 369 F.3d 293, 314 (3d Cir. 2004).
2. *Old Chief v. United States*, 519 U.S. 172, 187 (1997).

it may deserve.'"³ This book focuses on how to burnish that patina for your witnesses, and peel it away from your opponent's.

A jury trial is a unique experience. "The final period before a large trial, like the trial itself, involves late nights, multiplying tasks and resulting confusions that are hard to imagine for one who has not experienced them."⁴ This book identifies that key ingredients of success in that preparation and, therefore, later in front of the judge and jury.

As Sonny Liston's manager once said of his ward, "Sonny has his good points. It's his bad points that aren't so good." The purpose of this book is to make your points consistently good. It is a tribute to the author and the judicial contributors that it does this in a comprehensive, readable, and practical fashion.

Gregory P. Joseph
President, American College of Trial Lawyers (2010-11)
Chair, ABA Section of Litigation (1997-98)
New York, New York

---

3.   *United States v. Hebshie*, 2010 U.S. Dist. LEXIS 120746 (D. Mass. Nov. 15, 2010) (citation omitted).
4.   *Young v. City of Providence*, 404 F.3d 33, 41 (1st Cir. 2005).

INTRODUCTION

This volume has been designed for young trial lawyers eager to gain an appreciation of how to handle real problems encountered during jury and nonjury trials. Theories about trial advocacy abound and can be read about in numerous books. But as any experienced litigator knows, theory is often complicated, and sometimes compromised, by the realities of an actual trial.

For illustrative purposes, this book considers the key phases of trials, jury and nonjury (voir dire, opening statements, direct and cross-examination, and closing arguments), in light of three particular cases: one criminal jury trial, one civil jury trial, and one civil nonjury trial. The criminal case is *United States v. David Rosen*. The civil jury case is *Mary Jeanne Maffei v. Smedley, M.D., et al.*, and the nonjury civil trial is *Falls Road Community Association, Inc., et al. v. Baltimore County, Maryland, and Oregon, LLC*.

I have chosen to write about these trials in particular because they were vigorously contested by all parties and they offer many valuable lessons for students on opening statements, direct examination and cross-examination, the use of experts, and closing arguments, among other aspects of the trial. In discussing the cases, I will return repeatedly to the subject of rhetoric, which deserves some attention here at the outset.

It is helpful to think of any trial as one extended oral argument with component parts. Considered this way, trials clearly demand knowledge and dexterous application of rhetoric, the art of selecting the most effective means of persuasion. This is not to suggest that skills in direct examination, cross-examination, opening statement, and summation, and a command of rules and procedure, are passé. They most certainly are not, but cultivating the principles of rhetoric, and applying them to the case at hand, is foundational to every stage of trial advocacy. This book instructs and integrates principals of classical rhetoric with the principals of modern trial technique, in hopes of cultivating in the reader the skills required to achieve the highest level of courtroom advocacy.

CLASSIC RHETORICIANS

The following scholars and orators of antiquity are some of many who have influenced my thinking about trial technique. I will often draw upon their works as I tease out lessons from the particular trials at the center of this book.

Aristotle

Appreciation of the art of persuasion begins with Aristotle's *Rhetoric*. Aristotle (384–322 B.C.) identifies three elements of persuasion: the speaker, the argument, and the listener. He asserts that the listener is the most important component. He also identifies three modes of persuasion: ethos, the personal character of the speaker as perceived by the listener; logos, persuasion by logic; and pathos, persuasion by emotion. Aristotle suggests that the "whole affair of rhetoric is the impression to be made upon the audience." Today the capacity to match one's rhetoric to one's audience is enhanced by understanding human nature, as well as understanding the beliefs, attitudes, and emotions of those rendering decisions in our cases.

Demosthenes

A contemporary of Aristotle's, Demosthenes (383–322 B.C.) was the greatest orator of ancient times. His philippics against Philip of Macedon are legendary. Demosthenes assailed Philip of Macedonia's attacks on Athenian liberties, which eventually ended the era of Greek democracy.

The speeches of Demosthenes are robust with rhetorical questions and imaginary dialogues with his listeners. Consider this passage from one of his orations assailing Philip's aggressiveness and urging his countrymen to take up arms:

When, then, Athenians, when will you do your duty?

What must first happen? When there is a need for it.

What then should we consider what is not happening?

For in my opinion the greatest "need" is a sense of shame at the political situation. Or do you want, tell me, to go around and ask each other "Is there any news?"

Could there be anything more newsworthy than a fellow from Macedonia defeating Hellens in war and regulating their affairs? "Is Philip dead?" "No, he's not, but he's ill."

What difference does it make to you? If anything happens to him you will soon create another Philip, if this is how you attend to your business.[1]

With provocative questions and replies, Demosthenes' speech dramatizes debate about the current political situation and challenges the complacency of his fellow Athenians. Demosthenes blends logic and reasoning by employing many valuable stylistic devices. He was most effective when using simple words in short sentences:

Guard this: cleave to it; if you preserve this, you will never

Suffer any dreadful experience. What are you seeking?

Freedom. Do you not see that even Phillip's titles are

most alien to this? For every King and every tyrant is an

Enemy of freedom and a foe of the rule of law.[2]

---

1. 1. Philippic 1, quoted in R.P. Milns, *The Public Speeches of Demosthenes, in* DEMOSTHENES: STATESMEN AND ORATOR 212 (Ian Worthington ed., 2000); *See also* Paul Mark Sandler, JoAnne Epps, & Ronald Waicukauski, *Classical Rhetoric and the Modern Trial Lawyer*, LITIG. MAG. 16 (Winter 2010).
   2. *Id.*

Cicero

If we turn to the great advocates of ancient Rome, the name Cicero (106–43 B.C.) immediately comes to mind. He gave great attention to the arrangement of his speeches. Whereas others suggested that all arguments should have a beginning, a middle, and an end, Cicero favored a six-part structure: exordium (introduction), narration (presentation of the facts), confirmation (the argument), refutation (rebuttal), and peroration (closing argument).

In his work *In Re Inventione*, Cicero presents his ideas on preparation of the argument. He divides the argument into five parts:

1. Invention: the discovery of proper ways to present the case. This point underscores the importance of developing a theme or theory of the case early on.

2. Disposition: the arrangement of the argument. Here again we are reminded of the importance of carefully ordering how we present witnesses, ask questions, and structure openings and closings. In considering arrangement, Cicero recommends placing the strongest points first, following them with weaker arguments, and concluding with strong arguments. It is Cicero, then, who first articulates the essential doctrines of primacy and recency: we remember best that which we hear first and last.

3. Elocution: proper diction. Here Cicero calls attention to style, the form in which we express ideas.

4. Memory: Cicero never read from notes, but rather he devoted hours to preparation to ensure that he was well prepared. He then could be spontaneous in presenting the case.

5. Delivery: for Cicero, delivery involved gestures and movements in presenting the case. He would work through all five steps before presenting an argument.

Quintilian

No review of classical rhetoric would be complete without mentioning Quintilian (35–95 A.D.). His best-known work is his *Institutio Oratoria*. The work contributes ideas on the education of the advocate. Quintilian's conception of the education of the advocate is based on his belief that an advocate should be a "good man." He writes that, "ethos in all its forms requires the speaker to be a [person] of good character and courtesy."[3]

Like Aristotle and Cicero, Quintilian emphasized the importance of knowing the audience, the temperament of the judge, and the proper use of logic and emotion. He advised that assertions should be supported by facts or law, but also underscored the value of "charm"; he appreciated the importance of a well-timed smile, humor, and a courteous manner. He also urged beginning arguments with a concise statement crafted to draw in the listener. Here are some exemplary bold beginnings from Quintilian's advocacy: "The mother-in-law wedded her son-in-law: there were no witnesses, none to sanction the union and the omens were dark and sinister." Another: "Milo's slaves did what everyone would have wished their slaves to do under similar circumstances."[4] Quintilian's point about the first line is extremely important. Do not allow yourself to waste the first minutes of an opening statement with platitudes. Rather, dive into the heart of your case.

Regarding witness examination, Quintilian wrote that the advocate should put the witness through his or her paces thoroughly in private before the witness appears in court. What better way to heed Quintilian's advice then by conducting a mock trial either formally with a facilitator, or informally in the law office or a conference room? Consider Quintilian's reference to Cicero's view of advocacy:

[A]s soon as we have acquired the smoothness of structure and rhythm . . . we must proceed to lend brilliance to our style by frequent embellishments both of thought and words . . . with a view to making

---

3. QUINTILIAN, INSTITUTIO ORATORIA VI.2.18 (H.E. Butler trans., Harvard 1922).
4. QUINTILIAN, INSTITUTIO ORATORIA IV.2.121.

our audience regard the . . . [case] which we amplify as being as important as speech can make it.[5]

12 ESSENTIAL STEPS TO PERSUASIVE ARGUMENT

A close study of the above rhetoricians will reveal 12 essential steps toward persuasive argument:

1. Establish and focus on a goal.
2. Tailor your argument to the decision-maker.
3. Cultivate ethos.
4. Base your argument on reason.
5. Build the case with evidence, law, and policy.
6. Appeal to emotion.
7. Use the best medium for the message.
8. Strategically arrange your argument.
9. Argue with style.
10. Use strong delivery to enhance communication.
11. Concentrate on engaging the listener.
12. Understand the proper use of refutation and rebuttal.[6]

It is helpful to present an overview of these principals before examining them in the context of the three trials we will be discussing in the following chapters.

1. Establish and Focus on a Goal

Before preparing your case, it is essential that you establish precisely what you hope to achieve. Once the goal is established, develop a theme.

As you articulate the theme during trial you should focus on evidence and argument that develops or defends the theme. Do not fall victim to the distraction of extraneous facts, no matter how interesting they may be.

---

5. *Id.*
6. *See* RONALD WAICUKAUSKI, PAUL MARK SANDLER & JOANNE EPPS, THE 12 SECRETS OF PERSUASIVE ARGUMENT (ABA 2009).

2. Tailor Your Argument to the Decision-Maker

In any trial, the most important people in the room are those who will decide the outcome of the case—the jurors or the judge. It is essential that you understand these decision-makers as well as you possibly can. Adopt a receiver-centered approach. Mold your theme and presentation to conform to the intellectual and emotional mindset of the listeners. To accomplish this, you must be familiar, to the extent possible, with the way the listeners make decisions. Appreciating attitudes, predispositions, beliefs, and the fundamental building blocks of how a person forms judgments are all crucial aspects of advocacy.

For example, the belief that most people develop opinions based on first impressions might influence you to present the theme of your case during the first few minutes of your opening statement, taking advantage of the doctrine of primacy. Or if you know that a particular juror may have had unfortunate experiences with law enforcement officers, and if one of your witnesses is a police detective, you may want to humanize the detective in an attempt to overcome the juror's likely bias.

3. Cultivate Ethos

Ethos, the listener's impression of the speaker's character, is one of the most influential factors in argument. The higher the regard the judge or jury has for you, the more effective you can be. Demonstrating your integrity, knowledge of the issues, and goodwill enhances your ethos.

4. Base Your Argument on Reason

Distinguish between inductive and deductive arguments. In deductive arguments you focus on the premise and draw conclusions from that premise. For example, consider a syllogism, the major premise being that all cases alleging negligence must be filed within three years from the date of the negligence. The defendant argues that since the plaintiff filed suit five years after the date of the incident, a logical deductive conclusion is that the case is time barred.

Inductive argument focuses on inference; for example, if an EKG demonstrates serious cardiac issues, you may infer that the patient experienced chest pains.

A grasp of logic not only helps develop impenetrable arguments, but also allows you to identify weaknesses in the opposing case. An understanding of logic and logical fallacies is indispensible at trial.

5. Build the Case with Evidence, Law, and Policy

Notwithstanding the techniques of rhetoric, there is no substitute for substance. Develop fully the facts and law of your case. Also think about public policy considerations as you advance your theme. You may be able to persuade the court to invoke public policy to support a decision where the facts are not in your favor. For example, you are defending a case of fraud and infliction of emotional distress in a family law case. While the facts may be egregious, you might argue that as a matter of public policy the courts should not recognize these claims.

6. Appeal to Emotion

Emotion persuades. Appreciating the power of emotion is an important aspect of persuasion. Your case is an argument, but it is also a story, a narrative with emotional appeal. Take pains to humanize your client, even if it's a multinational corporation. No matter how technical the matter at hand, creating an emotional connection between you and the jury or judge can make the difference in your client's favor.

7. Use the Best Medium for the Message

Consider utilizing a variety of methods to communicate with the judge and jury. Demonstrative aids such as PowerPoint, video depositions, and diagrams can help you tell your story in a more memorable and effective fashion. As the saying goes, "Seeing is believing."

8. Strategically Arrange Your Argument

Whether it's the opening statement, direct examination, or cross-examination, your presentation must have an organizational structure that develops the theme and resonates with the listener.

When considering arrangement, appreciate primacy and recency: listeners generally remember best what they hear first and last.

9. Argue with Style

Style is the form into which we put the content of our ideas. When thinking of style, consider the application of metaphors, similes, and extended analogies. Also, consider schemes—unusual changes in word order for dramatic emphasis.

An example of a scheme is repeating a word or phrase at the beginning of a sentence several times in a row: "This is the case of the careless landlord. He was careless because he failed to fix the screen door on the porch. He was careless because he could not care about the small children who lived in the apartment. And he was careless because he failed to take remedial measures to repair the door after the accident."

Such dramatic flourishes can help you meet the challenge every courtroom advocate faces: captivating the decision-maker's attention at all times.

10. Use Strong Delivery to Enhance Communication

Delivery consists of your nonverbal communication. Consider facial expressions, eye contact, and how you use space in the courtroom.

Bear in mind that if you are permitted to approach the jury in argument, refrain from going too close, or jury members could feel that you are invading their space. Use gestures tactfully, and do not appear to be distancing yourself from your client.

11. Concentrate on Engaging the Listener

If you can involve the judge or jury in your quest for a just outcome, and if you can instill a sense of importance in the matter, you have an engaged listener. There are numerous ways to succeed in this regard. Consider elevating your particular case to one of universal importance. For example: "This case is not only about this young boy's breaking his leg on the escalator; it's also about the responsibility of corporate America to adhere to basic principles of safety."

12. Understand the Proper Use of Refutation and Rebuttal

The concept of immunization involves taking the wind out of the sails of the opposing case by explaining to the listener the weakness of your position early on and then dealing with that weakness as best you can. This technique prepares the listener for the opposing view and immediately presents your view to dispel any concern. For example: "The defense will argue that the failure to disclose the documents was a simple oversight. If so, why did the defendant not disclose the documents the following day, when he reviewed them to place in his filing cabinet?"

In the coming chapters, we will devote more time to these fundamental techniques, elaborate on their meaning, and explore their relationship with standard trial practice methodology.

The Cases

My aim is to illustrate the practical application of these 12 steps in examining the strategies and techniques employed in the three trials that gave rise to this volume.

I chose the *Rosen* case in part because of the subjects it involved—campaign finance, national politics, and Hollywood fundraising, among others—but primarily because the trial was rigorous and challenging. I selected the *Maffei* case because it illustrates the reality that most trials hinge on the credibility of witnesses, and because it showcases the critical importance of experts in trials of a technical nature. Both cases illustrate that, although criminal and civil cases have differences, employing the well-developed principles of rhetoric is fundamental to success at trial, no matter the nature of the litigation. Nonjury trials present their own challenges, and so I have included discussion of a dispute between a premiere Maryland restaurant and a neighborhood association.

I offer below a synopsis of each case. You will find this information useful as you read through the chapters that follow.

Background on the Cases
United States v. David Rosen

The criminal case discussed in this book was resolved in a jury trial presided over by Judge A. Howard Matz in the U.S. District Court for the Central District of California in May 2005. The government had indicted David Rosen for allegedly causing a false report to be filed with the Federal Election Commission (FEC) on behalf of a joint fundraising committee that included the national Democratic Senatorial Campaign Committee and the campaign committee for Hillary Rodham Clinton's 2000 campaign for the U.S. Senate. Rosen pleaded not guilty, and the jury acquitted him. I served as trial counsel for the defendant with the able assistance of Joseph E. Sandler of Sandler, Reiff & Young of Washington, D.C., and Michael Doyen of Munger, Tolles & Olsen in Los Angeles.

The case arose out of a lavish fundraising event billed as "A Tribute to William Jefferson Clinton." It involved a dinner and concert that included performances by Cher and Diana Ross, among others. A parade of celebrities attended, contributing tens of thousands of dollars to a joint fundraising committee established in part to support Hillary Clinton's bid for the U.S. Senate. The ensuing indictment focused on the role a young fundraiser played in organizing the event and whether he caused false reports about its costs to be filed with the FEC. David Rosen, the defendant, was the Clinton campaign staff person who, at the age of 33, went to Los Angeles to coordinate and oversee the gala on behalf of the joint fundraising committee. The entire event was put together in a few weeks.

The responsibility for raising money for Hillary Clinton's campaign fell to David Rosen, and the case centered around his fight against the injustice of being wrongfully accused of something he never did. Rosen was a victim of other people's motives, and never knew the cost of the production and concert expenses for this Hollywood gala. The costs for the event were hidden from him by two individuals, who participated with Stan Lee Media in underwriting and paying for the costs of this event, and they had their own agenda.

The gala was paid for in part by the joint fundraising committee, but most of the costs were underwritten by a startup Internet company, Stan Lee Media, that had been set up to distribute online versions of the works of Stan Lee, the creator of the Spider-Man comic book character. The company had been founded and was being run by Peter Paul, who, unbeknownst to the Clinton campaign, had been convicted years earlier on drug charges. The event was put together by a Hollywood promoter, Aaron Tonken. Tonken had made a name for himself by attracting celebrities to charitable fundraising events and had recently become involved in political fundraising.

The violation of law alleged by the government was based on highly complex and arcane rules established by the FEC. Under those rules, the joint committee could legally allow the company, Stan Lee Media, to pay for an unlimited amount of the costs of the event, but whatever amount was paid had to be reported, by the joint committee on its public disclosure reports to the FEC, as an in-kind contribution. Such an in-kind contribution also had to be accounted for by the joint committee in a complicated way that involved transferring funds from the account from which the Clinton campaign would obtain its share of the event's proceeds.

After the event, the joint committee reported about $600,000 in costs for the fundraising dinner and concert—about $350,000 was paid by Stan Lee Media, constituting an in-kind contribution to the joint committee, and about $250,000 was paid by the joint committee. In the meantime, the campaign discovered Paul's nefarious past. In the ensuing months, Paul was indicted for securities fraud in connection with his founding and operation of Stan Lee Media; he fled to Brazil, where he remained a fugitive for more than two years. Tonken, meanwhile, was charged by federal and state authorities in an unrelated matter with fraudulently pocketing the proceeds of charitable events and using proceeds from one event to cover the costs of another.

While he was a fugitive, Paul filed a civil lawsuit in California alleging that the true costs of the event paid by him and Stan Lee Media were close to $2 million, and that the joint committee and Clinton campaign had concealed those costs in their reports to the FEC. In the lawsuit he claimed that he had a secret deal with Bill Clinton, by which Bill Clinton would later come to work for Stan Lee Media (this never happened). Paul also claimed publicly that he had evidence that could incriminate Hillary Clinton in connection with the event. By 2003, Paul had been extradited and was in jail in the United States, talking to the U.S. Department of Justice.

Amid all this, it was an obscure staffer who eventually came under fire from federal prosecutors for "A Tribute to William Jefferson Clinton." David Rosen was indicted at the end of 2003 on four counts of aiding and abetting the making of false statements to the U.S. government, in violation of 18 U.S.C. § 1001. The government's theory was that Rosen knew that the costs had been underreported and deliberately caused the compliance officer for the joint committee to file the understated, incorrect costs with the FEC. The indictment was placed under seal for more than a year for reasons that remain in dispute: It seems likely that the government wanted to wait out the 2004 elections, but the government claimed that unsealing the indictment earlier would have forced it to reveal evidence in an unrelated investigation involving one of its witnesses. The indictment was unsealed in January 2005, and the trial took place in May 2005.

The trial was a colorful one, in large part because of the celebrities involved and the attention they attracted. Harold Ickes, a former deputy chief of staff in the Clinton White House, testified on behalf of Rosen, as did Stan Lee. Other Hollywood denizens, such as Gary Smith, a producer of the Emmy awards, testified, and Rosen took the witness stand in his own defense. Neither side called Paul or Tonken, and the admissibility of their criminal backgrounds was a hotly contested issue throughout.

The government's witnesses included Ray Reggie from New Orleans, the brother-in-law of Sen. Edward M. Kennedy (D-Mass.). Reggie had been charged with serious bank fraud in an unrelated case and, as part of his "cooperation" with the government required by his own plea agreement, Reggie secretly "wore a wire" during a dinner meeting with Rosen. Although Rosen said nothing at all helpful to the government even while he was being secretly taped, Reggie testified that on another, separate occasion Rosen had admitted to him that he intentionally underreported the costs of the gala. Difficult and interesting evidentiary issues were raised by the question of whether and how the existence and substance of the taped conversation could be revealed to the jury.

James Levin, a friend of Rosen's from Chicago, who had also been involved in fundraising for the Clinton campaigns and the Democratic Party, also testified. He, too, had pleaded guilty to serious federal felony charges, of defrauding the government in contracting matters, among other things, and was "cooperating" as part of his plea agreement. Like Reggie, he claimed Rosen had admitted underreporting the costs.

Another key witness for the prosecution was a Beverly Hills event planner named Bretta Nock. She had been employed by Tonken to help put together the event. She was the actual author of the spreadsheets from which the reported cost figures had been derived, and she claimed that Rosen had told her to enter understated figures.

Rosen explained at trial that Peter Paul, Aaron Tonken, and Bretta Nock, who were the ones who knew the true costs because they had actually incurred those costs, were also the ones who had provided the cost information to him. The defense argued that Rosen himself did not know the true costs and that Paul and Tonken purposely concealed them for their own reasons.

> In a sense, every trial presents variations of an essential problem: creating a convincing theme.

In demonstrating the defendant's innocence, counsel faced one key challenge at trial: How could the byzantine complexities of campaign finance law, the joint committee and Senate campaign's structure, and the twists and turns in the gala planning be boiled down to a convincing, defensible theme, one that would appeal to the jury's emotions and lead the jurors to acquit the defendant?

Mary Jeanne Maffei v. Angela Smedley, M.D., et al.

The civil case arose out of the death of Richard Maffei. Early on the morning of March 8, 2006, Mrs. Maffei drove her husband to the hospital emergency room. There he complained of closing of his throat, chest pain, and back pain.

The emergency room doctor diagnosed his condition as an ear infection, sore throat, and allergic reaction. She prescribed steroids and an antibiotic, advising that it would take some time for the medicine to take effect. He was discharged at 7:00 a.m.

He and his wife returned home. During the day, Mr. Maffei continued to feel worse. He succumbed at 11:00 p.m. from a dissection, or tear, of his aorta vessel to the heart. This dissection caused the aorta to burst. Blood poured into the pericardium, the sac around the heart, smothering the heart and preventing it from beating. This condition is known as cardiac tamponade, the official cause of his death.

In despair, Mrs. Maffei filed a wrongful death and survivorship case alleging medical malpractice against the hospital and the emergency room doctor. She maintained that the dissection was occurring while her husband was at the hospital. The failure of the doctor to detect the dissection was negligent. She claimed further that had the dissection been detected, her husband would have been able to undergo emergency corrective surgery. Then he would have survived to regain an active life and his work as a heavy crane operator.

The case went to trial in the Circuit Court for Baltimore County, Maryland, and was presided over by Judge Robert Cahill, Jr. The case against the hospital was settled, but the jury decided the case in favor of the doctor. I served as trial counsel for Mrs. Maffei with the fine assistance of my partner Eric Harlan of Shapiro Sher Guinot & Sandler.

The plaintiff's theory of the case against the doctor was that Mr. Maffei complained to the nurses and to the doctor that he was experiencing chest pain, which should have prompted the doctor to take a chest x-ray. This x-ray would have revealed a widening of the mediastinum, the cavity between the lungs. The abnormal x-ray would then have required a CAT scan. The CAT scan would have shown the dissection and immediate surgery would have saved Mr. Maffei's life.

The physician, however, denied negligence. She claimed that Mr. Maffei did not present symptoms of a dissected aorta. He did not complain to her about chest pain, as her notes in the medical records so reflect, but about pain in his throat and ear. The doctor further contended that the dissection was not occurring while Mr. Maffei was in the emergency room, and if it were, it was too minimal to reflect an abnormal x-ray. It was even more speculative, contended the doctor, that Mr. Maffei would have survived surgery.

The witnesses called by the plaintiff included Mrs. Mary Jeanne Maffei and Dr. Neal Shadoff, a well-known cardiologist. The defense witnesses included the defendant, Dr. Angela Smedley, and Dr. David L. Shank, a full-time emergency room doctor. Each of the witnesses testified in almost direct contradiction to the other side. Each was poised and earnest.

At the conclusion of the trial, the jury rendered a defense verdict. Mrs. Maffei was gratified that she had settled with the hospital and that she did her best for the memory of her husband.

Falls Road Community Association, Inc., et al. v. Baltimore
County, Maryland, and Oregon, LLC
Falls Road Community Association (FRCA) sued Baltimore County, Maryland (BCM), and Oregon, LLC (Oregon), its tenant on a historic site in rural Baltimore County. Oregon owns The Oregon Grille, a premiere, four-star restaurant located in a 19th-century farmhouse in Maryland's picturesque horse country, just north of Baltimore. The case was heard by Honorable Susan Souder in a three-day, nonjury trial in the Circuit Court of Baltimore County. The court ruled for the defendants.

Oregon has operated its restaurant since the mid-1990s on a parcel of land leased from the county's Department of Recreation and Parks. The parcel is approximately 2.6 acres and is part of a larger 420-acre lot owned by BCM. When BCM announced plans to lease the historic site to the restaurant, the FRCA complained and opposed the plan. The Board of Appeals of BCM considered formal objections by FRCA, and imposed certain restrictions on Oregon's use of the property. One of these restrictions was that the parking lot "shall consist of a non-paved surface such as stone or similar permeable surface unless otherwise required by law." The Board of Appeals also ordered that the restaurant could have 94 parking spaces, and limited the use of outdoor events including a prohibition of outdoor dining under canopies.

In the spring of 2006 the county received complaints from patrons of the restaurant about unsafe conditions in Oregon's parking lot. BCM investigated, and concluded that the parking lot required repaving to comply with The Americans with Disabilities Act. BCM then required its tenant to repave the lot at its expense. Oregon complied, but the repaved lot was not permeable. It was impermeable.

In its lawsuit FRCA sought mandamus against BCM and declaratory judgment against Oregon and BCM. FRCA alleged that BCM and Oregon violated zoning orders, regulations, and Orders of the Board of Appeals by changing the character of the parking lot from permeable to impermeable, enlarging the area for patron parking, and conducting outdoor dining under large canopies.

FRCA's goal was to require Oregon to remove the paving of the parking lot, and restore it to its permeable state, allowing for the particular drainage of water that historically was characteristic of the original parking lot. In its defense, Oregon claimed that BCM had ordered it to repave the lot at Oregon's expense for safety reasons, as the deteriorating condition of the lot had posed a hazard to restaurant guests. If the lot were to be repaved, Oregon argued, the BCM should be responsible. Regarding the enlarged parking area, Oregon argued that it did not violate existing zoning regulations, and that the outdoor dining was under tents and not large canopies, the former being permitted under the zoning regulations applying to the restaurant.

To help establish its case, FRCA called representatives of BCM familiar with the zoning relating to the restaurant, and with the various hearings over the years from which the orders had been issued governing the restaurant's land-use rights. Counsel for FRCA elicited testimony proving that the parking lot had been repaved and was now impermeable. One such witness was the director of the Parks Department, which serves as Oregon's landlord. On cross-examination by defense counsel, the director acknowledged that he had written a letter to the restaurant's owner on June 8, 2006, demanding that the tenant repave the lot in compliance with current safety standards.

The court ruled that the plaintiffs had met their burden of proof to show that the paving of the lot and number of parking spaces did, in fact, violate prior Board of Appeals orders, dated February 8, 1995, and July 2, 2004. But the court denied granting a declaratory judgment. The court based its decision on the law applying to declaratory judgment in Maryland, which stipulates that if declaratory judgment would not resolve a dispute between parties, declaratory relief should not be granted. In this case, the court found, declaratory judgment would not end the dispute. Given that BCM could not be subject to mandamus, that Oregon was not responsible for the lot's present condition (BCM was), and that the court was not going to order Oregon to repave the lot, a ruling in favor of the plaintiffs would do nothing to resolve the conflict. Thus, the court ruled in favor of the defendants. The plaintiffs appealed to the Court of Special Appeals of Maryland, and after oral argument, the appellate court affirmed the lower court's decision the basis of the opinion was on Oregon's original argument at trial that Plaintiffs did not exhaust administrative remedies. FRCA obtained a writ of certiorari from the Maryland Court of Appeals. The case is pending.[7]

VIEWS FROM THE BENCH

The renowned appellate lawyer John W. Davis once remarked that if fish could talk, who would ask an angler how to catch a fish? He added that since judges can talk, why ask a lawyer how to persuade?

This book is enhanced by the contributions of five judges, who were generous enough to offer their thoughts on opening statements, direct examinations and cross-examinations, closing arguments, and what judges want from trial lawyers. These writings, interspersed throughout the book, provide a rare view from the bench of the most common challenges trial attorneys face when they enter a courtroom. I sincerely thank Judges Marvin E. Aspen, Marvin J. Garbis, Paul W. Grimm, Mark A. Drummond, and W. Michel Pierson for their commentaries.

---

7. The Court of Appeals of Maryland in its review of the *Oregon* case "largely affirmed" the judgement, but remanded the case to the trial court to consider a surviving aspect of the case.

CHAPTER 1

VOIR DIRE

Voir dire is the process of selecting a jury. The term has its origin in the oath taken by jurors to speak the truth. The word *voir* is said to derive from the Latin word *verum*, meaning truth.

Many years ago a trial lawyer was known for stating confidently in open court during jury selection, "Your Honor, I have no need to strike any of these good people seated in the jury box today. They all are very satisfactory to the defense."

This same lawyer could not understand why he lost so many cases. Little did he know that he was skating on the edge of a cup. He lacked appreciation for the importance of jurors' predispositions, beliefs, and values. As a result, he viewed voir dire as an insignificant prologue to the trial. In fact, voir dire often predetermines a trial's outcome. Many cases are lost because the wrong juror was selected. You should try to prevent this from occurring by asking the proper voir dire questions to expose and eliminate those people with a bias that even the best argument will not overcome.

All of us possess predispositions to think and behave in a particular way. These attitudes are based largely on prior experiences, and they can play a major role in jurors' deliberations. A man who has been the subject of an overbearing search and seizure by the FBI might well harbor a grudge against FBI agents, for instance. Such a juror could understandably be predisposed to reject an argument that relies on an agent's testimony.

There are three main questions to ask about an attitude or predisposition encountered in a juror. First, is the attitude favorable, unfavorable, or neutral? Second, how intense is the attitude? Last, how important is the attitude to the person? The lower the importance, the more willing the person will be to change his or her views.

Like attitudes, beliefs also possess the dimensions of direction (ranging from complete belief to complete disbelief), intensity (the certainty with which the belief is held, from very certain to very uncertain), and importance.[1] Beliefs that are fundamental to our worldview can be called values. Values of truth, fairness, and family provide a foundation upon which many decisions are based. Core values also prove critical in the reception of arguments.

The human mind often acts like a filter, accepting those ideas that are consistent with preexisting attitudes and beliefs but rejecting those that are divergent. In the *Rosen* case, counsel on both sides had to consider how the potential jurors' political sensibilities would filter out certain arguments. A staunch Democrat sitting on the jury, for instance, might be expected to begin the case with a favorable view of the defendant, an aide to Hillary Clinton. This juror might also be receptive to the suggestion that the indictment against Rosen by a Republican-led Department of Justice had been politically motivated. On the other hand, a juror who did not hold positive views of Clinton might reject this idea.

In the *Maffei* case, counsel on both sides had to consider potential jurors' preexisting attitudes and beliefs about health care providers and how prior experiences would influence their view of the case, if at all. Certainly, the defense had to be concerned about jury sympathy, while the plaintiff had to be concerned about how a potential juror's respect for the medical community might cause the juror to filter out facts and arguments of the plaintiff.

In short, we tend to pay closer attention to and have better recall of messages that are consistent with our preexisting attitudes and beliefs. As a result, preexisting values tend to be reinforced over time, and they become harder to change. That's why voir dire is so crucial. We need to know the attitudes, beliefs, and values of the jurors. We need to know their likes and dislikes, to the extent relevant. The more we learn about them, the more effectively we can tailor our themes and arguments to suit the audience.

---

1. *See* RONALD WAICUKAUSKI, PAUL MARK SANDLER & JOANNE EPPS, THE 12 SECRETS OF PERSUASIVE ARGUMENT (ABA 2009).

Unfortunately, in most cases, what we can learn about jurors is very limited. The process allows for only superficial knowledge. Typically, the judge will call for the jury commissioner to send potential jurors to the courtroom. Depending on the nature and length of the case, the number of potential jurors varies. When a jury pool is seated, the clerk of the court will hand counsel a list of jurors present. The judge will then call the roll, and counsel will turn their chairs to face the jury pool, preparing to become as familiar as possible with the potential jurors. The roster will have brief facts about each individual, including occupation, education, and occupation of spouse. The judge then introduces the case and counsel and proceeds to read the voir dire questions that the attorneys have proposed (usually in advance through pretrial written submissions). A common question, which is closed-ended question, would be: "Is there any member of the jury panel who has knowledge of any facts relating to this case?" If jurors raise their hands, the judge might ask in open court the source of their knowledge or the judge might ask counsel and the juror to approach the bench for a private discussion. The judge will likely inquire about the potential juror's knowledge; whether he or she was influenced by the media; and whether the potential juror believes that he or she can keep an open mind if selected to serve. As this bench conference continues, some judges will then ask the attorneys whether they have other questions of their own. In some jurisdictions judges might ask open-ended questions. For example, "How do you feel about testimony of law enforcement officers as opposed to testimony by other witnesses who are not law enforcement officers? For example, do you think a law enforcement officer is more likely, less likely, or as likely to tell the truth as a witness who is not in law enforcement? What makes you feel the way you do about this?" Some jurisdictions have developed model voir dire questions to help counsel and the court recognize what is acceptable. At the end of this chapter are model questions used in New Jersey.

A lawyer who believes that a juror should be stricken for cause can so request during voir dire. Bear in mind that requests to strike for cause are unlimited in number. In contrast, so-called peremptory strikes are limited

We tend to pay closer attention to and have better recall of those messages that are consistent with our pre-existing attitudes and beliefs. As a result, pre-existing values tend to be reinforced over time and become harder to change. That's why *voir dire* is so crucial. We need to know the attitudes, beliefs, and values of the jurors.

by rules and in some instances by court discretion. Peremptory strikes may be used by counsel to strike any juror for almost any reason—for example, the potential juror is an accountant, or was a plaintiff in a prior lawsuit. Though one's latitude is wide here, it is unconstitutional to strike a juror on the basis of race, religion, or creed. These prohibited strikes are known as *Batson* strikes. If your opponent believes you have crossed the line in this regard, he or she may issue a *Batson* challenge, and the court will resolve the issue.

After asking the voir dire questions, the judge may or may not have a few additional questions of his or her own. Then the judge will call the jurors by number to stand and take a seat in the jury box. At this point, using no more than the allotted number of peremptory strikes, counsel can request that certain jurors be excused. The jury is then sworn, and the opening statements begin.

The problem with this procedure is that counsel has little information on which to base decisions about whom to strike. Jury selection becomes an exercise in "unpicking" jurors. You come into the courtroom with a rough understanding of both the ideal juror and the worst juror for your case. Then, based on little information, you do your best to recognize and discard the "bad apples."

Many lawyers have campaigned for a broader voir dire that would afford them more opportunity to question jurors individually. There has been little enthusiasm from the judiciary for such proposals. Arguments against an expanded voir dire range from the efficiency of judicial administration to the need to protect jurors from penetrating questions that violate their privacy, to the concern that lawyers would unfairly use the process to begin persuading jurors before evidence has been presented. Nevertheless numerous jurisdictions do permit individual voir dire. Under this procedure counsel ask questions to a group of prospective jurors or to the entire assembly of proposed jurors. In some of these jurisdictions the judge is not even present. It is essential that you ascertain the method used for voir dire in the court where you are presenting your case.

JURY QUESTIONNAIRE

Not all judges take a restrictive view of voir dire, however. Often in a cause *celebre*, a protracted process is permitted. Such was the case in *U.S. v. Rosen*. Judge Matz conducted a more elaborate voir dire than is typical. Counsel had proposed, and the court permitted, that the lawyers present a written jury questionnaire. Each juror was provided with the questionnaire and afforded ample time to complete it.

The questionnaire is confidential by order of the court and cannot be discussed. However, typical questions on a jury questionnaire explore the background of jurors, sometimes directly and sometimes indirectly. An indirect approach would be to ask jurors what newspapers they read and what television stations they watch; this information can indicate a great deal about a person's attitudes and beliefs. It can also be helpful to ask jurors whether they will give the presumption of innocence to a defendant as instructed by the judge, or whether they believe an individual who has been indicted is guilty simply because he or she has been indicted. The judge typically asks this question, but a juror answering it in writing may reveal much more than when answering orally in the courtroom. Not all judges will allow jury questionnaires in every case, but you should ask whether opposing counsel would support your request for a questionnaire, and then propose it to the court.

Regardless of whether you participate in individual voir dire or the judge asks the questions based on your written suggestions, consider asking questions that are indirect and that camouflage your real goal. Asking, "Is any member of the jury panel biased against the police?" may not elicit the same information as: "Have you or has anyone close to you ever been arrested or charged with a crime?"

To decide what questions to ask, you must first have a strong grasp of what type of juror you want. Who would be the perfect juror for your case, and who would be a nightmare juror? How do you make this assessment?

Mock Trials and Focus Groups

A mock trial or focus group can help you prepare for voir dire. There is no better way to explore how your overall case and all its parts will play before a jury. The mock trial, if done correctly, should reveal your strategy's general and particular flaws as well as its strengths. It will give you a sharper sense of how individuals will react to the evidence and arguments you present. This insight will prove invaluable to you during voir dire and the trial to come. There may also be value in a mock trial in a nonjury case. Engaging a retired judge to preside over a brief minitrial or to only hear proposed opening statements could well add value. In the *Oregon* case, counsel for Oregon presented portions of the case in a mock trial setting.

It is helpful to rely on jury consultants to run mock trials. If you communicate what you want to get out of the experience, a good consultant will design the process to fit your specific needs.

Always provide the consultant with a summary of the case from both sides, jury instructions, and a verdict sheet. It is helpful to also offer a draft of the pretrial order, which you should be developing by the time you are ready to present a mock trial.

The consultant will engage a research studio where you will eventually present the mock trial to a group of strangers. These strangers, selected by the studio, should match the profile of the actual jurors who will hear your real case. How can you be sure that the "mock jurors" will match the profile of the actual ones? You can't, but you can make an effort to come close. Within a month or two of the trial, contact the jury commissioner for the court. In some jurisdictions, you may be able to obtain a copy of the current jury list. If not, you should be able to offer a profile of the types of jurors called for jury duty in the court where the case is pending. Ask colleagues who try cases in the court for help or observe on your own. In most instances the jury consultant will know or investigate for you. Your jury consultant will pass the list or profile on to the studio or research center, which will recruit from its database people who match the profiles of the actual jurors. The participants are usually compensated from $50 to $100 per day.

The consultant can also arrange whatever number of jurors is required. If you want to watch more than one group deliberate, you can ask for 24 people. However numerous, the jurors will not know who the real party is or which side is seeking the benefits of the exercise. In some instances the jurors may believe that they have been selected to resolve an actual dispute and that their decision will be binding on the parties.

Before you come face to face with the group, you will want to consider which aspects of your case you should present. It isn't often that you can present the entire case or would even desire to do so if the upcoming trial is complex and lengthy. So be selective: focus on the key aspects of your case, such as the opening statement and closing argument, crucial witnesses, and any area about which you feel uncertain.

Once you know where you're going, the consultant can help you get there by developing questions for the mock jurors. You might want to ask them which among several witnesses were more credible and why. Or you might want comments on a particular defense. The consultant can ask some questions during the exercise and can ask others in a focus group session after the mock trial. These "in the moment" snapshots of jurors' responses will be of great value later on.

Your preparations for the mock trial should not be limited to your side of the case alone. To make the exercise worthwhile, give the opponent a fair shake by including opposing witnesses and opposing counsel. How can this be pulled off? Not authentically, of course, but you may have video depositions that would suffice. Alternatively, you could ask colleagues to portray opposing counsel and adverse witnesses.

After the mock trial is over, jurors hear instructions on the law and are ushered into separate rooms for deliberations. You, your client, and the consultant can usually watch the deliberations through a one-way mirror. This is your chance to observe what might well occur in the actual jury room. You'll be able to witness firsthand how the mock jurors evaluate the case, you, and your client.

After the jury reaches a conclusion and completes the verdict form, your consultant will lead a focus group while you and your client listen and watch through the one-way mirror.

This experience can be intense, as it is probably your first chance to hear fresh responses to your case. Listen carefully! These sessions are pure gold for the trial lawyer. You may not like everything you hear, so go into the exercise with an open mind—and always be willing to turn criticism into constructive change.

Mock trials are beneficial in more ways than one. The cost can range from $5,000 to $100,000, depending on the nature of the case and how extensively you design the exercise.

If your budget is very limited, you can work with the consultant to design an inexpensive project. For example, you can present opening statements and question one witness.

If you have no budget, you can assemble your office staff in the conference room for a few hours, present opening statements, and obtain comments. What if you have no colleagues or staff who will listen? Ask family members or friends to give you some of their time. (If all else fails, go to your dogs or cats. Line them up and present your case—the "throw your case to the dogs" technique.)

No matter how you pull it off, a mock trial can help you answer the key voir dire question: Who are the friendly jurors and who are the unfriendly ones? Once you see mock jurors grappling with the intricacies of the case, you will better understand what predispositions and beliefs can hurt you most.

Jury consultants can also play a direct role during jury selection. In the *Rosen* case, the defense asked and was granted permission to have its jury consultant sit at the counsel table. The consultant and counsel had prepared a profile of the types of jurors who would likely be receptive to the defense. Then, she assisted during voir dire in deciding which prospective jurors best fit the profile. She had reviewed the jury list and coded the list by numbers one to five. The goal was to exclude the fours and fives and to retain the ones and twos, and settle, only if necessary, for the threes.

Of course, hiring a jury consultant does not guarantee a successful result. There are some self-styled consultants whose work is not acceptable and whose guidance is no better than that you might receive from a stranger selected at random. And even well-conducted jury research can prove nearly useless if the pool is made up entirely of people who are predisposed against your case. But mock trials and jury consultants usually provide enlightening information. They enable you to identify and strike dangerous jurors. They also help you to deliver a more effective argument for the citizens left in the jury box after voir dire is over.

Voir Dire and the Internet

With more and more courthouses providing easy Internet access to attorneys, you may now have the opportunity to bring your laptop to the courtroom and conduct online searches on prospective jurors or seek information about them on Facebook or LinkedIn. A number of courts have ruled that it is perfectly fine for trial lawyers to bring their laptop computers to court and use them at the counsel table to conduct Internet research on prospective jurors. It is advisable to seek agreement with opposing counsel, and request permission in advance from the court to ensure that you do not provoke the court or hear cries of foul by opposing counsel.

If using the Internet in court during voir dire is not possible or practical, you may be in a jurisdiction where the jury commissioner will release the list of prospective jurors before trial. Then at your leisure you can investigate prospective jurors and use the information to fashion additional voir dire questions or develop a basis for striking a prospective juror either for cause or as a peremptory strike.

Consider also using the Internet to investigate jurors in more depth once they are seated in the jury box. Information gained may aid you in better understanding them and how you might best persuade them.

It is important to conduct juror research early and often. It is not unheard of for judges to dismiss a juror as late as the final throes of a case, if it is discovered that the juror did not respond accurately to a material question on voir dire.

Regardless of when you conduct Internet research on your jurors, you may find information that assists you with your case. With so many people broadcasting their political leanings, tastes, and habits online, trial lawyers can't afford to ignore the vast pool of information that jurors may have provided in public forums throughout cyberspace. It is therefore important to stay current with all the technology available and be prepared to use it to your advantage. Today it's Google with Wi-Fi access. Tomorrow, who knows?

Always remember that innovative voir dire techniques must be consistent with ethics and professional responsibility. For example: an ethics opinion of the New York State Bar Association has explained that a lawyer "may ethically view and access the Facebook and MySpace profiles of a party other than the lawyer's client in litigation as long as the party's profile is available to all members in the network and the lawyer neither 'friends' the other party nor directs someone else to do so."[2] While this opinion dealt with "parties" rather than "jurors," its reasoning is applicable to both:

> Obtaining information about a party available in the Facebook or MySpace profile is similar to obtaining information that is available in publicly accessible online or print media, or through a subscription research service such as Nexis or Factiva, and that is plainly permitted.[3]

Yet it is equally clear that "friending" a prospective juror, directing a third party to do so, or otherwise using deception to access a social networking website are all forbidden practices under the rules of professional conduct.[4] Interestingly, information on the Internet about potential jurors has caused some courts to impose responsibilities on counsel to conduct investigations and in some instances to communicate the results to the client.

Bear in mind that your voir dire must also conform to the practices within the jurisdiction and the court in which you are trying the case. In *Johnson v. McCullough*,[5] the court held that lawyers under some circumstances have a responsibility to perform online investigations of venire members. But other jurisdictions might not agree. Remember also that some jurisdictions permit counsel to conduct extensive voir dire; others do not. Following are representative model jury questions used in the

---

2. *See also* The Association of the Bar of the City of New York Committee of Professional Ethics, Formal Opinion 2012-2 ("Jury Research and Social Media"), which states that attorneys may use social media websites for juror research as long as no communication occurs between the lawyer and juror as a result of the research. In addition, attorneys must not use deception to gain access to a juror's website or obtain information.

3. *Id.*

4. *Id.*; *accord* Philadelphia Bar Op. 2009–02 (March 2009), 2009 WL 934623.

5. 306 S.W.3d 551 (Mo. 2010).

State of New Jersey which, like most states, does not normally permit lawyers to conduct voir dire.

MODEL JURY SELECTION QUESTIONS (STATE OF NEW JERSEY)
Standard Jury Voir Dire—Civil
[Revised as Promulgated by Directive #4–07]

1. In order to be qualified under New Jersey law to serve on a jury, a person must have certain qualifying characteristics. A juror must be:

Age 18 or older.

A citizen of the United States.

Able to read and understand the English language.

A resident of _____ County (*the summoning county*).

Also, a juror must not:

Have been convicted of any indictable offense in any state or federal court.

Have any physical or mental disability that would prevent the person from properly serving as a juror. Please consider that the Judiciary will provide reasonable accommodations consistent with the Americans with Disabilities Act (ADA).

Is there any one of you who does not meet these requirements?

2. a. This trial is expected to last for _____. Is there anything about the length or scheduling of the trial that would interfere with your ability to serve?

b. Do you have any medical, personal, or financial problem that would prevent you from serving on this jury?

c. Do any of you have a special need or require a reasonable accommodation to help you in listening, paying attention, reading printed materials, deliberating, or otherwise participating as a fair juror? The court will provide reasonable accommodations to your special needs but I will be aware of any such needs only if you let me know about them. My only purpose in asking you these circumstances relates to your ability to serve as a juror. If you have any such request, please raise your hand and I will speak to you at sidebar.

[Note: If a juror makes a request, contact the ADA Coordinator to see if the TCA can meet the request right away (e.g., providing a portable speaker system immediately) or if the juror's service should be deferred so that the TCA can arrange the accommodation timely (e.g., providing an ASL interpreter, which may require three or four months' reservation in advance).]

3. *Introduce the lawyers and the parties.* Do any of you know either/any of the lawyers? Has either/any of them or anyone in their office ever represented you or brought any action against you? Do you know Mr./Ms. _____? [Insert names of parties.]

4. *Read names of potential witnesses.* Do you know any of the potential witnesses? [Note: List witnesses' names here or attach a separate sheet.]

5. I have already briefly described the case. Do you know anything about this case from any source other than what I've just told you?

6. Are any of you familiar with the area or address of the incident?

7. Have you or any family members or close personal friends ever filed a claim or a lawsuit of any kind?

8. Has anyone ever filed a claim or a lawsuit against you or a member of your family or a close friend?

9. Have you or any family members or close personal friends either currently or in the past been involved as a party . . . as either a plaintiff or a defendant . . . in a lawsuit involving damages for personal injury?

10. A plaintiff is a person or corporation [or other entity] that has initiated a lawsuit. Do you have a bias for or against a plaintiff simply because the plaintiff has brought a lawsuit?

11. a. A defendant is a person or corporation [or other entity] against whom a lawsuit has been brought. Do you have a bias for or against a defendant simply because a lawsuit has been brought against that defendant?

[Ask if applicable.]

   b. The defendant is a corporation. Under the law, a corporation is entitled to be treated the same as anyone else and is entitled to be treated the same as a private individual. Would any of you have any difficulty in accepting that principle?

12. The court is aware that there has been a great deal of public discussion about something called tort reform (laws that restrict the right to sue or limit the amount recovered). Do you have an opinion, one way or another, on this subject?

13. If the law and evidence warranted, would you be able to render a verdict in favor of the plaintiff or defendant regardless of any sympathy you may have for either party?

14. Based on what I have told you, is there anything about this case or the nature of the claim itself that would interfere with your ability to be fair and impartial and to apply the law as instructed by the court?

15. Can you accept the law as explained by the court and apply it to the facts regardless of your personal beliefs about what the law is or should be?

16. Have you ever served on a trial jury before today, either in this state or in any state court or federal court?

17. Do you know anyone else in the jury box other than as a result of reporting here today?

18. Would your verdict in this case be influenced in any way by any factors other than the evidence in the courtroom, such as friendships or family relationships or the type of work you do?

19. Have you ever been a witness in a civil matter, regardless of whether it went to trial?

20. Have you ever testified in any court proceeding?

21. State law requires that a plaintiff has to prove fault of a defendant before he or she is entitled to recover money damages from that defendant. Do you have any difficulty accepting that concept?

Omnibus Qualification Questions (Two)

1. Is there anything, whether or not covered in the previous questions, that would affect your ability to be a fair and impartial juror or that would in any way be a problem for you in serving on this jury?

2. Is there anything else that you feel is important for the parties in this case to know about you?

Auto

1. How many of you are licensed drivers?
2. Have you or any family members or close personal friends ever been involved in a motor vehicle accident in which an injury resulted?
3. a. Have you or any family members or close personal friends ever been involved in litigation or filed a claim of any sort?

   b. Has anyone ever filed a claim or lawsuit against you or a family member or close personal friend?
4. Have you or any family members or close personal friends sustained an injury to the _____ or experienced chronic problems with _____?
5. [Ask if applicable.] Have you or any family members or close personal friends utilized the services of a chiropractor?
6. The court is aware that there has been a great deal of public discussion in print and in the media about automobile accident lawsuits and automobile accident claims. Do you have an opinion one way or another on this subject?

Slip and Fall

1. Is anyone a tenant?
2. Is anyone a landlord?
3. Is anyone a homeowner?
4. Have you or any family members or close personal friends ever been involved . . . as either a plaintiff or a defendant . . . in a slip-and-fall accident in which an injury resulted?
5. Have you or any family members or close personal friends ever been involved in litigation or filed a claim of any sort?
6. Have you or any family members or close personal friends sustained an injury to the _____ or have chronic problems with _____?

Medical Malpractice

Note: This information is not to be included on printed copies provided to jurors.

It is expected that the parties will submit a few specific questions seeking juror attitudes toward particular injury claims, such as pecuniary loss for wrongful death or a claim for emotional distress, if applicable, or juror attitudes about other particular types of claims, such as wrongful birth or informed consent issues. In particular, wrongful birth claims might require a questionnaire or separate voir dire to address attitudes about termination of pregnancy.

Before asking the questions below, explain that the trial involves a claim of medical negligence, which people sometimes refer to as medical malpractice, and that the terms both mean the same thing.

1. Have you or any family members or close personal friends ever had any experience, either very good or very bad, with a doctor or any other health care provider, that would make it difficult for you to sit as an impartial juror in this matter?

2. If the law and the evidence warranted, could you award damages for the plaintiff even if you felt sympathy for the doctor?

3. Regardless of the plaintiff's present condition, if the law and evidence warranted, could you render a verdict in favor of the defendant despite being sympathetic to the plaintiff?

4. Have you or any family members or close personal friends ever worked for one of the following: Attorneys, Doctors, Hospitals, or Physical Therapists, Any type of health care provider, Any ambulance / EMT / Rescue

5. Have you or any family members or close personal friends been employed in processing, investigating, or handling any type of medical or personal injury claims?

6. Is there anything that you may have read in the print media or seen on television or heard on the radio about medical negligence cases or caps or limits on jury verdicts or awards that would prevent you from deciding this case fairly and impartially on the facts presented?

7. This case involves a claim against the defendant for injuries suffered by the plaintiff as a result of alleged medical negligence. Do you have any existing opinions or strong feelings one way or another about such cases?

8. Have you or any members of your immediate family or close personal friends ever suffered any complications from [specify the medical field involved]?

9. Do you have any familiarity with [specify the type of medical condition involved] or any familiarity with the types of treatment available?

10. Are you, or have you ever been, related (by blood or marriage) to anyone affiliated with the health care field?

11. Have you or any family members or close personal friends ever had a dispute with respect to a health care issue of any kind with a doctor, chiropractor, dentist, nurse, hospital employee, technician, or other person employed in the health care field?

12. Have you or any family members or close personal friends ever brought a claim against a doctor, chiropractor, dentist, nurse, or hospital for an injury allegedly caused by a doctor, dentist, nurse, or hospital?

13. Have you or any relative or close personal friend ever considered bringing a medical or dental negligence action but did not do so?

14. Have you or any family members or close personal friends ever been involved with treatment that did not produce the desired outcome?

MODEL JURY SELECTION QUESTIONS
Standard Jury Voir Dire—Criminal
[Revised as Promulgated by Directive #4–07]

1. In order to be qualified under New Jersey law to serve on a jury, a person must have certain qualifying characteristics. A juror must be:

Age 18 or older.

A citizen of the United States.

Able to read and understand the English language.

A resident of _____ County (*the summoning county*).

Also, a juror must not:

Have been convicted of any indictable offense in any state or federal court.

Have any physical or mental disability that would prevent the person from properly serving as a juror. Please consider that the Judiciary will provide reasonable accommodations consistent with the Americans with Disabilities Act.

Is there any one of you who does not meet these requirements?

2. a. This trial is expected to last for _____. Is there anything about the length or scheduling of the trial that would interfere with your ability to serve?

b. Do you have any medical, personal, or financial problem that would prevent you from serving on this jury?

c. Do any of you have a special need or require a reasonable accommodation to help you in listening, paying attention, reading printed materials, deliberating, or otherwise participating as a fair juror? The court will provide reasonable accommodations to your special needs but I will be aware of any such needs only if you let me know about them. My only purpose in asking you these circumstances relates to your ability to serve as a juror. If you have any such request, please raise your hand and I will speak to you at sidebar.

[Note: If a juror makes a request, contact the ADA Coordinator to see if the TCA can meet the request right away (e.g., providing a portable speaker system immediately) or if the juror's service should be deferred so that the TCA can arrange the accommodation timely (e.g., providing an ASL interpreter, which may require three or four months' reservation in advance).]

3. *Introduce the lawyers and the parties.* Do any of you know either/any of the lawyers? Has either/any of them or anyone in their office ever represented you or brought any action against you? Do you know Mr./Ms. _____? [Insert names of parties.]

4. *Read names of potential witnesses.* Do you know any of the potential witnesses? [Note: List witnesses' names here or attach a separate sheet.]

5. I have already briefly described the case. Do you know anything about this case from any source other than what I've just told you?

6. Are any of you familiar with the area or address of the incident?

7. Have you ever served on a jury before today, here in New Jersey or in any state court or federal court?

8. Have you ever sat as a grand juror?

9. Do you know anyone else in the jury box other than as a result of reporting here today?

10. Would your verdict in this case be influenced in any way by any factors other than the evidence in the courtroom, such as friendships or family relationships or the type of work you do?

11. Is there anything about the nature of the charge itself that would interfere with your impartiality?

12. Have you ever been a witness in a criminal case, regardless of whether it went to trial?

13. Have you ever testified in any court proceeding?

14. Have you ever applied for a job as a state or local police officer or with a sheriff's department or county jail or state prison?

15. Have you, or any family member or close friend, ever worked for any agency such as a police department, prosecutor's office, the FBI, the DEA, or a sheriff's department, jail or prison, either in New Jersey or elsewhere?

16. As a general proposition, do you think that a police officer is more likely or less likely to tell the truth than a witness who is not a police officer?

17. Would any of you give greater or lesser weight to the testimony of a police officer merely because of his or her status as a police officer?

18. Have you or any family member or close friend ever been accused of committing an offense other than a minor motor vehicle offense?

19. Have you or any family member or close friend ever been the victim of a crime, whether it was reported to law enforcement or not?

20. Would you have any difficulty following the principle that the defendant on trial is presumed to be innocent and must be found not guilty of that charge unless each and every essential element of an offense charged is proved beyond a reasonable doubt?

21. The indictment is not evidence of guilt. It is simply a charging document. Would the fact that the defendant has been arrested and indicted, and is here in court facing these charges, cause you to have preconceived opinions on the defendant's guilt or innocence?

22. I have already given you the definition of reasonable doubt, and will explain it again at the end of the trial. Would any of you have any difficulty in voting not guilty if the State fails to prove the charge beyond a reasonable doubt?

23. If the State proves each element of the alleged offense(s) beyond a reasonable doubt, would you have any difficulty in returning a verdict of guilty?

24. The burden of proving each element of a crime beyond a reasonable doubt rests upon the prosecution and that burden never shifts to the defendant. The defendant in a criminal case has no obligation or duty to prove his/her innocence or offer any proof relating to his/her innocence. Would any of you have any difficulty in following these principles?

25. Would you have any difficulty or reluctance in accepting the law as explained by the court and applying it to the facts regardless of your personal beliefs about what the law should be or is?

26. Is there anything about this case, based on what I've told you, that would interfere with your ability to be fair and impartial?

27. A defendant in a criminal case has the absolute right to remain silent and has the absolute right not to testify. If a defendant chooses not to testify, the jury is prohibited from drawing any negative conclusions from that choice. The defendant is presumed innocent whether he testifies or not. Would any of you have any difficulty in following these principles?

[Note: The defendant has the right to waive this question. The defendant's decision in that regard should be discussed during the voir dire conference.]

Omnibus Qualification Questions (Two)

1. Is there anything, whether or not covered in the previous questions, that would affect your ability to be a fair and impartial juror or that would in any way be a problem for you in serving on this jury?

2. Is there anything else that you feel is important for the parties in this case to know about you? [6]

---

6. http://www.judiciary.state.nj.us/directive/2007/dir_04_07.pdf.

Learning Points for Chapter 1

- In analyzing a potential juror's attitude, think about three main things: (1) Is the attitude favorable, unfavorable, or neutral? (2) How intense is the attitude? and (3) How important is the attitude?
- Conduct a mock trial or focus group to help you assess the types of juror you want and don't want to have trying your case.
- Consider using a jury consultant to help set up your mock trial and perhaps to accompany you to assist with the actual voir dire.
- Stay current with the technological advances that can help you conduct your jury research: In many courthouses today, you can investigate potential jurors online as you conduct voir dire. Take advantage of all the opportunities that technology affords you, so long as they are consistent with ethics and professional responsibility.

CHAPTER 2

FIRST IMPRESSIONS— OPENING STATEMENTS

Ask a trial lawyer, judge, or jury what the most important part of a trial is. More often than not the answer will be the opening statement. Perhaps the basis of that answer is that most of us relinquish our first impressions reluctantly, if at all. Indeed, numerous surveys reveal that once juries are swayed by an opening statement, they usually do not change their minds. Whether the surveys are accurate or predictive of most cases is not susceptible to measurement—each case is unique. Nevertheless, trials can certainly be won or lost with the opening statement.

The opening statement presents the first opportunity to persuade the jury to decide in your favor. Every opening statement should be organized around the theme of your case. In developing your theme, consider elevating it to a universal principle that you believe will resonate with the listener's belief systems. For example, "This case is not only about young Scott Smith's fracture of his ankle on the escalator, but also about the need for corporations to be conscious of safety in developing new products." Creating an effective theme engages the listener and can help you explain the substance of your case; it's a way of telling a compelling story using your facts.

Arrange the opening to include a beginning, a middle, and an end. Take advantage of primacy and recency. We form significant impressions from what we hear first and last. Organize your case to accommodate these ideas. Make a favorable impression by advancing your most important facts first, placing less favorable facts in the middle, and concluding on a high note.

Bear in mind that the perceived character of the advocate—what Aristotle called *ethos*—is one of the important elements of persuasion. We can enhance our ethos during the opening statement and throughout the trial by being likable, respectful and sincere, honest and prepared, and courteous and fair, and being properly attired. We should also use plain English, and avoid ad hominem attacks and contentiousness. A strong ethos will help you unobtrusively form a bond with the jury.

In your eagerness to create a positive first impression, beware of overstating your case. Don't overpromise. If you refer to evidence, including documents that you plan to introduce, that evidence had better be admissible. Similarly, if you tell the jury that you will call a particular witness and fail to do so, you may injure your credibility.

From the advocate's perspective, opening statements are critical. From the judge's point of view, however, they are not decisive at all and must not be considered as such by the jurors. When giving instructions at the beginning or conclusion of a case, judges advise juries that what the lawyers say in opening statements and closing arguments is not evidence. The jury can decide the case only based on the testimony of the witnesses and on any documents or real evidence that the court admits.

"Arguing" the Case

The purpose of the opening statement, then, is to introduce what the lawyers will prove during the trial, and to do so in a way that engages and persuades the jurors. Complicating this task is the conventional prohibition against attorneys arguing the merits of the case and assuming that certain facts have already been established. For example, a defense lawyer is not permitted to say: "My client is innocent, and you should find him not guilty because witnesses against him are perjurers. This case is a miscarriage of justice." However, you must still couch the prediction of the evidence into an energetic "argument" so that the jury is leaning your way when the opening statements conclude.

One technique used by lawyers to "argue" the merits of a case is to preface their remarks with such phrases as "The evidence will show that. . . ." or "You will see from the evidence that. . . ." This way, counsel can usually escape objections and try to persuade the jury before the first witness is called.

For example, in the *Rosen* case, defense counsel told the jury during the opening statement: "The evidence will demonstrate that Mr. Rosen is an innocent victim of other people's motives. He did not know the true costs of the event because they were concealed from him by others who had their own agendas."

As helpful as they can be, avoid overusing phrases like "the evidence will show"; the last thing you want to be at the beginning of the trial is tedious. But note the subtle distinction between argument based on facts to be established and forcefully articulating your theory of the case. This is a fine line, one that should be heeded. If you do not refrain from arguing the merits of a case, opposing counsel and the court may intercede with an objection or an admonition.

In the *Rosen* case, Judge Matz interrupted defense counsel for arguing during the opening. Toward the end of the opening, counsel described how the prosecutors would characterize the fundraising event run by Rosen for Hillary Clinton's campaign for the U.S. Senate: they would attempt to paint the event as a failure and argue that Rosen was in danger of losing his job. In contrast, the defense would demonstrate that he was actually doing outstanding work and was not worried about his position with the Clinton campaign. Defense counsel went on to imply that the government's accusations were part of the "bizarre tragedy" of David Rosen's being wrongfully accused of something he did not do. That segment of the statement led to this exchange with the court:

MR. SANDLER: So the government will say, as a result of that he had a bad event, he was going to lose his job. It's a bizarre tragedy, bizarre.

THE COURT: Mr. Sandler . . . you can characterize what the evidence has proven at the end, with the adjectives.

MR. SANDLER: I beg your pardon.

THE COURT: Just anticipate, please. What you have been doing for the most part, what the evidence will show.

MR. SANDLER: I think the evidence will show all that I have said, ladies and gentlemen. Thank you, Your Honor.

This kind of interruption is generally undesirable. When the court calls into question an attorney's claims during the opening statement, the jurors may begin to look upon what that attorney says less favorably. It was thus important, in the above exchange, for counsel, before moving on, to suggest that the evidence would bear out his characterizations. In the end, the jury would agree that it did.

The prohibition against arguing the merits of a case raises an interesting question: Should lawyers object during opening statements?

If you feel you need to object, be sure you won't be overruled. It is better to stay quiet than to lose so small a battle at the outset. Being overruled can erode counsel's ethos with the jury or judge. Also, if counsel appears out of line, the opponent might adopt the goose-and-gander approach, by making improper comments of his or her own in the opening statement, though that does not mean the judge will allow improper argument.

On the other hand, objections during the opening statement in non-jury cases may not be as risky as in jury cases. A reasonable objection, even if overruled, should not cause the same potential rupture of ethos as it might before a jury. Judges in nonjury cases may be more prone to overrule objections to move the case along, and to be able to separate evidence from rhetoric at the time of rendering a decision. Consider this exchange between counsel and the court in the *Oregon Grille* case during the plaintiff's opening statement:

PLAINTIFF'S COUNSEL: The Board of Appeals, Your Honor, in July 2004, denied what it called the second bite of the apple and chastised the . . . ."

MR. SANDLER: Object, Your Honor. This is not evidence that's going to be proven.

THE COURT: What he says—

MR. SANDLER: It's argument.

THE COURT: —you know, obviously it's not evidence. It's something that he has some desire to say. We are just trying to get through it as quickly as we can. The objection is overruled."

No harm done. Perhaps if the case were before a jury, the judge would have sustained the objection, but the objection probably would not have been made.

In the *Maffei* case, the plaintiff's counsel began the opening statement with pure argument:

MR. SANDLER: Plaintiffs are ready for the opening statement, Your Honor.

May it please the Court, Members of the Jury, on March 8, 2006, Dr. Angela Smedley misdiagnosed the medical condition of the late Richard Maffei. He was 52 years old. He had registered at the emergency room of the hospital around 3:00 o'clock in the morning. He complained of a sudden feeling of closure at his throat, chest pain, and low back pain, as the medical records will so state. He was seen by Dr. Smedley and discharged around 7:00 o'clock in the morning. He didn't know it, but he was experiencing a medical emergency because he had a tear in the largest vessel of his heart, the aorta. The diagnosis of the doctor: ear infection, sore throat, allergic reaction; the prescription: steroids, antibiotics; head home, it will take a while for the medicine to kick in. But the medicine did not kick in. It could not. Mr. Maffei suffered a tear in his aorta. He died of a dissected aorta. But it didn't have to happen. It didn't have to happen, because all the doctor had to do was take a simple x-ray and from that x-ray the diagnosis could have been made.

Fortunately for plaintiff's counsel, there was no objection. If there had been, counsel could have cured the problem by adding, "The evidence will show. . . ."

Contrast the approach of counsel for the plaintiff with that of defense counsel at the outset of his opening. Defense counsel properly couched his argument in terms of what the evidence would show:

> MR. SHAW: Good morning, Ladies and Gentlemen of the Jury. My name is Ron Shaw. Together with Mr. Morrow, we represent Ms. Smedley. Obviously, if we agreed with the evidence that Mr. Sandler discussed, we wouldn't be here. There are two sides to the story. We strongly believe the evidence will show you, will convince you Dr. Smedley acted appropriately and did not commit medical malpractice. As you heard, this is a medical malpractice case and Dr. Smedley, we believe the evidence will show, treated Mr. Maffei appropriately and did not commit medical malpractice.

Both the plaintiff and defense introductions are examples of going to the heart of the matter at the inception.

OPENING STATEMENTS AND THE FIRST FIVE MINUTES

No one understands the power of first impressions like a trial lawyer. When you stand up to deliver an opening statement to the members of the jury, you are being scrutinized by unknown citizens—12 in a criminal case, six in a civil case—who have the power to determine your client's fate. Within the first five minutes of the opening, each of those citizens will have formed an impression of your case and of you. In those introductory minutes, every word you utter and every gesture you make should do the hard work of persuading the jury on your client's behalf.

The Primacy Effect

The essential challenge at the outset is to engage the listener's attention in order to capture the primacy effect. This doctrine holds that listeners remember best the information they hear first. If you cannot engage the jury immediately, you might as well not have presented the opening. Once you lose the jury's attention, it is difficult to regain.

Set the Stage

Within the first five minutes of the opening, your overarching theme should be obvious to the jury. There are many ways to present a theme, and the uniqueness of your case should determine the method you employ. One approach is to "set the stage": to provide the context in which the alleged events took place and draw the jurors into the drama you intend to unfold. This approach was employed effectively by the government in the *Rosen* case:

> Ladies and gentlemen, in August of 2000 Hillary Clinton's campaign for the United States Senate in New York was entering the stretch run. She was up against a well-financed challenger. The polls were tight. Money was tight. Running for the United States Senate in the United States is a very expensive proposition. Campaigning in a large, expensive media state like New York is particularly expensive. The responsibility for raising money for Hillary Clinton's campaign fell to this man seated at counsel table. His name is David Rosen.

"What This Case Is About"

You can also begin by bluntly articulating "what this case is about." This tactic was employed by the defense in the *Rosen* case:

> We would like to tell you what this case is really about. It's about David Rosen's fight against the injustice of his being wrongfully accused of something he never did. I will prove to you in this case he is innocent. He is the victim, an innocent victim, of other people's motives, and I will prove this. I will prove to you that David Rosen never knew, never knew the cost of the production and concert expenses for this Hollywood gala. And why didn't he know it, folks? The evidence will show he did not know it because those costs were concealed from him. They were hidden from him by two individuals. . . . These individuals participated with Stan Lee Media in underwriting, paying for the costs of this event and they had their own agenda.

Both these introductory statements have begun to stake out a general theme. For the prosecution, the case was about an aide's allegedly criminal response to the pressure of a high-stakes political campaign. For the defense, the case was about an innocent young man falling victim to the secret agendas of shady political operatives.

Properly Explain the Purpose

During the first segment of your opening, do not lose the opportunity to impress the jury or judge with your "argument" or case theme and the facts that support your theme. You can do this by taking time to explain the purpose of the opening statement or court procedure. However, if you feel it would be advantageous to make this explanation, save it for later in the opening. For example, you will want the jury to understand the required proof in the case, but discussion of the required proof need not appear at the very beginning of your opening statement unless it is the essential theme. You can work it in later.

Avoid introductions like the following; they are far too expository and almost patronizing:

> May it please the Court, counsel, and may it please you, ladies and gentlemen of the jury. It is at this stage of the proceedings that the attorneys for each side have an opportunity to make what is known as an opening statement. An opening statement is something like a preview, in that each lawyer can give the jury an outline of what he expects the evidence to establish. This preview that we give you might be something like a friend telling you what a movie was all about before you actually viewed it.[1]

Compare that opening with those made by the plaintiff and defendant in the *Maffei* case; after initially accusing the doctor of malpractice, plaintiff's counsel sought to shape the jurors' impression of this particular case:

---

1. ALAN MORILL, TRIAL DIPLOMACY (1973).

MR. SANDLER: Now, before I tell you exactly what we are going to prove in this case, I want to comment about the nature of this lawsuit. This suit is one that I would call professional negligence. Often we hear the term, malpractice, medical malpractice. I don't like the word "mal." It's an ancient Latin word meaning evil. We didn't bring this case to punish anybody or bring this case to say someone was bad. But that is medical negligence. We are required to live our lives, carefully. We drive cars. We go through a stop sign without stopping; someone gets hurt; we have a responsibility. This is a case of negligence. In essence, we have a lawsuit that deals with a wrongful death of the late Mr. Maffei, brought by Mrs. Maffei against the doctor for an adequate award, if there could ever be one for this type of loss.[2]

My name, as the judge told you, is Paul Sandler. With me is Eric Harlan. We represent Mrs. Maffei. She brings the case against the doctor and her employer, the physicians emergency group, Charles Physician Emergency Group, for negligence. It's a wrongful death case and right of survivorship case. What does that mean? Wrongful death, in a sense, is a fancy word to say Mrs. Maffei, because she lost her husband, has a right to sue for the loss of income he would have brought to her; her pain and suffering; and loss of companionship. Also, Mr. Maffei isn't here, so he can't speak, but his estate in law speaks for him. It's called a right of survivorship where he sues for his pain and suffering. That's the nature of the lawsuit. And under the circumstances of this case, when you go back to the jury room at the end of the case, you will find, and I'll prove to you, the negligence that brought about this horrible result.

And here is how defense counsel sought to shape the case, after initially asserting that the doctor did not commit malpractice:

MR. SHAW: Now, this is an important case to Mrs. Maffei, but it's also a very important case to Dr. Smedley. Mr. Sandler went first in his opening. He will go first in presenting the witnesses. We go second because the burden of proof is on Mr. Sandler and Mrs. Maffei. You will

---

2. Based in part on ALFRED S. JULIEN, OPENING STATEMENTS sec. 3H (1980).

hear the plaintiff's side of the story first and then our side. We ask you to please wait until you have heard all the evidence and keep an open mind before you make a decision in this case. But we strongly believe that what the evidence will show in this case is that the plaintiff's case is based on hindsight, because at the time that Mr. Maffei was in the emergency department, he did not have the full blown dissection that ultimately showed up. In fact, it wasn't until after he died and there was still mystery as to what had caused his death that an autopsy showed the diagnosis of aortic dissection was made.

The evidence will show the symptoms Mr. Maffei had while he was in the emergency department on March 8, 2006, were not typical of aortic dissection. He had throat complaints, he had an earache and a brief episode of low blood pressure. We'll see the low blood pressure only lasted ten minutes of the over four hours he was in the emergency department.

The nurses did report at various times complaints of chest pain, but I am going to show you in a few moments the nurses' notes about the chest pain and the throat pain. I'll show you those all came before Dr. Smedley saw Mr. Maffei and when Dr. Smedley saw Mr. Maffei, he explicitly denied having chest pain. I'll also show you the nurses' notes and you have to decide whether Dr. Smedley acted appropriately in trusting the nurses' notes.

Before planning an opening statement in nonjury cases and in other similar proceedings, such as arbitration or administrative hearings, consider first whether the judge or panel desires an opening statement. If so, try to shape the opening to conform with the court or arbitrator's particular predilections. Tailoring the argument to the decision-maker is always essential. In nonjury cases, there may be no need for rhetorical embellishment or lengthy presentation. The court may be familiar with the facts and proposed evidence by virtue of pretrial submissions.

In the *Oregon Grille* case, counsel did present opening statements. The attorneys were considerably quicker to plunge into the facts at hand than they likely would have been before a jury. Consider how the plaintiff's counsel commenced his opening:

MR. McCANN: Absolutely. Thank you, Your Honor.

First let me introduce my clients who are here today, Dennis Sutton and Kathleen House.

Both of those individuals, Your Honor, live in close proximity to the subject property. Mr. Sutton in particular. He is also a director of the Falls Road Community Association, which is also a plaintiff in the case, which you may or may not know, Your Honor, [is] a community association whose geographical boundaries encompass this property and which has actually been in existence some 50 years now as a community group.

The property itself, Your Honor, is 2.63 acres approximately. It's owned by Baltimore County. It sits at the southwest corner of Shawan Road and Beaver Dam Road. It's occupied presently by the Oregon Grille, a fine restaurant owned and operated by the defendant, Oregon LLC, which leases the property from Baltimore County.

The property itself is undoubtedly unique. It's part of the federally listed historic district. It's an RC 4 zone, which is a resource conservation zone, under the zoning regulations and which is designated for the protection of watersheds in the county. And a tributary actually runs right through this property, Your Honor, which is classified as a Use Three Stream, meaning that's a stream for naturally [produced] trout. The building itself is also a historic building. It's on the Baltimore County Landmarks list of historic buildings.

For all of this, Oregon LLC pays rent to Baltimore County, Your Honor, of approximately $415 per month, and has done this for many years.

What is here before you today, Your Honor, essentially, is to enforce certain legal restrictions that have been imposed upon Baltimore County and Oregon LLC. And the history of those legal restrictions, Your Honor, some are convoluted, but it's my job to make that as simple and clear as possible. And that's what I'll do now.

Compare the above plaintiff's opening to the commencement of the opening by defense counsel for Oregon LLC.

MR. SANDLER: May it please the Court.

As you know, I'm Paul Sandler. I represent Oregon Grille. And in these brief remarks I'm going to present to the court what I intend to prove in this case.

And first I'm going to prove to you that this case should not be in this court because the plaintiff did not exhaust their administrative remedies.

I will call a witness as an expert in zoning. He will testify that there's a clear remedy administratively available to the plaintiffs, which is Baltimore County zoning regulation 500.7.

What does that say? That says—I'll summarize. If neighbors have complaints about one another in terms of use of the property, they have a remedy, the zoning commissioner. And they can petition, not just write a letter but to have a petition and hearing.

Why is that significant? I'll prove to you in the case that under the declaratory judgment act, statutory courts and Judicial Proceedings Article 3–409, that if there is an available remedy for an aggrieved party that the court is prohibited from issuing a declaratory judgment. It's an axiomatic rule. That failure to exhaust remedies is not only a glaring defect that I will prove, but it also has an approved implication as to how this matter could be resolved.

The complete opening statement in the *Oregon Grill* case is concise, but defense counsel does take time to inject issues of emotion and public policy in hopes of gaining the judge's favor at the outset. For example, counsel states:

> In essence you will conclude at the end of the case that the plaintiff really wants to set back progress by 50 years. In other words, no longer is it desirable to have a safe, sound, attractive-looking parking lot, but rather unpaved. For what? So people can break their necks or so that a small business can't thrive?
>
> I will also prove to you that in terms of while the rest of the world is starving and they're almost at war, this court is now going to have to hear evidence from an expert that an umbrella is an umbrella, because the plaintiffs are upset about that.

Breaking a Spell

When a theme is powerfully presented, a lawyer can cast a spell over a jury. Whenever a spell is created by opposing counsel, it must be broken as soon as possible. Techniques for doing so vary. To do so in an opening statement, you may want to invoke a dramatic statement that shifts attention to your case, the theme of which is compellingly distinct from that of the opposing counsel. For example, in a case alleging sexual harassment, the defense could begin as follows: "Ladies and gentlemen, this case will demonstrate that just as it is important to eliminate sexual harassment in the workplace, it is equally important to eliminate false claims of harassment, which is exactly what we have here today."

Consider the remarks of the outstanding 19th-century advocate Joseph H. Choate in arguing in 1895 before the United States Supreme Court in *Pollock v. Farmer's Loan & Trust*.[3] The case involved the legality of the income tax. Choate persuaded the Court to strike down the act. It took the 16th Amendment to the U.S. Constitution to bring it back. But during the oral argument before the court, Choate was confronted with powerful oratory from opposing counsel at the Bar. Here is how he responded:

---

3. 15 S.Ct.673 (1895).

If the Court pleases, after Jupiter had thundered all around the sky, and had leveled everything and everybody by his prodigious bolts, Mercury came out from his hiding place and looked around to see how much damage had been done. He was quite familiar with the weapons of his Olympian friend. He had often felt their force, but he also knew it was largely stage thunder, manufactured for the particular occasion, and he went his round among the inhabitants of Olympus restoring the consciousness and dispelling the fears of both gods and men that had been prostrated by the crash. It is in this spirit that I follow my distinguished friend; and shall not undertake to cope with him by means of the same weapons, because I am not master of them.[4]

In the *Rosen* case, counsel for the defense drew upon a metaphor to break the spell cast by the government in its closing argument:

Listening to the Government reminds me of a young lawyer who approached her teacher to ask: How should I argue tomorrow's case? Argue the facts replied the teacher. What if the facts are against me? was the teacher's retort. Then argue the law. And if the facts and the law are both against me, what then? Pound the table, exclaimed the teacher. Members of the jury, that is just what the Government did in their closing remarks, they pounded the table.

Begin with a Question

Other techniques of introduction include clearly stating your purpose and asking a question central to the case. For example, "The government is going to ask you to take away the freedom of Sergeant Smith for defending our freedom. Now, what crime did he commit? His military working dog barked at people."[5]

---

4. Geoffrey Platt Jr., *Joseph Choate and the Imposition of Income Tax: The Man Whose Argument Won the Day*, 34 Sup. Ct. Hist. Soc'y Q. (2012).
5. Baltimore Sun, March 14, 2006, quoting Capt. Jason Duncan in the opening for the defense of Sgt. Michael J. Smith in the Abu Ghraib prison case.

Witnesses

There are times when you will want to mention particular witnesses and give the jury a brief overview of their testimony. In the *Rosen* case, early in its opening, the defense brought up one of the government's most valuable witnesses and sought to discredit him by mentioning that he had just signed a plea agreement in another criminal matter. The attempt there was to immunize the defense against the allegations that the witness would make later in the trial.

Compliments

You can also begin by paying a compliment to the jury or appealing to the jury's sense of self-importance: "In deciding this case you will be establishing the industry standard for the next 20 years."

Because your listeners' impressions of you bear on your persuasiveness, you should ingratiate yourself with the jury within the first five minutes of the opening. This isn't hard to do. A courteous smile and a word of gratitude can help you establish much-needed rapport. Keep in mind that you are engaged in a necessarily adversarial contest and that you need to avoid coming across as an egregiously antagonistic presence in the room. In the *Maffei* case, as seen above, plaintiff's counsel took care to avoid vilifying the physician, stating that the case was about professional negligence, not medical malpractice. Similarly, the defense counsel sought to avoid sympathy for the widow:

> MR. SHAW: Mr. Sandler told you that Mr. Maffei's death was tragic and we certainly agree that his death was tragic. Everyone in this room can agree his death was tragic. And all of us, Dr. Smedley, the legal team, everybody in the jury, everybody is obviously concerned about the tragedy. It would obviously be natural to have sympathy and compassion for Mrs. Maffei. But as His Honor will instruct you at the end of the case, you have to try as hard as you can to put the sympathy and compassion for Mrs. Maffei aside. That can't be the guiding rule for your decision in this case. Your decision in this case, as hard as it is, is going to have to be based on whether Dr. Smedley acted appropriately and whether she committed medical malpractice.

There are different opinions about whether you should thank the jury for its attention during the opening, but I believe doing so is important and can help humanize you and your client. A little courtesy can go a long way.

Ideally, within the first few minutes of your opening statement, each juror will have a favorable impression of you and a clear understanding of your overarching theme. Such themes are vital. In addition to drawing attention to your case, they can give the jurors a figurative lens through which to view all the information that is to follow and can help them organize it as you wish them to.

THE THEME AS ORGANIZING PRINCIPLE

The cornerstone of every opening statement is the theme of the case. The easiest way to develop a theme is to focus on the facts—what happened—and then reduce your client's view of those facts to a memorable, pithy expression that is consistent with what you believe are the jury's common experiences. The best themes are grounded on common sense and experiences shared by a broad spectrum of people, but particularly those people on the jury.

An effective theme is universal to the extent that it agrees with the value systems of the jurors and transcends the particular case. Presented with a theme they can relate to, jurors will more likely want to give you their support. It is far easier to engage people with an opening statement that places the case in the context of a larger ethical problem than with an opening that catalogues factual minutiae.

The theme governs how the evidence is marshaled for presentation. It helps you march through case preparation and the trial. For example, one of my rules on direct and cross is to avoid questions that are not helpful to developing or defending the theme. Frequently clients whisper or jot a note suggesting that I ask a particular question. Don't obey such a request if the question is geared only to embarrassing a witness but does not advance the theme or defend inroads to it.

In the trial of *United States v. Rosen*, in which the defendant was accused of underreporting donations connected with a fundraiser for Hillary Clinton's Senate campaign, the defense emphasized Rosen's position as a victim: "[This case is] about David Rosen's fight against the injustice of his being wrongfully accused." Brevity and emotional force are critical. The theme's mission is to help organize lots of information in an accessible fashion and to galvanize support.

In *Maffei*, the plaintiff's theme, stated at the outset of the opening, was that Mr. Maffei had complained to the doctor, and to the nurses before he saw the doctor, that he was experiencing chest pain, requiring the doctor to have taken a chest x-ray. This x-ray would have revealed a widening of the mediastinum, the cavity between the lungs. The abnormal x-ray would then require a CAT scan. The CAT scan would have shown the dissection and immediate surgery would have saved Mr. Maffei's life.

The theme of the defense, also stated at the outset of the opening, was that the doctor had complied with the standard of care; the patient had denied having chest pain at the time she saw him; there was no reason to call for an x-ray, and if one were taken it would have been normal, as any dissection occurring during the hospital visit would have been too small to detect. None of the signs of classic aortic dissection were present.

The plaintiff's theme in the *Oregon Grille* case was that the county and the restaurant violated zoning ordinances; the county was responsible for enforcing the ordinances; the restaurant was responsible, too, and was required to dissemble the parking lot and return it to its original state.

The theme of Oregon Grille's defense was that the county had ordered its tenant, Oregon LLC, to repave the parking lot, and a corollary theme was that the plaintiffs had failed to exhaust their administrative remedies.

In a nonjury trial, the length and delivery of the opening statement often are less elaborate and robust than in jury trials. Judges frequently are familiar with the case and are interested in going directly to the testimony. Some judges may permit an opening statement only out of courtesy. Consider the judge's reaction to opening statements in the *Oregon Grille* case:

THE COURT: Call your first witness:

PLAINTIFF'S COUNSEL: Actually I was going to give a brief opening statement, your Honor. I think it's necessary in this case because of—

THE COURT: All right. You go ahead and do opening. Then they will respond. And I will make a point of listening closely when we begin with the testimony, since opening statements are not evidence.
So go ahead.

Consider further the court's reaction when defense counsel objects during the plaintiff's opening:

The Board of Appeals, Your Honor, in July 2004 denied what it called the second bite of the apple and chastised the—

MR. SANDLER: Object, your Honor. This is not evidence that is going to be proven.

THE COURT: What he says—

MR. SANDLER: It's argument.

THE COURT: —you know, obviously it's not evidence. It's something that he has some desire to say. We are just trying to get through it as quickly as we can.

The objection is overruled.
PLAINTIFF'S COUNSEL: Thank you, Your Honor.

Proceeding under these circumstances calls for focusing the court immediately on the theme of the case and brevity. Nevertheless you have the opportunity to advance the case by preparing the court for the testimony. Hopefully the actual testimony will coincide with your remarks in the opening. Hence your credibility is preserved, and your points are reinforced by the testimony following your comments in the opening remarks. Objections during opening statements were discussed earlier in this chapter.

Arrangement

The theme will help you arrange your opening statement. Quintilian, the ancient Roman teacher of rhetoric, is reported to have compared arrangement in argument to generalship in battle. Unquestionably, the priority you give the topics you discuss in the opening statement can have a profound effect on the listener.

One approach is to divide your opening statement into three parts following your introduction: assertion, presentation, and conclusion. The assertion is where you stress the essential facts supporting your theme. In the presentation you elaborate with more detailed claims, and in the conclusion you bring the strands of "argument" together and leave the jury with a memorable impression of the essence of your case. Like an operatic motif, the theme should be sounded frequently and recognizably throughout the opening. You could move in the chronological order in which you expect the evidence to be developed, but you may be more effective by making your main points in service of the theme without dwelling on how facts will be presented later on.

More complex arrangements are sometimes appropriate. Consider the arrangement of argument preferred by classical rhetoricians such as Cicero and Quintilian:

Exordium (an introduction and "insinuation" in which you prepare the listener to receive the argument by ingratiating yourself with the jury or stating a stirring proposition to arrest attention);

Narration (recitation of the case);

Partition (an explanation of agreements and differences with opponent);

Argument (presenting the theory, facts, and law);

Refutation (explaining away opposing views); and

Peroration (summing up; inciting indignation against the opponent and sympathy or pity for the speaker).

In the *Oregon Grille* case, defense counsel arranged the opening statement according to the three-part model of assertion, presentation, and conclusion. The assertion stated the main points the defense would seek to prove.

And first I am going to prove to you that this case should not be in this court because the plaintiff did not exhaust administrative remedies. . . . We will also prove that the Oregon Grille Limited received the command from [its] landlord to pay the county for repaving the lot and thus cannot be responsible.

After these claims, defense in essence presented an argument to appeal to the sympathy of the court based upon the facts:

And I'm going to prove to you that there was a necessity to take action to solve a glaring problem with the parking lot. The parking lot, as you will hear from the evidence, was in deplorable condition, stone and sand created a hazard to the guests. Particularly to guests who are handicapped. There were rocks, ruts, and there were potholes. In the winter the parking lot could not be cleaned or shoveled because—or plowed because of the nature of the parking lot. It was a danger, a hazard, a danger and people complained, people tripped, and people were upset.

And then the opening concludes:

So, in conclusion, you will find first that the proper forum for this case is the zoning commissioner. You will also conclude based on the testimony that under existing law premises liability, Americans with Disabilities Act, local and state laws that it was proper and appropriate to have the lot repaved. And when the landlord presented the order to the tenant, tenant had to comply.

And finally counsel states,

You'll also hear testimony that if you were to declare that the regulations or the ordinances were not complied with, that there is no remedy that is presented in this case for you to exercise any affirmative granting of relief.

Demonstrative Aids

Studies show that we are far more persuaded by what we see than by what we hear. Demonstrative aids during your opening statement can enhance jury involvement, add potency to the learning environment, and make your statement more dynamic. You then increase the likelihood that your point of view will be understood and accepted.

Aids might include an organizational chart, crime scene photographs, or pictures of people important to the dispute. You may or may not decide to introduce them in evidence. Confirm in advance that any documents you show to the jury during the opening are admissible and consider available methods for displaying the aids that can help you emphasize your point, such as an ELMO, a large poster exhibit, or a Microsoft PowerPoint presentation. PowerPoint offers a variety of themes, transitions, and effects to easily create stunning presentations with minimal effort. The user, for instance, can add video, photos, and sound easily into the slides. Apple's Keynote offers similar functionality.

It is important to appreciate that a mediocre slide presentation is to be avoided at all costs. Blandly or poorly designed visual presentations can be difficult to read, distracting, or just plain boring. Take the time to consult with experts, if appropriate, to assure that your presentation is clear and engaging. PowerPoint has the advantage of displaying photographs, callouts, and highlighting, but these callouts (highlighted and enlarged sections of the document placed in the margins or as an overlay to the document itself) must be legible. In some cases, a blow-up of the document placed as close to the jury as the court permits might be preferable.

Many attorneys now use a tablet computer such as the iPad in the courtroom to view notes and outlines, but the devices can also display demonstrative evidence and aids to the jury or judge. Of course, as with a laptop computer, you will need a projector as well. There are applications (apps), such as TrialPad or ExhibitView, which feature robust trial presentation capability. These apps and others allow you to display or present graphs, photographs, time lines, and documents. A tablet can also be used as an electronic easel, allowing you to write with a stylist on the screen if you wish to circle or highlight a portion of an image.

It is also possible to use an iPad to display presentations wirelessly on a larger screen, freeing you from the podium, allowing you to move about the courtroom, presenting documents or slides when needed.

With the aid of a trial presentation specialist, Adobe Flash can create sophisticated self-contained interactive exhibits. This program creates presentations that resemble websites in that they allow you to click on links that take you to different screens within your presentation. With Adobe Flash, a programmer/designer can create complex and compact visuals combining documents, video, photos, graphics, and more. This has advantages when, for example, you wish to ask a health care provider to review a patient's entire hospitalization records. Calendar months can be presented and you can go month-to-month, day-to-day, and within each day you can press a button to reveal the medical records for that exact day or notes that relate to your case. If your opening statement involves complex information, Flash can help visualize it and thereby simplify it for the jury. A video time line, for instance, could help a juror keep track of when various events took place and what images you would like him or her to associate with those events.

Pictures seen early in the trial can have a lasting impact. They will stick in the memories of the jurors, who will likely come to associate them with certain ideas. With this in mind, in the *Rosen* trial, the defense used a projector to show jurors photos of two operatives, Peter Paul and Aaron Tonken, whom the defense would argue had concealed from the defendant key information about the expenses incurred by the Hollywood fundraiser. By presenting these images, the defense sought to focus the jurors' attention on their controversial actions, which would become central to the development of the theme. In the *Maffei* case, demonstrative aids came in handy, primarily as a way to simplify and clarify complicated technical information. All counsel referred to large color diagrams on poster boards, PowerPoint slides, and documents displayed by a document camera.

When involved with document-intensive cases, use of TrialDirector or Sanction may be desirable. In contrast to PowerPoint presentations that are scripted and follow a certain order, TrialDirector allows you to display the exhibits spontaneously in any order desired. TrialDirector

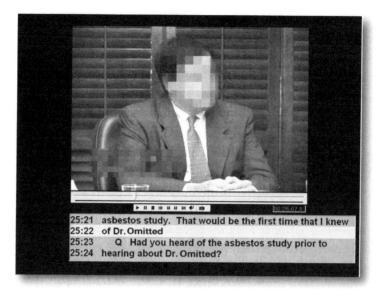

25:21   asbestos study. That would be the first time that I knew
25:22   of Dr. Omitted
25:23   Q   Had you heard of the asbestos study prior to
25:24   hearing about Dr. Omitted?

Figure 1

can also synchronize video-to-transcript and is often used to show the prior testimony of a witness for impeachment purposes, to underscore an admission, or display excerpts from deposition testimony of a witness who is not available for trial. (See Figure 1)

Demonstrative aids play an important role in opening statements in nonjury cases as well. While one might think a judge or arbitrator is perfectly capable of reviewing a document as opposed to viewing an enlarged version on a screen, this is not always the case. Having everyone view a document on a screen while it is being discussed helps you capture attention and emphasize your points. In the *Oregon Grille* case, counsel stipulated to exhibits and asked the court to refer to the exhibits during the trial. The judge was pleased to do so. During one part of the trial, counsel for the defense used an ELMO to portray the umbrellas that the defendant called canopies. (Canopies were prohibited under the zoning ordinances; umbrellas were not.)

A few words of caution about demonstrative aids during the opening statement: as helpful as they can be, using them excessively or unwisely can distract the jurors from your theme and clutter the jurors' minds with details better saved for later. Also, before you use the aids, consult with opposing counsel and ask the judge for permission. Having to fend off objections and a judge's disapproval during the opening can harm the jurors' impression of you.

Overstating the Case

While it is important to engage the jury with your theme during the opening statement, it is more important not to promise more than you can deliver. Doing so will destroy your credibility. What reaction can you expect from a jury if, in the opening statement, defense counsel says her client will take the stand and testify, but later the attorney decides otherwise? Once the credibility of counsel is undermined, the entire case is jeopardized.

Risking overstatement, the *Rosen* defense told the jury in its opening statement that it would call the defendant to the witness stand. Whether to call the defendant is a major decision that cannot usually be made until the prosecution concludes its case. Because making this pledge essentially requires you to follow through, no matter what, it is a dangerous tactic. The *Rosen* defense took the chance, in part because putting the defendant on the stand was one of the best ways to demonstrate his innocence and the overarching theme.

In the *Oregon Grille* case, counsel were careful not to overstate the case by representing to the court facts that would not be offered in evidence. Indeed, once the theme has been established in the opening statement, it can be seen as a guide for much of what the advocate does throughout the trial. The credibility of the theme must be vigorously protected every step of the way.

ETHOS, LOGOS, AND PATHOS

Opening statements, like closing arguments, are creatures of rhetoric—the art of using the most effective means of communication. The advocate who appreciates this will develop the opening in a manner that will enhance his or her ethos before the jury, appeal to the jurors' sense of pathos, and ground the case in sound logic, or logos. Ethos, pathos, and logos were the three pillars of argument for the great rhetoricians of antiquity. Attend to these elements of persuasion, and you will increase your chances of success.

Ethos

Because the opening statement is the first chance the jury gets to see you in action, it is the best opportunity to establish a strong ethos, which is the listeners' perception of you the advocate. While qualities such as honesty and integrity are part of one's ethos, the concept is broader. It includes such characteristics as the advocate's knowledge of the case, his or her sincerity, goodwill, and even the ability to convincingly demonstrate enthusiasm and emotion. Lawyers can enhance their ethos during trial by being likeable; respectful and sincere; honest and prepared; and courteous and fair; and being properly attired; using plain English; and by avoiding ad hominem attacks and contentiousness.

Ethos should be on the advocate's mind throughout the trial, as he or she tries to become the figure the jury identifies with and the central focus of attention in the courtroom. When you act with dignity and civility, your ethos rises. When you quibble and suffer admonitions from the judge, your ethos falls.

Qualities that enhance ethos include *integrity, knowledge, likability*, and *sincerity. Integrity* demands avoiding the assertion of facts that the jury is unlikely to believe. It also means appearing to the jury not as a zealous lawyer or hired gun, but as an advocate of justice, as an honest, sensible human being who avoids extreme positions. *Knowledge* here means familiarity with the case; demonstration of preparedness; familiarity with the sources of asserted facts or law; and the avoidance of logical fallacies. It will help, too, if you can deliver your arguments in a somewhat conversational style rather than reading them. *Likability* and *sincerity* consist of demonstrating interest in and care about your case; displaying civility and professionalism; and always speaking like you believe what you say.

In each of the three cases selected for discussion, all counsel attempted to maintain high ethos before judge and jury in opening statements. In the *Rosen* case, the government lawyer stroked jurors' sense of self-importance by speaking to them about their role as public representatives responsible for protecting the country from election law infractions.

Defense counsel took a different tack. Attempting to earn the jury's respect, the defense stated in the opening that the defendant Rosen would truthfully answer all questions put to him on the witness stand later in the trial. Making this statement early on was a risk, but it had the advantage of making the jurors' aware, throughout the case, that they would eventually receive an explanation of disputed events from the man charged with a crime.

In the *Maffei* case, plaintiff's counsel sought at the outset to gain the jury's respect by stating that he was not attacking the physician but simply trying to protect his client from negligence, which can happen without any harmful intent. The defense in that case proclaimed that the doctor was thorough and did everything possible and the defense portrayed the doctor as a likeable, sincere person who spared nothing to help the patient.

In the *Oregon Grille* case, counsel for both sides exhibited respect and courtesy to all those in the room and took the time to introduce their clients to the court. They were prepared and, in light of the judge's desire to get to the heart of the matter without wasting time, complied with her wishes.

Receiver-Centered Approach

Because your ethos as an advocate depends on how you are perceived by the judge and jury, it is crucial to tailor your opening statement to your listener. More important than you or your argument is the one you seek to persuade. Therefore, you should understand the factors that influence decision-making, such as a judge's or jury's attitudes and beliefs. Imagine stating in the opening statement that the police are exceedingly aggressive, when a member of the jury's cousin is a police officer who was seriously injured by an assailant. You may well have collided with a juror's attitude or belief.

All effort must be made to understand how the listeners will make judgments and how you can permeate their predispositions and prejudices. To the extent you can, shape your case to fit into what you believe are the mindset and emotions of the judge or jury. In other words, you and the judge or jury must become of one mind. Your audience must identify with you. As hard as it can be, you must try to know what judge or jury are looking for in your case. In short, you must be a detective and a psychologist.

During the 19th century in the United States, the luminary at the bar was Daniel Webster. He explained how he convinced juries ". . . by addressing the understanding of common men . . . I must use language perfectly intelligible to them. You will, therefore, find in my speeches to juries no hard words, no Latin phrases, no *fieri facias*."[6]

In England, during a time when Webster's advocacy reigned supreme in the United States, James Scarlett was a great figure of the British bar. The secret of his success was similar to Webster's. He blended his mind with the jury. Their thoughts were his thoughts. One juror was said to have remarked: "He is a lucky one, because he is always on the right side." He scored victories because there were "twelve Scarletts in the jury box."[7] Webster and Scarlett were great advocates because they understood their audiences, knew how to appeal to their listeners, and were liked and respected by them.

Of course, all of this is easier said than accomplished. In *Thinking Fast and Slow*, Daniel Kahneman, winner of the Nobel Prize in economics, illustrates some of the challenges we confront as advocates. He discusses the intuitive feelings and opinions all of us have about everything. Kahneman summarizes current studies on decision-making. He states that we have two modes of thinking: system one and system two.[8] The first system is automatic. It requires no work, causing one to operate automatically. For example we stand "automatically" when the judge enters the courtroom. System two allocates work and concentration. For example, the judge asks a probing question during our argument, and we work hard to respond. Others in the field contrast intuitive and rational thought.[9]

---

6. *See* Lloyd Paul Stryker, The Art of Advocacy 56 (1956); Robert Remini, Daniel Webster, The Man of His Time 80 (1997); Ronald Waicukauski, Paul Mark Sandler & JoAnne Epps, The Twelve Secrets of Persuasive Argument 14 (2010).

7. Stryker, *supra* note 6.

8. *See* Daniel Kahneman, Thinking Fast and Slow (2011).

9. *See, e.g.,* Jonathan Haidt, The Righteous Mind, Why Good People Are Divided by Politics and Religion (2013).

We know that in reaching decisions we tend to be "groupish" and strive for consistency. We use various devices to reach our decisions. We rely on our instincts, biases, and first impressions, which are often derived from attitudes and beliefs. Heuristics also aid us in our decisions. Heuristics are shortcuts based on substitution of easy facts for more difficult ones. An example: "Birds of a feather stick together." Thus, a defendant is likely to be guilty if he kept company with criminals."

Understanding how we render decisions helps us shape our arguments to meet the attitudes of listeners and lead them to our point of view. Sometimes this technique is known as "pacing." We signify to listeners that we understand and appreciate their opinion. Then we explain why that opinion should be modified.

Usually people like to make decisions on their own. We do not want to be told what to do or to be hit over the head with a two-by-four. Hence, rhetorical questions can be helpful. By asking a question without responding to it, the speaker leaves the answer up to the juror or judge. Another helpful device is the embedded request. Rather than say, "You must find her not guilty," you might say, "I am wondering, given this evidence, why would anyone find her guilty?" In other words, instead of yelling at little Tommy Jones, "Walk, don't run," we'll get further by saying to the boy, "I'm wondering, Tommy, if we should remember to walk when we are in the hallway." Posing the command in the form of a question, with a gentle preface, leaves room for the receiver of the message to feel less controlled and more independent.

Focusing on the people you wish to persuade is what's called a "receiver-centered" approach to persuasion. Adhering to it is tricky when it comes to jury trials. With a judge, you can at least study his or her prior opinions, sit in the courtroom and observe the judge at work, and seek information from the judge's colleagues. Getting a bead on a jury is more complicated. You can use your intuition, and rely on questionnaires and voir dire to give you some information. You can use the Internet to learn about jurors, but that most likely would occur after the jury is selected. There are judges, however, who will permit the use of computers and Internet searches of prospective jurors by counsel during voir dire. Before attempting to do this, seek permission from the court and consider the benefits of a jury consultant.

In *U.S. v. Rosen*, both sides sought to bolster their ethos and tailor their opening statements with the jurors in mind. To illustrate how the attorneys did so, we will consider how they handled Hillary Clinton's indirect involvement in the case.

The defendant had been the national finance director of Hillary Clinton's 2000 Senate campaign and had been accused by the government of causing a false fundraising report to be filed with the FEC. Clearly, there was the potential that some of the jurors would feel supportive of the Clintons and the Democratic Party, and that these feelings could affect their view of the evidence. The government thus delivered an opening that dealt with these suspected sympathies. The prosecutor emphatically stated that the case had nothing to do with Clinton. This was a smart approach. Clearly, the government wanted any jurors who did support Hillary Clinton to separate her from the defendant and the allegations against him.

If the government had neglected to address this concern, one can imagine that a Democratic-leaning juror might have sat through the trial internally resisting the prosecutor's efforts as an attack against Hillary Clinton's campaign, the Clintons themselves, or the Democrats in general. The prosecutor's ethos would have suffered greatly because of this.

While the government sought to distance the case from Hillary Clinton, the opening statement for the defense highlighted Rosen's relationship with the first lady after summarizing his background. The defense counsel's opening briefly touched on David Rosen's Chicago upbringing, his "loving family," and education. Rosen hadn't completed high school but had earned a GED and worked "all the way through his young life," at Burger King, Domino's Pizza, and as an encyclopedia salesman. He had also worked his way through college before becoming involved in politics. The defense's aim in making these comments during the opening was to portray Rosen as an industrious, earnest, self-reliant young man of humble roots.

Seconds after hearing how the defendant had worked as a pizza delivery-man and a burger flipper, the jurors received a three-sentence description of his entrance into Democratic politics and fundraising. Then they listened to the following story:

> [I]n 1999, an interesting phone call was received by Mr. Rosen. It was someone who was an official in the Democratic Party who wanted to know would he like to come to the White House, meet the first lady, and discuss being a fundraiser in her campaign for the United States Senate. And yes, folks, he was very excited.

> He went to the White House. The evidence will show he went into the Map Room of the White House, and there he met the first lady. He was ecstatic being in that room. It was very, very exciting. But he, of course, was not a child or a youngster, and was able to contain his enthusiasm. And he had lunch with the first lady around the pool of the White House, just the two of them, and they talked politics.

> And David Rosen was interested, and he was interested in helping the first lady become a United States Senator; and he was very, very excited when he was offered the position of being the national fundraiser director for her campaign.

In narrating the story just this way, the defense sought to help the jurors form their own vivid impression of David Rosen and this case; the goal was to forge an emotional connection between the jury and Rosen by showing the jurors that, just as they would have been excited to be summoned to the White House to lunch with the first lady, so too was the defendant. The defense provided details about the Map Room, the pool, and the need for self-composure, in an effort to demonstrate that Rosen was affected in ways the jurors could relate to, no matter their political affiliation.

Storytelling

Storytelling can be an effective technique of persuasion not only in opening statements, but also during witness examinations through your questions and the witnesses' answers, and in closing arguments. Stories can generate passion and sympathy for the characters, your clients.

Consider the role of the lawyer as storyteller in the following excerpt of *Passin' Through at 25*, by Louis L'Amour:

> In the smaller towns throughout the country trial lawyers were like stars in the theater. When court was setting, folks would drive or ride from miles around in their buckboards just to see the show and the trial lawyer played to us in the gallery as much as to the jury, and some of the more flamboyant lawyers had followings, who bragged them up and they told story after story about what they said or who they quoted. Most of the lawyers had read from the Bible and the classics and they could quote freely, and did. Some of them had a story for every occasion, and the story would often make the point when nothing else would.[10]

In any trial, there are at least two primary storytellers: the lead lawyers. Any advocate wants to be the most engaging, believable storyteller in the courtroom, the one who captures the jurors' attention and trust. Such authority is the very essence of ethos. Strategic appeals to emotion and rhetoric that embrace shared values can help establish such authority during the opening statement.

The lawyers in the *Maffei* case also sought to bolster their ethos and tailor their opening statements with the jurors in mind. The plaintiff stated that she was not accusing the doctor of being a bad person but of being negligent. The defense expressed sympathy for the widow but told the jury that the doctor had adhered to the standard of care and had not been negligent.

In the *Oregon Grille* case, counsel appreciated that the judge was not interested in histrionics. The defense attorney made brief, concise

---

10. *See* Judge Joseph F. Anderson, Jr., The Lost Art: An Advocate's Guide to Effective Closing Argument 32 (3d ed. 2008).

statements, provided the court with an exhibit book, and sat down. And as in any proceeding, counsel attempted to corroborate their arguments with the evidence.

Logos

For Aristotle, logic is one of the most important elements of argument. A well-constructed presentation based on logic is persuasive. On the other hand, a presentation poorly reasoned creates vulnerabilities that opposing counsel will likely exploit. Making a hasty generalization or false analogy during an opening statement can cause irreparable harm.

In developing your opening, keep in mind the patterns of inductive and deductive reasoning, the primary forms of logic.

Induction

Inductive reasoning relies upon an inference and contains new information not found in the premises. We go from the particular to the general or universal. For example, the defendant emerging from his car after the collision slurred his words and stumbled as he walked. One might infer that the defendant was intoxicated. With induction, the conclusion at best is probable. It is not always true, even when the premises are. The probability of conclusion depends on the strength of the inference. When using inductive reasoning, seek to strengthen your inferences and avoid relying on flimsy assumptions.

Inductive reasoning is often divided into the categories of generalization, analogy, and causal correlation. *Generalization* considers specific instances and then infers a general conclusion. For example, several instances of a particular type of lawn mower malfunctioning when used in cool weather might lead to the generalization that all such lawn mowers are deficient in cool weather. Of course, the refutation of the conclusion might be that an insufficient number of examples were drawn upon, or that the lawn mowers considered were not identical. In the *Maffei* case, the plaintiff's expert relied on generalization in coming to the conclusion that, given the expert's prior experience and a wealth of relevant data on similar cases, surgery would have saved Mr. Maffei's life. Again, to protect a generalization, be sure that the examples are both numerous and similar to matter in a dispute.

Analogical reasoning is based on observing similarity among a limited number of instances and then making inferences about additional, unobserved instances. In mediation, the magistrate judge reviews the court's prior awards of damages for cases similar to yours. The magistrate then concludes in private conference that your client should consider increasing the settlement offer. The magistrate used analogical reasoning in suggesting that your case would conclude as the others had. Analogical reasoning identifies a proper base point and then identifies the similarities between the base point and the present facts. A refutation would assert that the base point is too dissimilar to the present case and that, thus, the analogy is false.

Causal correlation involves inferring that a particular act caused a particular result. An example of this type of reasoning is as follows: Twenty people became ill after eating a single brand of chicken. One could conclude that the chicken caused the illness. Refutation might be that another cause was responsible for the illness, or that chronology of events does not prove effect.

Deduction

Deductive arguments focus on the premise. In deductive reasoning, a general premise leads to a specific conclusion that contains no new information. In contrast to inductive reasoning, we go from the general to the particular. If the argument's conclusion follows necessarily from a premise and contains no new information, the reasoning is deductive.

The most recognized form of deductive reasoning is the syllogism. It consists of two premises and a conclusion. For example:

1. Major premise: All lawsuits must be filed within three years from the date of event.
2. Minor premise: The case was filed four years after the event.
3. Conclusion: The case was filed too late and should be dismissed.

This example is often referred to as a categorical syllogism. What is true of the class is true of a member of the class. As long as the premises are true, the conclusion is valid; if the premises are false, so is the conclusion.

In the *Oregon Grille* case, the defense counsel used a deductive argument when he argued that the case should be dismissed, given the plaintiff's failure to exhaust administrative remedies.

1. Major premise: The Maryland Declaratory Act provides that a declaratory judgment is not a remedy if the aggrieved party has an administrative remedy.
2. Minor premise: An administrative remedy existed; counsel proved this by introducing the provision of the Baltimore County Code and by adducing testimony from an expert witness who explained the administrative remedy and its availability to the plaintiffs.
3. Conclusion: The case should be dismissed.

An interesting feature of a deductive argument is the enthymeme. An enthymeme is a major premise that is implied and need not be stated. The advocate appreciates that the listener subscribes to the unspoken first or major premise. In the *Oregon Grille* case, the defense opening incorporated an enthymeme. Counsel argued, in short, that the plaintiffs had other remedies and so the case should be dismissed. What was left unspoken was the major premise that under the Maryland Declaratory Act, if the aggrieved party has an available remedy, exhaustion of that remedy is required before suit can be initiated. The defense counted on the judge to understand this premise. Some things do not need to be explained.

Fallacies

Understanding the rules of logic enables you to tighten your arguments and to detect the weakness of opposing arguments, for example, logical fallacies. In the *Rosen* trial, the prosecution wove through its opening statement a kind of inductive reasoning that would assign a motive to Rosen for allegedly allowing false reports to be made to the FEC. The government's logic went like this: David Rosen was under pressure to keep expenses for fundraising events low. The expenses being incurred by this particular fundraiser were allegedly skyrocketing. Fearful of losing his job, Rosen therefore allegedly decided to file with the FEC reports that documented the expenses as lower than they actually were.

Now, every building has points of stress where beams must withstand pressure or the structure will fall. Similarly, logical arguments have points of stress—assertions that, if successfully rebuffed, endanger the entire argument. In the *Rosen* case, the logic of the prosecution's opening contained numerous such assertions, and the defense challenged them throughout the trial. The most vulnerable was the inference that because costs were high, Rosen was compelled to act unlawfully. The defense would argue that he did not, in fact, know the true costs because they were hidden from him.

Inferences are frequently vulnerable to attack. If listened to carefully, opening statements usually reveal the case's overarching logic and its points of stress. It is critical that you are prepared to defend your own inferences to the end and to counter those made by your opponents.

The way to spot fallacies in your argument or in that of your adversary is to keep your eye on the logical principles embedded within the rhetoric. Consider this syllogism: All parents who go to PTA meetings are honest; the defendant goes to PTA meetings. Therefore, he is honest and you can believe his testimony. It is easy to spot this fallacy. The major premise is not valid.

Numerous other fallacies are easy to spot. Here are some examples of common fallacies:

Red herring: Attention is distracted with irrelevant arguments.

Nonsequitur: The requested inference does not follow from the sample.

Post hoc ergo propter hoc: Chronology is used to explain causal correlation (after this, therefore because of this). You can avoid post hoc ergo propter hoc by ensuring that your causal correlation argument is based on more than a time sequence and that you have excluded other causes of the result.

Unlike circumstances in analogical reasoning: A case is compared to a previous case that bears no resemblance to it, and it is claimed that the cases should conclude in a similar fashion.

The straw man: This arises when your opponent describes your argument in an oversimplified or extreme form and then refutes it. For example, in a medical negligence case, defense counsel could set up a straw man by arguing, "The plaintiff expects doctors to be superhuman. He wants to use hindsight to hold them accountable for any outcome from a surgery."

Slippery slope: The argument assumes falsely that once you take a moderate first step, a catastrophic chain of events will follow. An example of a slippery slope argument in a medical negligence case would be plaintiff's counsel asserting that, "If you don't send a message by finding for the plaintiff, doctors will feel they can make mistakes and more patients will be harmed as a result."

False dilemma: This fallacy creates an issue and suggests only two alternatives when there are many. For example, in treating certain testimony, counsel might argue that "the testimony is false; it must have been a lie, as how could it be true?" But there exists another possibility—the witness made an honest mistake.

Composition: What is true of the separate parts is assumed to be necessarily true of the collective whole. For example, if a component was manufactured by a team of highly qualified individuals, the fact that they were each qualified does not mean, as a matter of logic, that the team itself was consistent in quality with every single component.

Pathos

While many of us take pride in making decisions based on logic, we all appreciate that most decisions are based in part on emotions. Abraham Lincoln once said during his trial lawyer days that, in order to persuade a person, one first had to capture the heart. Cicero once observed that we make most determinations through love or hatred, desire or anger, grief or joy, than from regard to truth. Invoking emotion in a trial requires a delicate balance with the jury. You do not want to be perceived as pandering, or as if you are trolling for sympathy.

Histrionics are never appropriate, but opening statements should make some emotional pull on the audience, however subtle. In the *Rosen* case, the defense's opening statement contained the following assertion regarding Rosen's initial response to the idea of the Hollywood fundraiser in question:

> David Rosen did not wish to go forward with this event. No, he didn't. He'll tell you that. He had reservations. . . . [B]ut it was all worked out and he was told, "Go forth, young man. Go west. Do this event." And when you meet him and he testifies, you will see his spunk, his enthusiasm, his dedication. He is a soldier, a trooper, and loyal, and a leader, and he went forward. But he never knew, like that poem of Alfred Lord Tennyson, that he was walking into the valley of trouble. Because when he went there, folks, he never knew what was going to come up and try to ruin him.

This segment of the opening cut to the emotional core of the defense's case. Throughout the trial, the defense sought to portray Rosen as an earnest, patriotic, and ambitious young man whose life was essentially sabotaged by the sinister machinations of political operatives. The historical allusions to America's 19th-century westward expansion and "The Charge of the Light Brigade" (wherein soldiers actually brave the "valley of death") were certainly hyperbolic in the context of a campaign finance dispute. Nevertheless, they were sprinkled in for their value as cultural shorthand for a whole set of emotional themes—patriotism, courage, optimism, loyalty, and betrayal.

There are many ways of telling the emotional side of your story during the opening statement. If the case concerns a traffic accident, you could describe the wreckage in vivid detail or tell an anecdote about your client's struggle to walk afterward. You needn't raise your voice or shed tears to get the message across. Rely on the power of understatement and allow the facts of your case to inspire the desired emotion. Rather than hit the jury over the head by reminding them how tragic your case is, show them by plainly describing what happened. Use photographs or videos if appropriate. Images of a disturbing incident shown during an opening statement may lodge themselves in a juror's memory and influence how he or she views the rest of the trial.

Emotion is an important aspect of communication. It stirs us to feel sad or happy, to feel pity or anger. Emotion persuades. However, avoid emotional appeals unless you can feel the emotion yourself. If you try to force pathos, the opening will come off as an act and will hurt your credibility. If the feeling is in you, it is far more likely to engage and help persuade the jury.

There are several techniques for the effective use of emotion as a means of persuasion: Sometimes the power of understatement is effective. Allow the jury to feel the emotion by the way you calmly and quietly present the opening statement or closing argument. Tell the jury what happened, or elicit testimony by crafting poignant questions for the witness. Let the witness testify about her life before the collision and how it changed afterward. Watch the reaction of the jury as you try to humanize the client. You may be able to determine how the testimony is developing. Showing a security video of a disturbing incident in closing, having shown it previously in the course of the trial, may be a perfect closing with no further comment.

Telling a story and using figurative analogies can be effective in creating the emotional mood that you desire. Sometimes a little drama may help. Consider the legendary plaintiff's personal injury lawyer Mo Leven's brief closing argument, perhaps somewhat embellished, which left the courtroom in an eerie silence in a case where his client lost the use of both hands.

> Ladies and Gentlemen of the Jury, all of us including my client and I took our lunch at the same restaurant during recess. I watched all of you and you perhaps watched my client and me. I saw how all of you dined using a knife and fork as did I. My client ate like a dog.[11]

Levin then sat down.

---

11. *See* The Best of Moe: Summations, Moe Levin (1908-1974) (1983)

Your opening statement's emotional efficacy depends on your credibility. Protecting your credibility demands moderation when it comes to pathos. A jury will reject maudlin arguments and come to distrust those who make them. To earn a jury's trust, present an opening built upon sound logic. If your logic is faulty, your efforts at pathos will appear merely irrational.

STYLE AND DELIVERY

Give two lawyers the same case for an opening, and in presenting it they will make two distinctly different impressions upon a jury. The difference will be a factor of variations in style and delivery.

The manner in which words are conveyed is as important as the words themselves. Preparations for the opening statement should always include some consideration of style and delivery. Body language, word choice, rhythm, the use of figurative language, and physical demonstrations of emotion can help persuade or dissuade jurors.

Supposedly, when Demosthenes was asked to rank the three most important parts of argument, he responded, "Delivery, delivery, and delivery." But if someone were to ask the same question today, the great advocates of our time would likely say, "Style, style, and style." Whichever you deem more important, delivery and style are two of the primary techniques that help us engage the listener.

Style

Style is the form into which we put the content of our ideas. Rhythm, diction, sentence structure, and other elements define one's style. An important element of style is figures of speech, such as metaphors and similes. They are an important element of style, infusing arguments with clarity and charm.

No conversation about opening statements—or any aspect of courtroom advocacy, for that matter—is complete without a discussion of style and delivery. While style is the form in which you present your ideas (language, analogies, the structure of an argument), delivery involves gestures, expression, the regulation of voice, and the like.

Rhythm, diction, sentence structure, and other elements define one's style. When thinking of style, consider figures of speech which include schemes and tropes. Schemes are a change in the order of words in a sentence for drama or emphasis. For example: "A fine man was the decedent." Or: "His reaction to observing the collision was horror, horror, horror." Tropes are a change in the ordinary signification of a word or expression: for example, the metaphor "The termination was a dagger to his heart" or the simile: "The termination was like a dagger to his heart."

In a helpful study of figures of speech, Ward Farnsworth in his *Classical English Rhetoric* divides figures of speech into repetition of words and phrases; structural matters; and dramatic devices. His categorization and examples are an excellent resource.[12]

Consider the application of the following schemes in the context of opening statements as well as the other aspects of trial:

Epizeuxis: Consecutive repetition of words
> "She felt sad, sad, sad after she spoke those words."
> "Remorse, remorse, remorse is what he feels as a result of his conduct."

Epimone: Consecutive repetition of phrases
> "This is the case of the careless landlord. This is the case of man who turned a cold shoulder to the very tenants whom he pledged to provide safe housing."
> "I shall prove to you that Mr. Jones knew when he signed the contract he had no intention of honoring it. I shall prove to you that Mr. Jones intended for Ms. Smith to rely on his representations that he would convey the business to her."

Anaphora: Repetition of words at the beginning of a sentence
> " Not guilty, not guilty should be your verdict."
> "Stop, stop, she cried, as he continued to taunt her."

Epistrophe: Repetition of words at the end of a sentence
> "The evidence of negligence will be clear and compelling. Based on the evidence your verdict will be clear and compelling."

---

12. *See* Ward Farnsworth, Farnsworth's Classical English Rhetoric (2011).

"I will prove that the Phoenix Company was negligent. The driver of the bus was negligent, and the board of directors was negligent."

Symploce: Repetition at the start and end of a sentence

"Her breach of the contract was reprehensible, and you should hold her accountable for her breach of this contract."

"You do not need to hear the testimony of Mr. Axem, but you do need to hear the testimony of his sister."

Anadiplosis: Repeating the ending of a sentence at the beginning of the next

"He saw the collision. Seeing the collision, he also saw that the defendant was speeding."

"He entered the building at ten o clock. When he entered the building at ten o clock, he carefully locked the door behind him."

Anastrophe: Changing the normal word order in a sentence

"An honest witness he will be."

"Fraud is what this case is about."

Parenthesis: Interruption of normal flow of words by inserting a phrase

"The evidence will show, and you will believe it, that the plaintiff herself contributed to her own injury."

"This event, and it is a shame, caused the collision."

Ellipsis: Deliberate omission of words implied from context

"All his hopes pointed to a successful venture for the partnership, but the defendant for himself."

"From the testimony of our expert you will find negligence, from negligence liability."

Aposiopesis: A sudden halt in speech for effect

"Her injuries, her injuries [silence] were too much to bear."

"Why did the collision occur? [silence] Because of the negligence of Mr. Jones."

Praeteritio: Saying things by not saying them

"I will not call him a fabricator, for he is the government's key witness."

"The lack of care by the defendant I should not mention, and I shall not speak of his recklessness, at this time as you will want to hear the evidence."

Metanoia: Correcting oneself

"You will believe; I am sorry; you will know from the evidence what occurred."

"The plaintiffs' crusade, no, their intense hatred of the defendant, is the reason for this case."

Prolepsis: Anticipating objections and meeting them

"Defense will claim contributory negligence. But the evidence will show otherwise."

"The plaintiff will present evidence that she was not in the office at the time of the incident. The defense will suggest otherwise based on the testimony of one witness, who was so intoxicated that he cannot be relied upon."

Metaphor, simile, and rhetorical questions are common tropes. Here are some examples.

Metaphor: An implied comparison between two things that are unlike in nature but have something in common. It derives from the Greek word "to transfer." Thus a metaphor involves a transfer of meaning such as calling one thing by the name of something else. It can take the form of an implied comparison between two things unlike in nature by having something in common. (The ship plowed the ocean.) It can take the form of a transfer of meaning by calling one thing by the name of something else. (Life is a journey.)

"The only way to stop a wild beast in the woods is to stab it in the heart. The only way to stop this corporate monster is to stab it in the pocketbook."

"He viciously pounced on every idea Smith suggested."

Simile: in contrast to a metaphor, which involves an implicit comparison, a simile is an explicit comparison using words introduced by as or like.

"The evidence of fraud is as clear as a fire bell in the night."

"Seeing the defendant rush toward her, she turned like an agile athlete to flee."

Erotema: Rhetorical question (one that does not call for an answer by the speaker, but by the listener)

"Look at her, Ladies and Gentlemen, does she look like the type of person to file a false claim?"

"Why do you think the plaintiff instituted this case, for her own health?"

Hypophora: Asking questions and answering them

"Why do you think that the plaintiff brought this case? Because she was desperate, and tired of enduring the brutality of her boss."

"Why do you think they filed this case—to protect the community? No, to harass Mr. Smith."

Alliteration: The repetition of an initial consonant sound

"We shall now discuss the grim, grueling audit of pain."

"The big, bad dilemma for the defense is that their theory defies logic."

Apostrophe: Breaking off discourse to address some absent person or thing, some abstract quality, or an inanimate object or a nonexistent character

"I do not ask 'Oh, Justice where are you,' because you, members of the jury, are in Justice's robe."

Irony: The use of words to convey the opposite of their literal meaning. A statement or situation where the meaning is contradicted by the appearance or presentation of the idea.

"His fault was that he loved art." (in a case in which the defendant is charged with stealing a painting from a museum)

Litotes: An understatement in which an affirmative is expressed by negating its opposite

"He was not untruthful and he was not insincere."

"He did not act without care in fulfilling his duties."

Metonymy: One word or phrase is substituted for another with which it is closely associated; such as describing something indirectly by referring to things around it.

"After the plaintiff purchased his new wheels (automobile), he
drove from the dealer directly home."
Synecdoche: A part is used to represent the whole (for example, ABCs
for alphabet) or the whole for a part
"Remember the presumption." (presumption of innocence)

Knowing these terms isn't at all necessary, but we should approach the
task of preparing our opening statement with an appreciation for the
power of style to rivet the listener's attention, turn abstract concepts into
vivid imagery, and arouse emotion. Without becoming precious about
our language, we can enliven even the dullest of topics with a touch of
stylistic playfulness.

Delivery

Whereas style is the choice of words we use to express ourselves, delivery
is the way we regulate our movement in presenting the argument. The
word for "delivery" in Greek means acting. Persuasive trial technique
employs a delivery appropriate and tailored to the listener. Rapping on a
table for effect may suit a jury under certain circumstances but will not
likely impress a judge in a nonjury case. Delivery in the context of trial
includes voice modulation, gestures, eye contact, body contact, facial
expressions, and movement in the courtroom, subject to the rules of the
judge hearing the case.

Varying voice modulation attracts attention. For example, when voice is
varied the same way periodically when referring to the same particular fact
or point, we help hold the interest of the listener and emphasize the point.

Consider in the *Oregon Grille* case whenever defense counsel during
opening statement referred to what he would prove, he enhanced slightly
his voice and inflection when he stated the words: "I will prove" or "I will
call a witness" and when stating those words: "And first I'm going to *prove
to you* that this case should not be in this Court. . . ." "We *will also prove* that
Oregon Grille received a command from the landlord to pave the parking lot; I *will call* an expert witness in zoning; we *will also prove*. . . ." Use
your voice as a means of persuasion. Showing earnestness by lowering or
raising your voice will influence how your argument is heard. Changing

voice modulation helps engage the listener. The speed and rhythm of your words also can have an impact on the listener. Changing the rate of speech to suit the occasion; pausing when making a critical point or hesitating when posing a rhetorical question can be effective means to engage the judge or jury.

Gestures appropriate to the situation and in good taste can create mood and rapport with the listener. Consider: "We shall prove that this man, this defendant [pointing to the defendant each time after stating the word "this"] pulled the trigger, setting in motion the horrible chain of events leading to the death of Mr. Jones." Other gestures may include using your hands by pointing to the judge or jury to emphasize a point. Refrain from pointing with a pen or pencil. Also, do not repeatedly remove and replace your glasses. It is distracting. To show the jury that you have a strong relationship with your client, place a reassuring arm on his or her shoulder. Similarly, by calling your next witness with outstretched arm, you indicate familiarity, suggesting the arrival of a credible friend. These gestures and others can be signals to the listener about your view of the case. There are an infinite number of ways to use gestures, including shaking your head one way or the other; removing your eye glasses to convey seriousness; opening your arms at a certain time to convey acceptance, or folding your arms to convey disbelief. One creative gesture was used by Sir Edward Marshall Hall, one of the great English barristers of the late 19th century and early 20th century. It was Hall who first explained reasonable doubt to the jury by personifying the scales of justice and with outstretched arms tiled one way and then another to illustrate the difference between preponderance of the evidence and reasonable doubt.

Avoid overusing a gesture or making an offensive one. For instance, try not to shake your head with disappointment when the judge rules against you or a witness testifies harmfully. Poor gestures drain your ethos.

Eye contact is another aspect of delivery, and an important one. Looking into someone else's eyes can signify sincerity and interest in them. Combined with gestures and facial expressions, eye contact can serve as a nonverbal cue about your view of the case and as a means of emphasizing points of argument. When using eye contact, refrain from staring or making someone feel uncomfortable. Vary your eye contact as appropriate to establish rapport with all members of the jury. If, for example, you know that juror number four is a former teacher and you are making a point about education, then might be the opportunity to look into the eyes of that juror as you appropriately modulate your voice and perhaps nod your head in a positive way.

Eye contact like other modes of delivery can be a two-way street. Gestures by the jury can often be telling. Consider the folklore of a trial lawyer that if the jury does not look at you upon returning to render its verdict, the case is lost.

Anchors are another helpful technique; an "anchor" is a kind of rhetorical shorthand for a point you want to emphasize without restating. By speaking in a certain way or making a certain gesture at the mention of a particular witness, for instance, you can concisely convey your disapproval of his testimony.

Facial expressions are another important aspect of delivery. A frown, a smile, like a picture, convey many words. Use facial expressions when appropriate to convey positive ideas as well as negative. Why not offer a smile when you thank the jury or at times during the trial when it is natural and helpful? Or why not a frown and a negative movement of the head when referring to a witness that you argue is untruthful?

Bear in mind that the wrong signal can send your case spiraling. If your client's guilt is written on your face or expressed in your mannerisms, the jury will not likely reward your client.

Movement in the courtroom is an important undertaking as well as a delicate one. The courtroom is controlled by the judge. It is essential that before trial you understand the judge's rules for moving about the courtroom, including approaching a witness to show an exhibit or moving to a place where you may need to display a PowerPoint presentation. While you may wish to pace while asking questions or presenting opening statements, the court may not permit you to do so. In the *Rosen* case, counsel were required to remain at the podium at all times; in the *Maffei* case, the lawyers were permitted to move anywhere in the courtroom, including very close to the jury. Counsel showed demonstrative aids to jurors within a few feet of them. In one instance, an expert testified about a large exhibit directly in front of the jury.

Sometimes moving in the courtroom keeps the jury alert and attentive. Well-timed maneuvers can even enhance your ethos. For example, if you walk up to the jury box and ask the witness to "tell *us* what you observed. . . ." you are identifying with the jury and showing control of the case, as you are not referring to notes when you are away from the podium.

Other than the demands of the court, there are no hard-and-fast rules about courtroom style and delivery, though you should always "be yourself." A lawyer who copies another's style or delivery may come off as insincere, contrived, and even foolish. That said, observing other advocates at work in the courtroom can teach you valuable lessons, and help you be more effective in your own way.

Humor and understatement can also be helpful. In *Rosen*, one of the prosecution's aims in opening statement was to portray the Clinton fundraiser in question as excessively lavish and expensive. Thus, the prosecutor mentioned a few of the more extraordinary features of the event, including the decision to give director's chairs to the guests:

> Someone came up with the idea to give away the chairs as souvenirs. You will hear that everyone had a director's chair with stencil on the back commemorating the event. Why don't we give away the chairs? That will be a nice touch. They gave away $35,000 worth of chairs.

Note that the attorney here did not explicitly say that this gesture was excessive. He leaves it up to the jurors to form their own opinion. This is apt; persuasion is most often accomplished when listeners arrive at a conclusion on their own. Thus, a light touch is preferable to a heavy-handed style.

All stylistic technique comes down to the essential challenge facing the trial lawyer during opening statement: to both engage and persuade the jurors at the same time. As an attorney plots out her opening statement, style and delivery should never be far from her mind.

Find a style and manner of delivery that is natural for you. Give attention to your choice of words and strive for simplicity devoid of legalese.

If you use concrete words, as opposed to abstract words, and verbs rather than nouns, you will be more effective.

Immunization

Just as it is sometimes appropriate to acknowledge that your listener may hold an adverse point of view, it may be helpful during the opening statement to mention facts or testimony that could cut against your case. This consideration is especially important to parties who open first. Nevertheless, in a criminal trial, the defense may want to touch upon damaging facts or testimony that the prosecution chose not to mention in its opening.

The doctrine of immunization comes into play here. You tell the listener in summary fashion about the expected adverse argument or testimony and then provide a response. In the *Rosen* case, defense counsel sought to immunize the jurors against a particular witness:

> Well, you're going to hear testimony from one of [Rosen's] friends, a Mr. Jim Levin. The government will call him. And this individual is going to say, David Rosen and I, we knew about this, and David told me that he was going to hide things and we'll keep it all secret. But the—you won't believe that, and I will prove to you that it's not credible. That individual, Mr. Jim Levin, just two days ago signed a plea agreement, because he has his own criminal problems. And in order to get benefit for himself he is coming to court; and he will talk to you about what David Rosen supposedly said to him.

The goal in thus flagging upcoming adverse testimony is to take the wind out of your opponent's sails. Immunization can be very helpful during the opening statement, providing one of the best chances to portray your opponent's case in a negative light.

Learning Points for Chapter 2

- "Argue" your case in your opening statement without running afoul of the rules.
- The five-minute rule: Capture the jurors' attention from the start with a compelling, memorable articulation of your overarching theme.
- Organize your opening in service to the theme.
- Consider visual aids that will make your theme more memorable and persuasive for the jurors.
- Avoid overstating your case.
- Ethos is everything: From the start, create a favorable impression of yourself among the jurors.
- Examine logical "stress points" in your arguments and in your adversary's, and tailor the opening to address these weaknesses.
- Strike an emotional chord with listeners without slipping into histrionics.
- Consider how your style and delivery serve your theme.
- Immunize your case against anticipated attacks.

CHAPTER 3

OPENING STATEMENT: A VIEW FROM THE BENCH

By the Hon. Marvin J. Garbis, United States District Judge, United States District Court for the District of Maryland

As a United States district judge, I have presided over dozens of federal trials. During my career as a trial attorney, I represented white-collar defendants in federal courts throughout the country. I have, accordingly, had the privilege of being counsel or judge in federal trials with some of the best and—inevitably—some of the other trial practitioners.

A study of the trial of *U.S. v. Rosen* affords the opportunity to consider and critique (with the benefit of 20–20 hindsight) some of the decisions made by highly skilled trial lawyers in a case challenging to both sides.

GOVERNMENT OPENING

In broad terms, the function of the prosecution's opening statement is to build credibility for the government's case and to set the stage for conviction. The prosecutor should present a clear theory of the case by means of which the jury will want to convict and have a logical and inevitable path toward conviction. In sum, when the prosecutor finishes an effective opening, the jury should be ready—if called upon to deliberate then and there—to return a prompt verdict for the government.

Inasmuch as the government opening is the first step in the case, the prosecutor will not know precisely what the defense will say but should, to the extent possible, anticipate and defuse the defense's opening.

In *Rosen*, government counsel presented a fine opening but, at least as to one witness, left an opening that defense counsel was able to exploit.

At the beginning of his opening statement, Peter Zeidenberg avoided a typical prosecution error. He did not, as I like to put it, "waste the honeymoon"—that is, provide nothing useful in the first minute or two, when the jury is particularly focused.

So many prosecutors—possibly to overcome nervousness and start with a comfortable litany—begin by introducing themselves and others (and sometimes, it seems, everyone in the courtroom). As a result, the first precious minute is squandered informing them of the name of the prosecutor, identifying the person sitting in front of the courtroom in a black robe, explaining exactly what the court reporter is doing with the small keyboard and where the witnesses will be seated, and on and on ad tedium until, at long last, something is actually said about the case to be tried.

In sharp contrast, Zeidenberg started with a bang:

> [I]n August of 2000 Hillary Clinton's campaign for the United States Senate in New York was entering the stretch run. She was up against a well-financed challenger. The polls were tight. Money was tight. Running for the United States Senate in the United States is a very expensive proposition. Campaigning in a large, expensive media state like New York is particularly expensive. The responsibility for raising money for Hillary Clinton's campaign fell to this man seated at counsel table. His name is David Rosen.

Right off the bat, the jury members knew that they were involved in an important trial that would transport them into the world of political fundraising in a high-profile case. There is no doubt that the jury's attention was riveted on Zeidenberg.

The prosecutor went on to do an effective job of explaining the nature of the case, making it clear that there was no contention that the donations were in and of themselves illegal, but that the charges were related to the false reporting of the costs of an in-kind donation underwriting a political fundraiser.

Zeidenberg laced his opening statement with references to the glamorous people and lifestyle associated with the fundraising event. The jury heard about planning for a $25,000 per couple dinner, big-name talent such as Cher and Diana Ross, guests such as Brad Pitt, John Travolta and Muhammad Ali, private jets, and all the rest.

The jury was told that costs spun out of control and rose to an amount in excess of a million dollars. According to the government, Rosen knew of the actual cost but deliberately caused substantially understated cost reports to be provided to Hillary Clinton's campaign headquarters. Therefore, he caused the filing of false reports with the Federal Election Commission.

The prosecutor knew that he had to establish a motive for Rosen to have understated the costs. He, therefore, had to explain why it made a difference whether Rosen accurately reported the costs. Zeidenberg put it this way:

> You might rightly ask yourselves, while you are sitting there, what's the big deal if [a donor] is paying for all this stuff? Isn't it free? . . . [Y]ou will hear, ladies and gentlemen, that there are some thing[s] called soft money and hard money . . . Hard money is what the campaign wanted and needed. . . .
>
> . . . [U]nder the law a certain percentage of money from that hard money account needs to be transferred from the hard money account to the soft money account . . . So that $1.1 million that [was the cost of the event would] have to be transferred from the campaign's hard money account to the soft money account. . . .
>
> . . . [A]nd David Rosen knew that there was going to be a negative impact on that hard money fund by taking a massive in-kind soft money donation . . . so he wanted that report to be smaller.

Narrow Focus

Finally, the prosecution—wisely—distanced its case from any accusation against Hillary Clinton and focused the jury solely upon David Rosen:

> [A]s his Honor told you, this case has nothing to do with Hillary Clinton. It is about David Rosen. You will hear no evidence that Hillary Clinton was involved in this in any way, shape or form. In fact, it's just the opposite. The evidence will show that David Rosen was trying to keep this information from the campaign because he was afraid if they found out how much he had spent he would be fired. . . .
>
> This case is about one question, and one question only: Did David Rosen deliberately cause a false filing and statement to be made to the Federal Election Commission concerning the in-kind donations made to that gala on August 12th, 2000?

The government's opening statement was a good one. However, as discussed below, the prosecutor did give the defense an opening to cast doubt on the government's case.

The Defense Opening

While the prosecution's objective is to prevail if the verdict were rendered immediately after its opening statement, usually the defense can go no further than to persuade the jury to defer judgment until all of the evidence is presented. After all, the government should start the trial with a rather solid theory of the case. On the other hand, the defense typically is not certain what will occur at trial and must, at all costs, avoid making promises to the jury that will not be kept. Furthermore, in many criminal cases, the defense is well advised to avoid making opening-statement disclosures that will help the government fine-tune its presentation.

Thus, in many cases, the defense should find a way to subtly prepare the jury to be receptive to its theory without being unduly specific and, hence, without restricting the defense's flexibility to respond to trial developments. Moreover, the bottom line is that the defense's opening statement, the evidence, and the final argument should be an effective, consistent, and confidence-building unitary presentation. The opening statement should lay out the theme of the case but retain flexibility without being too general.

Like the prosecutor, defense counsel avoided the mistake of starting with purely empty verbiage. However, unlike the prosecutor, Sandler chose not to begin his opening statement by addressing the case. Rather, he elected to commence with what is to me (but presumably not to juries) the shopworn "whole hand" cliché:

> If I were to show you my hand and ask you if you see it, some of [you] would say, sure, I see your hand; but in reality, you don't. You don't see my hand until I turn it all the way around. Then and only then do you see my hand.
>
> So like this case, you have not seen this case. All we have heard is what the prosecutor says he's going to prove.

(I must confess that I typically use the "whole hand" cliché in my initial instructions to the jury so that I simply don't have to listen to it from counsel anymore.)

"WHAT THIS CASE IS REALLY ABOUT"

Sandler then, after a sentence introducing himself and co-counsel, presented the electrifying statement that in my view should have been the first thing he said:

> [W]e would like to tell you what this case is really about. It's about David Rosen's fight against the injustice of his being wrongfully accused of something he never did. I will prove to you in this case he is innocent. He is [a] victim, an innocent victim, of other people's motives, and I will prove this. I will prove to you that David Rosen never knew, never knew the cost of the production and concert expenses for this Hollywood gala.

This unusual defense posture—taking on the burden to prove innocence—was effective and, realistically, had little downside. As a practical matter neither the prosecution in argument nor the judge in the instructions was going to try to shift the burden of proof to the defense. Moreover, the judge was, inevitably, going to repeatedly remind the jury that the government's burden was to prove guilt beyond a reasonable doubt. Yet, defense counsel was able to exhibit an extreme level of confidence in the innocence of his client. He carried this level of confidence throughout the opening statement.

Sandler proceeded to deflect an essential ingredient of the government's theory of the case—a motive for Rosen to have committed the crime. The prosecution, as noted above, contended that Rosen hid the costs from the campaign because he was concerned about being fired. Defense counsel—not quite meeting this head on (probably because he could not, but possibly because the point was better avoided than directly confronted)—stated in this regard:

> The evidence will show, and I will prove this to you, he gained not one penny from this underreporting. . . . I will prove to you and I will say to you that the government must concede this point, folks: The Hillary Clinton campaign gained no economic benefit from this at all. And to say that the campaign was coming into a stretch and money was tight and things were desperate is to be inaccurate. I will prove that to you.

Defense counsel also, of course, humanized the defendant with a review of his sympathetic personal background—a high school dropout who got a GED, held menial jobs flipping hamburgers at Burger King and delivering pizzas to work his way through college. Then, he attained various positions and, eventually, was thrilled to find himself working for Hillary Clinton. Sandler, however, made sure that the jury didn't have the impression that Rosen was enjoying an opulent lifestyle, even though he was working as a fundraiser: "Where did he live?" the attorney asked. "The evidence will show he did not live in the White House. He lived in a little room in New York City that was no bigger than a postage stamp."

Thus, the jury was presented with a solid working guy to whom they could relate. Nevertheless, the defense did not lack for problems.

DEALING WITH DIFFICULT FACTS

Defense counsel had to deal with the difficult fact that Rosen had been given luxurious hotel accommodations while in Los Angeles working on the campaign, but did not report the cost of this as a donation.

As the prosecutor put it:

> David Rosen incurred over $13,000 in hotel bills in the weeks leading up to the event. It's easy to rack up $13,000 in hotel bills when you're staying in hotels like The Hermitage and The Beverly Hills Hotel that charge $300 to $350 a night. He incurred those initially on his own credit card, never reported those expenses to the FEC as he was required to do. Later he tried to get someone, anyone, to pay them off. And you will hear he approached more than one individual trying to get them to pay off his bills. Eventually he settled on Aaron Tonken. And by pestering him for long enough, Aaron Tonken finally agreed to pay off that hotel bill. It's legal for a donor to pay off a hotel bill, but it has to be reported to the Federal Election Commission as an in-kind donation.

Sandler's response—delivered with supreme confidence:

> Now, when David Rosen stayed at the Beverly Hills Hotel, he will tell you he did not consider that a campaign contribution at all. He considered that this individual . . . was going to treat him because he was working hard, and he also loaned him his Porsche to drive back and forth during his work. . . .

> [A]nd it was very exciting for him, and he thought it was a nice idea. It didn't make him a criminal. It doesn't make him doing something wrong. He did not consider this to be a campaign contribution to the campaign, but for him, and this is how he conducted himself and he didn't hide it. . . .

> [T]here is no reason for him to have reported something that he thought was a personal gift to him. There was nothing that he did wrong in

that, and he did not conceal it or hide it and did not intend this to be an evil deed.

In this way, the hotel bill problem was smoothed over and presumably faded into the background during the course of the trial.

DEVELOPING A THEME

Sandler knew that he had to shift the blame for the underreporting of costs from Rosen to the donors. Thus, the defense had to develop the theme that the donors, Aaron Tonken and Peter Paul, hid the true costs from Rosen. Sandler used the tactic of pinning a label on them and never letting the jury forget that they were "concealers":

> I will prove to you that David Rosen never knew, never knew the cost of the production and concert expenses for this Hollywood gala.

> And why didn't he know it, folks? The evidence will show he did not know it because those costs were concealed from him. They were hidden from him by two individuals: Peter Paul, who you can see on the screen, and Aaron Tonkcn. . . .

> He met [at an event] three people for the first time in person: Peter Paul, one of the concealers; Aaron Tonken, another of the concealers; and Bretta Nock, joined at the hip with Aaron Tonken. . . .

> I will show you a letter from the concealer Tonken. . . .

> I will also prove to you that no one, except the concealers and those that were with them, knew what these costs were.

EXPLOITING AN OPENING

The government's opening statement provided an opportunity for the defense by not adequately addressing the fact that it was relying upon a "cooperating" witness. The prosecutor could have drawn the sting from the inevitable defense contention that the jury should not rely upon "bought and paid for" testimony from an admitted criminal. However, the prosecutor simply stated:

> Now, after the event, ladies and gentlemen, the FBI began investigating and they began questioning people. And David Rosen had a conversation with a witness, who you will hear from, and he told this witness that he wasn't worried. He said, it's their word against ours: Peter Paul, Aaron Tonken. They are liars. No one will believe them over me. And so he decided to ride it out.

This left an opening for Sandler to condition the jury to distrust an important government witness and, by implication, all of the prosecution's case. He did so with alacrity:

> Well, you're going to hear testimony from one of his friends, a Mr. Jim Levin. The court [sic] will call him. And this individual is going to say, David Rosen and I, we knew about this, and David told me that he was going to hide things and we'll keep it all secret. But the—you won't believe that, and I will prove to you that it's not credible. That individual, Mr. Jim Levin, just two days ago signed a plea agreement, because he has his own criminal problems. And in order to get benefit for himself he is coming to court, and he will talk to you about what David Rosen supposedly said to him. That's the type of evidence that you will hear from the government.

RISKY TACTIC

Finally, I note a most controversial tactical decision by Sandler. He made the jury a rarely heard promise:

> I will prove to you, through our witnesses, that David Rosen is innocent. And I will tell you this: David Rosen will testify. I am pledging that to you now. He will come to the witness stand. He will tell the judge, he will tell you, the jury, exactly why he did not do this and exactly what did occur. He will tell you that he is innocent and will relate to you in

his own words, answering all the questions Mr. Zeidenberg puts to him, under oath, and explain to you that he did not do this.

It may be difficult to hypothecate a tactical axiom in criminal trial advocacy that can be stated in absolute terms. If there is one, it is that the defense should never promise the jury in opening that the defendant will testify.

Typically, the most difficult decision for the defense in a criminal case is whether to have the defendant testify even though the defendant professes innocence. Experienced defense counsel well know the hazards of a defendant's testimony and that often inroads made in cross-examination of government witnesses can render the defendant's testimony unnecessary.

In my view, Sandler made a tactical error by promising the jury that Rosen would testify. He closed the door to the opportunity to decide that the case was going sufficiently well to avoid the risk of putting Rosen on the stand. He also ran the risk—one that criminal defense counsel can never fully foresee—that some unanticipated trial development, like an unexpected document, would make it difficult if not impossible for the defendant to testify effectively. Sandler could have had essentially the same benefit through a promise to "show," to "refute," or to "answer the government's allegations." Had he taken such a tack, he could have—if it became beneficial or necessary—kept Rosen off the witness stand without failing to live up to an unequivocal promise made to the jury.

Conclusion

The defense opening provides a splendid illustration of the trial lawyer's art. If, as I believe, Sandler varied from what experience has taught me is best, he may well have demonstrated that there are times when the lawyer fighting in the arena of the trial courtroom knows what to do better than any spectator. He may also, however, have proved that while every trial lawyer can make mistakes, a good one can often get away with them. I leave the wisdom vel non of Sandler's promising to call the defendant for the endless debates over tactics that trial lawyers seem to love so well.

In sum, I applaud Sandler's opening statement, which provided the foundation for the successful defense of Rosen, as can be seen when the presentation of evidence and the final arguments are examined.

CHAPTER 4

THE HEART OF THE TRIAL—DIRECT EXAMINATION

Direct examination is the heart of any trial. It is also one of the attorney's greatest challenges. A trial never feels more unpredictable than during witness examinations. The back-and-forth between attorney and witness, no matter how well both individuals have prepared, can easily go off track with the utterance of one undesirable answer or question. At any moment the exchange can be interrupted by the judge or opposing counsel. Add to this theatrical presentation the use of exhibits and PowerPoint presentations, and you have a lot of balls in the air.

Direct examinations demand extensive preparation on the part of any attorney, no matter how seasoned. This chapter will attempt to point out rhetorical techniques and strategies that have aided trial lawyers for ages. It will also discuss some of the ways lawyers can effectively structure examinations, introduce witnesses, and elicit the vivid, memorable testimony that wins cases.

To illustrate these pointers, I will refer to the direct examination of witnesses in the *Rosen* trial, including that of Rosen himself. David Rosen's acquittal relied greatly on his own testimony. How this direct unfolded will prove illustrative of various techniques commonly used by experienced trial attorneys. We refer also to the testimony of the parties in the *Maffei* and *Oregon* cases, whose testimony ran contrary to each other.

Succinctly put, the purposes of direct examination are to argue your case by engaging in dialogue with the witness, to advance the proof of your case, and to protect your witness from damaging cross-examination.

For direct examination to be effective, the attorney must understand precisely what he or she needs to convince the jury of at that moment in the trial. You cannot easily begin or even plan for an examination without having a comprehensive vision of how you want the trial to proceed, from start to finish—you should generally know what will happen throughout direct, and how it furthers your theme. You must have a believable story to tell, and this requires a firm grasp of the elements of proof required to win. Bear in mind that all of us enjoy a good story. In presenting direct examination, question the witness in a manner that creates interest and tells a story consistent with your theme.

Beyond developing this "vision" of the case—its theme, progression, and critical facts—you need to establish the credibility of your witnesses and elicit compelling and memorable testimony. The jurors should believe your witnesses and, during deliberation, remember what they said.

PREPARING YOURSELF AND THE WITNESSES

Few outstanding direct examinations happen by chance. They are almost always carefully prepared. Your knowledge and mastery of the case and of the other side's case are the first steps in preparing for direct examination. Do not underestimate the importance of understanding the other side's case by reviewing discovery responses, witness and exhibit lists, and any pretrial memoranda submitted by the other side. You do not want surprises at trial. Moreover, you cannot present your own case in a vacuum. By the time of trial, discovery is closed in civil cases and Jencks Act (the act that regulates certain discovery in criminal cases) material is usually available to the defense in criminal cases. You should have available document chronologies, event chronologies, and point-counterpoint outlines that help you keep fresh in mind the facts and issues of the case.

As discussed in Chapter 2, every case should have a theme that serves as the guide for the case development and especially the witness testimony. Your witnesses on direct should develop the theme and help you defend it.

Before you meet with a witness, prepare a list of questions or topics you plan to raise during direct and perhaps include the answers you antici-pate. Organize the exhibits you plan to show the witness so that you can review them together. Whether you use written questions or an outline at trial is a personal decision that depends on your experience and the complexities of the case.

Also prepare the questions or points that you anticipate will be covered on cross-examination. When preparing for direct, it is important to review these points with the witness not only to forewarn him or her, but also to help yourself prepare. You may improve your credibility and the witness's by meeting head-on some of the vulnerable aspects of the case.

When preparing your client or witness in support of your case, be conscious that the opposing party can call that witness as an adverse witness in its case. It is important to prepare your client and witnesses for this situation. Plan how to minimize disruption to your case and to the client's and witnesses' equanimity if any witnesses of yours are called by the opposing party. Under these circumstances, opposing counsel can pose leading questions. In the *Oregon* case, the counsel for the plaintiff called as an adverse witness the director of Parks and Recreation of Baltimore County, Maryland. He commenced with leading questions. Counsel objected, but the court overruled:

Q. Do you agree with me, Mr. Barrett, a supplemental leasing agreement imposes certain restrictive covenants for Oregon LLC's use of the property?"

SANDLER: Objection.

THE COURT: Sustained.

PLAINTIFF'S COUNSEL: Your Honor, this gentleman works for the county. He's obviously an adverse witness. He is called in my case. I should like to treat him as such.

THE COURT: So you would like to treat him as an adverse witness?

PLAINTIFF'S COUNSEL: Yes, Your Honor.

THE COURT: All right. The objection is overruled. You may lead the witness.

An important consideration is to what extent you will want to question the witness when the adverse party completes questioning. In the *Oregon* case the plaintiff called a defense witness in its case as its first witness. Defense counsel can redirect the witness immediately or recall the witness in the defendant's case. Sometimes counsel will do both: bring out a few points after the defense completes its questioning and later recall the witness in its case in chief. Remember that the *Oregon* case was nonjury. The defense conducted its complete examination of its witness immediately. There was no reason to recall the witness. Were there a jury in the box, defense counsel would have posed a few questions and recalled the witness in its own case. You may wonder how often one party will call in its own case the opposing party. While it does not happen every day, it does occur from time to time. The technique can be effective by catching the witness off guard, and disrupting the opposing side, but it is not without risks. The responding party can effectively strengthen its case by conducting a powerful examination of its own witness while on the stand, having been called by the opponent. For example, in the *Oregon* case, the plaintiff called the owner of the restaurant, then asked a series of questions designed to elicit testimony that the restaurant initiated the repaving of the parking lot. But taking the risk of calling the defendant in its case did not pan out. Observe:

Q. You are the owner of the Oregon Grille, correct?

. . .

Q. Do you recall receiving that letter? [Letter from Baltimore requiring repaving of the parking lot.]

A. Yes.

Q. Do you recall having a communication with Mr. Barrett [author of the letter and director of Parks and Planning for Baltimore County]?

A. There was some conversation, certainly.

Q. And in this conversation, am I correct, Mr. Cowman recommended to you that you hire a contractor to pave the parking lot yourself rather than go through the county bid process and allow the county to do it?

A. Your statement is incorrect.

Q. How is it incorrect?

A. My recollection of that was Mr. Barrett just sent Mr. Cowman saying that he was going to do the work. I did not select Mr. Cowman.

This was not the answer counsel for the plaintiff desired. The plaintiff wanted to show that the restaurant was pleased to undertake the repaving of the lot and even selected the contractor to undertake the work. Thus the defense that it was acting under compulsion was a pretext for violating the county ordinances. Further questioning attempting to improve the situation ensued:

Q. So you did not select Mr. Cowman to perform the work?

A. I'd never met Mr. Cowman. No.

Q. So in other words, it's your testimony, I take it, that the county hired Mr. Cowman to perform the work?

A. They directed him to me as the person that would be doing the work.

Calling this witness as an adverse party in the plaintiff's case did not achieve the result the plaintiff desired on the issue of who engaged the contractor to undertake the work. The plaintiff may have been better off not to have called the adverse party until cross-examination.

There are times when taking the risk is advisable—for example, when the plaintiff believes that to meet its burden of proof it must elicit facts from an adverse party.

How much you should share about your case with the witness depends on who the witness is—your client, one of the parties to the case, a witness under subpoena who has agreed to meet with you prior to trial, or an expert. Putting aside the expert for now, it may be helpful to orient the witness by explaining what information you seek from him or her and the importance of his or her testimony. Bear in mind that what you and the witness discuss may be the subject of inquiry by opposing counsel, either during trial or during deposition in civil cases. Be aware of any privilege or work-product doctrine protections and do not inadvertently waive them. If you believe a witness is hostile but still willing to see you, ask a colleague or assistant to accompany you while talking to the witness. The presence of someone else can thwart a witness from later claiming that you acted improperly during the meeting.

Practice the direct examination with the witness. Consider video recording the testimony for review, practicing before a small audience, or even staging a mock trial with a jury consultant. If you do so, also prepare your witness to anticipate questions about "rehearsals" during cross-examination or in a deposition if the case is civil. If your witness is asked on cross whether he or she practiced answering questions before a jury consultant, the witness should be prepared to respond, that is, to wait for an objection and not to disclose privileged communications unless directed to do so by the judge. Arguably, communications with a jury consultant or in "rehearsals" are protected by the attorney-client privilege or the work-product doctrine.[1]

When preparing your client and witnesses for direct examination, advise them to halt their testimony in court when an objection is stated, to wait

---

1. *See* Paul W. Grimm, Charles S. Fax, & Paul Mark Sandler, *Discovery of Jury Consultant, Focus Group Materials and Related Communications, in* DISCOVERY PROBLEMS AND THEIR SOLUTIONS, ch. 27 (3d ed. 2013).

for a ruling from the judge, and to answer questions directly without rambling or offering information beyond what the question calls for. Explain that you will have the chance to clarify their answers on redirect examination. Advise the witness to wait for counsel to complete the question before answering.

It is also important to alert clients and witnesses that in some courts all conversations in the courtroom are recorded or monitored even during recesses. Therefore, discreet conversation is important. Instances of embarrassment unfortunately abound. For example during the recess of one case, counsel explained to the client, in what counsel thought was a quiet tone, that the judge "did not know what he was doing." A few minutes later when the judge returned to the bench, he rendered a ruling on a motion beginning as follows while looking at counsel: "Although some in this courtroom believe I do not know "what I am doing. . . ." You do not want to be in the situation of the indiscreet lawyer.

You and your client should also be prepared for the occasion that could arise at trial when the judge intervenes and ask questions. Questions by the judge may or may not be helpful to your case. The ramifications may be different if the trial is jury or nonjury. One of the primary concerns when the court intervenes with questions is the effect it has on the jury. Most judges refrain from asking too many questions in jury trials, but they may be more active in a nonjury case. What if the judge asks a question that you believe is objectionable? Should you object? It depends on the importance of the objection balanced, against any harm to you in the eyes of the jury for appearing to criticize the judge. One approach is to ask for a sidebar conference with the judge. One attorney asked for such a conference, after the judge asked several questions. Counsel then objected, and the judge sustained the objection. Injecting some humor, the lawyer stated: "Your Honor, if you are going to take over my case, please don't lose it for me."

THE BOUNDS OF ETHICS

Of crucial importance in preparing your witness is emphasizing his or her obligation to testify truthfully. Making this obligation clear is your ethical and legal responsibility. Be aware of rules of professional responsibility.

Consider, for example, the American Bar Association Model Rules of Professional Conduct (2013 Edition), especially those rules concerning your obligations if your witness testifies untruthfully at trial. For example, Rule 3.3 of the Model Rules provides that a lawyer must not knowingly offer evidence that he or she knows to be false. If you, your client, or a witness called by you has offered material evidence and you learn of its falsity, you must take reasonable remedial measures, including, if necessary, disclosure to the tribunal. Moreover, with the exception of the testimony of a defendant in a criminal case, you may refuse to offer any evidence you reasonably believe to be false.

All young lawyers should be particularly aware of Rule 5.2 of the Model Rules of Professional Conduct—Responsibilities of a Subordinate Lawyer. If you know that a witness is lying while the partner with whom you are trying the case is questioning a witness at trial, you cannot avoid your responsibility by relying on the partner to take action regarding the testimony.

In meeting with witnesses whom you anticipate calling, consider Rule 4.2 of the Model Rules. This rule prohibits you from communicating about the case with any individual or entity represented in the case and with any employee or agent of such a person or entity. This rule appears straightforward—but what could result from your contacting a former employee who had managerial responsibility at a company you are litigating against? If your communication relates to the case, the communication could be in violation of the ethical rule and have serious implications for you and your client.

Attorneys have a duty to refrain from inquiring into areas that may be protected by the attorney-client privilege or the work-product doctrine. At least one court has held that when an attorney interviews a former employee, he or she should notify the former employer's counsel to permit him or her to obtain a protective order limiting the scope of the interview.[2]

Under Rule 3.4 of the ABA Model Rules of Professional Conduct—Fairness to Opposing Party and Counsel—you cannot unlawfully obstruct

---

2. Smith v. Kalamazoo Opthalmology, 322 F. Supp. 2d 883, 891–92 (W.D. Mich. 2004).

another party's access to evidence or unlawfully alter, destroy, or conceal a document or other material having potential evidentiary value. You cannot falsify evidence, counsel or assist a witness to testify falsely, or offer an inducement to a witness that is prohibited by law. In pretrial procedure, you cannot make a frivolous discovery request or fail to make a reasonably diligent effort to comply with a legally proper discovery request by an opposing party.

The rule provides that in trial, you may not allude to any matter that you do not reasonably believe is relevant or that will not be supported by admissible evidence; assert personal knowledge of facts in issue except when testifying as a witness; or state a personal opinion as to the justness of your case, the credibility of a witness, the culpability of a civil litigant, or the guilt or innocence of an accused.

Rule 3.4 also provides that you may not request a person other than a client to refrain from voluntarily giving relevant information to another party, unless (1) the person is a relative or an employee or other agent of a client and (2) you reasonably believe that the person's interests will not be adversely affected by refraining from giving such information.

These examples by no means exhaust the considerations of ethics in preparing for direct examination. A wise advocate should be familiar with all of the Model Rules of Professional Conduct.

BEWARE OF LEADING QUESTIONS
Ask Short Questions and Avoid Compound Questions
One of the challenges of direct examination is the prohibition of leading questions. The reason leading questions are prohibited on direct examination is that the jury must hear evidence from the witness and not from the lawyer.

Such questions can be posed only in limited circumstances, for example, when confronting a hostile witness, reviewing uncontroversial matters, questioning children or senior citizens, or introducing new topics in your examination with a topical oral sentence. The prohibition against leading questions on direct examination is one reason that direct examination is considered to be the most difficult part of a trial, and surprisingly, more difficult than most cross-examinations.

What then is the distinction between leading and nonleading questions? Simply stated, a leading question suggests the answer. A nonleading question does not. "It rained last night?" is a leading question. Some nonleading alternatives include, "Did it rain last night?" or "Do you recall whether or not it rained last night?"

Asking nonleading questions creates difficulties in controlling the testimony and the witness. When you ask skillful leading questions as permitted on cross-examination, you control the testimony by almost testifying for the witness: "It rained last night?" "You came home after midnight?" But when you must ask nonleading questions ("Can you tell us what the weather was last night?"), you could get more explanation than you wanted. ("Well, I can't recall, but I do remember that the road was very slippery, and cars were skidding all over the place.") Many lawyers have been stunned by a witness's response to an open-ended question on direct examination. Frequently even the most careful preparation of a witness is no safeguard against the witness's desultory response to your questions.

As you ask questions during direct, beware of the distinction between prohibited leading questions and leading questions that may be tolerated. These include questions that are used to save time, and do not relate to important facts or refer to facts that are generally in evidence. "You attended the Spago tea?" is leading, but it's more efficient than: "Did you attend the Spago tea at noon on June 11, 2000?" If the record is saturated with testimony that the witness was at the Spago tea on June 11 at noon, the shorter, leading question will probably be tolerated by opposing counsel and the court.

In the *Maffei* case, on direct examination of Mrs. Maffei, her counsel asked: "And then there was a time when he [Mr. Maffei] saw the doctor for the first time, is that correct?" There was no objection. The question was asked to transition from one topic to another and was innocuous. In the context of this examination an objection might have been annoying to the jury, and probably would have been overruled, with the judge commenting, "Let's not lead the witness, counsel." Sometimes objecting to a leading question can waste time, if not be outright annoying. For example, counsel for the plaintiff asked Mrs. Maffei on direct examination: "Now, Mrs. Maffei, the loss of your husband caused you emotional distress and unhappiness?" Defense counsel objected. The objection was sustained, but wasted time as counsel rephrased the question: "Do you feel that your husband's absence at home, his lack of companionship and being with you has affected your life?" There was no objection and the witness answered: "Dramatically." Then counsel asked her to explain.

Another exception to the rule against leading questions during direct examination, as discussed above, is when you are calling an adverse witness to the stand, or a witness turns adverse and the court permits you to lead the witness. Generally, however, leading questions should be avoided on direct and saved for cross-examination. Sometimes in the heat of trial you may have trouble asking a nonleading question after an objection is sustained. This predicament is not unusual. Don't panic. Try rephrasing the query using the word "whether." For example: "You then went to the bar after the reception?" could be rephrased: "Can you tell us whether you went to the bar after the reception?"

The best form of question on direct examination is a short question that produces a clear answer. Here is an example from the *Oregon* case:

Q. Did you receive a letter from the county in June 2006 relating to the parking lot at the restaurant?

A. Yes.

Q. Please turn to the exhibit book and to page 24. Can you identify Exhibit 22 in the book?

A. Yes.

Q. What is it?

A. The letter of June 8, 2006.

Q. Did you take any action based on the letter?

A. Yes.

Q. Tell us, what did you do?

A. I called Mr. Barrett.

Q. Why?

A. To discuss the county's demand that we repave the parking lot.

On the other hand, complex or compound questions are difficult to understand. They are objectionable. Often they produce ambiguous answers. For example, consider this compound question (slightly restated) discussed by Professor Stephen Saltzburg:[3] "Q. Do you know Tyra Jackson, and that she is the girlfriend . . . of the defendant?" A. "Yes." But to what does "Yes" refer? That the witness knows Tyra Jackson or that he knows she is the girlfriend of the defendant? This question spawned the appellate case of *United States v. Watson*,[4] which held that question to be prejudicial to the defendant and reversed his conviction.

MAKE IT MEMORABLE

For the jury members to be convinced of the merits of your case in direct examination, they must not only understand the testimony but also remember it; if the jurors remember favorable testimony, it indicates that your ideas may have penetrated their minds. As the case proceeds and other evidence is introduced, a juror's memory of prior testimony will affect how he or she receives new evidence and arguments.

One effective way to emphasize and help people remember a point is to repeat it, thereby using the technique of frequency to help the jury remember the testimony. In direct examination, one must learn to do this without violating the rules of evidence, which prohibit asking a question already asked and answered. In earlier times, lawyers would feign not hearing an answer and ask the question a second time. Or they would repeat the answer over the objection of opposing counsel. Such efforts

---

3. STEPHEN SALTZBURG, TRIAL TACTICS 54 (3d ed. 2012).
4. 171 F. 3d 695 (D.C. Cir. 1999).

are stilted and obvious. They can prevent a listener from developing confidence in reaching her or his own conclusions. They may also insult jurors' intelligence.

Looping and incorporation are more effective means of impressing the jurors with important facts on direct. Looping involves using the answer to the previous question in the subsequent question. Here is an example of looping taken from the direct examination of David Rosen:

> Q. When you arrived at the Spago tea, whom did you first meet?
>
> A. Aaron Tonken.
>
> Q. When you met Mr. Tonken, how much time did the two of you talk with one another?
>
> A. Fifteen minutes.

Incorporation is very similar. You incorporate a previous answer in your question without making it obvious. The testimony above continued as follows:

> Q. During the 15-minute conversation at your first meeting, did he discuss with you the costs of the gala?
>
> A. Absolutely not.

Consider this example from the direct examination of Mrs. Maffei in our civil case:

> Q. What concern did you have as you observed his symptoms?
>
> A. I was afraid he was having a heart attack.
>
> Q. Why were you afraid he was having a heart attack?
>
> A. Because of the symptoms he was having.

Q. What were the symptoms he was having, giving rise to your concern about a heart attack?

By using the techniques of looping and incorporation, you can help imprint certain testimony in the minds of the jurors.

One of the most effective means of presenting memorable testimony is by competent use of exhibits and demonstrative aids. Studies reveal that we are far more persuaded by what we see than by what we hear. The more you use demonstrative evidence to enhance the jury's involvement, the more memorable your direct examination will be. Juries want to see the exhibit or demonstrative aid as you are questioning the witness about it. Demonstrative aids are documents or drawings, including enlargements that are referenced but not moved into evidence. Sometimes enlargements of documents that receive frequent attention are moved into evidence. They must be clear and legible from a distance. There is even authority that certain colors resonate more than others. Selection of colors might depend on whether you are the plaintiff or the defendant and whether you are depicting conduct or facts that you wish the judge or jury to view favorably or unfavorably.

When using exhibits or demonstrative aids, it is helpful to obtain the testimony about the subject matter first and then introduce the exhibit. The appearance of the exhibit will help corroborate the witness's key points. After exhausting the witness's testimony on the subject, you can ask him or her to cover the same ground by reviewing and explaining the exhibit, which may well serve as a memory anchor for the jury.

Avoid using the exhibit or aid as the main point of your examination unless the exhibit is the central part of the case. In other words, elicit the testimony about the document first. Then invite the witness to examine the document or aid and to explain or answer your questions about the exhibit. This approach, as with looping and incorporation, employs the technique of frequency.

Visuals

Demonstrative aids, also discussed in Chapter 2, play an important role in the examination of witnesses on direct and on cross in both jury and nonjury cases. In the direct examination of David Rosen, he was asked to tell the jury about the organizational structure of the host group he believed was paying for the gala. Without any exhibits, such testimony would be hard to follow and dull. So defense counsel took the simple step of using employee photographs and an organizational chart. The witness referred to these exhibits during his testimony so that jurors were able to connect faces to names and responsibilities.

Similarly, the government, seeking to demonstrate the elaborate nature of the fundraiser, introduced one of the fancy director's chairs that guests sat in at the event. Rosen, the prosecution alleged, had complained about these chairs as being too expensive, a detail the prosecution emphasized to help establish the defendants' knowledge of the costs in question.

In the *Maffei* case, counsel for the parties extensively used demonstrative aids, and some of them were admitted into evidence. For example, to illustrate the difference between the normal flow of blood through the aorta and the flow with a dissection, counsel for the plaintiff used an enlarged diagram displayed on an easel. The court allowed it to be placed very close to and directly in front of the jury. During the direct examination of the experts, the court permitted counsel to invite the witnesses to step down from the stand and use the illustrations to explain their testimony. The scene in the courtroom became somewhat intimate as each expert and counsel all stood close to the jury. (See Figure 2)

Rarely will a scene like this be played out in court. Large illustrations, charts, or diagrams are seldom allowed so near the jury, and witnesses generally must work with illustrations from the stand. Still, as technology has evolved, there are many ways to display exhibits and work with demonstrative aids in the courtroom. For example, you can use Power-Point presentations to recreate time lines or to display exhibits during your examination. (See Figure 3) Computer-generated visuals such as animations, charts, pictures, and documents with highlighted text can be effective. (See Figure 4) Consider using an electronic interactive white board (see Figure 5) or an ELMO. The latter is a document camera used with a projector. The ELMO can project not only a two-dimensional image but also a three-dimensional image. (See Figure 6) Thus it can display physical evidence, like a gun alleged to be the murder weapon.

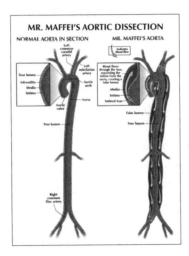

Figure 2

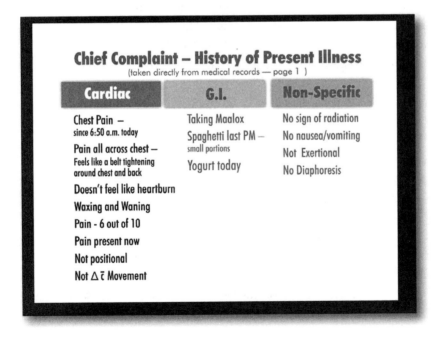

Figure 3

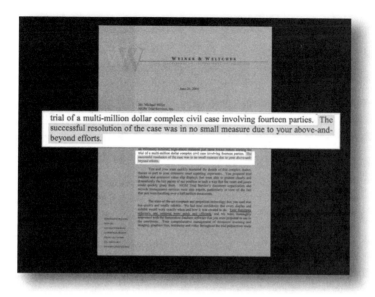

Figure 4

One advantage of the ELMO is that you can be more spontaneous in displaying documents than a PowerPoint presentation will allow, as they usually have a prearranged order. Most courtrooms have an ELMO available for counsel.[5]

When planning your examination (see Figure 3) and all phases of the case, you should consider whether you will use the documents or exhibits that already exist or whether you want to create exhibits to enhance your examination or argument. For example, in the *Maffei* case, counsel for the plaintiff created charts summarizing key points in the medical records. The summaries were admitted into evidence and displayed on the ELMO. An alternative approach could have been the use of the summaries as a demonstrative aid. Usually the court will agree to this if the summary has

---

5. *See* Ronald Waicukauski, Paul Mark Sandler & Jo Anne Epps, The Twelve Secrets of Persuasive Argument (2009).

Figure 5

been demonstrated as accurate. As a demonstrative aid, the summary is not in evidence; hence the jury does not review it during deliberations. But summaries can also be admitted in evidence, as distinguished from their use as demonstrative.

Once you decide upon the exhibits and demonstrative aids, the next step is to consider by what method to display them. Whichever method you use, keep the display simple, legible from a distance, and attractive. It may be important to visit the courtroom in advance to test the clarity and visibility of your exhibit as presented. If it is an enlargement not displayed electronically, you will want to be sure the jury will be able see it clearly at the distance it will be displayed. Also if the document is to be displayed electronically, know how to work the projector or have someone available who does. You do not want your ethos to suffer because of fumbling that slows down the trial.

Sometimes the judge will allow you to "publish the exhibit to the jury"—that is, show the document to the jurors and allow them to read it

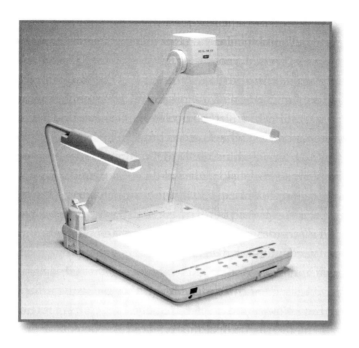

Figure 6

independently. You can imagine the time delay with this procedure. Don't rely on it unless your exhibit is a smoking gun.

You might also consider preparing a notebook of stipulated exhibits and asking the court whether you can give a copy to each juror so they will be able to follow along. The danger here is that the jurors will look at the notebooks when you want their full attention. In the *Maffei* case, for example, counsel prepared a notebook of medical records for the jurors to review during particular testimony of the medical experts, thus pulling their attention away at times from what the witnesses were saying.

In nonjury cases it may be more practical to give less attention to displaying visuals depending on the case and the judge. Providing the judge a book of exhibits and diagrams to review during the trial may be suitable for the case. On the other hand, computer programs and displays with counsel pointing to the screen may be an effective way to engage the judge. Counsel in the *Oregon* case, which was nonjury, provided the court with an exhibit book and several diagrams, but did not use a projector or PowerPoint display.

Engaging the Jury

Equally critical to how well the jury remembers key points is the style with which you and the witness make those points in court. You should always strive to elicit vivid and engaging testimony.

Clear, short, and precise questions asked in plain English are most useful in this regard. You can easily lose your audience with convoluted queries, and if you allow your witness to drone on and on about irrelevant matters, you forsake control of the argument you need to make a thorough direct examination.

Establish a rhythm of short questions and answers that help the jury follow the development of your argument. Vary the structure of your sentences by using closed- and open-ended questions to help retain interest and develop momentum. For example, an open-ended query like "Tell us what happened to you after you arrived at the tea" offers the witness an opportunity to assume some control, narrate past events, and thus enhance his or her credibility with the jurors. On the other hand, too much narration will be overbearing and tedious, if not objectionable. Break up the testimony with concise, closed-ended questions like "After the collision were you able to walk?" This helps you vary the pace of the examination and hold the interest of the jury.

Likewise, it is helpful to break up the examination with introductory and transitional phrases that help you and the jurors organize information. For example: "Now let's discuss the morning of the event." Or "Let's move on to the next day." The so-called break-down question is not a question at all but a short statement that serves as an oral topical sentence. Such statements, considered improper years ago, are now welcome and help everyone follow the testimony with interest. As explained below, using transition sentences to alert the jury or judge that you are moving to a new topic is a helpful technique to achieve clarity.

Do not read from written questions. Reading or even relying extensively on notes can prevent you from observing the witness and jury. You lose eye contact and the opportunity to alter your questions in the wake of an unexpected answer. To conduct careful but unscripted examinations, of course you must go into the courtroom with a very strong understanding of all the facts of the case. Without this understanding, your insecurity will force you to rely too much on notes, stumble over questions, hesitate, and miss opportunities. It is important to have your notes available, but don't allow them to become a crutch.

Style and Delivery

The elements of style and delivery presented in Chapter 2 apply to the examination of witnesses. Never discount speaking style and delivery as superficial elements of your case overall or your direct examinations in particular. As discussed, style is the form in which we put our ideas, the manner in which we convey the substance of our argument or questions to elicit testimony. Your choice of words and the use of open-ended questions or short staccato questions—these are aspects of style. Delivery involves how we regulate our voice, gestures, and demeanor. Style and delivery are critical instruments of persuasion. Before you even enter the courtroom, you should consider the tone you want to set during specific examinations, what expressions and gestures to use, and your demeanor, body language, and pacing.

Where you stand and how you move while conducting a direct examination are important. In the *Rosen* trial, Judge Matz required all counsel to remain at the podium, which was a distance of 15 feet from the jury. In this case, not being able to approach the jury or move about the courtroom limited the nonverbal modes of communication that are usually available to lawyers. In the *Maffei* case, on the other hand, the judge permitted counsel to stand close to the jury. In *Oregon*, the nonjury case, counsel spoke from the trial table, as the judge requested.

Prior to trial, it is prudent to ask the judge her or his preferences about where to stand when conducting examinations. When possible, it is often helpful to stand by the juror box while asking a witness to tell "us" about an event, as if you were part of the jury.

It can be difficult to control your body language so that it adheres to the overall impression you want to make. Facial expressions, in particular, can betray you. You may find yourself frowning or grimacing upon hearing an answer you did not want. Obviously, such slips undercut your credibility. How can they be avoided? If you can truly internalize conviction in your argument, your confidence in the face of contrary evidence is likely to be evident to jurors during examinations.

Your convictions about the case will also become evident as you vigorously engage a witness. A lack of conviction, on the other hand, and a lack of imagination, can lead to lazy questioning. A dull sequence might go like this: "Well, tell us what happened." "And then?" "What happened after that?" Generally, the examination will unfurl much more vividly if you take charge of it, tailoring questions to draw out compelling details you know are there, waiting to shine before the jury.

One final note about style during direct. Remember that you are not speaking to lawyers. You are trying to communicate with the witness and with the jurors. Stilted, lawyerly language is not desirable. For instance, a question like "Did there come a time when you returned home that evening?" comes off as formal and aloof. Also avoid arched questions such as: "What, if anything, did you do next?" and instructions such as "State your name for the record."

Authenticating Exhibits

When introducing exhibits during trial, it is important to understand the rules governing admissibility. Remember that the document itself is not evidence unless it has been introduced and authenticated. The basic principle in document authentication is to obtain testimony that the document accurately represents what it purports to depict.

According to Federal Rule of Evidence 901(a), authentication "is satisfied by evidence sufficient to support a finding that the matter in question is what the proponent claims." Authenticity "is in the category of relevancy dependent upon fulfillment of a condition of fact," and is governed by the procedure set forth in Federal Rule of Evidence 104(b). There are various requirements and techniques for authenticating documents and real evidence. For example, private writings, business records, and medical records each have their own requirements. But the essence of each requirement is that the exhibit is authentic.[6] Authentication is only a first step. The evidence must still satisfy numerous other rules of evidence: it must be relevant as well as authentic, it must not be hearsay or satisfy an exception, and of course its probative value must not be prejudicial.

The Federal Rules of Evidence do not address separately the admissibility of electronically stored evidence (ESI), so the same rules apply. Nevertheless, as with hard copy documents, nuances exist in authentication of ESI. Working with e-mails and other forms of ESI requires familiarity not only with the rules of evidence, but also the case law.[7] In *Lorraine v. Markel,* Judge Paul W. Grimm, then chief magistrate judge, analyzed the various methods of introducing ESI. E-mails may be self-authenticating. They may be admissible based on their distinctive characteristics such as their content, internal patterns, or other distinctive characteristics. Chain e-mails present more difficult problems. If they are introduced as a business record, under Federal Rule of Evidence 803(6), each participant in the chain must be acting in the regular course of business or qualify for admissibility by another exception to the rule against hearsay.

The introduction of other forms of ESI such as webpages and social media sources can be accomplished by various methods, including those used to introduce e-mails. For example, offering the evidence pursuant to Federal Rule of Evidence 901 (Requirement of Authentication or Identification) and 902 (self-authentication) are but two methods.[8] Notably, there are a few relatively inexpensive tools available to attorneys to assist with the admissibility of ESI, including the use of digital notaries and the Internet Archive Wayback Machine.[9] Authentication problems with ESI can best be resolved in pretrial conferences.

Given the challenges for authenticating Internet and social media sources of information, courts appear to be erring on the side of admissibility, and any concerns about the evidence itself—for example, contradictory

---

6. *See* PAUL MARK SANDLER & JAMES K. ARCHIBALD, MODEL WITNESS EXAMINATIONS (3d ed. 2010).

7. *See, e.g.,* Lorraine v. Markel Am. Ins. Co., 241 F.R.D. 534 (D. Md. 2007).

8. *See* Williams v. Long, 585 F. Supp. 2d 679 (D. Md. 2008) (Grimm, J.) (exhibits in the form of printed webpages were self-authenticating, and although hearsay, still met the requirements of the public records and reports exception to the hearsay rule).

9. http://www.archive.org/web/web.php.

testimony about whether or not someone authored a Facebook posting—is being left to the jurors to decide the weight that evidence should be given.[10] It is also important to be aware of the developing law that treats certain information stored on social media websites as "private" and subject to the Stored Communications Act.[11] Under this developing law, a civil subpoena would not be sufficient or, for that matter, appropriate for obtaining "private" information such as e-mails or instant message communications stored on a social media website or a private web-based e-mail account.[12]

In many trials today, such as the *Maffei* case, counsel agrees before the trial on the authenticity and admissibility of exhibits. In the *Rosen* case, many documents that needed to be authenticated could not be agreed upon, including photographs of the gala, receipts, invoices, and other business records. In the nonjury case of *Oregon*, all counsel agreed on the authenticity and admissibility of all exhibits.

In the following hypothetical example, defense counsel is introducing a budget to corroborate the witness's assertion that he did have a budget prepared for a political fundraising event held in his home:

Q. Mr. Jones, was a final budget prepared for the fundraising event at your home?

---

10. *See* Matthew A.S. Esworthy & Justin P. Murphy, *The ESI Tsunami: A Comprehensive Discussion about Electronically Stored Information in Government Investigations and Criminal Cases*, 27 ABA CRIM. J. MAG. (Apr. 1, 2012) (collecting cases on admissibility); People v. Lesser, H034189, 2011 WL 193460 (Cal. Ct. App. Jan. 21, 2011) (officer's testimony that he cut and pasted portions of Internet chat transcript was sufficient for admissibility); State v. Thompson, 777 N.W. 2d 617 (N.D. 2010) (victim's knowledge of defendant's cell phone number and defendant's "signature" on text messages sufficient to authenticate threatening text messages); People v. Valdez, No. G041904, 201 Cal. App. 4th 1429 (Dec. 16, 2011) (conviction upheld where the court correctly admitted a trial exhibit consisting of printouts of defendant's MySpace page, which the prosecution's gang expert relied on in forming his opinion that defendant was an active gang member); but see Commonwealth v. Koch, 2011 WL 4336634 (2011 PA Super 201, Sept. 16, 2011) (text messages found inadmissible because authentication requires more than mere confirmation that the cell phone belongs to a specific person).

11. *See* 18 U.S.C. § 2701.

12. *See* Theofel v. Farey-Jones, 359 F.3d 1066, 1071–72, 1077 (9th Cir. 2004) (finding that an overbroad civil subpoena to plaintiff's Internet service provider violated the Stored Communications Act).

A. Yes, it was.

Q. Did the final budget itemize proposed expenses for the fundraising dinner at your home?

A. Yes.

Q. Do you recall the particular expenses that were itemized?

A. Most of them.

Q. What were they?

A. $500 for the caterer; $150 for refreshments; and $100 for miscellaneous costs.

Q. Mr. Jones, can you identify Exhibit 24 for identification?

A. Yes.

Q. What is it?

A. This is the formal budget for the event.

Q. Who prepared it?

A. I did.

Q. When did you prepare it?

A. One month before the event.

Q. Does this budget reflect the very costs you just described for the jury?

A. It does.

Q. Is this the final budget that you prepared for the event?

A. Yes, it is.

Q. Your Honor, I move into evidence as defendant's Exhibit 24, the final budget, Exhibit 24 for identification.

Mr. Jones, will you please read the expenses reflected on the budget?

A. $500 for the caterer; $150 for refreshments; and $100 for miscellaneous costs.

Q. Thank you.

Notice that the witness first testified without referring to the document, and then counsel introduced the document to emphasize the substance of the testimony. The jury in effect heard testimony on the matter twice and hopefully would better remember it as a result.

This technique can be trickier if the witness does not recall the information in a document on his own. Imagine that Jones cannot remember the costs of the fundraiser. In that instance, counsel would have to rely on what is known as the doctrine of present recollection revived:

Q. Mr. Jones, were budgets prepared to itemize proposed expenses for the fundraising dinner at your home?

A. Yes.

Q. Do you recall the particular expenses that were itemized?

A. I am sorry, it has been a while, and I just don't recall.

Q. Is there anything that would refresh your recollection?

A. If I could see the budget, that might help.

Q. Please examine Exhibit 24 for identification—the budget—and tell us whether that refreshes your recollection?

A. It does.

Q. Now please tell us the particular expenses that were itemized.

The key circumstances permitting a lawyer to present a witness with a document to refresh a recollection are:

1. The witness cannot recall the particular facts inquired about;
2. A document or memory aid might help the witness recall the facts in question; and
3. After reviewing the document, the witness's memory will be refreshed.

Remember that the document is not evidence unless it is authenticated and introduced.

If your witness's recollection is not refreshed after reviewing the document, you can still introduce the document as a prior hearsay statement pursuant to the doctrine of past recollection recorded. To accomplish this, counsel should elicit testimony that the writing was made or adopted by the witness at the time when the witness had a clear recollection. The testimony should also state that the document was accurate at the time the witness adopted the writing, that the witness presently vouches for the accuracy of the writing, and that the witness lacks sufficient recollection to testify fully and accurately about the events referred to in the document.

Hopefully you will have had the opportunity to prepare your witness before trial, and the need to stimulate memory from a document will not arise. There are occasions when you cannot prepare a witness, however, and understanding how to use documents to stimulate memory is important.

Authenticating documents before a jury, particularly in exhibit-heavy cases, can be time-consuming. Many courts, according to court rules or practice, will require you and your opposing counsel to agree to the extent practical on authentication and admissibility prior to trial. Generally, you don't want to wrangle over authentication. Do you really want to require opposing counsel to subpoena the bank to send a witness to authenticate bank records? But just because you are willing to stipulate to authenticity of an exhibit does not mean that you desire to agree to its admissibility. The document may contain hearsay or be irrelevant. Under those circumstances, you would stipulate to authenticity but not to admissibility.

If the court requests it, you will have to submit the joint list of stipulations before trial. The court usually requests this by way of a proposed pretrial order submitted jointly by counsel. The court might decide to consider objections to exhibits in advance to avoid lawyers haggling over documents before the jury. Most judges, however, will wait until the exhibit is offered so as to consider the matter in the context of the trial.

STRUCTURING THE EXAMINATION

Listeners remember best what they hear first and last. Keep this maxim in mind as you plan the order in which you will call your witnesses. You will want to begin and end your case with strong witnesses. Less desirable witnesses belong in the middle of the lineup. Carried further, the concepts of primacy and recency suggest that individual witness examinations should begin and end forcefully, with the weaker portions in the middle.

Remember that direct examination is how you argue your case. You don't want the argument to consist of a string of disorganized questions and answers. Plot the direct as you would your opening statement or closing argument, with a clear introduction, presentation, and conclusion. More specifically, the direct examination can be divided as follows:

1. *The introduction*, where you establish the credibility of the witness and attempt to predispose the jurors to believe him or her;
2. *The context of the witness's testimony*, where you demonstrate that the witness is qualified to present credible testimony on the topics upon which the witness is called to testify;

3. *The main substance of the testimony*, where you advance the points you wish to argue or assert;

4. *Immunization*, where you pose questions that opposing counsel might ask on cross-examination to take the wind out of his or her sails; and

5. *The conclusion*, where you drive home your most important points in a memorable fashion.

Introduction

The introduction should often be warm and humanizing. Usually, but not always, you will want to introduce the witness to the jury by asking questions about the witness's background, including education, work experience, and occupation. This introductory phase helps you establish the witness's credibility and humanizes the witness. If the witness is your client, the introduction is critical.

In the introductory portion of David Rosen's testimony, the questions and answers portray the background of a hard-working young man who sold encyclopedias for a living and worked his way through school:

Q. And how do you explain what your occupation or work is, sir?

A. I'm a fundraiser.

Q. Mr. Rosen, would you briefly tell the jury your educational background?

A. I have two years of high school, I have a GED, and I graduated college with a B.A. in political science.

Q. And what about your work experience? When did you have, for example, the first job you can remember?

A. My first job was [at] 14 years old. I was a caddy at Olympia Fields Country Club in Olympia Fields.

Q. Can you give us a chronology of your work experience?

A. I caddied for two summers. When I was a sophomore in high school, I took a job at Burger King. After my sophomore year, a friend of mine called and presented me with an opportunity to work at a ski resort/ summer resort in northern Wisconsin—Cable, Wisconsin. It was a job where I was a recreation director, and I took the job. I worked with a bunch of college students. Actually, my sister Ruth worked that summer too, and we organized activities for the guests there, from preschool through seniors, volleyball games, softball games, things to keep them busy. And after that summer was over, the college students returned to college; and the owner, Tony Wise, offered me a job at the resort full time to work through the winter.

Q. Did that, then, mean you dropped out of school?

A. I did. I dropped out of high school.

Q. And you then worked?

A. I—in Illinois, they had a law that you couldn't take the GED prior to your class's graduation, and in Wisconsin, they let you take the GED. So I took the GED. I worked at Telemark Lodge. I taught skiing to kids, and after—after about a year and a half, the Telemark Lodge went bankrupt.

Q. What did you do?

A. I took my GED in hand and went to the University of Wisconsin in Eau Clair, Wisconsin, and they admitted me on a probationary basis. Academic probation, it was called.

Q. Now we're focusing on your work. Were you working at that time?

A. I'm sorry. I wasn't sure.

Q. Where?

A. I delivered pizzas for Domino's.

Q. And for how long did you occupy that job or did that job occupy your time?

A. It was—I was going to school and working full-time. So it was a year.

Q. Did you work your way through school, these schools?

A. Yes, sir.

Q. Did you have other jobs after the pizza job?

A. I did. I transferred—after I was accepted as a full-time student, it was easy for me to transfer schools—I transferred to the University of South Florida in Tampa, and there was an advertisement for summer work outside of one of my sociology classes, and it said, "Summer job. Pays well." I went to the interview. I took the job. It was a college summer work program that taught students how to sell and manage, and I took that job, and all the—it was a college exchange program where they hired 4,000 students from 500 universities, and they participated in this exchange program, and they taught us how to sell, and we sold books.

Q. Where did you sell these books?

A. All over the country. . . . The students from Florida sold in upstate New York, and the students from New York sold somewhere else. They were, they were, like, encyclopedias, but they covered math, English, social studies, and science. More like for homework.

Q. Try to bring us current.

A. I'm sorry.

Q. In terms of the work that you did over the years.

A. I sold books for 10 summers. I was going to school part-time sometimes, full-time sometimes, and at one point I entered the full-time management program, moved to Baton Rouge, Louisiana. I was recruiting off the Louisiana schools, hiring and training the students, and then I'd take them off to sell during the summertime. And then my dad had a heart attack, and I moved back to Chicago, and I took—I wanted to be closer to where he was. I took a job selling law books to lawyers for Clark, Boardman & Callahan; and after about seven months at that job I decided I needed to complete my undergraduate degree. So I went back to school. I enrolled at DePaul University, which is where I finished up.

It is worth noting that the content of the testimony transcends the facts of Rosen's resume. It contains many emotional cues and hints at his values. That he returns home to his father after the heart attack, for instance, indicates that he is a caring son. The story of his job at the ski resort suggests leadership ability, a fun-loving personality, and a certain independence, even as it explains the surprising fact that he did not graduate from high school. In preparing a witness for testimony, keep in mind that jurors remember details that may not be critical to the logic of your case, but that can predispose people to believe or disbelieve a witness.

Q. Were you working while you were at DePaul?

A. I wasn't. I had money saved.

Q. Did you then take on a position after college?

A. I did. It was a volunteer. At my last quarter at DePaul, David Wilhelm came to teach a class, and he was a friend—did Bill Clinton's, President Clinton's '92 campaign, and a bunch of other campaigns. He was very well known. While studying political science at DePaul, I became excited about politics, wanted to get into politics, and David Wilhelm opened up a volunteer spot for me on the Clinton/Gore campaign.

In this exchange, the defense counsel allowed the witness to speak at length in response to a few open-ended questions. For many witnesses, this technique could be a bad idea, but in this instance, the defense needed the jury to gain an appreciation for the kind of man Rosen was, and what experiences had led to his career in political fundraising. Counsel steps in here and there to underscore an important point ("Did you work your way through school, these schools?") or guide the testimony down the chronological path. But for the most part, the witness himself tells the story, in his own voice, and beginning with his most youthful and humble work experiences.

The importance of allowing the witness on direct examination a degree of freedom of expression helps establish the witness's credibility. The jury can observe that the lawyer is not testifying for the witness, as is sometimes the perception on cross-examination. But beware of the "runaway witness." When the lawyer asks an open-ended question, and the witness runs off course, away from the main purpose of the question, trouble soon follows. You need to balance the witness's freedom to testify in his or her own voice with your need to control the course of the testimony. Which is why, in the previous example, the lawyer stepped in to ask a few pointed questions.

This brings us again to the subject of ethos. If the jury finds your witness to be likable and sincere, you and your witness enjoy a rising ethos. With nonexpert witnesses, ethos is complex and highly subjective. In addition to the substance of what the witness says, his or her body language, manner of speaking, word choice, and dress can all affect his or her ethos with the jury.

Contrast the seriousness and depth of the Rosen introduction with that of Stan Lee, a witness whom the defense wanted the jury to believe but who had a less significant role than Rosen:

Q. Good afternoon, Mr. Lee. I would first ask you to describe to the ladies and gentlemen of the jury what your occupation is, what you do.

A. I am basically a writer, and I have a new company now. I am the chairman of the company.

Q. What's the name of that company?

A. It's called POW, P-O-W, Entertainment, and we do television movies, DVDs, that sort of thing.

Q. Mr. Lee, how young are you at this time, sir?

A. Eighty-two years.

Q. And for how long have you been a writer?

A. Just about all my life.

Q. And have you lived in the Los Angeles vicinity most of your life, sir?

A. Twenty-five years.

Note what counsel did not ask here: He did not ask about POW Entertainment and Mr. Lee's role as "chairman." Instead, counsel zeroed in on the witness's fame as a writer and creator of popular characters in hopes of enhancing the jurors' interest in hearing what he had to say. Ultimately, this is one of the most important goals of the introduction—to excite the jury about what is coming next.

Q. Now, with the court's indulgence, I would like to ask if you've ever heard of a character known as Spider-Man?

A. Yes.

Q. And how is it you heard of that character, sir?

A. Well, I was the cocreator of Spider-Man.

Q. And have you heard of a character known as the Incredible Hulk? And that's definitely not me I acknowledge, but—

(Laughter in the courtroom.)

A. Yes, I have. Same reason.

Q. And can we ask, my last little dalliance, sir, about—have you ever heard of the X-Men?

A. Yes.

Q. And why is that?

A. I created that too.

Here the attorney plays a more active role in directing the testimony and setting the tone. With Rosen, the defense counsel allowed the witness's voice to dominate, but with Stan Lee, counsel intentionally interjects his personality and sense of humor. Doing so at appropriate moments can go a long way to improve an attorney's ethos, particularly if the proceedings appear to be boring the jurors. Had counsel simply asked, "Did you, sir, create Spider-Man, the Incredible Hulk, and the X-Men?" the testimony would have been less engaging.

Never underestimate the power of humor. In addition to making testimony more pleasurable for you and everyone in the room, it can aid you in your quest to persuade. On the flip side, an off-color, poorly timed, or unsuccessful attempt at humor can sink your ethos in a second.

Counsel in civil cases often demonstrate the same principle; they introduce their clients in a warm humanizing way to develop a rapport not only between their clients and the jury, but also between themselves and the jury. The jury's view of the lawyer is as important as its view of the client.

Compare the manner in which counsel in the *Maffei* case introduced their clients:

Q. Good morning.

A. Good morning.

Q. You want to introduce yourself again to the jury, please?

A. Good morning, again. My name is Mary Jean Maffei. I was married to Richard Maffei.

Q. You are the plaintiff in this case?

A. Yes, I am.

Q. Why did you become a plaintiff and bring this lawsuit that we are here today to hear about?

A. I actually did not understand how my husband could have left the hospital without a proper diagnosis based on the severe symptoms he had.

Q. Are you a resident of Baltimore County?

A. Yes, I am.

Q. And exactly what neighborhood do you live in?

A. I live in Perry Hall.

Q. How long have you lived at that address, Mrs. Maffei?

A. Twelve years.

Q. Do you now live alone?

A. Shortly after Rick died, I asked my son to move back home.

Q. And you were married prior to your marriage with Mr. Maffei?

A. Yes, I was.

Q. How old is your son now?

A. He's 33.

Q. And how is his health?

A. His health is fine. He was born with a hearing impairment, but other than that, he's a normal kid.

Q. I think the most difficult question I always ask of a witness in trial is coming up now. How young are you?

A. I'm 56.

Q. And tell us what occupation, if any, you now have?

A. I am a secretary.

Q. Where do you work?

A. I work for Bravo Health.

Q. What is Bravo Health?

A. Bravo Health is a supplemental insurance carrier for people on Medicare.

Q. And how long have you been employed there?

A. Almost two years.

Q. What do you do exactly?

A. I am the secretary for the senior executive vice president and chief medical officer.

Q. So what hours do you work?

A. Seven-thirty to five.

Q. And in your capacity as an assistant, what are the responsibilities that you have?

A. We work with extensive meetings, scheduling, typing, filing; we also work with his ten direct reports with all matters of their needs.

Q. Do you like your work?

A. Yes, I do.

Q. Do you like the people you work with?

A. Very much.

Q. Do you ever interact with any of them during the day?

A. Yes, occasionally.

Q. Where do you usually have lunch, for example?

A. We eat lunch at our desks; we don't go out.

Q. Do you ever socialize or meet with the people at work outside of work?

A. Occasionally.

Q. What are some of the circumstances that would cause that to arise when you would meet with people?

A. We have gone to parties at individuals' homes, cookouts, holiday parties.

Q. What is your educational background?

A. High school, twelfth grade.

Q. Where did you go to high school?

A. Parkville High School.

Q. Did you start work right after high school?

A. Yes.

Q. Mrs. Maffei, in terms of your activities generally when you are not working, I'd like to hear about some of the things that interest you generally?

A. Generally?

Q. What do you do with yourself, in other words?

A. Generally, I am a homebody, so I do a lot things just around the house, gardening, cooking, spend a lot of time with my family, Rick's family, lot of time with my two nieces.

Q. And how old are the nieces now?

A. They are 12 and 14.

Q. What is the date, if you can recall, that your husband passed away?

A. March 8th, 2006.

Counsel in his introduction of Mrs. Maffei wanted to present her as a working lady who had endured a terrible loss, but at the same time had struggled to overcome that loss as opposed to wallowing in self pity.

Q. Now, Mrs. Maffei, you and your husband were married for how long on that date?

A. At the time of his death, it was eight and a half years.

Q. I would like to talk to you a little bit about your husband and show a few pictures that might help our discussion. Why don't you take a second to describe your husband to the jury?

A. He was the most loving, kind, generous man I think I have ever known. He treated me better than I ever thought anybody could be treated. He loved me completely. I loved him. We did everything together. You looked forward to when you came home at night, saw that smile, got a hug. And those are things I miss terribly.

Q. Let's show some pictures, if we could, just so we could put him in his environment. Okay. Why don't you show us, where is Rick? Is your husband in this picture?

A. Yes, he's the one in the baseball cap.

Q. On the far right?

A. Yes.

Q. And who is he with?

A. He's with all of his brothers and sisters and his mother.

Q. Is that the young lady there second to the left?

A. Yes, it is.

Q. Is she with us today?

A. Yes, she is.

Q. How old is she?

A. Seventy-nine.

Q. And let's see, let's not take too much time with this, but let's go to another one. That's a picture we saw in the opening statement with you and your husband?

A. Yes.

Q. How tall was he?

A. Six-foot.

Q. How much did he weigh?

A. Approximately 230 on average.

> The photographs introduced the jury to the late Mr. Maffei and made vivid and memorable the relationships that had been severed by his death.

Q. What did he do for employment?
We may have heard it, but we'd like to have you state it.

A. He was a heavy equipment operator by trade.

Q. What does a heavy equipment operator do?

A. He can run cranes, backhoes, loaders, bulldozers, most big earth-moving equipment.

Q. How would you describe his work ethic or the hours that he would work?

A. Impeccable. He took great pride in his work. He did the best he always could do. He was there whenever they needed him with no question.

Q. If we were to take a day in the life of Mr. Rick Maffei, what time would he leave for work?

A. Five o'clock in the morning.

Q. Generally, what time would he come home?

A. He was home by four, generally, if he worked a single shift.

Q. What were some of his interests outside of work?

A. He, since the age of 16, was an avid trap shooter. He absolutely loved doing that. He did it almost weekly.

Q. Did you ever go with him?

A. Yes, all the time.

Q. Where would he go for that?

A. He belonged to a private club in Carney, Maryland, Carney Rod and Gun Club. Then they would have other clubs around Maryland that they would go to occasionally.

Q. And what were some of his other interests?

A. He loved goose hunting. Even if he wasn't hunting, he just loved to go out in the environment just to watch.

Q. You didn't go goose hunting with him, did you?

A. No.

Q. Did he have other interests with family, for example?

A. We spent a lot of time with both families.

Q. Did he have any interaction with your nieces?

A. Constantly.

When the defense called Dr. Smedley to the witness stand, not only did counsel wish to portray his client as an outstanding individual but also as a competent physician. The attorney's challenge was to offset any momentum gained by the plaintiff through the direct examination of Mrs. Maffei and her supporting witnesses.

Q. Now, we've already heard your name mentioned a number of times during this trial. But the jury hasn't heard from you, so I want to ask you some background questions and then we'll talk about the events of March 8, 2006. You are an emergency physician, is that correct?

A. Yes, I'm an emergency medicine physician.

Q. Keep your voice up, please. And how long have you been practicing emergency medicine since you completed training?

A. I completed my residency in 1999. So I've been practicing post-residency for the last nine, almost ten years.

Q. Okay. And tell us about your educational background, beginning from college.

A. I went to college undergrad at Loyola College here in Baltimore.

Q. Did you grow up in Maryland?

A. I moved around a lot as a kid. Both my parents are from Baltimore, born and raised, so we had connections here.

Q. And is that why you came back to Loyola for college?

A. Yes. I still have other family around here as well. And in addition to that, my husband is from this area. And we were together at that time so—

Q. And after you—when did you complete Loyola College?

A. I finished in May of 1992.

Q. And then you went on to medical school?

A. That's correct.

Q. Where?

A. I went to University of Maryland Medical School here in downtown Baltimore.

Q. That's a four-year program?

A. Correct.

Q. And you completed that in what year? 1996?

A. Yes, I finished in 1996.

Q. So after you completed medical school, tell us about your training.

A. After medical school, I applied for residency and . . . did my residency [at University of Maryland] from '96 through '99.

Q. And tell us about what your residency consisted of.

A. The residency is a three-year period. In the first year of your residency, you spend your time divided between the intensive care units, the emergency department, the medical floors, orthopedics, the cardiac care unit, the surgical wards, ERs both at the VA and again at University. So our first year is spent sort of all over the hospital. Our last two years are focused in the emergency room. Again at several different institutions, we spend some time at Mercy, at the VA, and again back at University. Our last year of training is spent primarily at University, some time down at Children's Hospital down in D.C. as well. And as senior resident, so to speak, we are also responsible for running the ERs, supervising interns, and then reporting back to our attendings.

Q. Did you receive any portion of your training at Maryland Shock Trauma?

A. Yes, we spent our time both second year and third year over at the Shock Trauma Center to learn more about sort of what we think of as the Baltimore Gun and Knife Club, a lot of shootings, motor vehicle crashes, things of that nature.

Q. Okay. And what happened after you completed your residency? You went into practice?

A. That's correct. After I finished at University of Maryland, I went to work up at Greater Baltimore Medical Center in the emergency room.

The defendant here was portrayed as a competent physician, thorough and experienced in the emergency room. The cold transcript, of course, cannot portray the witness' demeanor and how it resonated with the jury. It is important in preparing witnesses for testimony to underscore the importance of conveying honesty, sincerity, and a likeable personality. In this respect, both parties in the *Maffei* case presented well.

Often the introductory portion of the direct examination is treated casually. This is a mistake especially when, as in most cases, credibility is an underlying issue. For the jury to have confidence in your case, it must not only *like* your client but also *trust* your client. The introduction is the place where you begin. Remember it is hard to undo a first impression.

In bench trials it may not be necessary to go into great detail introducing the witness, but certainly it should not be overlooked. In the *Oregon* case, the plaintiff called a county official to the stand. Counsel briefly introduced the witness as follows:

Q. Mr. Barrett, what is your position with Baltimore County?

A. Director of Parks and Recreation.

Q. How long have you held that position?

A. Nearly eight years.

Q. Were you employed by the county prior to that?

A. I was, sir.

Q. And in what capacity?

A. Senior executive assistant to the Baltimore County executive.

Q. And what did you do in that position?

A. I worked directly for the county executive.

Q. Doing what sort of things?

A. Policy, administrative duties, oversaw some of the department. . . .

This introduction—brief, and to the point—presents the witness as someone of responsibility whom the judge should find believable. Such an examination is a question-and-answer "argument" that says to the judge:

"You can believe this witness because he is trustworthy, was relied on by the county executive, and is a leader and a community servant."

Context of the Witness's Testimony

After you introduce the witness, it is helpful to question the witness about his or her relationship to the matters at hand. Before you ask the witness to describe something, you want to carefully establish his or her authority on the matter.

If the witness is an eyewitness, you might establish the foundation for his or her ability to accurately observe the event in question. Use your questioning to let the jury know, for example, whether the witness had a clear view and has excellent eyesight, is not on any medications, and has no personal interest in the case. Or, if you're trying to foster doubt about the eyewitness testimony, you might establish that the witness knew well the subject matter of the testimony, or was well acquainted with the individuals to whom the testimony referred.

Consider how the government developed the context of the testimony of Christopher Fickes, one of the witnesses called to testify against Rosen. Fickes was Rosen's friend and had worked for him. The government called Fickes to establish Rosen's sophisticated understanding of political fundraising and to establish Fickes' direct observation of Rosen's alleged bad conduct.

Q. Prior to going to law school, can you tell the ladies and gentlemen how it is you were employed?

A. Yeah. I started working on political campaigns after I graduated college, and after one year on a campaign in Iowa, I moved to Chicago to work on the fundraising team for the "Gore for President" campaign under Mr. Rosen's watch there.

Q. And when you say "Mr. Rosen," are you referring to the gentleman seated here at counsel table?

A. Yes.

Q. When was it that you graduated college, sir?

A. 1998.

Q. And can you tell us what you did when you were in Chicago working with Mr. Rosen?

A. Yeah, I worked largely in a support capacity. He ran the Midwest region for the Gore fundraising operation, and I would just help him put together fundraising events, coordinate the logistics for the fundraising events, track the contributions, and just be a general support staffer.

Q. Where did you go to, in terms of your employment? Where did you go after working on the Gore campaign?

A. After that we went to—we moved to the Senator Hillary Clinton campaign in New York.

Q. Approximately when was that?

A. That was at the end of 1999.

Q. When you say "we," who are you referring to?

A. Mr. Rosen and myself.

Q. Now, can you tell us what kind of a relationship you had with Mr. Rosen?

A. Yeah, it was a, you know—over the, I guess, three-plus years that I worked with him, I think we had a very good working relationship. We spent a lot of time together working on events. It was a pretty—the job is just—wasn't an eight-hour workday. So we spent a great deal of time together, and I think we worked together very well.

Q. After you completed working on Mrs. Clinton's campaign, did you continue to work with David Rosen?

A. Yes. After that campaign, we moved—well, I'm from Chicago originally. So I moved back to Chicago, and he opened up a campaign fundraising consulting business, and I helped him with that.

Q. What was the name of that organization?

A. It was known as the Competence Group.

Perhaps the most important answer given was regarding the nature of Fickes' relationship to the defendant. The assertion that the two spent a lot of time together over the years and had a good working relationship was important. It grounded Fickes as someone who had no reason to hold any grudges against him.

Q. What was your position with the Competence Group?

A. I think the business card said vice president.

Q. When you left—when was it that you left the Competence Group?

A. In about the middle of 2002.

Q. Why did you leave it?

A. I had decided to go to law school. So that was—at that time I—that was the time it's done.

The prosecutor's purpose here was to establish the witness's credibility on the subject of David Rosen. The government wanted Fickes to offer proof that Rosen was responsible for collecting donation information for an event and should have reported certain expenses as in-kind contributions, and it was important to establish that Fickes knew Rosen well enough to have that proof.

In Mrs. Maffei's case, to develop the context for her testimony about the substantive matters at hand, plaintiff's counsel demonstrated that Mrs. Maffei was present with her husband at the hospital and that he had complained of chest pain to nurses before seeing the doctor.

Q. Tell us what occurred after you and your husband arrived at the hospital?

A. When we got there, they called a triage nurse immediately and they took him in the back. He never sat down. They took me to registration.

Q. How long were you at registration?

A. Approximately 15 minutes.

Q. And after that time, where did you go?

A. I asked if I could go where he was and they said, "Give us a few minutes." I waited in the waiting room for ten to 15 minutes.

Q. That's about 25 minutes between registration and waiting?

A. Give or take a few minutes.

Q. Other than that 25 minutes, were you with your husband the entire time?

A. Absolutely every minute.

Q. Where was he, where did you go to find him?

A. As soon as you leave the waiting room of the emergency room, there are two double doors that go back into the emergency room and immediately inside of those doors to the left is a little alcove that had a gurney and a curtain there and that's where he was.

Q. When you saw him on this gurney behind a curtain, was he lying down on the gurney or was he sitting up?

A. At that time I believe he was lying down.

Q. Now, did you at any time before he saw the doctor, tell anyone in the hospital your view of what was happening to him?

A. Yes.

Q. Tell us about that.

A. When we came into the hospital, we had said he had chest and back pain with tightness in his upper chest. I believe that's why they took him back immediately. I also had that conversation with the nurse that was with him.

Q. Did you have occasion to have any discussions with them about your husband's condition?

A. I did.

Q. What concern did you have as you observed his symptoms?

A. I was afraid he was having a heart attack.

Q. Why?

A. Because of the symptoms he was having.

Q. What were the symptoms as you understood them, please?

A. Chest pain, severe back pain, and tightness in the base of his neck and throat.

When it was the defense's turn on direct, the attorneys also sought to create suitable context for the doctor's testimony. In particular, counsel elicited facts about the defendant's experience and practices when seeing patients so that ultimately the jury would accept her critical assertion that Mr. Maffei had *not* told her that he'd been suffering chest pain.

Counsel desired to establish the predicate for Mrs. Maffei's subsequent substantive testimony: the reason she brought her husband to the hospital and what he told the doctor about his complaints.

Q. And how long did you work at GBMC?

A. I worked at GBMC for the next, I guess, seven years through the fall, almost the same time in the fall of 2006.

Q. Can you estimate for me prior to March of 2006 about how many patients you had seen or patient encounters you had experienced in the emergency department after you completed your training and started practicing?

A. After residency?

Q. Yes, ma'am.

A. Many. I would see between, depending on the volumes, 12 to sometimes 20 patients in the evening or night, and I worked about three days a week. So calculating that out, I'd say probably thousands.

Q. Okay. And during that period of time, can you tell us if you had any experience prior to March of 2006 with patients who had aortic dissections?

A. I did have some experience with patients with aortic dissection. I had seen them both at Maryland and at GBMC.

Q. We heard prior to today about the—testimony about the frequency or infrequency of aortic dissection in the general population. What is your experience with that and what is your training and knowledge as far as the frequency of aortic dissection in the general population?

A. Aortic dissection is a rare entity, but it's a deadly one that we are taught about in detail, and one of the reasons we also ask detailed histories if there's any question of chest pain.

Q. Do you have a number of patients that you can recall that at some point who were under care were diagnosed with aortic dissection prior to March of 2006?

In the *Oregon* case the plaintiff's counsel wants Mr. Barrett, who was introduced as the director of Parks and Recreation, to testify that the lease agreement between the county and Oregon required the parking lot of the restaurant to be nonpaved such as stone or a similar permeable surface. To give context to the testimony counsel posed the following questions:

Q. Are you familiar with the property that is the subject of this case?

A. Yes, sir.

Q. Where is it situated?

A. The southeast corner of Shawan and Beaver Dam Road.

Q. Are you familiar with the property reflected in the photograph? Do you recognize Defendant's Exhibit 17 as an accurate aerial photograph of the Oregon Grille property as it looks today?

A. Yes.

Q. Please describe the property.

The witness describes the property, pointing out streams and various buildings as well as explaining that the entire property owned by the county is acres, but that the restaurant sits on a smaller allocated acreage.

In presenting the context in which a witness will testify, always ask yourself, "Why should the jury believe what the witness is about to testify?" Your answer to that question will help you develop the testimony. For example, for the defendant in the *Maffei* case, the answer to the question is that the doctor was an experienced emergency room doctor who had treated hundreds of patients and had familiarity with dissected aortas. In the *Oregon* case, Mr. Barrett knows the property, including the location of streams and the bucolic nature of the environment. He is well equipped to answer questions relating to preserving the environment as allegedly required by the county.

Substance of the Witness's Testimony

After providing a foundation for a witness's authority, move on to the topics that prove your case or defend against your adversary's attacks. Always keep your audience in mind as you construct your questions. While you have been immersed in the facts of the case for weeks or months, the dispute is all new to the jurors. If you forget the story you are trying to tell and become mired in arcane detail, you are likely to lose people along the way. The challenge is to marshal the facts selectively so that the direct examination focuses on what is most important. How do you know what is most important? Go back to your theme. Bring out those facts that support the theory of your case.

In the *Rosen* case, the core argument for the defense was that Rosen did not conceal the costs of the so-called Hollywood Gala; rather, he was the victim of the event's sponsors' concealment, and he had no motive to cause any false reports to be filed with the Federal Election Commission.

But the government developed many sub-themes in efforts to thwart this argument. For example, the government wanted the jury to believe that Rosen was part of the planning group for the event and that he was very enthusiastic about it. Defense counsel wanted to prove that he had no enthusiasm for the event and in fact had no part in developing the idea, and even opposed it.

Some context: James Levin was a government witness. He was a friend of President Clinton and active as an adviser and fundraiser on the Hillary Clinton Senate campaign. He was also a former friend of the defendant. Levin played an important role in the case, and his direct was initially damaging for the defense. He testified about his first meeting with Aaron Tonken, the donor who would later bank-roll the Hollywood Gala. He also testified that at this meeting Rosen and others were excited about planning the gala. The meeting took place in the year 2000 at a private fundraising event in Chicago (the Tullman event) that featured a performance by Olivia Newton-John. The events of that night were the subject of the government's direct of Levin, as excerpted below:

Q. And why is it you were at the event?

A. I was asked to come to the event by a woman who worked at the White House for the first lady by the name of Kelly Craighead who wanted me to meet Aaron Tonken.

Q. And did you meet Aaron Tonken at the event?

A. Yes, I did.

Q. And what was your reason for meeting Aaron Tonken?

A. To gauge whether he was for real and could be helpful with future events for us.

Q. And did you eventually meet Mr. Tonken?

A. Yes, I did.

Q. What happened? Were you alone or were you with anyone else?

A. No. We went out after the fundraiser with both Mr. Tonken, myself, Kelly Craighead, and David Rosen.

Q. Now just going back, I don't know if you answered this question: Whose event was that fundraiser with Olivia Newton-John in 2000 from the campaign? Who was supervising that?

A. That was—that was—David Rosen was.

Q. And where was it that you—do you recall where exactly you and Mr. Rosen, Ms. Craighead, and Aaron Tonken went?

A. It was on, I believe, Alston Avenue. It was an industrial-type loft building, and it was in the gallery or art space for a—one of our donors, Howard Tullman.

Q. And your purpose in going out with—the four of you going out was what?

A. To meet with Mr. Tonken and to—to find out if he was credible and if he could—and what he was capable of doing for us in the future.

Q. What was—what did he propose to you all?

A. He proposed to do a very large star-studded gala or event for the first lady in California.

Q. And what was Mr. Rosen's reaction?

SANDLER: Objection.

THE COURT: Overruled.

Q. You can only state what Mr. Rosen said or any—any reaction that you noticed physically, but not what you think was his thinking.

A. We were all verbally excited about the idea.

Q. And in the course of that evening, did Mr. Tonken bring up expenses that he had already expended for bringing in Olivia Newton-John?

A. Yes.

Q. Can you tell us about what he told you all?

A. Well, Mr. Tonken is a very gregarious person and a very—

Q. You can continue.

A. He stated that he had paid for Ms. Olivia Newton-John's travel to come by private plane, and he had paid for her suite at—I believe it was the Peninsula or Four Seasons hotel. And he also said that he had to pay for her sister's suite, who she brought along, and her entourage.

Q. What was Mr. Rosen's reaction—when that information was conveyed? What did he say?

MR. SANDLER: Objection.

THE COURT: Overruled.

That we didn't hear that; "you didn't tell me that."

Here we see the prosecutor doing an effective job moving the testimony swiftly to the critical testimony—that these four individuals met in a loft, where David Rosen allegedly became excited about the idea of a Hollywood fundraiser and also allegedly turned a blind eye to in-kind contributions made by Tonken in connection with the Chicago event that had just concluded that evening. The testimony is precise, to the point, and damaging.

Defense counsel was forced to respond and did so, not only in cross-examining Levin (which is discussed in Chapter 7, on cross-examination), but also in the direct examination of the defendant, David Rosen:

Q. At the event, when the event ended, the Tullman event, did you go out drinking with Jim Levin?

A. No.

Q. Did you go out drinking with Kelly Craighead?

A. No.

Q. Did you go with them and discuss costs of Olivia Newton-John?

A. No, sir.

Q. Did you go there and hear conversation about costs and say at this—

MR. ZEIDENBERG: Objection. Leading.

THE COURT: Overruled.

Q. [By Mr. Sandler] Did you go after the loft to this alleged separate get-together and hear complaints by Aaron Tonken about costs of Olivia Newton-John?

A. No.

Q. Now, the prosecutors pointed out through witnesses and Mr. Jim Levin, in particular, that you were at a separate meeting with him and Mr. Tonken and Ms. Craighead after the Tullman event. Did you hear that?

A. I did hear that.

Q. Were you at such a meeting, sir?

A. No, sir. I left right from the event. I was in the van with Mrs. Clinton, with the Secret Service, and we went to the Ebelings' residence; and after meeting Tom, I retired. I had an event the night before, I had an event the next morning, and I was dead tired.

Note in the above the use of repetition to drill a point home. Defense counsel wants the jury to know and believe and remember that the meeting between Rosen, Levin, Craighead, and Tonken did not take place, as Levin testified. But this refutation is elicited in pieces, with rapid, rhythmic, and repetitive questions.

Rosen's testimony on this topic continued as follows:

Q. All right. I want to talk to you now, if I could, about the first time you learned that there might be an event in August of 2000. Okay?

A. Okay.

Q. All right. Tell the jury, when did you first learn about the idea of an event in August 2000?

A. It was the next day. We woke up at the Ebelings, we attended a breakfast, and Kelly always traveled with Mrs. Clinton. She was her— Kelly Craighead was Mrs. Clinton's trip director. And Kelly had mentioned it to me, and then Jim Levin called me on my cell phone, and then Aaron Tonken called me on my cell phone, and they had all talked about this gala, potential gala during the convention.

> Note the way counsel introduces the new subject, by asking the witness at the end of the sentence, "Okay?" It is a simple technique, but provides a pause that is helpful for jurors trying to keep lots of information straight in their heads.

Q. By the way, the night before the Tullman event, when you went to the Ebelings' home with the first lady and escort, did Kelly Craighead accompany you?

A. No, she went out with Jim Levin and Aaron Tonken. They invited me to go. I didn't go.

Q. And did she eventually—did you eventually see her the next day?

A. I did.

Q. What were the circumstances?

A. She traveled with Mrs. Clinton everywhere she went. We had an event the next morning.

After moving ahead by asking Rosen how he first heard about the gala idea, counsel backtracks and asks about the previous night and Kelly Craighead's whereabouts. This was called for because Rosen had just testified that Craighead "always traveled" with Mrs. Clinton, and some clarification was needed. But by switching subjects so quickly, attorneys risk losing or confusing jurors.

Q. So when you heard about this proposed event, were the people advising you about the event enthusiastic?

A. Yes.

Q. What was your reaction, Mr. Rosen?

A. I was less than enthusiastic.

Q. Why? Tell the jury.

A. I didn't know how, with the other events planned, we would be able to participate in such a large event; and I thought there would be some resistance from Vice President Gore's campaign, like we were raising some of his money or intruding on his convention; and I also thought there might be some resistance from the people that were raising money directly for the convention itself here in Los Angeles.

Q. And time was a factor as well?

A. Yes.

Q. So did these issues or considerations that you just told us about get resolved?

A. They did.

Frequently, direct examination involves the testimony of a corroborating witness. In addition to Rosen refuting Levin's testimony, the defense called friends of Mrs. Clinton who corroborated Rosen's testimony that he did not go drinking with Levin but was with the first lady the entire time.
Here is an excerpt of the direct examination of Thomas Ebeling:

Q. Do you recall the approximate time when your wife and the senator did return from the Tullman event?

A. I would only guess at this point it was 10:00, 10:30, 11:00 o'clock at night.

Q. Do you remember who came back to your house directly from the event?

A. Well, there's always the Secret Service, and there was Mrs. Clinton, my wife, and David Rosen.

Q. Are you sure David Rosen came back with them?

A. I do, because David and I had a conversation in my kitchen.

Q. And how long did that conversation last?

A. Oh, maybe 10, 15 minutes.

Q. Can you tell the jury whether or not at some point he went to sleep?

A. After a while, I think—well, he went upstairs and retired, and Mrs. Clinton and I went into our family room and had a discussion. And then shortly after that, we all went to bed.

Another claim of the government was that Rosen and Levin entered into a pact to both lie about Rosen's alleged reporting of costs he knew to be inaccurate. Here is the substance of the direct examination of Levin on this point, presented by the prosecutor:

Q. And subsequent to that, did you have a meeting at a restaurant with David Rosen in which some of these same issues were discussed?

A. Yes, we did.

Q. Do you recall—what's your best recollection of what that conversation was?

A. I don't remember. It was sometime thereafter, not too long thereafter.

Q. Are you talking about 2001 at this point, if the gala was August of 2000?

A. I would imagine it's 2001. I am not sure.

Q. And how was it that you arranged to meet? Whose idea was it?

A. We both agreed that we should meet and talk but not on a cell phone.

Q. What was the point of your meeting?

A. To discuss the ongoing lawsuit [referring to a civil suit relating to the Hollywood Gala filed by Peter Paul against the Clintons and others] and the ongoing allegations by Peter Paul.

Q. Can you tell us about your meeting with Mr. Rosen and what was discussed?

A. We both agreed that both him and I were very credible and that Peter Paul and Aaron Tonken were not and that whose word in the end would people believe, them or us, and we were much more credible, much more believable; and they were just trying to paint a story to get themselves out of trouble; and we'd stick the line; and if we stick the line we won't have a problem, but we had to stay together.

Q. And your view of what you call your line, which was stick together and say you told the truth, was that, in fact, the truth?

SANDLER: Objection; it's vague as to what he is referring to.

THE COURT: Sustained.

Q. What was the story or the line that you and David Rosen agreed you were going to stick to?

A. That we had no understanding, we had no interpretation, and we did not know that Peter Paul's allegations of spending $1.2 million on this event was even remotely true.

Q. And was that line that you came up with, that you didn't know, was that the truth?

A. No.

Here is how on direct examination of David Rosen the defense addressed Levin's testimony:

Q. Did you ever talk to Jim Levin and tell him that there was illegal activity going on?

A. Absolutely not.

Q. Did you ever suggest to him that the costs—this will never be the cost of the gala?

A. No, I never said that.

Q. Did you ever have an occasion to sit down with Mr. Levin and talk about a pact that he won't say anything and you won't say anything and you would go forward?

A. No.

All these questions are asked in such a way that they elicit a concise and certain "no." They do not call for any explanation, and the witness gives none. Such questioning is helpful when you want to emphasize a position. Again, repetition is invaluable in direct examination if not overplayed.

The hotly contested facts in dispute in the *Maffei* case were whether the emergency room doctor had misdiagnosed Mr. Maffei. From the plaintiff's viewpoint the outcome hinged on whether the plaintiff could prove that Mr. Maffei had told the doctor that he was experiencing chest pains. Here is how Mrs. Maffei testified about this important aspect of the case:

Q. Let's now talk about the time your husband first saw the doctor.

A. Yes.

Q. Can you tell us about that?

A. Yes. Dr. Smedley walked in and said that she had the results of the blood test and that said negative, he was not having a heart attack, which I was very relieved.

Q. Did you react, other than your internal sense of being relieved, did you make any comments or say anything?

A. Yes, I was still concerned what all the symptoms were.

Q. I'm talking about your being relieved. Did you tell the doctor, that's a better question, did you state to your husband or to the doctor you were relieved?

A. Just, thank God, I just, thank God.

Q. Thank God for what?

A. That he wasn't having a heart attack.

Q. Was that from a blood test, is that what you are telling us?

A. Yes.

Q. Did you or your husband engage in further conversation with Dr. Smedley?

A. Yes she asked him questions and they talked.

Q. Tell us what they discussed?

A. She asked where Rick worked and he stated Sparrows Point.

Q. All right.

A. And she said, "I assume there is a lot of toxic stuff there" and he said, "I guess," you know. And she thought that possibly this was a reaction to something he had been around.

Q. Were you present during the discussions between the doctor and your husband about his symptoms?

A. Yes, I was.

Q. And do you recall whether your husband discussed with the doctor his symptoms and how he was feeling?

A. Yes, he did.

Q. What do you recall [about] what your husband said at that time when the doctor asked him about his symptoms and how he was feeling?

A. I recall him specifically telling her that he had a severe pain in his chest and back and felt the squeezing in the base of his neck and throat and it felt like heavy pressure.

Here, the questions go directly to the key dispute—what Dr. Smedley was told about Mr. Maffei's symptoms—and questions calling for short answers are used to slow down the testimony for the jurors, and keep their attention focused.

Q. Mrs. Maffei, did you make any comments about his symptoms to the doctor?

A. I did.

Q. What did you say to the doctor?

A. I asked if she would do an MRI.

Q. Was that the first meeting or was that at a later meeting?

A. I believe it was the first, but I can't be sure.

Q. Why did you ask for an MRI?

A. I still wasn't convinced there was nothing wrong with him. You don't get the severe chest and back pain for no reason. If it wasn't his heart, what was it? And I didn't know anything else to ask for.

Q. What was the response when you asked about an MRI?

A. She told me, no, we could not do that because it was a nonemergency procedure that we should see his primary care doctor [about].

Q. So, how long did the doctor spend on this first meeting with you and your husband?

A. Five minutes or so. I mean, you know, she checked him out; we talked.

Q. Were you under the impression, at least based on this meeting, that Dr. Smedley had ruled out a myocardial infarction or heart attack?

A. Yes.

Q. And did she ask, do you recall any other discussion?

A. At some point, at the second meeting, she started asking about a sore throat, which he never had a sore throat, but she said, "have you been around anyone with strep?" Ironically, the week before, Rick and I were taking care of my sister's children for the week and the youngest had strep throat. So she said she would do a strep test, but really believed that wasn't the problem.

Q. Do you recall any discussion at the second meeting between Dr. Smedley and your husband whether the doctor asked him about whether he was experiencing chest pain?

A. Yes.

Q. And what do you recall about that discussion?

A. He described he had a sharp pain in his chest that went through to his back and this tightness in his throat and he talked to her about this and I talked to her about this.

Q. Well, when you talked to her about it, again, did you or did he point to any area in the abdomen where he was referencing this pain?

A. He kept taking his hand with a squeezing motion at the base of his throat and upper chest.

There is an elliptical quality to this testimony. It does not build up to a climax or tell a story, but does vividly describe that Mr. Maffei demonstrated chest pain. Though compelling, the testimony would be aggressively countered by the defense when the emergency room doctor took the stand and gave exactly the opposite testimony.

Q. Now, I'd like to direct your attention to the day in question. It was a tragic day for Mr. Maffei and for Mrs. Maffei. But I'd like to ask you about your recollection. Do you have an independent recollection, do you have a memory distinct from the medical records of Mr. Maffei and your encounter with Mr. Maffei that day?

A. I do remember my encounter with Mr. Maffei that day.

Q. That's now a little over three years ago. Can you tell us, tell the ladies and gentlemen, you've probably seen hundreds of patients since that time, how you have an independent recollection or memory of Mr. Maffei and your encounter with him that night?

A. I remember my encounter with Mr. Maffei because I remember talking to him. He was very calm, he was—his appearance was benign. And he had symptoms that were consistent with his physical exam. He had a red throat, he had a sore ear. And so when I found out what happened, I was shocked.

Q. When did you find out that Mr. Maffei had died?

A. I found out the following—the day after he had passed.

Q. I'm sorry. I interrupted you. You were telling us why you remember Mr. Maffei.

A. Yes. Cause it was just I couldn't think of what could have happened that would precipitate that, his death. He looked so well. When he left in the morning, his vital signs were all stable and there was nothing in the history that he gave that would indicate why he would have died.

Q. Okay. I'd like to go over with you some of the medical records; particularly the medical records that you would have seen and the medical records you would have created. When do you begin the care of or encounter a patient that comes into the emergency department?

A. I encounter the patient when they're brought back into the room. Or if there's nothing that the nurse is concerned about, then they bring them out of triage in the hallway area to evaluate the patient. In general after the patient is brought back, the patients are placed in an order of which the nurse in triage considers important, then I pick up the chart from a rack and go see the patient.

Q. What did you do when you first walked into the room with Mr. Maffei or any patient? What did you do initially?

A. I walk in the room, I look at the patient. I want to see if they look like they're in distress, any intervention I need to do right away generally on the monitor board there, repeat the last blood pressure again and the heart rate. If they're on a monitor, I can see the limit up on the monitor. And, well, when you walk in, I do a global assessment to make sure there's nothing I need to do right then to [stabilize] him. I also introduce myself to the patient so they know who I am, and they can correct me if I pronounce their name incorrectly. And in Mr. Maffei's case, while I was doing that, I also put the blood pressure cuff on and took his blood pressure. Because I wanted to be sure that again, that his blood pressure was stable and that that repeat blood pressure was the accurate one.

Q. What was his blood pressure when you retook it?

A. I did not write the number of the blood pressure down. Again, I took it to reassure myself that it was normal. And the nurses continued recording the vital signs, and they again remained normal.

Q. You didn't write down that you retook the blood pressure. How is it that you can testify today that you retook his blood pressure?

A. Because I remember that I retook his blood pressure and I remember that it was normal.

Q. Okay. And then what would you have done?

A. So once I had done those things, normally I would sit down, if there's a chair, and I ask patients why they came to the emergency department.

Q. Okay. And what did Mr. Maffei tell you?

A. Mr. Maffei told me that he had come in because around nine o'clock that night, he had a somewhat sudden onset of a sensation of his throat closing and feeling sore. He said it sort of happened over ten minutes or so, and that it was pain deep in his throat here.

Q. And what else did he tell you?

A. Well, after he told me that, I specifically wanted to ask him some other questions because clearly the triage note reflected that he had chest pain. And he didn't report that to me initially as why he came to the emergency room. And so I wanted to clarify that. So I—at that time I asked him how he had been feeling. And in particular at the time as well, Mrs. Maffei was also very concerned about him. So I wanted to clarify the chest pain. So I asked him, you know, are there any symptoms he's been having, has he been sweaty, has he been nauseated. He said no. He didn't appear short of breath and told me he wasn't feeling short of breath. And though I also specifically asked him about chest pain, he hadn't brought it up. And he told me he wasn't having chest pain and that he hadn't been having chest pain. And I said was it in your chest or your throat, [because] this can be confusing. So I specifically said are you having chest pain or is it in your throat, and he told me it was in his throat.

Q. And you also wrote—here read this. Fifty two—

A. It's 52-year-old white male comes in complaining of onset at 9 p.m. of sense of throat closing and sore. Rapid onset over about ten minutes.

Q. So the zero with the line through it means no or none?

A. Right. No nausea, no shortness of breath.

Q. That looks like SCO, that's SOB, shortness of breath?

A. Yes, shortness of breath. No chest pain. This is just an additional clarification of his throat pain. Because I want to make sure the throat pain wasn't something that was exertional because that can reflect more concern for something cardiac. The pain was not associated with exertion. Other than we talked—talked further about why he could have had this sudden sense of his throat closing, work allergens, anything he was exposed to at work because I became concerned with this more rapid onset that he potentially was having an allergic reaction, which he said there was certainly things at work that would cause him to have a respiratory reaction, it could cause a breathing reaction. And then we also talked about because he had this sore throat if he had any exposures to that. And he said his niece visited about a week ago and had strep throat.

Q. Now, we heard testimony from Mrs. Maffei yesterday that Mrs. Maffei and/or Mr. Maffei told you that he was having chest pain when you saw Mr. Maffei at 5:55 a.m. Do you recall that?

A. Mr. Maffei told me that he did not have chest pain. I asked him on more than one occasion. I particularly want to clarify, as I said, because chest pain is never a complaint I would ignore or not take seriously. There are some very dangerous things that kill folks when they have chest pain. There are many diagnoses that you need to rule out when someone has chest pain. He didn't have chest pain when I asked him directly. He was appropriately alert, he was perfectly communicative and able to tell me what was wrong with him. And he denied to me that he had chest pain.

Q. Did you ask Mr. Maffei if he had chest pain earlier that evening that had brought him to the emergency department?

A. I asked him if he had been having chest pain earlier and he said no. And I particularly again asked, when I do my review of systems, any chest pain, and he had not been having chest pain.

Q. Let's talk about the back pain. Mrs. Maffei described yesterday that Mr. Maffei was having severe back pain and that was also mentioned to you. What do you recall, if anything, about that?

A. Well—

Q. Did he describe severe back pain to you that also started around that evening?

A. No. Again, I spoke with him about the back pain because it was in the triage note. And that was when we talked about the nature of the back pain and was it like his kidney stones or not. You know, how long has he been progressing. And he told me he had had problems with the back in distant past that he'd seen an orthopedist for, that things progressively were getting worse over the last year or so.

Q. And then the next thing you would have done would have been what?

A. This is called the Review of Systems. And this is just where, you know, we kind of go through a laundry list of other problems that he may or may not be having so—

Q. Did you find—I'm not going to go through each and every one of these.

A. Okay.

Q. But it's—there's one, two, three—there's more than ten categories here. So you—would you have asked him—how did you find out the information? To respond to this by asking these questions?

A. Right I asked them, and then any things [he confirmed] I would back slash.

Q. Let's direct your attention specifically to CV. What does that mean?

A. That's cardiovascular.

Q. And then it's CR, that's—

A. Chest pain.

Q. And you drew a line through that. Why did you draw a line through that?

A. Again, because I asked him and he told me he wasn't having chest pain and he didn't have chest pain.

Q. And then you would have moved onto the physical examination?

A. Uh-huh.

. . .

Q. Now, based upon your history, based on your review of symptoms, based upon your physical examination, did you have any suspicion that Mr. Maffei had an aortic dissection in progress?

A. No, I had no suspicions that he was having an aortic dissection or any cardiac problem or chest-pain-related medical condition.

. . .

Q. Okay. Let me show you what's been marked as Defense Exhibit 6, without my reading glasses. There are a number of signs and symptoms to aortic dissection that you can see in a patient in an emergency department, correct?

A. Huh?

Q. Of this diagram?

A. I've seen that, yes.

Q. And these are various signs and symptoms that could be presented of an aortic dissection, including chest pain, excruciating chest pain, sudden chest pain, excruciating, ripping, tearing chest pain, shortness of breath, pale skin, sense of impending doom, extreme anxiety, sweating, heart murmur, nausea, vomiting, upper extremity pain, lower extremity pain, upper extremity weakness or paralysis, upper extremity meaning the arms, right?

A. Uh-huh.

Q. Lower extremity meaning the legs, abdominal pain, and stroke. Did Mr. Maffei have any of those when you saw him and examined him and took a history—

A. No.

Q. On March 8, 2006?

A. No, he had none of those signs and symptoms.

Q. What diagnosis did you make based upon your history and physical, review of the symptoms, and the laboratory work and EKG that were done on Mr. Maffei?

A. I made a diagnosis of recall otitis media, which is an ear infection, based on ear pain and redness of the ear, and sore throat, which is a pharyngitis, which is based upon the redness of the throat, his throat discomfort. He had been exposed to strep. And so I decided that I would treat him presumptively on the conservative side, to cover him for his ear infection and strep throat. Although most likely the symptoms are related to a viral infection, I don't like to wait and not treat them. I went ahead and started him on amoxicillin. The other concern was the feeling of closing in this throat, that concern he had reacted to something at work. That night when he came in, he was given—he was given Benadryl and steroids via a medrol dose pack. . . .

In presenting the testimony of their parties, each counsel utilized the basic principles of argument although in dialogue form. Working with counsel, each witness introduced herself effectively, presented the context for her testimony, and then testified about the substance of the case.

Mrs. Maffei's point was that she had great concern for her husband, she was present when he met with the doctor, and she heard him testify about his chest pain; she stated he had complained about chest pain to the nurses prior to visiting, which is reflected on the hospital records, and that the doctor should have diagnosed dissected aorta.

The doctor's responsive argument through testimony was that she is a thorough physician and caring toward her patients; she said she clearly remembered Mr. Maffei and that he not only specifically did not complain of chest pain but denied having chest pain. Furthermore, she noted in her medical records at the time of the visit that he did not have chest pain. Implied in her testimony is that she would not have anticipated his death at that time, and that she would not have stated in her records at the time that he denied having chest pain if such were not the case.

Immunization

It may be wise to ask questions the jury would expect your adversary to ask. Queries that may seem at first glance antithetical to your theme, if handled well, will only enhance your ethos and your witness's ethos in the courtroom.

This brings us to the technique of immunization, a means of taking the wind out of the opponent's sails. By being the first to recognize that you have a problem with your side of the case, you can then communicate to the jury that, when properly understood, the problem is minor or certainly not significant enough to cause the jury to decide against your client. Immunizations, of course, involve injecting a small amount of an infectious agent into the body to fight against the full disease.

For example, two of the government witnesses in *Rosen*, James Levin and Ray Reggie, had recently pleaded guilty to felony charges involving fraud. Rather than wait for their witnesses to be impeached on cross-examination, the prosecution elicited testimony on direct about the charges and subsequent pleas. In so doing, the prosecution sought to "immunize" its witnesses from attack by emphasizing that regardless of their wrongdoing, the witnesses were testifying truthfully about Rosen's alleged criminal conduct.

In immunizing a client against the claims of a witness, there may be the temptation to attack the witness as mendacious. Doing so can easily backfire, however, particularly if the witness appears credible. Nevertheless, it is important to meet the claims head on.

Whereas immunization defends against claims before they are articulated, refutation involves rebutting an adverse claim or testimony after it is revealed.

In *Rosen*, Whitney Burns, the compliance officer for the Democratic Senatorial Campaign Committee and a government witness in the case, testified that David Rosen had told her to reduce the recorded costs for the gala by $100,000. She also claimed that Rosen had told her Cher would not be attending and so further reductions could be made. (Cher did, in fact, attend.) On direct examination, Rosen specifically refuted these points.

Rosen did not, however, characterize Burns as a liar. He simply insisted that she had misunderstood him. At the time Rosen discussed the matter with her, he was talking hurriedly over the telephone. He testified that there was never a doubt that Cher would be attending, but that the gala would save money because Cher's band would not be coming. Rosen also explained that he had told Burns that the actual cost of the concert was $100,000 less than reflected on the budget she had been discussing with him. These responses were couched in the form of question and answer.

By addressing these matters on direct, defense counsel prevented prosecution from making a big show by throwing Burns' testimony at Rosen on cross. The claims had already been fully explained.

Similarly the defense in the *Maffei* case, seeking to refute the plaintiff's claims about the doctor's failure to order a chest x-ray, presented the following testimony:

Q. Now, Mr. Sandler, read to the jury from your deposition taken previously where you stated that if a patient comes in with chest pain, you would order a chest x-ray.

A. Yes.

Q. Is that accurate?

A. I would order a chest x-ray in a patient that came in with chest pain. That's routine practice, do an EKG and chest x-ray.

Q. Why didn't you order a chest x-ray in Mr. Maffei's case?

A. I didn't order a chest x-ray because Mr. Maffei told me he wasn't having chest pain. He was calm, cooperative, he was in no respiratory distress, no respiratory complaint. There was no cough that would have pushed me to do that because of a concern for pneumonia or anything of that nature. So once I had spoken to Mr. Maffei and clarified his history, and he had clearly told me told me he didn't have chest pain, at that point there was no reason for me to order a chest x-ray.

Asking these series of questions on direct examination of the doctor, defense counsel not only refuted testimony on direct examination in the plaintiff's case, but also immunized the doctor from cross-examination on the topic of not ordering a chest x-ray.

Conclusion

Always try to end your direct examination on a high note. Each examination calls for its own conclusion. Consider the conclusion of Rosen's direct examination:

Q. Mr. Rosen, I want you to tell the jury specifically the answers to some of these last questions I am going to pose to you. At any time—at any time during the Senate campaign and your work for the campaign, did you intend to cause a false statement to be filed with the Federal Election Commission or any governmental agency?

A. Absolutely not.

Q. Did you ever intend to falsify or cause the falsification of any documents to anyone?

A. No.

Q. Did you ever intend to violate any laws?

A. No.

Q. Do you believe, sir, in all and full honesty that you performed your work honestly?

A. Yes.

Q. With diligence?

A. With diligence.

Q. With sincerity?

A. Yes, sir.

Q. Are you innocent of the charges against you?

A. Yes. I am 100 percent innocent of these charges.

MR. SANDLER: Your Honor, thank you for the opportunity.

We have already touched on the virtues of rhythm and repetition in testimony, but here it is evident that these techniques can evoke the witness's emotion and, potentially, jurors' sympathy for the defendant in his most essential and important claim: his innocence. In concluding the direct, counsel did not merely ask for an affirmation of innocence, but also an affirmation of a job well done on Rosen's part. Again, the witness touches on the themes of diligence and sincerity that were hinted at in the introduction portion of the testimony.

Counsel concluded Mrs. Maffei's testimony by asking her to describe how her husband died:

A. And when I got to the bottom of the stairs, I saw him on the floor at a very odd angle in front of the sofa like with his butt up in the air like when you were getting up off a chair and flat on his face on the floor. His glasses had come off. And he was bleeding from the mouth and the nose.

Q. You were obviously terrified and upset. Did you call 911?

A. Immediately.

Q. Did you call, go to a neighbor's?

A. The 911 operator asked if he was breathing and I said, I don't think so, but I am not sure. She said, "Turn him over." And I couldn't because his legs somehow got wedged from the knees down under the sofa. He was stuck. She said, "Is anybody home with you?" And I said no. She said, "Do you have a neighbor close that can help you?" We live in townhomes. I said yeah. She said, "Go get help now." I ran out the door in my nightgown, screaming, pounding on the neighbor's door. They came immediately to assist me.

Q. And your husband died?

A. Yes.

Q. So, let's come forward a bit and just ask you, how [are] you doing now with all of this?

A. I am getting better. I am starting to try to pull my life together.

Q. Did you seek any counseling or help for your emotional anguish, ma'am?

A. Yes.

Q. I apologize for having to bring numbers to the table in light of what you just testified to, but do you feel that your husband's absence at the home and his lack of companionship, lack of being with you has affected you in your life?

> This testimony forms an evocative image of the man's last minutes.

A. Dramatically.

Q. How are some of the ways it's affected you?

A. He was the love of my life. He was the person I never thought I would meet. He fulfilled my life in every way and I don't have that anymore.

Q. Over the years when you were married, did he ever give you advice or give you guidance?

A. I think we gave it to each other.

Q. What are some of the things you'd go to him and talk over with him that are not so personal that we can at least share?

A. We absolutely shared everything together from every day work experiences to finances, to our hopes and dreams of where our life would go.

We met later in life, so we were hoping to make up for lost time with spending our lives together.

It would be easy for jurors to be touched by the widow's grief. Such pathos, especially when evoked in a memorable fashion, is often essential to effective witness examination.

REDIRECT EXAMINATION

After cross-examination you have the opportunity to conduct redirect. If you do so, be selective. You may not want to redirect on a topic if your case theme and theory were not harmed by it, or you have another witness to combat harmful facts elicited on cross. You may also feel that the topic, whether harmful or not, was covered in depth to the point that you do not want to draw any more attention to it and make matters worse, hoping that in closing argument you can resolve the matter.

After extensive cross-examination of Mr. Rosen in his case, defense counsel did not conduct any redirect examination at all. The reasoning here was two-fold: first, counsel believed there was no major point to cover on a redirect examination, and second, foregoing redirect examination was a way to communicate to the jury confidence in the witness' direct examination and how well he stood the cross-examination.

In the *Maffei* case, brief questions were asked of Mrs. Maffei on redirect examination that related to a discrepancy in the medical record and the date of death of her husband. The redirect examination was not extensive.

From the introduction to the establishment of context, to the substance of the testimony, to immunization and refutation, to the conclusion, the direct examination is a complex performance that must be *designed to persuade*. Unpredictable testimony may surface and opposing counsel will occasionally object, but the attorney on direct has a great deal of latitude with which to employ the most persuasive means of eliciting advantageous, credible, and memorable testimony. That freedom will help you win your case. It is wise to acknowledge this latitude, to appreciate your options, and to recognize the many techniques at your disposal. Only then will you be equipped to make the best choices for your particular case and witness

Learning Points for Chapter 4

- Do your homework: Prepare yourself and your witnesses thoroughly for direct and cross-examinations.
- Remember to prove elements of each claim or defense.
- Use nonleading questions.
- Maintain an easy control of the testimony with a mix of closed-ended and open-ended questions.
- Does your witness appear sincere and likable? Do what you can to make sure that he or she does. A high ethos is critical to success.
- Style and delivery matter. Consider body language and tone, use plain language, and coach your witness on his or her own delivery.
- Be vivid. What counts in the end is what jurors remember. Ask detailed questions to draw out engaging, memorable testimony, and find ways of repeating key information (e.g., looping and incorporation).
- Use demonstrative evidence to concentrate jurors' attention on, and anchor their memory of, important testimony.
- Prepare to authenticate exhibits if you do not have an agreement.
- Immunize the witness against anticipated attacks on cross-examination.
- Begin and end each examination with your strongest testimony, and arrange your lineup of witnesses likewise.

CHAPTER 5

DIRECT EXAMINATION—A VIEW FROM THE BENCH

By the Hon. Paul W. Grimm, United States District Judge, United States District Court for the District of Maryland

Much more difficult than opening, closing, and cross-examination, where the lawyer's skill, preparation, and individual *ethos* are center stage, direct examination requires the lawyer to have the talent, confidence, and courage to leave the limelight to the witness, and to abandon the security of control for the risky but essential goal of persuading the jury through the logic, emotion, and character of the witnesses and exhibits. This is essential because, as the Supreme Court observed not long ago, testimonial and documentary evidence "tells a colorful story with descriptive richness . . . and as its pieces come together a narrative gains momentum, with power not only to support conclusions but to sustain the willingness of jurors to draw the inferences . . . to reach an honest verdict."[1]

There are structural challenges to the conduct of effective direct examination: nonleading questions must be used, the lawyer is vulnerable to the witness interjecting harmful testimony despite careful advance preparation, and the narrative flow may be interrupted by the need to authenticate and admit documentary or demonstrative evidence. However, astute counsel can turn these potential hurdles into advantages. If the use of nonleading questions deprives the lawyer of the control that leading questions

---

1. Old Chief v. United States, 519 U.S. 172, 187 (1997).

afford, it provides the unmistakable benefit of allowing the development of the *ethos* of the witness before the jury, enabling the witness to be humanized and accepted by the jury. The introductory examination of the defendant, Rosen, at pages 105–108, for example, highlights that he was a hard-working man who had overcome the lack of a high school education to put himself through college and become a successful fundraiser. The result is a warm and human portrayal of the defendant, which is essential to instilling in a jury a willingness to accept the defense's theory of the case over the prosecution's. Similarly, the example on page 109, of the examination of Stan Lee, was aided by the self-deprecating humor of the examiner and portrays a legend of the entertainment industry, 82 years "young," in a lighter vein. This enhanced the jury's interest in his testimony, and overcame any appearance of the witness as a self-important "big shot" from Hollywood.

As noted in Chapter 4, organization and focus are important elements of direct examination. Direct examinations often include an introduction to the witness (developing his or her *ethos*); the context of the witness in the larger case (helping to advance the theme of the defense and establish the witness's personal knowledge of the underlying events); the substantive content of the testimony (providing the *logos*, or logic, of the witness's contribution); an immunization to draw the sting from any weaknesses that an adversary will attempt to exploit on cross (thereby enhancing the ethos of the witness and the examiner); and a strong conclusion (which builds the *pathos*, or emotion, of the presentation).

A bedrock obligation, one that is often overlooked, is to plan the direct examination to prove the essential elements of a claim or affirmative defense. Meeting this obligation ensures that each witness contributes to the twin goals of presenting evidence to support the lawyer's burden of proof, and doing so with a quality that has the weight to persuade the jury to accept this evidence as proof. As pointed out in Chapter 4, questioning techniques such as looping, incorporation, and using short and open-ended questions will help the novice lawyer meet the evidentiary burdens of proof in nonabstract terms that are easily adapted to any case.

As discussed, proof and persuasion have not one dimension, but three: ethos, pathos, and logos. Every question asked adds to or detracts from the ethos of the witness as well as the lawyer conducting the direct examination. Is the lawyer confident, prepared, focused, and respectful of the witness, court, and jury, but not afraid to demonstrate an appropriate amount of humor when called for? Or is she nervous, overbearing, self-impressed, or inattentive? The questioning techniques described in Chapter 4 will help attorneys develop the pathos of a case by maintaining a rhythm, pace, and tone that, as noted in *Old Chief* (cited on page 147), gives the evidence a "force beyond any linear scheme of reasoning . . . as its pieces come together [and] a narrative gains momentum." And, as careful attention to the elements of proof of each claim and defense and the proper authentication of documents and exhibits result in the admission of essential evidence, the *logos* or logic of the case becomes compelling.

Here are some additional practice tips that you may wish to consider in the form of dos and don'ts from the view of the court:

1. When you prepare for your direct examination, make a list of all the things that the witness can be expected to testify to that will advance the proof of your case, paying particular attention to the elements of proof for each claim or defense that you must prove. As part of this process identify all exhibits or demonstrative evidence you will use during the examination. Once you have done this, prepare a list of all the things that you think that the witness may say during cross-examination that could be harmful to your case. Knowing this, you are now in a good position to outline your direct examination, anticipating the most persuasive manner in which to present the positive points and immunize the negative ones. This outline will help you prepare the witness when you meet before trial and minimize the risk of an unexpected poor outcome.

2. When considering how to conduct direct examination by avoiding leading questions, phrase questions using "who, what, where, when, how"; "describe"; and "explain." Use of these words makes it more likely that the witness will be testifying, rather than the lawyer "suggesting" the answer. Moreover, when the witness answers without suggestions from the lawyer, the *ethos* of the witness is enhanced, and the jury can begin to understand and relate to him or her. With this

understanding comes the willingness of the jury to give persuasive weight to what the witness has said. Additionally, remember that the prohibition against leading questions during direct is not absolute. Federal Rule of Evidence 611(c) provides that leading questions may be asked during direct to develop the testimony. Examples include background questions, questions about matters that are not contested, foundational questions to admit evidence under Rule 104(a), transitional questions from one topic to another, questioning a child witness or elderly witness, or when questioning a witness who has difficulty discussing a sensitive or emotional topic.

3. If at all possible, avoid writing out questions verbatim. Doing so increases the likelihood that you will be reading the questions, not interacting face-to-face with the witness or observing the reaction of the jury to the testimony. If you have carefully prepared and have a good outline, you will be able to frame the questions as you ask them and, by carefully listening to the witness's answer, you are better able to take advantage of the techniques of looping and incorporation discussed in Chapter 4.

4. Pace your examination to make sure that it proceeds at a speed that is neither too fast, which the jury cannot follow, or too slow, which could cause you to lose the jury's attention. Remember that when juries give feedback to judges after trials are over, they frequently complain that the lawyers took too long to "get to the point" of the examination, and needlessly asked repetitive questions. If you are doing your job the right way, the jurors will be paying attention and will appreciate it if you give them credit for their intelligence.

5. If you are using an exhibit during the examination of a witness, make sure you have thought about how to present it so that the jury sees it. Juries do not like it when a lawyer is huddled over a witness who is looking at an exhibit that the jury cannot see. Once you have laid the foundation to get an exhibit admitted, try to avoid examining the witness about the substance of the exhibit unless the jury knows what it says. Use of audiovisual aids such as document presentation equipment keeps jurors engaged

and allows them to see an exhibit while the witness describes its importance to the litigation. This technology works much better than "publishing" an exhibit to the jury after the witness has finished describing it.

CHAPTER 6

DEUS EX MACHINA— THE EXPERT WITNESS

In classical Greek drama, when the hero was in grave straits, an immortal would often come to his aid. The god would be lowered onto the stage from above by a machine and save the day—hence the Latin term describing the Greek experience of the deus ex machina (god from the machine).

While today's trial lawyers don't have the deus ex machina, they may have the next best thing: the expert witness. The well-qualified expert can do what the deus ex machina did so many centuries ago—save the day and destroy the adversary—not by force of arms but by rendering a lethal opinion.

The advantages of using an expert at trial are numerous. In many cases—such as tort cases—an expert may be necessary to prove an element of the cause of action. In a medical malpractice case, for instance, an expert can help counsel argue that the botched surgery was caused by the defendant's failure to comply with the standards of the profession. In other instances, the expert will help explain complicated facts with which the judge or jury is not familiar. How a propane furnace operates and why it malfunctioned, for example, may be territory only an expert can cover adequately. The value of the expert is heightened because he or she is permitted to render opinion testimony. Lay witnesses, with limited exceptions, may not render opinions.

These advantages make experts indispensable at trial. Many trials evolve into a so-called battle of the experts. A distinguished person capable of winning the jury's confidence can give one side the edge it needs to win. This was precisely the situation in the *Maffei* case. Two well-qualified physicians testified diametrically opposite each other as to whether the emergency room doctor violated standards of care by not discovering Mr. Maffei's dissected aorta.

In the *Rosen* trial, experts, while not a decisive factor, proved critical in decoding for the jurors the intricacies of campaign finance law and how it should be applied to the circumstances in question. Both sides called upon campaign finance experts to support their theme. Later in this chapter, we will look at the defense's presentation of an expert in an effort to refute the prosecution's explanation of the defendant's motivation for allegedly concealing fundraising expenses from the FEC.

But the examination of the expert is actually the end of a complex process. Selecting an expert, complying with evidentiary rules, overcoming discovery snags, and preparing the witness all precede your expert's appearance in the courtroom.

BEFORE TRIAL—CHOOSE WISELY

Sometimes the urgency to locate an expert obfuscates the importance of selecting the right one. Before you choose any expert, you need to develop your theory of the case and then use that theory to identify what you specifically need from the expert(s). The more time you have to select the witness, the better.

There are several ways to locate experts. You can ask a colleague or friend for suggestions or use the Internet to examine the many groups offering a stable of experts. You can also contact bar associations that retain directories of experts, and review depositions given by potential witnesses. Still another technique is to draw upon the assistance of a consultant to help locate a credible witness.

Before interviewing the candidate, be certain that you have developed the theory of your case and have a clear idea of the opinions you seek from him or her. Leap forward in your mind to the trial. Imagine the closing argument and how you plan to describe to the jury the views of your expert. This exercise helps you focus precisely on the unique needs of your case.

One question frequently asked is: who should retain the expert—the lawyer or client? There is no uniform answer, but many lawyers prefer to sign the engagement letter along with a written agreement stating that the client is responsible for payment of the expert's fees. In the absence of such an agreement, the lawyer would likely need to pay the expert if the client failed to do so. If there is no agreement in place explicitly stating that the lawyer is not responsible for these fees, refusal to do so could result in difficulties in retaining experts in the future.

Retaining the right witness is just the beginning. Turning an expert's knowledge into winning testimony demands deep familiarity with the rules of evidence that govern experts. If experts are akin to the deus ex machina of old, the attorney is surely the one up on the catwalk, lowering the apparatus before the jury.

Types of Experts

Bear in mind that there are three types of experts (other than good or bad ones): the testifying expert, the hybrid/fact expert, and the consultant or nontestifying expert. The hybrid/fact expert is one who has firsthand knowledge and will also render opinions. The consultant expert can be retained to render advice, teach counsel about complicated subjects, and suggest testifying experts to retain.

One key difference between the testifying expert and the nontestifying expert in civil cases is that the latter is exempt from discovery and cannot be deposed. Under federal rules, the mandatory disclosure requirements applicable to a hybrid/fact expert are minimal compared to the full mandatory disclosure requirements for testifying experts.

ESSENTIAL RULES AND CASE LAW

Working with expert witnesses is much easier if you have an authoritative grasp of applicable rules and case law. Generally, expert testimony is admissible only when it can assist the judge or the jury in understanding the evidence or determining pertinent facts. But the standard used to scrutinize expert testimony in federal court is distinct from that employed in some state courts. Anyone working with experts must appreciate the differences.

The federal standard is iterated in a trilogy of U.S. Supreme Court decisions: *Kumbo Tire Co. v. Carmichael*,[1] *General Electric Co. v. Joiner*,[2] and *Daubert v. Merrell Dow Pharmaceuticals Inc.*[3] Federal Rule of Evidence 702 is derived from the principles enunciated in these cases, which instruct that the judge serves as the gatekeeper for the admissibility of expert testimony.

Rule 702, Testimony by Expert Witnesses, provides as follows.

A witness who is qualified as an expert by knowledge, skill, experience, training, or education may testify in the form of an opinion or otherwise if:

(a) the expert's scientific, technical, or other specialized knowledge will help the trier of fact to understand the evidence or to determine a fact in issue;
(b) the testimony is based on sufficient facts or data;
(c) the testimony is the product of reliable principles and methods; and
(d) the expert has reliably applied the principles and methods to the facts of the case.

The decisions assert that the following factors should be used in considering the admissibility of expert testimony: (1) whether the pertinent theory or technique has been tested; (2) whether the theory or technique has been subject to peer-reviewed publication; (3) the known or potential error rate and whether standards or controls exist for the operation of the theory or technique; and (4) whether the theory or technique is generally accepted in the scientific community.

These standards are applicable to all cases, but not every standard will be relevant in every case. For example, an accountant testifying about lost income will be evaluated differently from a scientist testifying that tests in rats reveal a causal connection between irradiation and death.

---

1. 526 U.S. 137 (1999).
2. 522 U.S. 136 (1997).
3. 509 U.S. 579 (1993).

Most states have adopted the federal standard governing admissibility of expert testimony, or have deemed the federal standard to be consistent with their own law. But several states continue to adhere to the rule set forth in *Frye v. United States*.[4] Under *Frye*, expert testimony must be sufficiently established to have gained general acceptance in the particular field to which it pertains. This was the same test applied in federal courts until the advent of *Daubert* and the revisions of Federal Rule of Evidence 702 precipitated by *Daubert* and its progeny. States continuing to apply the *Frye* standard include Illinois,[5] Maryland,[6] New York,[7] and Pennsylvania.[8]

Thus, while under *Daubert* and Federal Rule 702 the court as gatekeeper must scrutinize the foundation of expert testimony to evaluate methodology and basis, *Frye* and the states applying it have established a framework for the admission of such testimony based on minimal standards of general acceptance. This latter approach under *Frye* is much easier for the proponent of expert testimony to satisfy, and it does not place as much of a burden on trial judges. The question arises: Does *Frye* infuse the system with inappropriate expert testimony causing mistaken results? This debate continues.

The Expert's Basis

State and federal rules of evidence also diverge slightly when it comes to the admissibility of information on which expert opinions rely.

Many state rules and Federal Rule of Evidence 703 provide that the expert witness may base opinions on the following: firsthand knowledge; facts that the expert does not personally know but that consist of evidence made known during trial; or facts presented before trial that the expert does not personally know, if of a type reasonably relied upon by experts in the field.

---

4. 293 F. 1013 (D.C. Cir. 1923).
5. *In re* Commitment of Sandry, 857 N.E.2d 295, 307–08 (Ill. App. 2006).
6. Clemons v. State, 896 A.2d 1059, 1078 (2006).
7. Zito v. Zabarsky, 812 N.Y.S.2d 535, 537 (N.Y. App. 2006).
8. Commonwealth v. Dengler, 890 A.2d 372, 381 (2005).

The rules become complicated regarding opinions based on facts or data that the expert does not know firsthand. In such testimony, the particular facts or data need not be admissible (though they can be); for example, an expert can voice an opinion based on inadmissible hearsay.

Under Federal Rule 703, an expert cannot recite this inadmissible hearsay when rendering an opinion or its basis. The federal rules prevent counsel from presenting evidence that would otherwise be prohibited but for the fact that it served as the basis of expert testimony.

Imagine an expert witness offering an opinion about a company's taxes. After the opinion is given, counsel may ask the witness to explain his basis. Under the federal rule, the witness may state his basis to be an interview with the company's chief financial officer. The follow-up question—"What did the CFO tell you?"—would be objectionable in federal court during direct examination, but acceptable during the cross, according to Federal Rule of Evidence 705.

In many state courts, however, expert witnesses can recite otherwise inadmissible hearsay as a basis for an opinion. In these states, the witness above could, in rendering his basis, tell the court what the CFO said, subject to the court's discretion to exclude it. Most state courts' websites include links to their rules of evidence. Many state bar associations also contain court rules or links to them.

Another important concept is codified in Federal Rule of Evidence 705 and many state court rules: an expert may render an opinion and provide reasons without offering a basis unless the court requires otherwise. The expert may have no firsthand knowledge of facts underlying an opinion but is nevertheless permitted to render it.

For example, the court could allow the following question: "Dr. Bentley, do you have an opinion based on a reasonable degree of medical certainty about whether Mr. Hanks was of sound and disposing mind, capable of signing a deed, with an understanding of the nature of his act?" Before the advent of Rule 705, the expert would have had to discuss the facts relating to Hanks' condition or at least confront them in a hypothetical question. But under Federal Rule of Evidence 705, Dr. Bentley could simply respond, "Yes, Mr. Hanks was of sound mind."

Trial lawyers who avoid raising the basis of an expert's opinion, however, may be walking on thin ice. If opposing counsel eviscerates the expert's underlying basis on cross-examination, the witness's opinion may be deemed unreasonable and therefore inadmissible.

Ultimate Issue

Often in trial, opposing counsel, concerned that the jury is mesmerized by an expert's testimony, will object on the basis that the expert is rendering an opinion on the ultimate issue of the case—for example, "he must be innocent because. . . ."

Nevertheless, numerous state court rules and Federal Rule of Evidence 704 provide that an expert's testimony is not objectionable because it "embraces" the ultimate issue in the case. The rules do, however, prevent an expert from testifying about whether a defendant in a criminal case possessed the mental state or condition constituting an element of the crime charged.

In trials won and lost on the basis of what experts say, you can wield these complex evidentiary rules as shields—to deflect damaging testimony—or swords—to reveal lethal opinions. The better you know the rules, the better your case will be.

Experts and Discovery in Civil Cases

The great thing about expert witnesses is that they are experts. Most likely, they know all there is to know about the subject matter your case involves, at least in part, or you wouldn't have hired them. You may well be tempted to huddle with these brilliant minds and involve them in your litigation strategy and preparations.

To some extent this instinct is correct, especially in cases dealing with issues unfamiliar to you. If you're handling a medical malpractice suit such as the *Maffei* case, revolving around a subject that might not be familiar to the jury, a good expert can become a valuable guide through the intricacies of cardiology. Especially in very technical litigation, you should consider your expert a full member of the team. You can review deposition testimony with your expert and ask him or her for help in planning the deposition of adverse witnesses. Sometimes it is helpful to invite your expert to sit in during depositions so that you can obtain immediate advice.

But be careful. Much of what you communicate to your expert may be subject to discovery. Even information you consider protected under the attorney-client privilege or work-product doctrine may be discoverable if you share the information with the expert.

Before opening communications with an expert, be sure to familiarize yourself with the rules of civil procedure and evidence. The challenges of discovery relating to experts can leave you in turmoil unless you meld knowledge of the rules with local customs and case strategy. Rule 26 of the Federal Rules of Civil Procedure extends the work-product protection to drafts of expert reports. They are not discoverable. Rule 26 also protects from discovery, with exceptions, communications between a party's counsel and a retained expert who intends to present testimony. There are three exceptions to the protected communications:

1. Communications that relate to compensation for the expert's study or testimony;
2. The identification of facts or data that the party's attorney provided and that the expert considered in forming the opinions to be expressed; and
3. The identifications of assumptions that the party's attorney provided and that the expert relied on in forming the opinions to be expressed.

Notwithstanding Federal Rule of Civil Procedure 26, many state jurisdictions do not protect from discovery communications between a party's counsel and a retained expert who intends to present testimony. Rules of procedure and case law in these jurisdictions permit opposing counsel to inquire about such communications. For example, whereas the federal rules protect expert reports from disclosure, many state jurisdictions do not. Nor would many state jurisdictions protect from disclosure correspondence sent to an expert by counsel.

Thus it is imperative to know the rules pertaining to your case, and the consequences of showing any material to a testifying expert. Is the communication discoverable or not? If so, could the communication, if produced in discovery, damage your case irreparably? Similarly, unless you're absolutely sure they're protected, do not have conversations with the expert that you do not want disclosed. Be mindful of any writing used to refresh an expert's memory prior to or during testimony. Rule 612 of the Federal Rules of Evidence provides that the opposing party has a right to the production of such material. In many state courts, however, the counterpart to this rule requires production of the writing only if it is used during the trial. There are many such differences between state and federal rules of evidence governing discovery and disclosure. The requirements also vary according to the type of expert (testifying, hybrid/ fact, or nontestifying or consultant expert).

Full Disclosure

The disclosure requirements under Rule 26 of the Federal Rules of Civil Procedure for those witnesses required to provide a written report for experts retained to testify are complex. Read and study the rule. You must disclose the expert's name as well as a written report explaining, among other things:

- a complete statement of all opinions to be expressed and the basis and reasons for the opinions;
- the facts or data considered by the witness in forming these opinions;
- any exhibits to be used in conjunction with the opinions;
- the qualifications of the witness, including a list of publications written within the preceding 10 years;
- a list of any other cases in which the witness has provided expert testimony, either in trial or deposition, in the preceding four years;
- a statement of the compensation to be paid for the study and testimony in the case.

These disclosures may not be enough if you later develop additional opinions or evidence of importance. In that case, be sure to supplement the original disclosure or you may have to go to trial without your expert. Rule 37(c) of the Federal Rules of Civil Procedure provides for the exclusion of expert testimony if it is not properly disclosed to opposing counsel.

The federal requirements for hybrid/fact experts (for example, a physician who treated the plaintiff and will also render opinions) also require disclosures, but they are not as extensive as those required by the retained expert who will present testimony. The hybrid/fact expert must disclose the subject matter; the anticipated testimony; and a summary of the facts and opinions to which he or she is expected to testify.

If you want more information about testifying experts than what is provided through mandatory disclosures, you may use depositions, interrogatories, and document requests to gather such information.

Experts engaged to consult but not to testify are usually immune from discovery, though extreme circumstances can arise to pierce this immunity. For example, what if a testifying expert engages in extensive meetings with a nontestifying expert? The opinions shared between them could be brought to light to the detriment of your case.

In numerous state courts, there are fewer mandatory disclosure requirements for experts (both testifying and nontestifying). The expert may prepare a report but is not required to do so. Thus, more detailed written discovery is involved in obtaining information about experts. For example, Maryland Rule of Civil Procedure 2–402(g)(1) provides that a party may require by interrogatories: the identification of experts expected to testify, the subject of the testimony, the findings and opinions about which the expert is expected to testify, the grounds of each opinion, and a report made by the expert, if one was prepared.

While these procedural and evidentiary matters are arcane, ignoring their intricacies can be devastating. If you write your neurosurgeon expert detailed letters about your client, you may find your own words coming back at you in court. Ultimately, you want to get the most out of your expert's knowledge without compromising your case.

Prior to trial, counsel may challenge the admissibility of adverse expert testimony by filing a "*Daubert* challenge" in federal court. This challenge may result in a hearing upon memoranda to determine whether the expert's testimony comports with rules and case law. If making such a challenge, courts appreciate counsel providing the name of the expert; a brief summary of the opinion challenged, including a reference to the source of the opinion, for example, expert disclosure or deposition testimony; a brief description of the methodology or reasoning used by the expert to reach the challenged opinion, including a reference to the source material; a brief explanation of the basis of the challenge to the reasoning or methodology used by the expert, including a reference to the source material used for the challenge; a discussion of the known or potential error rate associated with the methodology employed by the expert, if known; a summary of the relevant peer review material, if available, with citations to sources; and a discussion of whether the methods or principles used have been generally accepted within the relevant community, with citations and references.[9]

Lay Witness Opinions

Before we move on, it is important to remember that experts are not the only witnesses allowed to express opinions at trial. There are limited exceptions when lay witnesses may do so as well.

Rules of evidence provide that a lay witness may render an opinion if it is rationally based on the perception of the witness and if the opinion would help clarify the witness's testimony or the determination of a fact in issue.[10] Nonexpert witnesses are permitted to express opinions on a variety of topics including the value of real property, the appearance of persons or things, the identity of individuals, the competency of individuals, feelings, degrees of light or darkness, sound, size, weight, distance, and a number of other matters, including intoxication.

Whenever you elicit nonexpert opinion testimony, you should take care to demonstrate that the lay witness has a sufficient basis to express the opinion. Moreover, even if the opinion is rationally based, it will not usually be admitted if it is superfluous or otherwise inappropriate. For instance, a witness's opinion about the veracity of another witness's testimony is not admissible.

Presenting lay witness opinions is essentially about justifying them to the court. If you fail to do the job well, the opinion becomes vulnerable to opposing counsel and an alert judge. Indeed, if you want to impeach

---

9. *See* Samuel v. Ford, 96 F. Supp. 2d 491 (D. Md. 2000).
10. FED. R. EVID. 701.

an opposing witness's nonexpert opinion, pursue any weak point in the opinion's basis.

THE EXPERT AT TRIAL

If the expert witness is to the attorney what deus ex machina was to the classical Greek dramatist, the breathtaking entrance usually comes at trial. That is when the lawyer lowers the all-powerful witness before the judge and jury in hopes that the expert will deliver a potent opinion capable of knocking out the adversary.

But the deus ex machina is a dramatic convention that can, with one false move, come off unconvincingly. The wires can get tangled, the god's plaster head might wobble, and the whole mannequin could come crashing from the theater rafters into a comic heap on the stage. The same can happen to your witness. A poorly articulated question or answer might open up the door for an eviscerating cross-examination, and suddenly your immortal from on high doesn't look so mighty.

Preparation goes a long way in setting the stage for a convincing performance. If you have selected the right expert and made sure that the opinions are defensible and in congruence with your overall strategy, you will likely find your expert to be resilient and capable of bolstering your case.

Introduce the Expert

Your first object in presenting expert testimony at trial is to qualify the expert. It may feel as if you're going overboard while you're detailing the expert's qualifications, but it is more dangerous to be cavalier and take for granted the judge and jury's esteem for your witness. Allow the witness to catalogue his or her credentials, each one more impressive than the next. If the witness has written articles and given lectures about surgery, allow him or her to say how many. If the witness serves on the boards of professional associations or has written a book in the area of specialty, solicit this information. By the end of the presentation, you should have thoroughly impressed the jury that your expert is an authoritative and respected figure in his or her specialty.

After you present the qualifications of your expert and ask the court to accept that person as an expert, opposing counsel has the right to voir dire or to question the witness about his or her qualifications. Usually, major objections to expert testimony are resolved before trial, as previously discussed.

In the *Rosen* trial, both sides called upon campaign experts to support their theme. Here is an excerpt from the testimony of Jane Hedgepeth, a campaign finance consultant called by the defense:

A. I am a self-employed compliance consultant. I help people with record-keeping and reporting of—of contributions and expenditures.

Q. What kind of people do you provide assistance to?

A. Federal and Texas candidates, parties, other kinds of political committees.

Q. And the reports you are talking about, are those submitted to federal agencies?

A. To federal agencies and state agencies.

Q. And what federal agencies?

A. The Federal Election Commission.

Q. How many—how many FEC reports have you been involved with, very roughly? Tens? Hundreds?

A. Roughly, hundreds.

Q. How long have you been involved in the business of compliance reports?

A. I have been doing compliance over 20 years, since 1983.

Q. Have you been involved in providing any training with respect to a compliance report?

A. Yes, sir. I have helped to do training both in Texas and also for the Democratic National Committee and for the Association of State Democratic Chairs, including helping to draft manuals for state party committees.

Here, the expert is allowed not merely to summarize her professional background but also to specify the length of time she has worked within a narrow specialty, and to name clients. (In nonjury cases you may find it more effective to introduce into evidence the curriculum vitae of your expert.) Compare this for example to the procedure for qualifying the expert in the *Oregon* case, which was nonjury. Notice a relatively brief examination on qualifications and the introduction of the expert's curriculum vitae—technically not admissible, but rarely objected to in a nonjury trial. Sometimes even in jury trials counsel will stipulate to the admission of curricula vitae.

As in *Rosen*, counsel in the *Maffei* case devoted considerable time to establishing the experts' credentials and explaining the expert's profession and work in a way that the jurors could easily understand. This challenge in *Maffei*, however, was far more time-consuming; the case was a battle of the experts, so both sides went to great pains to build up the experts' authority. Note the gradual introduction and explanation of key terms, the use of the visual aid, and the discussion of the expert's past experience as a witness in other trials.

Q. Would you please as you get seated introduce yourself to the jury?

A. I am Neal Shadoff.

Q. Your occupation is what, sir?

A. I am a cardiologist.

Q. What does a cardiologist do?

A. A cardiologist deals with the diagnosis and treatment of both diseases of the heart and diseases of the circulation in the body.

Q. What is the difference between a cardiologist and what we hear as cardiac surgeon?

A. A cardiac surgeon or heart surgeon is a physician who not only deals with the diagnosis of heart problems, but deals with the treatments by doing operations, surgery.

Q. What's your current address?

A. I practice at 201 Cedar Southeast in Albuquerque, New Mexico, which is the site of the Presbyterian Heart Group.

Q. Are you affiliated with that group?

A. I am, I am a member of that group.

Q. Are you licensed in the state of New Mexico?

A. Yes, sir.

Q. To practice medicine?

A. That's correct.

Q. To practice cardiology?

A. Yes.

Q. What is your educational background, Doctor?

A. I went to Colby College in Waterville, Maine, and I received a bachelor's degree in chemistry with honors and I then went into the combined scientific master's degree and medical degree at Boston University. I went from that part of my education, graduating from medical school, to do an internship and residency in internal medicine at the University of Colorado and I stayed there as a junior faculty member as chief medical resident. I then went from the University of Colorado and I did a cardiology fellowship, which is further training in cardiology specifically, and I did that at Duke University and then I stayed on as a faculty member at Duke University, running the catheterization laboratory at the Durham, Virginia Medical Center.

Q. What is a catheterization laboratory?

A. A catheterization laboratory is a place in the hospital where diagnostic procedures are done to make pictures of the arteries by inserting tubes through the skin and injecting dye.

Q. Do you have more than one license in terms of practicing medicine or have you in your career in states other than New Mexico?

A. Yes, of course, I was licensed in North Carolina when I practiced at Duke and licensed in Colorado when I was at the University of Colorado.

Q. What does board certified mean?

A. That is a level of competence that you achieve by taking tests in your area of specialty.

Q. Are you board certified in any particular aspects of medicine?

A. I am.

Q. Would you tell us what?

A. I am board certified in three different areas.

Q. What are they?

A. First, I am board certified in internal medicine and its specialties. And then I am specifically board certified in cardiovascular disease, and then, finally, I am board certified in interventional cardiology. I think I need to explain that.

Q. You anticipate me; I was going to ask.

A. I told you that part of what I do is make diagnoses of patients who have heart and circulation problems and the other part of what I do is try and fix those problems by inserting balloons inside arteries and then expanding open little metal scaffolds, what we call stents, little rolls of chain link fence. And inserting the balloon and opening blocked arteries and inserting those little metal scaffolds, what we call stents, that's called interventional cardiology. I am intervening, doing something to help the patient.

Q. Have you testified in court as an expert witness before, Dr. Shadoff?

A. Yes, I have.

Q. How many times have you testified in court roughly?

A. About 50 or 60 times.

Q. When you testified in court in those 50 or 60 times, have you ever been excluded or prevented from being qualified as an expert, sir?

A. No.

Q. When you testified in court as an expert witness on these occasions, have you testified for the plaintiff in the past?

A. I have.

Q. Have you testified for the defendant in the past?

A. Yes, I have.

Q. How would you state the ratio as between plaintiff and defense in terms of your testifying in court?

A. It's probably an even split, about 50 percent of each.

Q. And do you have criteria before you would become involved in the case in terms of your medical acuity and integrity?

A. Yes, of course.

Q. Can you elaborate?

A. Well, first, it would have to be something that's involving either a specialty of internal medicine or more specifically heart disease, cardiovascular disease, and then I would review the records and render an opinion as to what I thought had occurred in that specific situation.

Q. Have you ever turned down the request of a party to testify as an expert in any particular case and render an opinion?

A. Yes, many times.

Q. Why?

A. Well, for instance, if it were on the side of the defense, it would be because I didn't think that the care standard had been met, I didn't think I could defend that standard. And if it were on the side of the plaintiff, it was because I thought that the care standard had been met.

Q. Can you tell us whether you have written any papers or studies in the field of cardiology or related fields?

A. Yes, I have—a number.

> It can be very persuasive to a jury to articulate that an expert witness has turned down testifying on matters with which he or she disagrees.

Q. How many?

A. Probably about a dozen different papers and articles in total.

Q. Where do these articles appear?

A. They appear in two locations, medical journals—medical magazines—that are educational, and there are a series of book chapters.

Q. Can you tell us or describe your current practice so that we, the jury and I, understand what is it you really do on a regular basis?

A. My practice is what I would call a clinical practice, which is that I see and take care of patients every day. And it's combined into a practice of making diagnoses, seeing patients for the first time who have some complaint and I don't know what it is until I see them, and then treating those patients. So, it's about 40 or 50 percent of the time seeing patients and doing consultations and the rest of the time doing procedures that I've described to make diagnoses.

Q. Have you ever made diagnoses of related heart issues in emergency rooms?

A. Yes, that's a large part of my practice, since that's the most common way that patients enter into the medical system when they have an urgent problem.

Q. You were here, were you not, during the opening statement of counsel for the defendant?

A. Yes, I was.

Q. Did you hear counsel state that the plaintiff was not calling an emergency room doctor, do you recall that?

A. I did.

Q. Do you feel you are qualified to give an opinion to this jury in issues that relate to the heart and emergency rooms?

A. Yes.

Q. Why?

A. Because it's what I do very frequently. . . .

Q. So, we have heard in opening statements, but now we are in the testifying stage, I am going to ask you if you understand what a dissected aorta is?

A. Yes, I do.

Q. What is a dissected aorta?

A. An aortic dissection or dissected aorta is a tear in the lining of the aorta that allows blood to get into the wrong space. First, I think it might be helpful if I drew a picture and explained this.

Q. Sure, if the court will allow you to come to the easel?

MR. SHAW: Are we going beyond voir dire at this point?

THE COURT: I'll allow some leeway here before voir dire, before I give you an opportunity for voir dire.

(The witness approached the jury box.)

THE WITNESS: The aorta simply is a tube or a pipe and it is the main artery that arises from the heart from which every other artery

Defense counsel's objection might just as well have been sustained, as the next series of questions tread on the expert's substantive testimony.

branches out. If you think of it as a tree, there's a main trunk and there are branches and even the branches can have branches. It extends from the heart.

Q. Doctor, I think you may have to come on the side so that everyone can see. I think that would be helpful.

A. What I'd like to do is show you this in a simple way. Looking down the barrel of the tube, so I'll just cut across one spot, and the aorta has really three layers, an outer layer, you have heard the fancy term, adventitial, but it's the outer layer that is the strong part of the aorta, and it has an inner layer that is actually very thin, it's only a few cells thin. So you can't really see that with the naked eye; you'd have to look at that under a microscope. And then a middle layer, which is comprised of support tissue and muscle. The reason the muscle is there is because it's the gas pedal and brake of the aorta and blood flowing.

The aorta has the ability to expand when there is a need for blood flow in the body to increase and contract when we are resting and we don't need that much blood flow. And the regulator, gas pedal and brake, is the muscle layer in the middle. That's what the aorta is.

An aortic dissection, which is really what your question was, is a tear in the lining of the aorta that allows the blood to get into the wrong channel. There is no channel here, this is normally muscle. It spreads because the blood is coming out at a relatively high pressure. You have heard those numbers of our blood pressure; 120 means 120 millimeters of pressure. So we are talking about a consequential amount of pressure, that's eight atmospheres, that's 120 millimeters of mercury pounding into this space where there is a tear.

Q. Please take your seat and thank you for the explanation.

(The witness resumed the stand.)

Q. Are you familiar with dissected aortas as they may or do occur in the emergency room environment?

A. Yes, I am.

Q. How are you so familiar?

A. I have seen myself and made the diagnosis somewhere between ten and 20 times. And within our large practice, there [has] been more than double that amount that I have been familiar with.

Q. Have you been engaged in the past in teaching or lecturing on the topics of cardiology, which is your specialty?

A. Yes, I have.

Q. Where are some of the places you have lectured?

A. Well, first of all, until just this past year, I have been a faculty member at the University of New Mexico in the division of cardiology, so for the last 24 years, I have lectured at the university. But I have really lectured worldwide in terms of talking about heart intervention and angioplasty, the balloon procedures. And that would really include virtually every continent I have taught those procedures in: China, in France, Germany, in Australia, Japan, and South America.

Q. How many years have you been practicing medicine, Doctor?

A. Well, really, started my training in 1978, so it's a little bit more than 30 years now.

Q. In the 30 years of your practice in cardiology, can you give us a feel, using that term, of how many patients you have seen with heart issues or conditions? Hundreds? Thousands?

A. Well, it's in the range of 50,000 different patients.

Q. Have these patients, many of them, been seen by you in an emergency room, on call or visits to emergency rooms to check out patients?

A. Probably a third started that way.

Q. Let me ask you a question about the dissected aorta for a minute. Are there classic symptoms of a dissected aorta?

A. There are.

Q. What would they be?

A. Really the one classic symptom would be chest pain; everything else continues from that.

Q. What are some of those that continue from that?

A. It depends on where this false channel, this expansion, tracks. So, for instance, if it tracks up into one of the arm arteries, someone might feel the pain tracking into their arm or into the carotid artery into the neck.

Q. I have to ask you about a carotid artery.

A. The carotid arteries are two large arteries that feed both the brain as well as the scalp, the tongue, the teeth, the ears, and the skull. And they arise from the aorta on the left side and from a different artery, the right arm artery on the right side and at the level of our Adam's apple, they fork. One fork goes up into the brain, the other fork goes to the tongue and the jaw and ears and scalp and skull.

Q. Do all dissected aortas display the classical symptoms?

A. No, but I think that more than 95 percent of people who have an aortic dissection will have chest discomfort of some kind or another.

Q. Are you aware that I have engaged you to review the matter of the death of Richard Maffei and express opinions about his medical care and cause of death?

A. Yes.

Q. Are you familiar with the standards of practice or care among the emergency room's physicians in Baltimore County or similar emergency rooms in March of '06 when physicians such as Dr. Smedley were presented with symptoms that Mr. Maffei demonstrated when he visited the hospital on March 8, 2006?

A. Yes, I am.

Q. Are you familiar with the standard of care and practice of Baltimore County physicians in emergency rooms when they have nurses' notes that precede the consultation?

A. Yes, I am.

Q. Do you believe that you are qualified to give opinions today on the standard of care in Baltimore County in 2006 and whether that standard was breached by a particular physician?

MR SHAW: Objection.

THE COURT: Overruled.

Q. Such as Dr. Smedley?

A. Yes.

Q. Why do you think you are qualified to give such opinions, sir?

A. Because I believe that my almost daily interaction with emergency room physicians regarding evaluation of chest pain and potential heart problems allows me to do that and I believe that there really is only one standard in the United States, because we are all trained the same way and with Internet and with the medical journals that are available, we are all exposed to the same information, we all take the same tests to become certified, therefore, the standard of care is no different to me in Baltimore, Maryland, or Albuquerque, New Mexico, or Los Angeles, California, or New York City. It's one standard.

Q. Do you believe you are qualified to express opinions regarding the care provided to Mr. Maffei in the emergency room of GBMC on March 8, 2006?

MR. SHAW: Objection.

THE COURT: Overruled.

THE WITNESS: I do.

Q. Do you believe you are qualified to give an opinion based upon the records of the cause of death?

MR SHAW: Objection.

THE COURT: Overruled.

A. I do.

Q. Were you asked by me to form an opinion about the likelihood or not of Mr. Maffei surviving if his aortic dissection had been diagnosed in March of 2006?

A. Yes.

Q. Do you feel qualified to give an opinion, whatever that opinion may be?

A. Yes.

Q. Why do you suggest you are so qualified, sir?

A. Based on my education, my own experience in taking care of patients with aortic dissection, and my knowledge in general of medical literature, what is published as a result of other people's experience.

Q. Were you also asked to form an opinion by me about the life expectancy of Mr. Maffei, if his dissected aorta had been diagnosed on March 8, 2006, in the emergency room?

A. Yes, I was.

Q. Do you think you are qualified to render that opinion?

A. I do.

Q. Why is that? Why do you believe you are qualified for that?

A. Again, based on my education, my experience, and my understanding of other people's experience.

Q. Have I also asked you to consider and render an opinion about whether Mr. Maffei could have returned to work if he had survived the aortic dissection?

A. Yes, you did.

Q. Do you believe you are qualified to render such an opinion?

A. Yes.

Q. Why do you believe you are so qualified?

A. Very same reasons I have outlined before.

Q. Now, at some point, Doctor, we do have your curriculum vitae, which would be Exhibit 27 and that

> In a case as complex as this one, separating the medical issues and establishing the witness's credibility to address each one can help make each issue more memorable.

is in evidence and is there any aspect of your curriculum vitae Exhibit 27 that you think would help us understand your qualifications to answer the questions related to opinions?

A. I think it's really what I have described for you, which is my educational background, my training, and current practice over an extended period of time.

Q. So, am I correct that dissected aortas and their symptoms are no strangers to you?

A. That's correct. In fact, they are no stranger to any cardiologist, not just me.

MR SANDLER: Your Honor, I am going to submit and then offer for voir dire to counsel Dr. Shadoff as an expert in the field of cardiology, in the evaluation, diagnosis, and treatment of patients with cardiac disease, including dissected aortas, outcomes, life expectancy of such patients with cardiac disease, and the ability to work upon discovery and treatment.

Because the opinion the above expert had been called upon to render was relatively complex, counsel needed to take the introduction slowly, establishing piece by piece the expert's authority. Note the expert's reliance upon a visual aid to illustrate what he knows. This is particularly helpful in testimony that risks becoming mired in specialized terminology. Finally, in these concluding sections of the introduction, counsel asks the expert to state for the record that he is qualified to render several distinct opinions. Keeping these opinions distinct in the jurors' minds helps clarify the core issues of the case, as counsel wants to present them.

Consider the very brief questioning of Oregon's expert, since the case was nonjury and the judge could obtain a solid understanding of the expert's qualifications by reading his curriculum vitae:

Q. Mr. Kaplow, what is your profession?

A. Real estate attorney.

Q. How long have you been a real estate attorney?

A. Just over 25 years.

Q. Do you practice in Baltimore County?

A. Yes, I do.

Q. And what in particular can we tell the court about your expertise in zoning matters in Baltimore County?

A. My practice is concentrated on land use and environmental law for 24 years, always based in Baltimore County, the vast majority of our work in central Maryland.

Q. Have you authored articles in the field of zoning and real estate?

A. I have authored more than 200 articles in the last ten years on land use and environmental law, including a recently published law review article on the subject.

Q. Do you believe that you have a familiarity with the Baltimore County zoning regulations?

A. I do.

Q. Let me show you Exhibit 32 for identification, and ask if you could identify it.

A. This is a copy of my curriculum vitae.

MR. SANDLER: Unless there is an objection I am offering the curriculum vitae into evidence to save time.

THE COURT: It will be admitted.

MR. SANDLER: I submit Mr. Kaplow as an expert in the area of Baltimore County zoning and real estate law.

THE COURT: Will there be any voir dire, Mr. McCann?

The Climactic Question

Once the preliminaries are out of the way, you will want to build the testimony toward the key question, the one designed to elicit the opinion. You should not ask this too soon. Better to set the stage and allow the witness to articulate the circumstances from which the opinion arose.

While a formulism is dangerous to consider as a rule, it is helpful to think of the basic questions to ask the expert witness on direct examination in this fashion:

Q. Did you receive an assignment from me?

Q. What was that assignment?

Q. Did you complete the assignment?

Q. What did you do to complete the assignment?

Q. How many hours did you devote to your work?

Q. Tell us please what opinions (or conclusions) you reached; or

Q. Do you have an opinion based on a reasonable degree of certainty (or probability) as to what caused the injuries you diagnosed?

Q. What is the basis of that opinion?

Q. Why did you reach that conclusion on that basis?

Q. Were you in court when the expert for the plaintiff rendered her opinion on the cause of the plaintiff's injuries?

Q. Do you agree with that opinion?

Q. Why not?[11]

In the *Rosen* case, the defense's primary aim in calling Hedgepeth as an expert was to argue that the Clinton campaign had nothing to gain by concealing costs from the FEC, as the prosecution was alleging Rosen had

---

11. *See* Model Witness Examinations ch. 6 (3d ed. 2010).

done. In this context, the defense sought Hedgepeth's informed opinion that even if the costs of throwing the Hollywood gala had exceeded the funds it had raised, the event would still not be considered a loss because such events could be paid for through an account wholly separate from accounts used to finance the senatorial campaign.

Q. Ms. Hedgepeth, have you heard the phrase "a wash" in terms of fundraising events?

A. Yes.

Q. Do you have an understanding of what it would mean for a fundraising event to be a wash?

A. Yes.

Q. What would that mean?

A. When the committee—the organization pays out as much as it took in and makes no money, then you would characterize—or I would characterize the event as a wash. It didn't make any money.

Q. But an event like the Hollywood tribute, which took in a million dollars, becomes a wash merely because in-kind expenses went from $400,000 to a million or $2 million?

A. No, sir.

Q. And why is that?

A. Because the committee was not paying the bills directly.

The witness went on to explain, in more technical detail, why the committee was not paying the bills directly. The testimony thus helped the defense to refute the motivation the prosecution was attempting to pin on Rosen. Interestingly, in the exchange above, counsel is comfortable asking a leading question that implies an answer favorable to the prosecution: "But an event like the Hollywood tribute . . . becomes a wash. . . ?" The expert then refutes this idea, granting Rosen's position more credibility. Here the defense is subtly playing the devil's advocate against its own case to immunize the defendant against one of the prosecution's critical arguments.

In presenting expert testimony, you may also consider the value of your expert relying on a learned treatise. While the treatise itself is not admissible, the expert can testify about its contents and demonstrate how it supports the opinion. By the same token, consider the use of learned treatises to cross-examine the opposing expert to demonstrate that the opinion is inconsistent with published findings.

Interestingly, modern rules of evidence that permit the expert to render an opinion without disclosing underlying facts eliminate the need for the hypothetical question. Nevertheless, the value in posing such questions is that they can help organize the facts of the case for the jury in the way you want them organized.

Q. Ms. Hedgepeth, assume that the fundraiser asked the host to itemize the expenses of a tea or dinner. Assume further that the host gave to the fundraiser inaccurate information. Do you have an opinion whether under those circumstances the fundraiser is responsible for reporting the inaccurate information, if he in good faith relies on the honesty of the host?

A. I do.

Q. What is your opinion?

A. Under the circumstances you described, the fundraiser is not responsible for reporting the information.

This example illustrates the beauty of hypotheticals: they can be carefully tailored to present a circumstance that sheds only favorable light on your client. The question above is not only about the expert's opinion about responsibility in a given situation, but implicitly about Rosen's "good faith" reliance on Aaron Tonken and Peter Paul's "honesty."

In the *Maffei* case, the attorneys had to work a bit harder to elicit the necessary opinions. Not unusual, this "battle of experts" became highly complicated and both sides labored to build up to climactic questions gradually. Consider the testimony below of Dr. Shadoff, the plaintiff's expert cardiologist. Having successfully introduced the physician as a credentialed and articulate witness, counsel goes on to solicit his opinion.

> Q. Did you hear counsel state to the jury that when Mr. Maffei was in the hospital, the dissection was so slight, it would never have shown up on an x-ray, meaning there would not be any signs or irregularity of the x-ray?

> A. Yes, I heard that.

> Q. Is that correct? Do you agree with that?

> This question is inappropriate to fact witnesses, but since experts render opinions, it was proper in this context; there was no objection.

> A. Absolutely not.

> Q. Just briefly will you explain?

> A. Because the symptoms that he described could only come from the fact that that dissection already involved the artery going up into the neck or else he wouldn't have had neck pain and ear discomfort and already involve the artery going down through the back towards the right leg or else he wouldn't have had back discomfort.

> Q. Were you here when counsel said to the jury, wait a second, the nurses didn't ask for an x-ray. Look at this, five out of 10, there was no x-ray, and then waved his hand as if that meant the doctor didn't have the responsibility if chest pain existed to take an x-ray. Did you hear that?

A. Yes, I did.

Q. Do you agree with that?

A. No.

Q. Why?

A. The ultimate responsibility is [with] the physician to order the test.

Q. Tell us whether you have an opinion to a reasonable degree of medical certainty whether or not if the nurse fails to take a particular test or administer a certain procedure and those same conditions exist at a later time when the doctor is examining and looking at the patient that the fact that the nurses didn't do a test or procedure, the doctor doesn't have to have the responsibility to do so?

A. I do have an opinion.

MR. SHAW: Objection, Your Honor.

THE COURT: Overruled.

Q. What is that opinion?

A. That it's still ultimately the doctor's responsibility.

Q. You were here in opening statement when defense's counsel stated that the tear that Mr. Maffei had when he was in the hospital was so slight that there couldn't have been any kind of showing on an x-ray because it would not have been the so-called dissection. You remember that?

A. I was.

Q. Is that correct?

A. No.

Q. Why not?

A. Again, because this tear would have been of a size to create this false channel, this double barrel to the aorta based on the symptoms that were reported and, therefore, would have been easily visible on a chest x-ray.

Q. Did you hear counsel state there was confusion in the nurses' notes about chest pain?

A. I did.

Q. Did you read those notes?

A. I did.

Q. Did you read them carefully in relationship to the assignment I asked you to undertake?

A. I did.

Q. Did you conclude there was confusion about the existence of chest pain?

MR. SHAW: Objection.

THE COURT: Overruled.

A. No, there were three different nurses plus a registration clerk that documented chest pain.

Q. Thank you. Now let's talk about why we are here. . . . Do you have an opinion based on a reasonable degree of medical certainty about the cause of death of Mr. Maffei?

A. Yes, I do.

Q. Did you form that opinion by studying the medical records in the case?

A. Yes, I did.

Q. What is your opinion of the cause of his death?

A. The cause of death for Mr. Maffei was aortic dissection, and then finally rupture of the aorta into the sac around the heart, the pericardial sac, and that led to this entity that we call cardiac tamponade, which means the heart has been compressed, it's been squeezed so it neither has the ability to fill or to pump.

Q. Are you able to give us an opinion based on a reasonable degree of medical certainty as to whether or not Mr. Maffei's death could have been avoided at the time that he died?

A. Yes, I can.

Q. What is that opinion?

A. His death was avoidable.

Q. What is the basis of that opinion?

A. It's based on my education and experience with this disease process.

Q. Can you state your reasons?

A. The opinion is that, had the proper diagnosis been made prior to releasing him from the hospital, a surgical procedure could have been done to correct the dissection and, importantly, in this situation, prevent this rupture.

Q. How could it have been diagnosed, Doctor? Or how would it have been diagnosed?

A. Well, the first step would have been a chest x-ray.

Q. Why a chest x-ray?

A. Because with aortic dissection, if a chest x-ray shows an abnormality, the silhouette of the heart and vascular structures, then you have a very high level of suspicion that aortic dissection has occurred and it would lead you to do further testing.

Q. What type of further testing?

A. It could come into three categories. The easiest test everyone is aware of is a CAT scan test with an injection of dye to outline the aorta. It's a very simple test that would take maybe 15 minutes to do.

Q. What would have been revealed in the CAT scan?

A. The CAT scan would have demonstrated the aorta had a tear and that tear extended up into the left carotid artery and the left arm artery and around down into the abdomen and the belly, tracking into the right leg.

Q. I am going to ask you to tell us what the x-ray would have revealed and then to show us what the x-ray, if it were taken, would have shown to someone looking at the x-ray, that would have been a sign in the x-ray that there was a problem that would warrant further testing?

A. Much more likely than not, given his symptoms, that x-ray would have shown a widening of the vascular artery structures that we see as a silhouette or a shadow.

At this point, counsel called attention to a blow-up of a chest x-ray, propped on an easel located close to the jury box. Counsel then asked Dr. Shadoff to step down from the stand and show the jury what he thought would have been observed on a chest x-ray of Richard Maffei had the emergency room doctor ordered one. Note that counsel asked the witness to explain first, followed by the assistance of the visual aid. This repetition presumably helped the jury remember the details better—a technique that takes advantage of the "frequency" doctrine.

After that, counsel presented to Dr. Shadoff a copy of the autopsy report, which supported the physician's testimony on what an x-ray of Mr. Maffei's chest would have shown. This further confirmed the expert's authority on the subject. Counsel followed with other questions to Dr. Shadoff to convey how Dr. Smedley, in whose care Maffei had been, failed to follow established standards of care:

Q. Assume that Dr. Smedley, when she took the history of the patient, Mr. Maffei, did not want to or seek to acquire the information about chest pain that was in the medical nursing notes other than looking at the first note, triage note. [Does] that conform with the standard of care?

A. No, I do not believe it does.

Q. Why?

A. Well, prior to her seeing the patient, there were a number of nursing notes that would have been helpful in his evaluation.

Q. Are you aware of, let's look at page 23 of Exhibit 8. Are you aware that Dr. Smedley noted on the page that the patient denied having current chest pain?

A. Yes.

Q. Would you read that document carefully?

A. I did.

Q. Assume that the patient also told Dr. Smedley, no, not only don't I have chest pain now but I never ever, ever had chest pain in the past, whether that is documented on the record?

A. It's not specifically documented.

Q. Had the patient really said that, should that have been documented?

MR. SHAW: Objection, Your Honor.

THE COURT: Sustained.

Q. Can you tell us whether you have an opinion based upon a reasonable degree of medical certainty that if the patient ever denied having chest pain in the past, it's a standard of reasonable care to have it documented on the records?

MR. SHAW: Objection.

THE COURT: Sustained.

Q. Do you believe that—strike that. Let me rephrase this. Assuming that a physician is told that a patient did not have chest pain and never had chest pain, but the nursing note and other records revealed chest pain, whether the doctor has an obligation to probe and to question the patient about his denying chest pain when the chest pain was in the record and evidenced by hospital records of that day?

A. Yes, I have an opinion about that.

Q. And what is that opinion?

A. That when there is contradictory information, it's up to the doctor to settle that and document that.

Q. . . . And was it documented here?

A. No.

An important lesson to be learned here is do not be deterred by sustained objections. Try other, proper ways to introduce the evidence. Here, to avoid another objection from the defense, plaintiff's counsel used the technique of a hypothetical question. This type of question asks the expert to assume facts and then render an opinion. The assumed facts must either be in evidence at the time or introduced subsequently. Otherwise, the opposing side will point out in the closing argument that the foundation of the expert's opinion—the facts the expert was asked to assume—has been undercut.

Hypothetical questions are largely out of vogue as the Federal Rules of Evidence and some state rules of evidence do not require the expert to state a basis or facts supporting an opinion. However, as discussed, it is effective practice to elicit the basis of your expert's opinion—and sometimes the best way to do this is with a hypothetical.

Here is another example of a hypothetical question in the context of a civil case:

Doctor, I will ask you what is known as a hypothetical question. This question will request that you give an opinion based on facts as submitted in this case. Please follow closely the statement of facts that I present to you, assume it to be true, and then I will ask you to express an opinion based upon those facts. Assume a man 89 years of age cannot stand up straight and needs a cane. He suffered a stroke at the age of 87, and since that time he constantly babbles and talks to himself. He professes frequently that he is the pope. Now, Doctor, assuming all these facts and conditions as being true, do you have an opinion based on reasonable medical certainty as to whether this man, on June 6, 2003, was of sound and disposing mind, capable of signing a deed with an understanding of the nature of his act, its effect, and the natural objects of his bounty?

In many cases, an elaborate question such as this will prove more effective than simply asking: "Do you believe the gentleman was of sound and disposing mind?" Finally, here is an example of a hypothetical question from the *Oregon* trial posed to Oregon's environmental expert by counsel for Oregon:

> Q. My last question is what we call a hypothetical question. I'd like you to assume as accurate the following facts I unfold, and then I'm going to ask you your opinion. Assume that for some reason it was determined or decided that the paved lot on the Oregon Grille restaurant was to be dug up, crushed up, destroyed so that there could be a grass covering or a gravel covering with stones and sand. Assume those facts to be true. Do you have an opinion based upon reasonable certainty whether there would be any negative impact on the environment?

Why ask the expert to assume facts rather than just asking the ultimate question? There are two reasons. First if you want to develop a basis for the opinion, the facts may not be in evidence at the time the question is posed. Second, presenting the hypothetical with a statement of the facts to be assumed provides the opportunity for you to "testify."

The above excerpts demonstrate an inevitable truth: notwithstanding the metaphor, you cannot, in the end, rely on the deus ex machina expert to save the day on his or her own. You must strategically present the witness yourself. Expertise carelessly handled can backfire against your client. No matter how well informed your experts may be, opinions are just that—opinions—and are therefore inherently fallible and subject to doubt.

If done well, however, your direct examination of the expert will transform him or her, in the jurors' minds, into a convincingly authoritative voice, one that can turn the verdict in your favor during deliberations. The process of achieving that dramatic effect begins well before trial, starting with the selection of the expert, the mastery of the evidentiary rules, and the successful handling of discovery skirmishes. By the time you reach the courtroom, your expert should be ready to shine and bolster your case.

Learning Points for Chapter 6

- Appreciate the distinction between the trial expert, hybrid/fact expert, and nontestifying consultant.
- Particularly in civil cases, be careful in working with experts that you do not waive the attorney-client privilege or work-product doctrine.
- Remember to qualify the expert; in doing so, bring out his or her credentials so as to impress the jury.
- Be familiar with the rules and case law relating to expert testimony.
- After the expert renders the opinion, ask for the basis and reasons to impress the jury, even if not required to do so by the rules.
- Insist that you and the expert speak plainly, avoid jargon, and clearly explain any unfamiliar terms; do not allow the expert to talk down to the jury.
- Use a hypothetical question when appropriate.
- Request that the expert use exhibits and demonstrative aids.
- Structure the examination to build up to the "ultimate issue" in a dramatic and convincing fashion.

CHAPTER 7

"A LEGAL ENGINE FOR TRUTH"—CROSS-EXAMINATION

Cross-examination is something like a chain saw; in the hands of a novice, it can dismember a case with a single mistake. The unprepared and unschooled should think twice before taking hold of what has been described by jurist and evidentiary expert John Henry Wigmore as "the greatest legal engine ever invented for the discovery of the truth." But for those who take the time to study, rehearse, and prepare, cross-examination should be embraced as an unparalleled opportunity to stymie your adversary's case and advance your own.

The first step in getting a grip on that chain saw is to understand the overarching purpose of cross-examination. As with direct, you want to continue arguing your case to the jury. Thematic questions are critical. With laser-like precision, every question posed should advance your theme or protect it against adverse testimony. When cross-examining, you must also have a goal specific to that witness and that particular moment in the trial. You might want to neutralize or render incredible a witness's harmful testimony by demonstrating that he has a faulty memory or did not observe accurately. Or your goal might be to show that the witness is biased. You may want to compel an opposing expert to say that your own expert's writings are authoritative. Whatever your goal may be, every question should help you develop or defend your theme. Otherwise, consider the question a misfire.

What goes into a winning cross-examination? There are thousands of tips out there, but ingredients often left out of the conversation are poise, intuition, and an appreciation of human nature. These qualities are vital to the trial advocate. Many believe that they cannot be taught or studied in books. To some extent this is true, but they can be developed through experience over the years. The more comfortable you feel with the core cross-examination techniques, the greater your confidence will be, and the keener your instincts.

FOUR STEPS TO POWERFUL CROSS-EXAMINATIONS

In any cross-examination, the witness, if not your enemy, is certainly not your friend. He is usually resistant to control and liable to say things that could prove damaging to your case. Acknowledging this, excellent cross-examiners willfully impose a predetermined structure upon the exchange, eliciting testimony that drives home very specific points, but doing so without offending the jurors with an overbearing manner. To be successful, you need to:

1. Select only those topics that will be most advantageous to your case;
2. Arrange your topics and points strategically;
3. Control the witness; and
4. Conduct the cross-examination with a delivery and style that is consistent with your specific goals.

The end result should be that your argument prevails with the jury and your courtroom ethos remains high. Put another way, after the cross, the jury should like and trust you more than it does the witness.

Selectivity

Cross-examination is limited in most instances to the subject matter of the direct and matters affecting the witness's credibility. Within this framework, it is important to know which arguments you wish to advance or protect. The key is to be selective, to exclude all subjects that will clutter the record with trivia, cloud the jurors' impressions, and deprive the cross of persuasive force.

Preparation is a must when it comes to strategically selecting topics for cross-examination. In advance of trial, you cannot know exactly what any given witness will say on direct. However, you can and should anticipate the general theme of the witness's direct and even specific points he or she will make, evaluate this anticipated testimony, and then list those topics you hope to work with at trial with that particular witness. You can develop your own system of notation, but it may be helpful to arrange the trial notebook so that each topic of interest has a separate page, with sub-topics or questions listed below. As you listen to the direct examination of the witness, you may be able to add to these notes to ready yourself for the cross.

Such preparation will get you only so far. It will not substitute for careful listening or the capacity to imagine what it is like to be a particular witness. An attentive nature and insight into each witness's point of view will help as you decide what to ask and how to ask it. However, always select a few topics that you believe you can handle successfully in cross before trial; modify them as necessary as the trial unfolds.

Before you begin making detailed topic lists, first decide whether you should question the witness at all. Better not to cross at all than to cross and fail. A hostile witness can give more harmful answers on cross than on direct. That is what Emory Buckner meant when he said, "More cross-examinations are suicidal than homicidal."

So, when you have no need to cross-examine, do not hesitate to say, "I have no questions for this witness." This strategy might apply when the witness has not hurt your case and cross-examining the witness could lead to damaging testimony. Sometimes in that situation you may decide on "an apparent cross," which involves asking a few harmless questions to give the impression that you are engaged in the process, or because you believe that posing a few questions will help you sustain a strong ethos with the jury.

Another reason for not cross-examining is that the witness has testified inaccurately, thus establishing a foundation for you to call another witness to contradict or impeach the testimony. If you cross-examine in this situation, the mistaken witness may change his testimony and deprive you of an opportunity to call your own witness to set the record straight in a more potent manner.

If you do proceed to cross-examine, do so with a brief agenda when appropriate. Ask yourself, "What should the juror remember from this scene? What phrases should stick in his or her mind? What anecdotes or ideas or descriptions should linger? With what overall impression of the witness do I want to leave the juror?" Answering these questions will help you select your questions. It will also help you control the witnesses when it is time to question them.

Arrangement

Once you select your topics, you should consider the order in which you will address them. Bearing in mind the concepts of primacy and recency—people remember best what they hear first and last—try to begin and finish your cross with the strongest testimony.

Beyond that, there are no hard and fast rules for arrangement. Sometimes the last point of the direct, which is fresh in the minds of the jury, must be addressed right away. A direct attack on the credibility of the witness may be in order if the witness just offered explicit evidence against your client but also demonstrably lied. Opening with an aggressive strike to discredit the witness can set a hostile tone, which may or may not be desirable. Depending on the situation, you might begin the cross-examination in a cordial manner to enhance your credibility with the jury.

Because you cannot be sure what will happen during direct, a certain degree of structured spontaneity can be helpful. Be ready to abandon a planned order and quickly reshuffle your questions. When you prepare, try organizing your topics on separate pages so you can flip between them in your trial notebook as the need arises.

Beware of concluding with a series of floundering, repetitive, or unnecessary questions. When you stand up to begin, know precisely what you want to accomplish. Once you have made your desired points, sit down. Many cross-examinations turn to ruination when one question too many is asked.

Controlling the Witness

Generally, the cross-examined witness does not want your client to prevail. With every question you ask, you take a certain risk of receiving an answer adverse to your case. The more finely honed the question, the lower the risk. Ultimately, it is a question of controlling the witness.

Control is more subtle and difficult than dominating or abusing the witness by interrupting, berating, or attacking him or her. Control over the testimony should not be as evident to jurors as more aggressive tactics would be, but you'll know you have it when the answers you're looking for come forth.

The best technique for control is the leading question, which is prohibited in direct examination but permitted in cross. As discussed in Chapter 4, a leading question suggests its answer. ("It rained that night; isn't that true?" Even better: "It rained last night?") Nonleading questions do not. ("Tell us whether or not it rained that night.") Leading questions tend to be short, affirmative questions containing a statement that compels a favorable response, if not by the witness, at least in the minds of the jurors. Here are some examples:

Q. You were driving the green car?

A. Yes.

Q. You stopped at the red light?

A. Yes.

Q. You then turned left after the light turned green?

A. Yes.

Observe that the statement is a question, and your voice inflection should so demonstrate. Strive for "yes" answers when appropriate and "no" answers as a second preference. Thus, you establish a rhythm and in effect testify for the witness as you continue to develop your case theme. If you've presented your case effectively, you and the jury will know the answers to your questions on cross before the witness answers.

For variety you may wish to consider "true or false" questions as counsel did in the *Oregon* case while still maintaining control:

Q. True or false: The county ordered the tenant, Oregon Grille, LLC, to repave the lot?

A. True.

Q. True or false: The county ordered Oregon Grille, LLC, to repave the lot because the county believed the parking lot was not in compliance with the ADA?

A. True.

Q. True or false: The county operated in a businesslike fashion in the ordinary course of business to protect the citizens of the county when it ordered the repaving?

A. True.

But the best-laid plans may go astray. The witness may dodge your efforts to control the examination even with your leading questions.

With your mind processing so much information during a trial, it is easy to lose track of what exactly the witness is saying during cross. This endangers your case. You must stay in the moment, homing in on every word the witness utters. When a witness does dodge questions on cross-examination, many lawyers simply move on to their next query or ask the judge to intervene. Avoid these approaches. If needed, repeat your question. If the witness still evades, try this approach: "I appreciate your response but will you please answer my question." Or: "You did not answer what I asked. I asked whether you attended the party the night of February 12. Now will you please answer the question?" For a more dramatic effect, you could write your question on a blackboard and focus everyone's attention on it. Rarely should you ask the court for help. You may lose control, and perhaps respect, when you cannot obtain the answers on your own.

Expect opposing counsel to object with "Asked and answered your Honor." The court might well admonish the witness to answer the question, or if you are being hyper-technical the court may sustain the objection.

Another problem challenging your control sometimes arises early in the examination when the witness answers specifically your question but gives you the "wrong answer." You must regain control and demonstrate that giving the wrong answer is unacceptable for you and the witness. Of course you can always try to impeach the witness and go on a frontal attack, but doing so is not always appropriate or may be too aggressive. Another approach is the gentle reminder to the witness that you have the power to command the proper answer. Consider the following excerpt from the cross-examination of the defendant doctor in the *Maffei* case. Plaintiff's lawyer wanted to emphasize that the sensation of his throat closing was the main concern of Mr. Maffei when he first met with the emergency room doctor. The doctor at first did not agree.

Q. Good morning, Doctor.

A. Good morning.

Q. Now, on the day of Mr. Maffei's death, which was the 8th of March of 2006, you were the emergency room doctor at GBMC when he arrived?

A. That's correct.

Q. And you had worked that night, the evening or night shift?

A. The overnight shift. That's 11 at night to seven in the morning.

Q. And at the time that Dr. Maffei was seen by you, you agree you were the only doctor available at the time?

A. At the time I saw him.

Q. And when you did see him, did you agree he was worried about the sense of closing in his throat, which he felt was more than just a sore throat, isn't that true?

A. No, that's not true.

Q. Let's see if I can refresh your recollection, Doctor. You gave prior testimony in a deposition in this case?

A. Yes. (Nodding head.)

Q. And you were represented by counsel during the deposition?

A. Yes.

Q. And the lawyers for Mrs. Maffei questioned you?

A. Yes, sir.

Q. And you were under oath then?

A. Yes, sir.

Q. And you're under oath now?

A. Yes, sir.

Q. You were asked on Page 113, line 18 of your deposition, which you have before you, a question.

A. Yes, sir.

Q. Do you see where you said, "Okay. There are a couple different aspects of that. He was more worried about the sense of closing in his throat which he felt was more than just a sore throat?"

A. Yes.

Q. Does that refresh your recollection that Mr. Maffei was more worried about the sense of closing in his throat?

A. Yes, sir.

Q. So when he felt he was more worried about the sense of closing in his throat, his wife was also present, isn't that true?

A. His wife was present.

This aspect of the examination of the doctor was not designed to impeach her or embarrass her but to convey to her that counsel had support for all questions posed and that if she did not give the answer counsel sought,

This question was asked not only to lead into another subject matter but also to loop back to the previous answer to take advantage of the doctrine of frequency.

he would lead her to the desired answer, perhaps causing her embarrassment and jury disfavor.

Upon occasion, you will want to ask open-ended questions, particularly when you have at your disposal prior testimony, such as a deposition or grand jury transcript. Then if the witness strays from the correct answer, you can rein him in either by refreshing his recollection, or by the more extreme measure of impeachment, discussed below. In general, though, asking open-ended questions risks giving the witness more control than you want him to have.

Avoid, too, posing questions unless both you and the jury already know the answer, based on what you have previously presented. Breaking this rule can lead to surprise testimony damaging to your case. Surprise testimony isn't always bad, of course; sometimes it can help your case. But the stakes are too high during cross-examination to take this risk.

Of course, there are exceptions. One particular exception is when a question's answer, regardless of what it is, cannot hurt or can only help your case. For example, assume that it has previously been established that the mother of the defendant knew her son was using illegal drugs. When cross-examining the mother, you might want to ask questions like "You knew your son was using drugs? Did it concern you that he was using these drugs?" If the answer is yes, you have an admission. If the answer is no, you may have established a lack of credibility.

One last word on this subject: The importance of concision is great. To maintain an engaging rhythm and momentum that keeps the witness under your control, you should avoid convoluted questions that tie your tongue and confuse the witness and jurors. One query of that sort can throw a wrench in the works.

Delivery and Style

Good cross-examiners are good listeners. If you can hear the subtleties of testimony and imagine what the witness is thinking, you are more likely to make smart, split-second decisions that lead to favorable answers. Some of the most critical decisions you have to make concern style and delivery: How will you approach the witness? What tone of voice will you use? Will you immediately lunge for the jugular with a harsh line of questioning, or will you smile and joke with the witness as you cross-examine him or her?

These decisions are largely intuitive and come, in part, from listening closely—noticing the witness's every word, expression, and modulation in tone during direct—but you should also be sensitive to the jurors' evolving views of the particular witness and the case as a whole. In the context of cross-examination, where the potential for conflict is high, the jurors will be watching you closely, gauging in the back of their minds whether they like and trust you more than the witness. Your style can have a great impact on their thinking.

You would not want to attack fiercely a witness who has just impressed listeners as credible and sympathetic—unless, that is, you are sure that you can expose the witness as mendacious. A witness you know is not testifying honestly might merit an aggressive approach. In such instances, you will want to speak in a firm, calm voice as you ask a series of short, driving questions that builds suspense and elicits the desired revelation. When appropriate, take your time to draw out vivid, memorable details that will resonate later in the trial. And always use plain language, avoiding legalese that will likely turn the jurors off.

Remember, too, that juries do not like discourteous lawyers. (They may not like lawyers at all—a subject for another book.) Do not bully a witness or cause him or her to appear in a poor light without strong justification, and always allow the witness to answer fully. Trying to force a witness to answer yes or no when he or she is eager to elaborate is unfair and generally frowned upon by judges and jurors. Often a more effective approach is to "kill them with kindness"; a polite, even friendly, cross-examination can reveal helpful information even while destroying the credibility of the witness.

In the cross-examination of Mrs. Maffei in the civil case, defense counsel's manner was respectful of Mrs. Maffei:

Q. Good morning, Mrs. Maffei. You know I have to ask you some questions in follow up?

A. Yes, I do.

Q. If you need a break for any reason, let me know. I recognize your loss, but in a court of law, I am obligated to ask you some follow-up questions.

Should you write down and read your questions? Notes can be helpful as a preparation tool; sometimes the act of writing questions in advance will help you remember or phrase them better. But reading questions or fussing over notes interferes with the task of watching and listening to the witness and so should be avoided. Letting go of your notes during cross-examination may feel scary at first, but that is how you will eventually build the confidence necessary to excel at this challenging aspect of trial practice.

SPECIFIC GOALS OF CROSS-EXAMINATION

As discussed, every time you stand up to cross-examine a witness, you should have a few key goals you want to satisfy before you sit down. Every case is unique, of course, but there are certain situations that are common enough that they can be categorized. This section presents a series of frequent cross-examination challenges, and using real examples from the *Rosen* case and others, it illustrates how they can be met successfully.

Use Adverse Witness Testimony to Develop Your Own Case Independently

Eliciting favorable testimony to advance or defend your theme need not be confrontational. The term "hitchhiking" refers to the practice of using an adverse witness to argue your theme beyond the subjects that were narrowly addressed on direct.

In the *Rosen* case the defense claimed that Aaron Tonken and Peter Paul, the organizing sponsors of the gala, intentionally reported incorrect event costs. During the cross-examination of one of the government's important witnesses, event planner Bretta Nock, defense counsel sought to highlight Tonken's history of mismanaging funds for charitable events. Counsel proceeded as follows:

Q. Were there any problems or questions by the sponsors of those events on the charities that you worked on with Mr. Tonken?

A. I believe there came to be some problems, but that was directly with Aaron and the sponsors. I didn't have involvement.

Q. I am not suggesting that there were any complaints against you, Ms. Nock. I am just talking about complaints about the events themselves.

A. Yes—by the sponsors.

Q. And what were the nature of these complaints by those sponsors?

A. It depended on the—the event.

Q. Well, let's take them one at a time. Do you want to tell me each event where there was a problem raised or expressed by the sponsor?

A. I don't recall. I would have to—I don't recall exactly what the complaints were from what sponsors.

Q. Were the complaints relating to the—the proper procedures used to track funds and contributions?

A. Yes.

Q. Were the complaints relating that perhaps Mr. Tonken misused funds?

A. Yes.

Q. Not you, I am talking about Mr. Tonken.

A. Oh, absolutely, yes.

Q. And there were complaints that Mr. Tonken cheated the sponsors?

A. Yes.

Q. Complaints that he stole from them?

A. I don't know if that was a complaint.

Q. A complaint that he misrepresented to them?

A. Yes. . . .

Q. When was the last time you had a conversation with Mr. Tonken?

A. I don't recall.

In this exchange, counsel posed numerous open-ended questions to Nock. The general rule for cross-examination of the need to control the witness with short, leading questions answered with a simple yes could be set aside in this instance, because counsel had prior testimony from the witness that contained the expected answers.

Q. Do you know where Mr. Tonken now resides?

A. Yes.

Q. Where is that?

A. He is incarcerated.

Q. And is he incarcerated for conduct that relates to his involvement in sponsoring events like charitable—charitable events?

A. Absolutely.

When you have high confidence that an open-ended question will elicit favorable testimony, you should feel free to ask away. When a witness provides a favorable answer without being pressed by a leading question, that testimony may have even greater value.

There are similar situations when obtaining helpful testimony is not so easy. If, for example, you pursue a line of questioning stemming from prior testimony, but the witness fails to recall what he or she said earlier, you may need to use the transcript to refresh recollection, as the attorney does in the following instance:

Q. Doctor, you agree that you examined Jenny Barnes on only one occasion?

A. Yes.

Q. You know that Dr. Smith examined her 12 times over an 18-month period?

A. No, I do not.

Q. Doctor, do you remember testifying in your deposition last year that you were aware that Dr. Smith examined Ms. Barnes at least 12 times?

A. No.

Q. Let me read what you what you said. [Counsel reads from deposition.] Does that refresh your recollection that Dr. Smith did examine Jenny Barnes 12 times over an 18-month period?

A. Yes.

These questions did not place the witness in the position of being discredited, and in the above situation the cross led to testimony that helped establish Dr. Smith as a more reliable witness than the physician on the stand. If the doctor had continued to insist that he did not remember the testimony, the transcript would have helped counsel impeach the witness.

Reveal Discrepancies between Direct Examination Testimony and the Facts

Like the goal above, this one is critical to many cross-examination scenarios. At issue in the *Rosen* case was whether the defendant David Rosen procured from a vendor a fake invoice, one that the vendor, upon request, had reduced to an amount lower than what was actually owed. The government claimed the sum owed and paid to the vendor was actually $400,000, while the records indicated only $200,000. This detail came into play as the prosecutors sought to prove that Rosen had falsified the reported costs of the gala. On direct, the event planner, Bretta Nock, testified as follows:

Q. And what was your conversation—what do you recall about your conversation with Mr. Rosen about that invoice?

A. Again, that any line item that was going on my budget without my direct knowledge I needed substantiation for.

Q. Did he make any suggestions to you?

A. Yeah, absolutely, to call Black Ink Productions and obtain that invoice [in the amount of $200,000 as opposed to $400,000].

Q. Who specifically did he ask—suggest that you speak to?

A. I don't know specifically—Allan Baumrucker was the person that I spoke to.

Q. And did you request an invoice?

A. Yes.

Q. And what do you recall saying to Mr. Baumrucker?

A. That I needed an invoice to reflect the $200,000 that was in the line item of the final budget. . . .

Q. And eventually did you receive an invoice from Mr. Baumrucker?

A. Yes.

Q. What is it that you did with it once you obtained it?

A. I forwarded it on to the New York Senate 2000.

Q. And do you recall whether or not Mr. Rosen knew you were sending it to New York Senate 2000?

A. Yes, he did.

Q. How do you know that?

A. Per our conversation, I believe.

Q. When you obtained that invoice from Mr. Baumrucker for $200,000 for—to cover your line item, did you believe that that was a true cost of what Black Ink invoice—Black Ink Productions' costs truly were in connection with the gala?

A. After everything, all was said and done, no.

This testimony was potentially quite damaging to the defense. If the jurors believed that Nock had, on Rosen's instruction and with his knowledge, procured and filed a false invoice, the government's case would have been essentially made. Defense counsel had to undermine the testimony, and it sought to do so with a few simple questions concerning Nock's responsibilities as the event planner. Among them:

Q. All right; and my question is do you have any written document, know of any written document that you have in your possession or that you have given to anyone else that suggests the $200,000 entry [in the final budget] came from anyone but you? That's the question.

A. I believe not.

Q. All right. And you prepared this budget on your computer; isn't that correct?

A. Yes. . . .

Q. Do you agree with me that Rosen would rely on you to obtain and provide invoices and costs to him?

A. Yes.

The argument defense counsel is developing here is that if Rosen were responsible for a fraudulent invoice, Nock would have a note to that effect because she prepared the budget and reported the invoices. The heart of the government's case rested on the theme that Rosen derived and reported the costs, but here Nock testifies that Rosen relied on her for this information.

Notice that, unlike the example in the section above, the questions asked in this portion of the cross are somewhat more aggressive, controlling, and specific. As you approach the very central questions of a trial, you want to be very precise about the testimony you elicit.

For further study, let's consider two excerpts of the cross-examination of the expert for the defense, Dr. Shank, in the *Maffei* case. Again, the plaintiff's theory of the case claimed that Dr. Smedley, the ER doctor, should have x-rayed Mr. Maffei's heart because he complained of chest pain. The x-ray would have revealed an abnormality sufficient to require an MRI, which would then have revealed the dissection of the aorta. The doctor contended that Mr. Maffei denied ever having chest pain when she saw him, and this denial is reflected in her notes. Thus there was no reason for an x-ray. But plaintiff's expert during trial testified that Dr. Smedley should have been more aggressive in resolving the conflict between what Mr. Maffei allegedly told Dr. Smedley about not experiencing chest pain and the hospital records, which reflected that he did complain of chest pain upon admission to the emergency room.

Dr. Shank testified on direct examination that if a dissection were occurring while Mr. Maffei was at the hospital, it was so minimal that it could not be detected; an x-ray would have revealed no meaningful abnormality if any, and that the doctor properly ruled out chest pain so that an x-ray was not called for.

Plaintiff's counsel in cross-examination of Dr. Shank wanted to undercut his testimony. During his deposition, Dr. Shank conceded that an x-ray would have revealed a minor abnormality, although not one that would warrant an MRI. He also testified during his deposition that in medical school training he had learned that if there is a conflict about a patient's complaints contained in the hospital medical record and what the patient tells the emergency room doctor, the doctor must be very aggressive and thorough in resolving the conflict. Nevertheless on direct he testifies differently.

Q. Good afternoon. You would agree, would you not, that when Mr. Maffei presented at the hospital that day, he had, if not a full dissection, as you would call it, at least a minimal dissection of his aorta?

A. Based on what we retrospectively know and, and the Paul Harvey end of the story and the autopsy results, I could go back and say that, yes, sir, he had a small dissection when he was there.

Q. And you would agree, would you not, that we call it a minimal dissection?

A. Based on the autopsy report, yes, sir, I think that and, and the entire clinical picture that I went through.

Q. The next question I want to ask you is whether or not you agree with me that if an x-ray had been taken, that there would have been a minimal abnormality on the x-ray?

A. I would not have expected any minimal abnormality based on anything that was happening, the way of the dissection. Now, what you can have when I look at his cardiogram—and we didn't discuss the cardiogram—the cardiogram has some changes that we call LVD, which means the left ventricle is enlarged, and that usually happens—not always, but usually happens because there's some high blood pressure. When you have some blood pressure, even if it's not terribly elevated, it can cause the aorta to somewhat uncoil, and instead of being a nice smooth thing, it can be a little tortuous. So and, so, you can get—when you take an x-ray of someone who's had high blood pressure, you can look at something that looks minimally abnormal. It's not abnormal to the extent we would expect if someone has a wide mediastinum.

Q. Let me just ask it again. Do you agree with me that if he, with his minimal dissection, as you described it, or as you would, or as you've stated that he would have had at this hospital, that he would have—if an x-ray were taken, it would have been minimally abnormal?

A. No, sir, not based on the dissection—that's why—

Q. I'll ask the question differently: had his x-ray been taken at all for any reason, would you agree that his x-ray would have been minimally abnormal?

A. Yes, sir. I told Mr. Harlan [at] my deposition that, that it could have been. If there had been some slight uncoiling in the aorta from hypertension, that has, does not have anything to do with what it would have been abnormal from the perspective of a dissection, I understand.

Q. And I only have one other topic to cover with you; it's very simple. I think that you said that as an emergency room doctor, you have seen hundreds of patients, is that correct?

A. Actually, I've seen a little over a hundred thousand.

Q. Thousands of patients?

A. Yes, sir.

Q. And would you agree with me that in the thousands of patients that you see, or have seen, that you have had occasion to treat a patient in the emergency room where the notes identify the patient complaining of a particular symptom and then the patient, upon your conference with him or her, denies ever having such symptoms?

A. I'm sorry I didn't follow your—I was okay with you 'til you got to the end would you repeat that for me?

Q. I will be happy to: you agree with me with the thousands of patients that you see in the emergency room that you have frequently encountered where they have identified [a] particular symptom reflected in the notes you're looking at, and then the patient upon your examination denies ever having that symptom?

A. . . . I can't remember the last time [someone] brought me a list of symptoms. It's a verbal exchange.

Q. Let me ask the question again: Have you ever seen a patient who presented to you or denied having symptoms that they previously told nurses or other people [about]?

A. Oh, yes, sir. I talked about that earlier.

A. I misunderstood the question.

Q. No big deal. But that's happened to you frequently?

A. Yes, sir, it does.

Q. And, in fact, it happened so frequently as an emergency room doctor, that you have developed a personal professional approach to that situation, isn't that true?

A. Yes, sir.

Q. In fact, if you see a triage note, for example, that says chest pain and the patient says to you no chest pain, you don' t just move on, isn't that true?

A. No, I go and talk to the patient, and I take a specific history, as did Dr. Smedley, to try to find out exactly what's involved in their complaint.

Q. You also talk to the nurse and ask the patient to reconcile the discrepancy, isn't that true?

A. Yes, I do that sometimes if I think there's a need. I don't always do it, but I frequently do it. What I happen to do doesn't determine what somebody may or may not happen to do. That happens to be my personal approach.

Q. Well, in fact, it's so engrained in your style that, isn't it true, that you do that regularly?

A. That happens to be my approach, to do it frequently. I don't always do it, but I do it frequently.

Q. Frequently enough so that you recall going away, back to medical school in terms of that process when residents and interns are trained and you remember being so trained, so it stayed with you, isn't that correct?

A. No, sir, what we were talking about there's a little bit different. What we were talking about there was the fact that patients often give different people different histories. And what I was referencing in that specific section was, as a medical opportunity you would go in, you, you'd take this exhaustive history and do everything real well, try to confront the attending physician and the resident, walk in the patient room and attempting this something different than they told you [an] hour earlier. So that was a little different than what you were initially talking about of getting a different history and then reconcile it with a different nurse, two sort of totally different things.

Q. Well, you do, when you were confronted with a person who did, no, I didn't, tell me—let me read, let me ask you this in context.

A. Sure. Could I go to the page that you're on?

Q. Well, I'm looking at page 436 of your deposition.

A. Yes, sir, I'm there.

Q. Okay. So just to make it clear, it's quite frequent that you will have a note in front of you about chest pain, for example, okay?

A. You mean the triage nurse note?

Q. Yes. You can use it.

A. I understand what you meant now. I misunderstood you.

Q. Exactly.

A. Yes, sir, you're correct.

Q. And that you would have a patient say I don't have chest pain, correct?

A. Yes, sir.

Q. And that happens frequently?

A. It does.

Q. And your approach is not to just document no chest pain and move on, but you try to resolve it, the discrepancy; isn't that true?

A. Yes, sir. And I try to describe it initially with the patient.

Q. All right. Well, I appreciate—let me just ask my question—

A. Okay.

Q. —and you can answer, and then on redirect you can explain. So— okay. Well, you've established that frequently you have a situation where there's a discrepancy, correct?

A. Yes, sir. I wasn't sure that, if that was a fact or an estimate.

Q. I'm sorry?

Obviously this seems repetitive, but keep asking your question until it's answered correctly. Your witness may become a bit flustered and defensive, but that can work in your favor; it can affect their ethos in the minds of the jurors.

A. Yes, sir.

Q. And then what you do in dictating your notes is you identify the situation, correct, what you, you—

A. Well, I—

A. I just, I—in fact, it's a sore—well, it, it's a scenario that you encounter, and it's a scenario where you say to the patient, for example, tell me, Mr. Jones, about your chest pain. And he, if he says, "No, I don't have chest pain," you say, "Well, the nurse said that's the reason you're here." And he says, "No, I don't have chest pain," you then say that's a dramatic situation, right, and, and that you, it's not unusual and that you go and document that and reconcile that; isn't that correct?

A. Yes, sir. I seek to reconcile the difference in what I'm being told.

Q. When you reconcile it, it's not unusual for you to talk to a nurse or engage the nurse, isn't that correct?

A. I sometimes do. I don't always, but I sometimes do.

Q. I see. My question, is it not unusual for you to do that?

A. That would be correct, it wouldn't be unusual.

Q. Okay, I have no further questions.

The examples illustrate repeating the question until the witness answers properly. Remember, counsel was in possession of prior deposition testimony by the witness giving the desired answer and which was used to control the testimony. Although deposition testimony is not available in a criminal case, often counsel has grand jury testimony, affidavits, or other prior statements, such as police reports or, in federal cases, 302s (investigation reports of agents).

Use the Testimony of the Witness to Corroborate the Favorable Testimony of Other Witnesses

This goal of cross-examination can be pursued when you want to corroborate the testimony of one of your witnesses or, more potently, the helpful testimony of an adverse witness. When cross-examining Bretta Nock, the defense obtained helpful testimony concerning Rosen's character.

Q. In your work with David Rosen, were you satisfied at the time, the year 2000, that he wanted to make sure that everything was done ethically and properly?

A. Yes.

Q. And would it be your testimony before the jury that he was always concerned about following the correct campaign finance protocol?

A. Yes.

To bolster this testimony, defense counsel put similar questions to Christopher Fickes, another government witness, later in the trial:

Q. In all the years that you worked with David Rosen, did he ever tell you or suggest that you do something illegal?

A. No.

Q. Did he ever tell you during the years you worked with him to do something unethical?

A. No.

Repetition is a powerful tool. When you have a strong point to make about an individual, particularly about a defendant's character, take advantage of every opportunity you have to make it. The more often jurors hear that your client is highly respected as an ethical, upstanding citizen, the more likely they are to take this assertion into account during deliberations. This technique is particularly helpful during cross-examination, even if it does not touch upon the topics adverse counsel dealt with on direct.

Use the Testimony of One Witness to Discredit the Unfavorable Testimony of a Previous Witness

This goal often comes into play in cases involving a large number of witnesses. The *Rosen* case was certainly that. The cross-examination of one government witness proved vital in discrediting the testimony of another. Remember that Bretta Nock testified that Rosen had asked her to call the vendor to obtain the fake invoice. The government called the vendor to the witness stand. But on cross-examination, the vendor, Baumrucker, testified that Nock told him that someone else had asked her to make the call:

Q. Mr. Baumrucker, when Ms. Nock called you for the invoice, she told you who had asked her to call?

A. Yes.

Q. She told you Jim Levin, friend of the president, asked her to call?

A. Yes.

Like this excerpt, the cross of Baumrucker was short and to the point. The above testimony was the crucial detail, and to avoid cluttering the jurors' memory of the witness, defense counsel limited questions to the essential.

Impeachment—Discrediting the Witness's Testimony or the Witness

While many attorneys view cross-examination as the art of impeachment, impeachment is only one technique. It is also the last technique you should consider using. It is often difficult to achieve successfully; and it may not be the most desirable way to achieve your primary objectives of protecting/advancing your theme while maintaining the favor of the jury. Most juries do not appreciate attacks on witnesses unless such attacks are well deserved, and if you try and fail to impeach, you may discredit yourself.

In general, it is easier to obtain admissions or concessions from a witness than to impeach him or her. For example, if a witness's testimony differs from his or her prior statements, you could attempt to portray the witness as a perjurer, but if he or she is highly sympathetic and claims that the discrepancy is simply a matter of faulty memory, you might appear to be something of an ogre before the jury if you attack. A better approach would be to refresh the witness's recollection and move on.

Here are some examples of impeachment:

The witness lacks capacity or personal knowledge or demonstrates weaknesses in the capacity to perceive or remember.

To show lack of capacity you may be able to demonstrate that the witness is on medication or was not of sound mind either when testifying on direct or at the time of the event in question. To demonstrate lack of perception, you can show that the witness lacked the ability to perceive accurately what he or she testified to on direct. For example, the night was dark, and therefore the witness could not have seen or observed what he or she testified about. There may also be occasions when you can impeach testimony by showing that the witness's recollection is faulty. For example, the event occurred so long ago that the witness just does not have a clear recollection.

The witness is biased, prejudiced, or interested in the outcome of the proceeding, or the witness has a motive to testify falsely.

"You are the defendant's mother? You love your son, don't you?" This is a common line of questioning in cases involving family members or friends interested in protecting a defendant, who happens to be a loved one. Impeachment in such situations can be a delicate business; roughing up a teary-eyed mother could turn you into monster in the jurors' eyes.

More often you encounter witnesses with selfish motives, in which case impeachment is easier. The *Rosen* case involved one Raymond Reggie, a media consultant from New Orleans and a brother-in-law of Senator Ted Kennedy. Reggie had become involved in the gala, and at trial he testified on direct that Rosen told him on many occasions that the costs of the event "crushed him." He also testified that Rosen was upset with the high costs for the producer. To show bias and motive, the defense cross-examined Reggie as follows:

Q. Now, before you testified today, you had a number of meetings with the prosecutors in this case; isn't that correct?

A. I met with them, yes, sir.

Q. And you reviewed what you would testify to; isn't that correct?

A. That's correct.

Q. Now, it is true, is it not, that when you were preparing for your testimony, you were conscious of the fact that you entered into an agreement with the government for your plea bargain? Isn't that correct?

A. Yes, sir.

Q. And I'm going to show you Exhibit 520, which is stipulated for the defense, and ask if this is not your plea bargain agreement. Is that it? Does that look like it's the agreement?

A. Yes, sir. . . .

A. That's it, sir. That's my signature.

Q. And [you] had a lawyer negotiate that agreement on your behalf; is that correct?

A. Yes, sir.

Q. And as you said earlier, it is your hope that you will not receive the harshest sentence, but to get a reduced sentence; isn't that correct?

A. That's correct.

In this situation, a little goes a long way. Simply pointing out the reality of the plea agreement and the witness's desire for a lighter sentence is enough. If the attorney here were to follow up with a question like, "Aren't you, then, biased against the defendant by your motivation to cooperate with the prosecution?", the witness could fight back by exclaiming, to the horror of the defense, "No, sir, I want to see that man brought to justice!" When the motive or bias is self-evident, be satisfied that the jurors get the message and move on.

> The witness has made statements in the past that are inconsistent with the witness's present testimony.

Once the witness testifies contrary to a prior statement, you have the basis to impeach. One of the most important steps in this situation is locking in the witness. As the situation allows, you might ask: "Is it your testimony that the light was green?" or "Did you just tell us. . . ?" In other words, have the witness reaffirm the testimony that is inconsistent with the prior statement. This approach allows you to strengthen the foundation for impeachment and gives the impression that you are being fair in giving the witness the opportunity to have his or her say. At other times you may not want to allow the witness to repeat his contradictory assertions; it may be preferable to go directly to the impeachment with the prior statement.

The National Institute for Trial Advocacy (NITA) and Judge Mark Drummond characterize the steps of impeachment by prior inconsistent statement as the three Cs: Commit, Credit, and Confront.

> First commit the witness to his or her trial testimony. For example: "Did you just tell the jury that the traffic light was red?"

Second, credit the prior testimony before trial. For example: "Do you remember reading and signing interrogatories in this case?" "You signed them under oath?" "Were you satisfied at the time that your answers were accurate and true?"

Third, confront the witness with the prior inconsistent document or statement. For example: "Please read to us question number 3 and your answer." "What color was the traffic light? The light was green."

There are at least two ways to impeach when a witness has made statements in the past that are inconsistent with the witness's present testimony: by a prior oral or written statement and by extrinsic evidence.

Here is an instance of impeachment using a prior written statement in the context of a civil case:

In this example, the defendant, a radio station, had terminated the plaintiff for stealing hundreds of compact discs. The plaintiff then sued for breach of contract, contending that, as program director for the station, he was entitled to take as many CDs as he wished. Every year, the station would receive thousands of CDs, many of which were discarded. But at trial the station's coordinator contends that the plaintiff never held the position of program director. The plaintiff's counsel cross-examines the witness as follows:

Q. Ms. Smith, you were the station coordinator of WZB Radio in the spring of 2007?

A. Yes.

Q. What were your responsibilities as station coordinator?

A. I was in charge of making all personnel appointments and coordinating the staff.

Q. Was there a position of program director at the station in 2007?

A. Yes.

Q. Who occupied that position?

A. It was vacant.

Q. Would it be accurate to say that the plaintiff, John Reeves, was the program director during the spring of 2007?

A. No, he was not.

Q. You appointed him as program director of WZB?

A. No.

Q. Didn't you circulate a memorandum in the spring of 2007 announcing the appointment of Reeves to the position of program director?

A. No.

Q. Would the clerk please mark this document? Ms. Smith, I show you what has been marked Plaintiff's Exhibit 1 for identification and ask you to review the document and tell us whether your signature appears at the bottom?

A. Yes, it does.

Q. Did you prepare this document?

A. Yes, I did.

Q. What is the date at the top of the document?

A. May 1, 2007.

Q. Your Honor, we offer Plaintiff's Exhibit 1 for identification in evidence. Would you please read for us, Ms. Smith, the first paragraph of Plaintiff's Exhibit 1?

A. "On this date, effective immediately, I appoint John Reeves as program director of WZB Radio. Please join me in extending to him our congratulations."

Q. No further questions.

Again, there's no need to reach further than this. Counsel would be foolish to demand of Smith why she was trying to mislead the jury. Cutting it off here, with the witness in a clearly uncomfortable position, discredits her sufficiently and allows the plaintiff's case to move forward.

Here is an example of impeaching using deposition testimony.

Cynthia Wright, an alleged witness to an accident, is on the witness stand. She is the aunt of Lindsey, the infant plaintiff in a suit for negligence against Wright's landlord. The lawsuit alleges that the child touched and fell through a broken second-story screen door that the landlord had negligently failed to repair. On direct, the plaintiff's witness testifies that she saw the child touch the door and that the door fell solely because Lindsey touched it.

The cross-examination on behalf of the landlord proceeds:

Q. Ms. Wright, is it your testimony that you saw the infant plaintiff touch the screen door and fall through the kitchen door onto the porch, and then from the porch onto the ground?

A. Yes.

Q. Ms. Wright, do you recall that you were summoned to appear in my office over one year ago?

A. Yes.

Q. Do you remember coming to the office with an attorney?

A. Yes.

Q. Do you recall that we met in my library and that a court reporter was there who took down questions that I asked you as well as your answers to those questions?

A. Yes.

Q. The testimony that was taken down by the court reporter was taken down or recorded the same way as in this court, except there was no judge or jury present, is that correct?

A. Yes.

Q. And you were under oath then just as you are now?

A. Yes.

Q. The lawyer that accompanied you to my office for what was your deposition is the same lawyer who represents you now, is that correct?

A. Yes.

Q. When you finished testifying, your testimony was typed up by the court reporter word for word as you gave it and was submitted to you to read and to correct any mistakes, isn't that true?

A. Yes.

Q. Did you in fact read your deposition?

A. Yes.

Q. You did find mistakes in the transcript, did you not?

A. Yes.

Q. And you made notes of the corrections you felt had to be made, didn't you?

A. Yes.

Q. And then you signed your deposition as corrected by you before a notary public, isn't that true?

A. Yes.

Q. I am now going to read to you beginning at line 7 on page 81 of the transcript of the testimony as typed by the court reporter and corrected by you:

Q. Prior to the accident involving the infant plaintiff, where were you, Ms. Wright?

A. I was in the bedroom looking after my little boy.

Q. When was the last time you had seen the infant plaintiff prior to the accident?

A. After we had breakfast, she was playing with the other children staying with me, and I went to nurse my baby.

Q. Am I correct in understanding that your testimony is that after breakfast you left the infant plaintiff with the other children and that you went into the bedroom to nurse the baby and that you did not see the infant plaintiff until after the fall?

A. Yes.

Q. Now, Ms. Wright, what I have read was your testimony under oath on April 14, 2006, wasn't it?

A. I cannot remember what I said at the time, but I suppose that what you read is what I said, if that's what it says.

> The series of detailed questions about the deposition (the court reporter, the oath-taking, the entire setup) creates suspense and focuses the jurors' attention on what clearly will be testimony of significance.

Q. Well, you are not suggesting that what I read was anything but your previous testimony, are you?

A. No.

Q. We can agree now that in April of 2006 you testified under oath in your deposition that you did not see the child touch the door?

A. I guess so.

Q. Is that a yes?

A. Yes.

Q. We can now agree that after breakfast when you left the children you did not see Lindsey until after the fall?

A. Yes.

Note that the tone here is somewhat confrontational. The same goal could be achieved differently, more efficiently, and with less drama. For example:

Q. Ms. Wright, you just testified that you saw the infant touch the screen door and fall?

A. Yes.

Q. But you testified under oath over a year ago in your deposition that you were—and I quote—at the time of the incident you were "in another room looking after my little boy."

A. I do not recall that.

Q. You do remember that you gave a deposition last year?

A. Yes.

Q. Would it refresh your recollection if I were to read your testimony to you on this issue?

A. Sure.

Q. [Counsel reads the relevant deposition testimony.] Does that refresh your recollection that you did not see the child touch the screen door or fall?

A. I guess.

Q. Is that a yes?

A. Yes.

This approach may be less memorable, but would be preferable if you were concerned about appearing overbearing before the jurors. The information you elicit on cross is critical, but so is the manner in which you do so.

Note that in both the examples about the baby and the screen door, as well as in the radio station case, the cross-examiner begins by letting the witness repeat the core assertion made on direct. Only then, after establishing a sound foundation for impeachment, does the attorney present the witness with the prior written statement.

In the *Maffei* case, on direct examination Mrs. Maffei testified that she expected her husband to continue working for another 15 years. Defense counsel wanted to demonstrate that such may not have been Mr. Maffei's intentions:

Q. You remember that we took your deposition in this case in September, September 18, 2007?

A. Yes.

Q. About a year and a half ago?

A. Uh-huh. (Nodding head up and down.)

Q. And at one point we were, I believe it was me asking you questions about Mr. Maffei. I asked you questions concerning how long he planned to work. On page 38 at line ten you said, I quote: "He wanted to I believe work another year and a half when he could have retired with full pension from the union, but we didn't know if that was going to be possible financially. And then he was going to try to open a business with his brother."

Q. What type of business?

A. Drywall.

Q. Is that accurate?

A. Yes.

Q. So as of sometime before March of 2006, Mr. Maffei had told you he planned to work roughly another year and a half?

A. No, that's not what he said. He said he would like to, if he could.

Q. You said: "He wanted to I believe work another year and a half when he could have retired with full pension from the union." Correct?

A. If he could afford to go into business for himself.

Q. But he had discussed that with his brother?

A. Yes.

Q. The drywall business?

A. Uh-huh. (Nodding head up and down.)

Impeachment with Extrinsic Evidence

Often there is no handy transcript or memo from which to read, and the mistaken witness does not so readily recall what he or she has said or written in the past. Between the action at issue and the trial, many years may have passed, and the specific conversations and correspondence around which the case may pivot have long since faded in memory.

U.S. v. Rosen was just such a case. The investigation leading to the indictment began in 2001, and the trial took place in 2006. The critical question of the fake invoice centered jurors' attention on conversations that took place more than four years earlier. The event planner and government witness, Bretta Nock, had testified on direct that the defendant, David Rosen, had asked her to procure the falsified invoice from a production company. But the defense knew that, in her initial contact with law enforcement officers investigating the matter, she had said she could not recall if it was Rosen who had asked for the invoice. Defense gave her the opportunity to testify accordingly, but her memory seemed to fail her.

Q. When was the first time that you met with the representatives of the government about this case?

A. I don't recall. I believe it was in 2001, but I don't recall.

Q. Do you recall [a] discussion with them about the invoice from Mr. Baumrucker? Did they ask you about that?

A. I would have to know exactly. I don't recall exactly when.

Q. Well, let me be specific. Can you recall whether you had a meeting with the representatives of the government on January 9, 2002, where you discussed the facts of this case?

A. I don't recall the exact meeting, but I knew I met with them several times, yes.

Q. Do you recall discussing the invoice that you were shown on direct examination from Mr. Baumrucker?

A. I don't recall the exact conversation.

Q. Do you recall whether or not you told the government—didn't you tell the government that you could not recall if Rosen had asked you to get the invoice from Black Ink Productions? Do you remember saying that?

A. I don't recall.

Q. Do you recall telling the federal agents that—or Mr. Smith, specifically, that it could have been Bretta Nock who asked for the invoice? . . . Excuse me—Whitney Burns. . . .

A. No, it would not have been Whitney Burns, I don't believe.

Subsequently, the defense called to the stand a law enforcement officer, Agent David Smith, who had contacted Nock about the Rosen matter. The officer did, in fact, confirm that the event planner had told him at their first meeting that she had no recollection of Rosen asking her to procure a falsified invoice. Additionally, the vendor, Baumrucker, testified that Nock had told him that it had been James Levin, another government witness, who had requested the falsified invoice.

This extrinsic evidence refuted the critical government claim that Rosen had engaged in an underhanded attempt to acquire a fake invoice to falsify the costs of the Clinton fundraising gala. With not one but two witnesses contradicting Nock's testimony, the star prosecution witness dimmed before the jury. Note that the impeachment did not require hostile confrontation. Primarily, defense counsel relied on casting her memory of events into doubt. In the above cross-examination, she repeats several times that she could not recall this or that conversation, leading jurors, the defense hoped, to question how precisely she could remember who had asked her for the fake invoice.

Establishing Flawed Character—Prior Bad Acts or Prior Conviction

Unsavory characters make for rich cross-examinations. The prosecution in *U.S. v. Rosen* based much of its case on convicted felons. One of them was Raymond Reggie, Senator Kennedy's brother-in-law. He had been convicted of bank fraud and, to reduce his sentence, had agreed to converse with Rosen about the fundraiser while secretly wearing a wire. On direct, Reggie said the expected: that Rosen admitted to him that he had understated the costs of the gala. But on cross-examination, Reggie's character was the focus:

Q. . . . I'd like to talk to you about the particular crimes that you pled guilty to.

A. Yes, sir.

Q. One of them was check kiting; is that correct?

A. That's correct.

Q. What was the average size of the check that you wrote in the check-kiting scheme?

A. The average-sized check for my company?

Q. For whomever that you were writing checks that caused you to be committing the crime.

A. The gross revenues of our company were $60 million that year, so there were a significant amount of checks. I couldn't tell you how many—1999 we grossed $60 million. So for me to be able to say that— we probably had some checks for $20, as you suggested, and we had some for millions of dollars.

Q. Okay. So you'd be writing checks for a million dollars, recognizing, in your heart, that it was wrong because it was violating the law; isn't that true?

A. Yes, sir.

Q. All right. With regard to the bankruptcy—I'm sorry, the bank fraud, am I correct, because I thought I had read that you had engaged a fictitious person to contact the bank to pretend that person had a valid contract with your company. Is that correct?

A. Yes, sir.

Q. And you knew at the time that was wrong.

A. Yes, sir.

Q. It was false.

A. Yes, sir.

Q. Fake.

A. Yes, sir.

Q. Made up.

A. Yes, sir.

The questions about the fraud elicit valuable details that not only reveal the extent of Reggie's crime, but also suggest that he is an innately dishonest person.

Q. And you have a custom and practice for some reason that I don't have to get into of make-believing when it suits you; isn't that true? . . .

A. I take full responsibility, sir, for what we did and having an employee sign a voucher saying that the invoices were accurate and accounted for. But I really—I guess I don't understand your question.

Q. Well, do you recall impersonating a police officer one night? That's specific enough for you, isn't it?

A. That is a charge, yes, sir.

Q. Okay. You admitted to that; isn't that true?

A. Absolutely not.

Here defense counsel has no hesitation in taking an aggressive tone. Given the seriousness of the witness's claims on direct, and the black marks on his reputation, the defense had no choice but to go on the offensive.

The cross-examiner takes a somewhat dangerous leap, extrapolating that Reggie has a practice of "make-believing" when it suits him. If the witness had been the least bit sympathetic, such a question would be foolish; the jury could quickly side against the attorney. But in this situation, counsel felt at liberty to confront the witness with a certain moral outrage that was perhaps shared by the jurors.

Such assaults are rarely justified. When impeaching a person's character, execute the cross with conviction. If your questions arise from genuine abhorrence or frustration, the testimony will more likely hit its mark. The danger, of course, is that you lose control of your emotions and strike too hard. Even in the midst of a confrontation such as the one above, maintain your cool.

Impeachment by Exaggeration or Improbability
The goal here is to lead or allow the witness to testify in such a way that he or she exaggerates, thus causing the testimony to appear improbable.

Consider the following from the *Rosen* case: James Levin testified that, as a friend of President Clinton, he attended the fundraising gala to keep an eye on matters and report to the president. He testified on direct that he had observed problems with rising costs, and that Rosen had complained about the matter. To discredit this testimony, defense counsel cross-examined Levin about his arrangement with the president:

Q. Well, when you were the eyes and ears of the president, was it to make sure everything went right?

A. Correct.

Q. Correct. That there was nothing to be alarmed about, that there were no major problems; isn't that true?

A. Yes.

Q. So when you're at the gala and you're telling the jury that there are all kinds of issues with costs and that you were getting concerned that the costs were spiraling, was that something that was significant to you?

A. Yes.

Q. And when it was significant to you, was it also significant to you that your dear friend the president of the United States was relying upon you to be his eyes and ears?

A. I'm sorry. Do you want to ask me the question again? I don't know.

Q. Was it also of significance to you that your dear friend the former president of the United States asked you to be his eyes and ears at this event?

A. It would be significant, yes.

Q. And how many times did you call or notify the president of the United States that things were amiss at the gala or the planning of the gala?

A. We had no conversations about it before the gala.

Q. So it's your testimony that you never reported to him that there was a problem, correct?

A. Correct.

The inference here is that it is improbable that Levin was concerned about costs or problems or he surely would have reported his concerns to the president. There is also a more subtle point being made in the nature of the questions about his "dear friend the former president": that Levin is perhaps exaggerating his closeness to the president and putting on airs. The desired effect here is to raise questions about Levin's character.

In the *Maffei* case, as discussed, one of the arguments of plaintiff was that the defendant limited her review of the nurse's notes to only the triage notes, which reported among other complaints a complaint of chest pain intensity of 3 on a scale of 1 through 10. The plaintiff's view was that if the doctor had reviewed those notes of complaints of chest pain, she would have ordered the x-ray. Dr. Smedley testified that she did not need to review the other notes because she met directly with Mr. Maffei. At the meeting Mr. Maffei allegedly denied present chest pain and prior chest pain.

The plaintiff's expert witness testified that the ER doctor breached the standard of care by not reviewing the prior notes and by not reconciling with the patient his prior complaints of chest pain with the prior notes of the nurses. When cross-examining the defendant, plaintiff's counsel demonstrates the improbability of the defendant's version of the facts:

Q. It is true, is it not, that prior to your meeting with Mr. Maffei, you did not see the complete nurses notes?

A. I saw the triage note and the written notes on there. I didn't see the other entries that were placed in the computer following that as we discussed prior to this.

Q. I'm going to show you a summary of the notes.

A. Yes.

Q. All right. Do you feel comfortable looking at it this way, Doctor?

A. Sure.

Q. So you did see the triage note, right?

A. I did.

Q. And that showed chest pain of 3 out of 10.

A. Okay.

Q. And when you saw that note, you—you were concerned then, were you not, about a heart condition?

A. When I read the triage note, I was. That's why I was wanting to go see him right away and talk to him myself.

Q. And you also had concern when you [saw] the triage note that he [might] have an aortic condition, isn't that true?

A. There are a number of serious conditions that can cause chest pain. Those are two of [the] things that can cause chest pain, a ruptured esophagus, and a collapsed lung, pneumonia, pulmonary embolism, there's a whole wide range of things that are a serious cause of chest pain. So as I said, I always take chest pain seriously and always further question folks about it when they come in complaining of chest pain.

Q. When you saw the triage note with chest pain, 3 out of 10, you were concerned about an aortic problem, isn't that true? Yes or no.

A. Again, yes. That's one of the many things that can cause chest pain.

Q. Is it yes though, that you were concerned about an aortic problem at that time when you saw the triage note?

A. That was not my primary concern, but yes. I believe I said yes.

Q. Now, when you had a concern about an aortic condition, and you saw chest pain, it is true, is it not, that you did not administer a chest x-ray.

A. It's sort of a—a convoluted answer. I did not administer a chest x-ray because it's my practice to see a patient and take a thorough history and physical, which is more reliable than that particular diagnostic study, to rule out an aortic dissection. So before I would have ordered a chest x-ray, I would have gone in and spoke[n] to the patient, which I did. And after I spoke to the patient and he told me he wasn't having chest pain, there was no reason to order a chest x-ray.

Q. Is your answer to my question that when you saw the throat/chest 3 out of 10 and had a concern about an aortic dissection, you did not ask for an x-ray or take an x-ray?

A. I didn't take an x-ray because as soon as I picked up the chart, I walked in and talked to Mr. Maffei. It's more important for me to assess his condition than to sit at the computer. So no, when I saw the triage note, I did not order a chest x-ray I went to assess the patient.

Q. So you agree then you did not take the x-ray.

A. You're correct.

Q. You did not take an x-ray.

Q. Thank you. Now, you could have seen, had you wanted to, other notes relating to Mr. Maffei's stay at the hospital, isn't that true?

A. Yes there are other notes I could see related to Mr. Maffei's stay at the hospital.

Q. And had you looked at other notes—they were available to you if you wanted to, isn't that correct?

A. The notes were on the computer as noted.

Q. Is the answer yes?

A. Yes.

Q. And you could have seen a note that had a chest pain that was 5 out of 10, isn't that correct?

A. I could have seen that note had I been looking at the computer.

Q. Is the answer yes?

A. Yes.

Q. And you could have seen that the chest pain was radiating to the neck, isn't that true?

A. Yes, that's true.

Q. And you could also have seen that the chest pain duration was one to three hours, correct?

A. Yes, correct.

Q. Now, do you agree with me had you—had you seen this note coupled with the previous triage note, that you did see, would your concern have increased?

These repeated questions about the doctor's exam of Mr. Maffei were designed to make jurors question how thoroughly she discussed the chest pain with him.

A. No. I already had a level of concern based on the triage note. So it wouldn't have increased my concern any further. I'm always very concerned, as I said, when there's a complaint of chest pain. That wouldn't have made me more concerned.

Q. Did you see the next note: chest pain—2 out of 10?

A. No, I did not.

Q. Had you seen that note, which was even later, would that have increased your concern?

A. Again, no. I was concerned about chest pain, and that's why I went to see Mr. Maffei and asked him directly. It would not have increased my concern because my concern was already high.

A. I'm testifying that I was already very concerned.

Q. If you had seen that the chest pain was radiating to the neck, would that have enhanced your concern?

A. My answer is no, because I was already most concerned.

Q. And you stated I believe that not only did Mr. Maffei tell you that he did not have currently chest pain, but that he had not had chest pain prior, isn't that your testimony?

A. That's correct. I did a detailed chest pain history because of concerning components.

Q. Isn't it true, please look at your notes from the day in question that while you may have stated he had no current chest pain, you do not document that he denied having prior chest pain.

A. Part of Review of Systems, I document chest pain to indicate that I have additionally asked chest pain questions above and beyond, which is why both places it says chest pain. So it's documented in that sense. Is the word prior chest pain written? No, but did I ask him? Yes.

Q. But you didn't document it, correct?

A. I document it by documenting in the Review of Systems.

Q. Show me where one reading there can see that you're documenting his statement to you if he said that, that he did not have prior chest pain.

A. All right.

Q. Show me where.

A. Okay. As I said, I didn't write prior, but this is something that's called a Review of Systems. It means I have reviewed the symptoms that he's been having. So there's no place that it's written that I asked him if he had prior chest pain. It is implied in the Review of Systems that I asked him those questions, and I did.

Q. Doesn't this say at the top "Circle at Present"?

The point of the cross-examination was to present the improbability of the doctor's testimony that she thoroughly questioned Mr. Maffei about the inconsistency between his prior complaints of chest pain and his allegedly telling the doctor than he had neither current nor prior pain in his chest. The argument is that if the doctor had fulfilled her obligation under the standard of care she would have documented her discussion, in detail.

Historical Examples

The annals of legal history offer hundreds of examples of effective trial strategy. Before we close our comments on cross-examination, we would like to cite two particularly valuable illustrations of impeachment. We would also encourage readers to reach beyond what we offer in this volume and wade into the little-consulted but fascinating records of historic trials. They reveal how much our legal system has changed and how much has remained the same.

In the trial of Queen Caroline in 1820, King George IV charged her with adultery. The great luminary at the bar of the day, Henry Brougham, later Lord Chancellor, appeared for her defense in the House of Lords. Brougham was confronted with one Theodoro Majocchi, an Italian servant who presented some of the strongest testimony against the queen. If his testimony were believed, it was more than sufficient to establish the queen's guilt. At first, Majocchi appeared immune to Brougham's cross-examination. But then the advocate asked him a series of questions that, if he were truly an eyewitness to wrongdoing, he would surely be able to answer. Majocchi responded "non mi ricordo," "non mi ricordo" (I do not remember) over and over. The repetition threw his testimony into doubt, for it seemed the servant could remember precious little about the alleged adultery. For example, Majocchi could not recall the position of the rooms of the queen and her alleged paramour, Bartolomeo Bergami. This was striking in that the case against the queen relied in part on the position of the queen's and Bergami's rooms, signifying closeness and mutual communication.

In closing argument, Brougham demonstrated that Majocchi's repeated answers, "non mi ricordo" defied belief. He argued:

> Theodore Majocchi, of happy memory, will be long known in this country and everywhere else, much after the manner in which the ancient sages have reached in our day, whose names are lost in the celebrity of the little saying by which each is now distinguished by mankind, and in which they were known to have embodied in the practical result of their own experience and wisdom. . . . My Lords, this person is a witness of great importance. He was the first called and the latest examined; continuing by the case and accompanying it throughout. . . .
>
> There is an end, then of innocent forgetfulness, if when I come to ask where the rest slept, he either tells me, "I do not know," or "I do not recollect;" because he had known and must have recollected when he presumed to say to my learned friends, "these two rooms were alone, near and connected, and others were distant and apart;" when he said that, he affirmed his recollection of the proximity of those rooms and the remoteness of the others. He swore that at first and afterward said, "I know not"; "I recollect not" and perjured himself as plainly as if he had told your Lordships one day that he saw a person and the next day he never saw him in his life.[1]

Though Brougham had not truly impeached the Italian servant on cross, he discredited him thoroughly in closing argument. Surely the jury (the House of Lords) appreciated that Majocchi's answers made it improbable that he had witnessed adultery. The power of understatement in developing the pattern of answers—"non mi ricordo," "non mi ricordo"—was Brougham's method of tacitly arguing, "Do not believe him."

A similar strategy was employed by prominent Chicago lawyer Weymouth Kirkland in the early 1900s when he was called upon to defend an insurance company in a case where the plaintiff claimed entitlement to

---

1. John Lord Campbell, Lives of the Lord Chancellors and Keepers of the Great Seal of England 318–19 (London, John Murray 1869).

funds based on the death of a policyholder. As Lloyd Paul Stryker points out in *The Art of Advocacy*, the defense asserted that there was no death and the policyholder did not fall from a ship and drown. Rather, he walked off the ship very much alive.

A key witness for the plaintiff was the ship's cook. Here is how Stryker reports the cross-examination:

Q. How long had you known Peck (the policyholder)?

A. Fifteen years.

Q. You knew him well?

A. Yes, sir.

Q. How did you happen to see his body?

A. I looked out of the porthole.

Q. You recognized it beyond doubt as the body of Peck?

A. Yes, sir.

Q. Did you make any outcry when you saw the body?

A. No, sir.

Q. Did you ask the captain to stop the ship?

A. No, sir.

Q. What were you doing when you happened to look out the window and saw the body?

A. I was peeling potatoes.

Q. And when the body of your old friend, Peck, floated by, you just kept on peeling potatoes?

A. Yes, sir.

During closing argument Kirkland went to town. He did not argue to the jury that the cook's testimony was false. Instead he took a potato and a knife from his pocket (you could bring knives into the courtroom in those days), rested his foot on a chair and began to peel the potato. As he did this, he said to the jury, "What ho! What have we here? Who is this floating past? As I live and breathe, if it isn't my old friend Peck! I shall tell the captain about this in the morning. In the meantime, I must go right on peeling my potatoes." As in the example from the Queen Caroline case, Kirkland waited until the closing argument to enjoy the fruits of his slyly effective cross.

THE LAW OF IMPEACHMENT
The techniques of impeachment cannot be mastered without appreciating the technicalities of the rules of impeachment.

Rules vary by jurisdiction, so be sure you are up to speed on them wherever you happen to be trying a case. Many state court rules provide that a prior written statement examined in state court must be shown to the witness, and the witness must be given an opportunity to explain or deny it before the end of the cross-examination.

On the other hand Rule 613(a) of the Federal Rules of Evidence does not require that the witness be shown a prior inconsistent written statement before the conclusion of the examination, but the party must on request show it or disclose its content to an adverse party's attorney. Also when impeaching with extrinsic evidence under the federal rule, you are not required to permit the witness to examine the statement. Under the federal rule, the opportunity for the witness to examine and explain the document may be left to counsel on redirect.

In addition to following rules of evidence, counsel must adhere to ethical obligations concerning cross-examination. For example, in the ABA Model Rules of Professional Conduct, Rule 3.4(e) prohibits you from stating any matter that you have no reasonable basis to believe is relevant to the case or will not be supported by admissible evidence. The American College of Trial Lawyers Code of Trial Conduct, Rule 20(g), provides that a lawyer should not ask improper questions or attempt to place before the jury any evidence that is improper.

In cases in which you have any doubt about the propriety of any disclosure to the jury, a request should be made to approach the bench and obtain a ruling out of the jury's hearing. You can be held in contempt for asking a question that calls for inadmissible evidence. For example, asking a question that implies that the plaintiff was drunk at the time of the accident, when there was no supporting evidence, would constitute a prejudicial error that could not be cured by a jury instruction. Similarly, a prosecutor's question on cross-examination that implies prior criminal conduct by a witness without any evidentiary foundation is improper under ethical standards.

Numerous situations can get you into trouble on cross. It would be improper for counsel to ask, "Isn't it true that you told X you saw Y shoot Z?" leaving the impression that such was the case and then not calling X to establish the fact when it was denied. It is a reversible error for the prosecutor to ask a question suggesting that the defendant has a long criminal record when she does not. It is improper for defense counsel to ask a rape victim if she had been raped before. In almost every case, there will be off-limits questions, and only broad familiarity with ethical obligations and rules will save you from making this kind of mistake.

Beware, too, of conflicts of interest. Sometimes an attorney will encounter adverse witnesses who are also clients, former clients, or expert witnesses the attorney is using in another matter. It is unethical to skewer a client or former client on the witness stand in the interest of defending another client. A cross-examining lawyer is ethically prohibited from revealing client confidences or privileged information. A devastating cross of an opposing expert might boomerang against the cross-examiner's client in a second case in which the expert is serving the attorney. Fortunately, conflict situations like this are rare, but if a conflict arises, it should be recognized as early as possible so that it may be remedied by obtaining the consent of the client or former client to be cross-examined. If consent is not feasible, the attorney could raise the issue with the court and consider withdrawal from the case.

Learning Points for Chapter 7

Cross-examination is difficult, but it is critical to the administration of justice. At the beginning of this chapter, I cited Wigmore's statement that cross-examination is the greatest legal engine for the discovery of truth. I would moderate this assertion by saying it is the greatest legal engine for fairness. The jury trial system recognizes human fallibility. Mendaciousness, forgetfulness, vanity, greed, fear, selfishness, and other vices surface when normal people climb into the witness stand and testify under oath. What they say in rehearsed, sometimes scripted, direct examinations frequently must be countered. To receive a truly fair trial, clients rely on strong advocacy in the wake of threatening attacks made on direct. Each stage of a trial is crucial, but cross-examination represents the moment when clients most need their attorneys to perform well. Such heavy responsibility demands rigorous preparation and the willingness to hone the necessary skills throughout one's career.

- Decide whether you need to ask any questions at all on cross.
- Have a specific objective for the testimony you want to obtain.
- Be sure that your objective advances or protects your theme.
- Be selective in deciding what topics to cover.
- Use short leading questions to control the witness.
- Strive for answers of yes or no, preferably yes.
- Remember the doctrines of primacy and recency.
- Beware of open-ended questions; ask them only when appropriate.
- Watch and listen to the witness on direct.
- Be spontaneous.
- When impeaching, remember to "lock in the witness" by having the witness confirm the prior statement.
- Know when to sit down.

CHAPTER 8

CROSS-EXAMINATION—A VIEW FROM THE BENCH

By the Hon. Mark A. Drummond, Circuit Judge, Eighth Judicial Circuit of Illinois

I got a chuckle out of the chainsaw analogy for cross-examination. Sandler once told me that he bought a chain saw, only to have a close friend take it away from him for fear that he was in greater danger from the saw than were the trees. The friend knew Sandler's skills lay in cutting witnesses, as opposed to oaks, down to size.

So, taking his four steps, let's see if I can match them to some common chainsaw wisdom and carry the analogy through. The reader should know that this is by no means an exhaustive treatment of this topic. However, since part of the title of this book is *A Handbook for Young Lawyers*, I thought I would try to distill the things I wish I had known about cross-examination on the day I cross-examined my first witness. Here's what nearly 20 years of trying cases coupled with 10 years of watching others do it, topped off with 23 years as an instructor for the National Institute for Trial Advocacy (NITA), has taught me. May you find something of value in it.

SANDLER'S STEP ONE: SELECT THOSE TOPICS
MOST ADVANTAGEOUS TO YOUR CASE
Chainsaw Wisdom: Keep the Bar in Solid Wood

I tell young attorneys that the gold standard of cross is the ability to ask a single-fact, leading question from an "island of safety" (IOS). An IOS is like solid wood. It may be a deposition, statement, record, or another witness that you know will testify to certain facts. It is solid, does not change, and can be relied upon if impeachment is necessary.

The young attorney must:

Assemble all of the IOSs;

Know what they say or contain; and

Be able to get to the IOS quickly at trial.

Your discovery has undoubtedly produced all kinds of information that you will need at your fingertips in order to do a proper cross-examination. Each adverse witness had a tab in my trial notebook. Directly behind my cross-examination outline, which I will touch on later, were the IOSs. I always had four copies: one highlighted copy for me with any notes I needed; one for opposing counsel so he or she could not interrupt the rhythm of my cross with "Your Honor, I don't know what counsel is giving to the witness!"; one for the witness if it was required by the court or, even if not required, if I wanted to give it to him or her to show fairness or to gauge the witness's reaction; and one for the judge. Trust me, judges like to look at this stuff, especially the impeaching stuff. After all, we have nothing else to do while sitting there.

I always used different colored highlighters for my own trial notebook. I would highlight or underline the various topic areas with the same color. For example, I might have a topic area concerning a witness's ability to see. Let's say I used a blue highlighter for this topic. Blue would be used for the witness's statement in the deposition that "It was kind of foggy that night," for the witness's statement to the police officer that he was "... about 200 feet away," and for the accident report showing that the conditions and time were "2:00 a.m. with light fog and light drizzle."

At the front of the trial notebook I would create a legend by simply swiping each color I used and writing next to that color the corresponding topic area. There may be many topic areas in a single document, and using different-colored highlighters allowed me to get to each topic quickly. Only highlight your copy of the IOS. The copies for opposing counsel, the judge and the witness should not be highlighted. Since I am a visual learner, this system worked best for me.

For every case, I would construct a proof chart. This would give me a visual of what I needed to prove. The prima facie elements of my case were listed from top to bottom along the side of the vertical axis and included all topics that built my case. Across the top were all the IOSs from which I could get those elements or points. If I found only one check mark for a crucial element to my case and saw above it that this element could come only from a witness on cross-examination, it told me that I might need to buttress my proof on that point. For example, it might prompt me to send out a request to admit facts or genuine documents or to see if I could find another witness, seek a stipulation, or find another IOS in addition to the adverse witness. If at all possible, I never wanted to go into trial where my whole case could fall apart if I did not get an admission out of a witness on cross. If the other side decided not to call that witness and I did not have that person under subpoena, that would be a real problem.

As has been pointed out, cross-examination must be fluid because it depends on what comes out in direct examination. Only by having a rock-solid (sorry, I mean wood-solid) knowledge of the facts in the IOSs can the cross-examiner have the luxury of really listening carefully to the direct and knowing whether or not it is accurate. The last thing you want to be doing at the counsel table is fumbling through hundreds of pages of depositions or documents because you are unsure whether what was just said on direct examination is exactly true.

STEP TWO: ARRANGE YOUR TOPICS AND POINTS STRATEGICALLY
Chainsaw Wisdom: Determine the Felling Direction and a Clear Fall Path

For me, strategically arranging my points on cross-examination involved creating a cross-examination outline. When I say outline, I mean outline. For a case that you have been living with for years, you should know the facts. All you should need for trial is a simple, easy-to-read outline in order to list the sequencing of topics and questions.

My outline tips are as follows:

1. It Must Be Big and Bold
   Too often, I see young attorneys bring outlines to the podium that they have written the night before while they were seated at a desk. Their cross-examination questions are written out word for word and can be read only while sitting with their face no more than two feet above the paper. They conduct their cross hunched over, desperately trying to read every word of their highly detailed, complete sentences.

2. Headlines on the Left
   My cross-examination outlines were constructed using a thick felt tip pen so that I could catch my next point from a standing position with a simple glance to the outline. The headlines or topic areas would be in the left margin and were not too highly detailed. The simple words "Did Do/Did Not Do" would prompt my headlining for a question such as "Now Ms. Watson, let us turn to everything you did do and did not do after the accident."

3. Ending Words in the Middle with Anchors to IOSs to the Right
   The meat of the cross-examination was in the middle of the paper and was usually limited to just the main point or the ending words of the cross-examination sentence. The first line might just be the word—ambulance—without quotation marks around the word. The lack of quotation marks around the word told me that it was not a statement from the witness. To the right of the word I might have the reference: Police report: No ambulance requested. The next

line might read "No Emergency Room," which tells me that it is a direct quote from the witness and to the right would be Dep (short for deposition) and, p. (page) 27, ln (line) 12.

The actual outline would look something like this:

Did Do/Did Not Do

No Ambulance	Police report:
"No emergency room"	No ambulance requested
"Did not go home"	Pl's Dep. p. 27, ln 12
Did go somewhere, "McDonald's"	Pl's Dep. p. 5, ln 2
	Pl's Dep. p. 5, ln 6–7
	Smith Dep. p. 23, ln 12
	Jones Dep. p. 12, ln 23
	(Note: 3 IOSs)

STEP THREE: CONTROL THE WITNESS
Chainsaw Wisdom: Hold the Chainsaw with Both Hands

Entire chapters of books have been devoted to the issue of witness control. My guiding light on this topic is Vilfredo Pareto, the Italian economist credited with creating the 80/20 rule, or what is known as Pareto's Principle. I may be going out on a limb here (sorry, I can't help myself), but I truly believe that 80 percent of the problems with witness control can be cured if the attorney will simply learn how to ask a single-fact leading question from an IOS and then be patient enough to use the witness control device of repetition.

What the novice attorney tends to do is to take the good, concrete, and solid facts contained in the IOSs and mix them with other facts, paraphrase, expand, make conclusions, or, even worse, use words that might even have less impact than those actually written in the IOS.

An example is the best way to illustrate this point. The outline above was used at trial in a "dart-out" case. The plaintiff was running in and out of parked cars with some of her friends. She darted out in front of my driver and, fortunately for her, my driver slammed on the brakes in time so that the force of the car simply knocked her to the pavement.

I knew from the depositions that she went to McDonald's after the accident with her two friends who were at the scene. Two days later she drove to the emergency room where she was prescribed bed rest and Tylenol No. 3. Three weeks later she was at the chiropractor's office, and several thousands of dollars worth of adjustments later we were in court.

Early in my career, I might have made the mistake of asking her on cross-examination using, of course, a tone dripping with sarcasm, "Well, Ms. Watson you must not have been very hurt because you ended up at McDonald's that night with your two friends." This would be a mistake. It contains more than one fact and a conclusion. Unless the IOS (her deposition) says, "I must not have been very hurt, because I ended up at McDonald's with my two friends," it is not wise to ask that question.

Instead, I look at my trial outline and see the words "Did Do/Did Not Do" which cue me to say, "Now, Miss Watson, I want to ask you some questions about everything you did do and everything you did not do after the accident." The word in the middle is "ambulance." This one word is all that is necessary to cue me to ask, "You didn't ask for an ambulance?"

Now, what's her response in a real courtroom? She doesn't look sheepish and say, "You're right, Mr. Drummond, I didn't ask for an ambulance." No, you get something like, "Well, I really didn't start hurting until two days later." You simply repeat the question, but this time more slowly and softly, "You didn't ask for an ambulance?" Again, she may respond, "Well, like I just said, I didn't start hurting until two days later." You go back a third time, even more softly and slowly, "You didn't ask for an ambulance?" By this point, one of two things happens. Either the judge becomes frustrated and tells her to answer the question, or you see the jury squirming in their seats and you know the thought, "*Oh, just answer the question!*" is screaming through their minds.

Even if she persists in her original answer, you have made your point. You can then just as politely say, "So Ms. Watson, the answer to my question would be 'No, I didn't ask for an ambulance.'" Why does the jury or the judge hold it against her and not against you? Because you have asked a single-fact, leading question for which you are entitled to a yes or no answer, and the more she tries to dodge that simple question, the better it is for you. I cannot agree with Sandler more when he says, "If you've presented your case effectively, you and the jury will know the answers to your questions on cross before the witness answers."

STEP FOUR: CONDUCT CROSS WITH DELIVERY AND STYLE CONSISTENT WITH YOUR GOALS
Chainsaw Wisdom: Find the Right Saw to Fit Your Needs

I once told a young attorney in a NITA training course that "You can't treat every adverse witness who gets on that stand as if God placed them on this earth for the sole purpose of messing with your case." This young man would go after 80-year-old occurrence witnesses who had no stake or bias in the case with hammer and tongs.

Someone once told me that if you want to impress, it is always good to throw in a quote from Shakespeare. So here's your Shakespeare: Hamlet cautions the Player against overacting by advising, ". . . suit the action to the word, the word to the action."[1] At trial, fit the cross to the witness, the witness to the cross.

In most cases, the jury is far behind the attorney in terms of their feelings toward witnesses. Accordingly, the old saw of constructive first and only then destructive is usually good advice. There are exceptions. If you have a "red light/green light" case and the witness has testified contrary to a previous statement, you may have to start your cross with impeachment since the only issue is "red light/green light."

However, in most cases it is best to get as much good stuff as you can out of the witness before you start tearing the witness down. Remember always that the jurors tend to identify with and sympathize with the poor lay witness who just happened to be in the wrong place at the wrong time and ended up as a witness in a trial. Many of the jurors feel as the witness does. It takes them a long time to build as much animosity as you may have for a particular witness. The jurors may have less of a concern for the parties since the parties have a stake in the outcome. They rarely identify with the attorney unless they really, really like you and, hopefully, they will.

---

1. WILLIAM SHAKESPEARE, HAMLET, act 3, sc. 2.

CHAPTER 9

TYING IT ALL TOGETHER—CLOSING ARGUMENT

The purpose of the closing argument is to incite jurors to render the decision you request. It is not about impressing listeners with your eloquence. According to the apocryphal tale, when listeners heard Demosthenes, they would remark, "What a pretty speech." After hearing Cicero, they would remark, "Let us march." A closing argument should provoke the jury to march into the jury room and render a verdict for your client.

The challenge of closing argument is not merely to summarize what you have proved, but to *unify*, to gather together disparate facts and testimony and present a cohesive narrative pointing jurors to one inevitable conclusion. During the trial, evidence often appears disconnected. Facts and documents rarely surface according to the precise chronology and structure you would like because the case must be presented witness by witness. Closing argument is your chance to bind the facts together and tell a story. They don't teach storytelling in law school, but the skill is essential to courtroom advocacy, particularly closing arguments.

Too often advocates approach the closing argument as logicians. Logical reasoning should indeed be at the heart of every closing argument, but it is not an end in itself. All good stories appeal to our emotions, and so do good closing arguments. At the crux of strong closings are adroit, controlled appeals to both logic and emotion. Pulling off such appeals effectively rests on the power of your delivery.

DELIVERY, DELIVERY, DELIVERY

At no stage of the trial is your delivery more important than in the closing argument. Blending the substance of your argument with a compelling delivery requires attention to various classical rhetorical elements discussed earlier in this book, including ethos, pathos, logos, figurative analogy, rhetorical question, diction, and nonverbal communication. Marshalling these various tools to present cohesive arguments is truly an art form. Some of the most outstanding examples of the art have been handed down from antiquity. Aristotle's *Rhetoric*, the oratory and writings of Cicero, and the work of Quintilian remain invaluable teaching tools for advocates today. Consult these sources as you hone your advocacy skills.

This chapter will first consider some of the key elements of effective closing arguments, drawing on examples from the *Rosen* case to illustrate. I will then point out the most important legal rules concerning closing and finally discuss how to structure this final presentation before the jury.

The Power of Pathos

Cicero said it well: "Mankind makes far more determinations by hatred, or love, or desire, or anger, or grief, or joy, or feelings . . . than from regard to truth, or any settled maxim or principle."[1]

In appealing to the heart of your listener, you should consider the listener's feelings and his or her likely reaction to what you say. This is much easier said than done.

It can be difficult to rise above the moment and take into account the full narrative arc of your case and the emotional state it has provoked in the jurors. We are prone to assume too much in our favor. Take a step back. Acknowledge that certain appeals along the way may have missed their mark, and that jurors' minds have strayed or been persuaded in part by your opponent. Acknowledge that at this juncture jurors may feel conflicted, confused, or anxious as they approach the moment where they must finally act. As an advocate, you want to meet jurors where they stand to help provoke an emotional response most advantageous to your client.

---

1. CICERO, DE ORATORE XLII (Harvard Univ. Press 1988).

Which is not to say you should overtly manipulate their feelings. Hyperbole or injurious language in a direct effort to incite the listener can prove harmful. The power of understatement is far more potent. Instead of describing in gory detail the terrible injuries the plaintiff received as a result of the defendant's negligence, discuss in a factual manner the client's limitations that resulted from the injuries. Allow the jury to draw its own conclusions by the way you summarize the nature of the harm. In other words, don't hit the listener over the head with a two-by-four. Allow the audience to be emotionally engaged, not manipulated.

Figurative Analogies

Figurative analogies are a powerful way to achieve this end. Unlike literal analogies, which compare cases that are similar in relevant characteristics, a figurative analogy is a kind of story, sometimes a metaphor, developed to compare unlike characteristics. Everyone enjoys a story. Listeners, judges, and juries often create their own narratives in making decisions. A figurative analogy in a closing argument can help the listener accept your points as the narrative of the case, thus allowing him or her to subconsciously come to the conclusion you desire.

In appealing to the heart of your listener, you should consider the listener's feelings and his or her likely reaction to what you say. This is much easier said than done. As advocate, you want to meet jurors where they stand to help provoke an emotional response most advantageous to your client.

When a listener believes he or she has come to a conclusion independently, your argument and case theory become more acceptable. When you use a figurative analogy, it is important that you relate the facts of your case to the analogy's elements. Frequently, analogies are left undeveloped; hence, their full effectiveness is lost.

A number of tried-and-true figurative analogies are passed among trial attorneys. Don't be shy in using such material. Defense counsel relied on one familiar analogy in the *Rosen* case to illustrate the concept of reasonable doubt and bring up the subject of holes in the government's case:

Let's assume you go home tonight and you have a box, and you put a cat in the box and a mouse. You close the lid. You come back an hour later, the mouse is gone. One could firmly believe that the cat ate the mouse. What if you come back later and you put the same—it has to be the same cat this time. You put the cat in a box and the mouse, close the lid, come back an hour later again, and there are holes in the box. No longer would you firmly believe the cat ate the mouse. And I want to talk to you now about some of the holes in the government's case, about the burden they failed to meet.

Such analogies can hold the jury's attention and encourage your audience to envision the case in terms that are favorable to your client. The parallels between the case and the analogy may surprise the jurors and cast the decision in a new light. A figurative analogy is a general comparison, a broad-brush image of the case that will remain in the jurors' minds and hopefully shape the decision in your favor.

You may want to deploy an analogy to counter a specific witness's testimony. In *U.S. v. Rosen*, the prosecution's case relied in part on the testimony of James Levin. In closing argument, the defense took special time to attack him. He had admitted on cross that at one time in the recent past he had stated that the charges against Rosen were "BS." The defense took some liberties with this slang as it developed the following analogy:

> There was a fellow, every week he took his great-uncle to a restaurant. His uncle loved beef stew, and it was his favorite meal, and it was the nephew's favorite night. And they [went] to a wonderful new restaurant, advertis[ing] the best beef stew in the world. [T]he great-uncle puts his fork into the beef stew when it is served. He tastes it, and the meat is rancid. Now what is he required to do? Poke around and find some beef that's really good, credible, tasteful, or send it all back? And that's what he did: He sent it back.

> And as far as Jim Levin is concerned—I am not trying to be cute; I am trying to illustrate a point—he should be sent all the way back home. You should believe nothing of what he said. And instead of saying BS

for what he said it stood for, I say "BS" to you—beef stew—as far as Mr. Levin is concerned, because his testimony totally lacked credibility. Not only did he admittedly cheat the school system in Chicago, defrauded them, inflated bills—but he lied blatantly on the witness stand. He lied about everything he said David said.

He admitted to you—it's like he came here and said, "Hello, I am one of the biggest liars and frauds and cheats in my community. I duped everyone, and now I am going to tell you something, so believe me." It's not because he pled guilty and had a criminal deal with the government that should cause you to be suspicious. It's because, we use the term, the cut of his jib: how he acted and conducted himself on the witness stand and what he said to you about himself. "I am a fraud. Don't believe me."

Notice how this analogy seeks an emotional response from the jury. The key image of the beef stew tale is that of the outraged uncle rejecting a rancid meal. Counsel thus encourages the jurors to reject Levin with a sense of moral disgust. Figurative analogies that arouse visceral responses are likely to stick in jurors' memories.

Rhetorical Questions
Like a figurative analogy, a rhetorical question can help engage listeners and give each one the independence to reach his or her own conclusion. Consider this rhetorical question used by the *Rosen* defense in closing argument:

I commented about the role of Peter Paul and Aaron Tonken, and I told you they aren't here, and you know that as well as I do. You saw the video. You have heard the evidence about where they live now, what they are. I wonder why they didn't call them?

The defense desired the jury to conclude that the government should have called the witnesses but did not because the witnesses would not have helped the prosecution.

Here is a second example concerning the event planner and prosecution witness Bretta Nock: "Do you think that when the agents visited Bretta Nock she had any concerns about herself? Do you think that, based on the evidence, Bretta Nock had any issue to deal with?"

One of the defense's key assertions was that Nock was responsible for giving Rosen accurate cost figures, and that she failed him in this regard. Thus, when the government interviewed her so many times, she would render testimony to protect herself.

Rhetorical questions such as these help make the jurors feel that they are thinking for themselves and arriving at conclusions independently. In planning a rhetorical question, be sure it does not highlight a weakness in your own case or raise issues that you did not intend to address. In other words, don't structure a rhetorical question so that opposing counsel can answer it in a way that is consistent with his or her case. The thought-provoking rhetorical question must be used carefully to invoke the conclusion you desire.

Nonverbal Communication

Perhaps no aspect of your closing argument influences your delivery and overall ethos more than nonverbal communication. How you dress, even the color of your clothes, use of eye contact, variations in the tone and volume of your voice, and use of the space can have a huge impact on the audience.

In the closing argument, strive to match nonverbal cues with your message. Nothing can be more disconcerting to a client, judge, or jury than an advocate who cracks a smile or rolls his eyes when his argument should be deadly serious. Similarly, if you argue passionately for your cause but the jury observes body language conveying hostility between you and your client, the perceived discrepancy will greatly diminish your appeal.

Your client's body language also matters. An apocryphal trial tale illustrates how subtle nonverbal cues can influence a jury. A trial lawyer during closing argument passionately argues reasonable doubt in a murder case: "Ladies and gentlemen, you must have reasonable doubt. The state has not even produced the body—no corpus delicti as the saying goes. As a matter of fact, in 30 seconds the so-called decedent will walk right through the courtroom door." Counsel then looks in the direction of the doors and glances at his watch. After the passage of 30 seconds, he says: "Well, you looked, and that proves you have reasonable doubt." The jury then deliberates and promptly returns a verdict of guilty. Stunned and on the verge of tears, the defense attorney asks the jury: "How could you not acquit on the basis of reasonable doubt? All of you looked at the doors." The foreman responded: "Yes, this is true. We all looked, even you did, but your client did not."

Diction

As you present your closing argument, rely on vivid language that most powerfully and effectively communicates the message you want your listeners to receive. Do you want to characterize the event as an automobile accident or an automobile collision? In general, the Harry Truman approach of plain speaking is advisable.

Sometimes lawyers will attempt to sabotage words used by the opposing side. In the opening statement in the *Rosen* case, the defense called Aaron Tonken and Peter Paul "concealers," saying they concealed the true costs of the event from the defendant. In closing, the prosecutor turned the word against Rosen: "Ladies and gentlemen, the evidence is overwhelming. David Rosen is the true concealer in this case."

The prosecution's language with regard to the jury was highly respectful. He repeatedly referred to them as "ladies and gentlemen," and was always using the phrase, "I submit to you" as he made his assertions. This stylistic decision helped convey to the jurors the seriousness of their task and projected high respect for the rule of law. By contrast, the defense emphasized the human and emotional and relied on a more folksy approach: "And then you have to ask yourself, wearing the hat of common sense, well, maybe he made a mistake. Maybe he was rushing around. Maybe it happened. But does it look from the evidence or the facts there that he intended to do it?"

An overstylized performance can be just as damning as a dull one. Shakespeare knew this well. Before your next foray on the stage of justice, consider Hamlet's wise counsel to the Players:

Speak the speech, I pray you, as I pronounced it to you, trippingly on the tongue; but if you mouth it, as many of our players do, I had as lief the town-crier spoke my lines. Nor do not saw the air too much with your hand, thus; but use all gently, for in the very torrent, tempest, and (as I may say) whirlwind of your passion, you must acquire and beget a temperance that may give it smoothness. Oh, it offends me to the soul to hear a robustious periwig-pated fellow tear a passion to tatters, to very rags, to split the ears of the groundlings, who for the most part are capable of nothing but inexplicable dumb shows and noise. I would have such a fellow whipped for o'erdoing. Termagant. It out-herods Herod. Pray you, avoid it.[2]

GENERAL RULES

The law on closing provides wide latitude for delivery of the closing argument, but limitations apply. Here are some cardinal rules.

You must confine your argument to the facts of the case and reasonable inferences from the evidence. For example, you cannot tell the jury what a nonwitness might have said on the stand but you can make inferences about his or her absence from the trial. Hence, in closing arguments in the *Rosen* case, neither prosecutor nor defense counsel inferred what Peter Paul or Aaron Tonken would have testified since neither man was called as a witness. The defense, however, inferred that the government should have called the men as witnesses but did not because they would not have helped the prosecution:

> I commented about the role of Peter Paul and Aaron Tonken, and I told you they aren't here, and you know that as well as I do. You saw the video. You have heard the evidence about where they live now, what they are. I wonder why they didn't call them?

Similarly, you may not refer to excluded evidence or facts not established. For example, Reggie, a prosecution witness, had worn a "wire" and covertly taped a conversation with Rosen on behalf of the

---

2. WILLIAM SHAKESPEARE, HAMLET act 3, sc. 2.

government. This fact was in evidence, but the tape was not. Rosen's defense counsel stated to the jury in closing argument: "I would have liked to introduce the wiretap to you, but it was prohibited by the Rules of Evidence." The prosecution objected, and the judge properly sustained the objection, telling counsel to refrain from comment on evidentiary rulings. Had the defense referred to the wiretap without the matter having been in evidence, the mistake of the defense would have been far more serious.

Another rule prohibits you from misstating the evidence. Though this rule may be self-evident, breaking it is easy to do when you are caught up in the exuberance of persuasion. When your opponents object on the basis that you are misstating the evidence, the court may caution the jury that it is entitled to use its recollection of the facts and not accept counsel's rendition. Consider the following colloquy from the defense's closing argument in the *Rosen* case:

> I asked Mr. Reggie in court about an incident of impersonating a police officer and asked if he put this light on the top of his car, and what did he say? He was a commissioner himself of police.

The prosecutor objected, and the court instructed the jury:

> [L]adies and gentlemen . . . as I instructed you in the jury instructions, if there is a different recollection you have, yours controls. Lawyers are expected to account for the evidence in a fair-minded way and [are entitled] to draw reasonable inferences from that. You will be the judges of just what he said and whether he said what counsel has just referred to.

This kind of slip damages an advocate's ethos. The ease with which one can misstate or mischaracterize evidence reinforces how important it is to truly master the evidence, to internalize it to the point where mistakes are unlikely.

Any personal attacks during closing argument should be calibrated to the specific situation and individual. Beware of petty or brazen insults, particularly in civil disputes. Calling a defendant a "pig" for wanting more alimony, for instance, could turn off many jurors. Though closing argument is often the place where you want to express forcefully your views of a particular individual, you must maintain control and speak with integrity and professionalism.

Speaking of professionalism, you may never personally attack opposing counsel. For example, you cannot suggest that "counsel should be ashamed of his client" or "ashamed of himself." You would be better served by complimenting opposing counsel on presenting his or her views well before carefully dismantling his or her case. You cannot appeal to passion or prejudice that is not based on the evidence. To do so would be in bad taste. It would also precipitate a sustainable objection.

As you strive to persuade the jurors to see the case through your eyes, you may be tempted to say something like this: "Put yourself in this man's shoes! How would you feel if you were suddenly accused of a crime you did not commit?" But such statements, often referred to as "golden rule arguments," are prohibited. You cannot ask the jurors to put themselves in the place of any of the parties to the case. You are also prohibited from calling a juror by name. In closing argument, you often want to connect in a powerful way with the jurors, but rules such as these force you to find more inventive ways of doing so.

Furthermore, you may not directly express your personal belief or opinion during closing argument. In criminal cases, the ABA Standards for Criminal Justice and the Model Rules of Professional Responsibility provide that neither the prosecutor nor the defense counsel should express personal belief about the truth or falsity of testimony, or about the guilt of the defendant. That does not mean you cannot impress upon jurors that you feel very strongly about your case. It is often merely a matter of semantics and delivery. Instead of stating, "I believe the evidence proves guilt," state, "The evidence shows . . . ," and do so in such a way that it communicates your personal conviction. You may also vouch for the credibility of witnesses without explicitly injecting your personal opinion. For example: "You saw Rosen on the witness stand and listened to his testimony. . . . You observed his demeanor. You could see he was telling the truth."

You are also permitted to argue the law, particularly the law upon which the judge instructs the jury regarding burdens of proof. However, whether you can read or recite general law to the jury is not uniformly agreed upon. When in doubt, the best practice is to seek advance court approval. In the *Rosen* case, defense counsel stated during closing:

> But my job is not to prove to you David [Rosen]'s innocence, although the evidence cries out for that. I want to invite your attention to another instruction of the judge's, and that is about reasonable doubt. There is no question that the government has the burden of proving its case beyond a reasonable doubt.

In criminal cases, reasonable doubt is strictly defined. Therefore, you may not be able to explain the meaning of doubt as you would wish. Many courts prohibit arguing "reasonable doubt to a moral certainty." Some courts will not allow counsel to define reasonable doubt at all, but only permit repeating the judge's definition recited in the jury instructions. Most courts, however, will permit counsel to discuss reasonable doubt as it relates to their case as long as they do not attempt to define it.

In civil cases if you are arguing for damages, know whether the law in your jurisdiction allows a per diem argument. This type of argument presents a method of calculating damages for pain and suffering based on a specific dollar amount per day, month, or year. The jury is asked to consider what one might pay to be free from pain for a day and use that amount of money as a basis to calculate the plaintiff experiencing pain and suffering over an extended period of time.

For example, in the *Maffei* case, counsel for the plaintiff argued as follows:

> So I ask you to consider the total of $684,382 as the compensatory damages for Mrs. Maffei based upon what happened to her husband.

There's another category of damages, which we call noneconomic damages. And you have within your discretion to award for emotional distress, pain, and suffering.

And you can and should consider Mrs. Maffei's mental anguish, emotional pain and suffering, loss of society, loss of companionship, loss of marital care, loss of attention, loss of advice or counsel.

That number can be as high as a trillion, which would be ridiculous, or it can be as low as a zero, which I suggest to you would also be ridiculous. Somewhere in between is the proper amount.

I am not going to suggest to you a particular figure. That is within your discretion. Because in your role as a jury you, in a sense, wear an invisible robe because you're the judge of this case.

However, I'm going to suggest to you as follows, that if you were to examine her pain and suffering every day and consider, if some people go to a dentist for root canal work, they may pay seventy-five dollars for a day to be free of pain. Everyone is different.

But you can understand that if one would pay seventy-five dollars a day to be free from pain and Mrs. Maffei's mental anguish continues day by day by day, week by week by week, that you might want to consider the example I just presented to you as a frame of reference for rendering to her an adequate award for her pain and suffering. And you should also consider that Ms. Maffei said to you very candidly, she feels she is on the upswing. And that's good.

So in terms of a specific dollar amount that you should give for her emotional suffering, use your discretion wisely to render a fair award. You are the judges, you are the jury. And I respectfully suggest to do what is right and what's fair, to give Mrs. Maffei an adequate award for the loss of her husband.

Also I also remind you that Mr. Maffei himself cannot speak to you. But his wife is here to speak for him. He suffered as well, pain and suffering. And he is entitled too. He had a horrible day; he's no longer here. And we're talking about someone's life, someone who deserved your full and careful attention, as you are giving it.

You may and should, when appropriate, use demonstrative aids to advance your argument. As discussed in Chapter 2 on opening statements, visual aids are often integral to a winning argument. This is especially true with complex subject matter that can be easily understood when mapped out visually. At the conclusion of *U.S. v. Rosen*, which revolved around various details about specific expenditures, defense counsel relied upon budget documents presented to the jury with an ELMO projector. Similarly, you may want to refer to the verdict form and review it for the jury and argue how the facts of the case apply to the instructions. Show the verdict form to the jury on the projector as you present your explanation.

These and other rules pertaining to the closing argument should be kept in mind when you plan your presentation. In your final words to the jury, you want your ethos to continue to rise. Objections from opposing counsel and judges will throw you off your stride and possibly diminish the jurors' view of your case.

ARRANGEMENT

When planning your closing, arrangement of your points is key. Because we remember best what we hear first and last, the closing argument, like the opening statement, should be delivered with an impressive introduction and conclusion and with a strong grasp of tone, style, and language. Use the same principles in developing your closing argument as you did in your opening statement.

While there are many ways to structure closing arguments, every closing must have a beginning, a middle, and an end. This arrangement can be augmented as follows: introduction, where you capture attention and restate the theme; argument, encompassing: assertion (where you state a major proposition or claim), presentation (where you justify assertions with evidence, logic, and emotion, as well as refute opposing points), and conclusion; and a peroration.

Introduction

The introduction of your closing argument should make a powerful impression on the jury. Here is the time to reorient the jury to your theme and reestablish shared values. Just as with the opening statement, the first five minutes of the closing argument are crucial. Do your best to capture the attention of the jury from the very first words.

There are a number of ways to begin. You can leap into the main point of your case without a buildup. For example: "In this case an innocent man who loved his wife dearly is now falsely accused of hiring someone to kill his wife. Let me tell you about Donald Patapsco." You could also begin by asking a question or by telling a story. The use of humor and suspense can help you captivate your audience. However you choose to begin, speak with an engaging, personable style that feels comfortable to you.

If you are speaking second, a reference to the previous speaker may be a helpful transition, and you may need to "break the spell" created by the first speaker. A dramatic statement, a compelling question, or an appeal to the listener's sense of importance can help shift attention to your case. Here are excerpts from the government's and the defense's introductions in their closing arguments in *Rosen*. Observe that the prosecutor, in describing what the case is about, seeks to raise the stakes beyond Rosen's alleged wrongdoing:

> However you choose to begin, speak with an engaging, personable style that feels comfortable to you.

Thank you, Your Honor, counsel. Ladies and gentlemen, let me start by thanking you all for your service. You sat through a lot to get you to this stage, and if you can believe it, my job now is to try and make things a little simpler for you.

So, ladies and gentlemen, let me just tell you that this case is about one thing: This case is about the public's right to know. The case is about the public's right to know who is paying how much to their elected officials.

The case is about the public's right to know how much Peter Paul is paying to a national campaign. The case is about the public's right to know how much Aaron Tonken is paying to a national campaign finance director.

Ladies and gentlemen, this case is about the public's right to know the truth, and the defendant, David Rosen's, continued and intentional obstruction of that public right.

And what is this case not about? Well, the case is not about sloppy or negligent record-keeping. The evidence is clear that David Rosen knew what was and what wasn't being reported to Whitney Burns, and he knew he was feeding specific lies to Whitney Burns.

The case is also not about anybody's responsibilities except the defendant's. All the attempts to blame the contributor is a transparent dodge, and the evidence shows that all of the talk of Peter Paul and Aaron Tonken and Bretta Nock concealing is without any support in the evidence.

Next, the case is not about exact numbers, because you don't have to know whether this cost $1.1 million or $1.2 million to know that it was a lot more than half a million, and you don't have to know the exact number to know that any number of types of costs were left out, never reported as required.

So, finally, ladies and gentlemen, despite all the difficult testimony that you heard and that you sat very patiently through, let me relieve you and say this case is not about benefits. This case is not about whether the campaign benefited from the defendant's lies. The question of benefits in this case is only one of motive. And, ladies and gentlemen, the government does not have to prove motive to you.

The question of benefits is not part of the government's proof, and it's not something that you need to wrestle with to determine that David Rosen is guilty beyond a reasonable doubt of causing Whitney Burns's reports to be false.

I'll say it again: Motive is not an element of the government's case. We don't have to prove any benefit to the campaign or anyone. But motive is helpful to understanding the big picture, and the bottom line is that the evidence shows and the defendant finally admitted on cross-examination that there were clear potential benefits to Hillary Clinton's campaign for underreporting soft money in-kind contributions. But, still, that's not what this case is about.

And so, ladies and gentlemen, since we've discussed what the case is not about, let's get back to what it is, and let's talk about the story that the evidence told throughout the case.

And we're going to do that by asking three questions: First, what did the defendant do? Second, why did he do it? Third, why does it matter?

First we'll talk about what the defendant did, what were the lies; and after that we'll talk briefly about why he did it, the motives that help you understand the bigger picture.

And, finally, we'll talk about why all of this matters. How did it affect the very function and role of the Federal Election Commission? And that's when we'll come back to the public's right to know. What did he do? Why did he do it? Why does it matter?

This is a strong, concise, and effective introduction. The prosecutor grabs the jurors' attention by lifting the case high above the nitty-gritty details. In saying that the case is about the public's right to know, he appeals to the jurors' patriotism and sense of civic duty. They are being called upon now to protect something precious to the republic, and that is no small thing. Also notable is the way the prosecutor adroitly anticipates the opponent's line of attack. He attempts to immunize his case by repeating that the case is not about motive, which is precisely the issue the defense will soon seize at the beginning of its closing argument. Finally, the prosecutor does a fine job of outlining the story he is about to tell, relying on three central questions. The use of questions engages the jurors in the process and acknowledges that they, too, are thinking through these problems.

Like the prosecutor, the defense begins by thanking the jurors for their service. (This is a common practice, though a judge will sometimes instruct counsel not to thank the jury, reserving that pleasure for the court.) Unlike the prosecution, the defense turns this expression of gratitude into an elaborate appeal to their sense of patriotism and civic duty, commenting on their duty to protect the innocent from oppression:

> May it please the court, members of the jury, good afternoon. As you know, I represent David Rosen, and I want to echo the words of Judge Matz and the prosecutor about thanking you for your patience. Serving on a jury is one of the most important public services any citizen can give. The right to trial by jury is so precious to our society, it's been mentioned no less than four times in the text of the United States Constitution.

> We have a jury of citizens in criminal trials to prevent oppression by government officials. And because we have citizens, such as you, serving on juries as the last check and balance in government, the government cannot be unrestrained in its power over all of us. It's very, very vital that we preserve trial by jury, and that's why everyone thanks you and that's why we stand when you come and go, out of respect for you and the vital role that the citizen plays in cases just like this.

> Now, in a short time you will take this case with you to the jury room. You have been sitting here for about three weeks in what, up until now,

has been a silent role in a somewhat unique criminal trial. Soon, you will render a verdict which will be fair, just, and equitable, and it's my purpose at this time, to the extent the court allows me, to proceed to review with you the salient materials of evidence superimposed by the instructions that the judge has given.

And first I ask you this; what is the issue in this case that you, the jury, will decide?

Is David Rosen charged with stealing money that belongs to others? No.

Is he charged with inflicting physical harm or violence? No.

Is he charged with causing innocent people to suffer economically or lose their jobs? No.

As the judge has instructed you, he is charged with causing false information to be filed before the Federal Election Commission. He has been charged with willfully, knowingly, and deliberately making false statements and that he had knowledge of these statements and intended to do it.

In other words, he sat down one day and said, "Okay, I am 33 years old. I have a very important job. I am afraid that I could get fired and, let's see, I think I'll risk my whole career, my family, and jeopardize everything. I'm going to lie. I am intentionally going to deceive people," so for what? He's scared for his job?

First of all, Mr. Ickes came from Washington to tell you he had no reason to be. Secondly, even if he were, many people sometimes are concerned for this or that. There is no evidence here that he had such a concern.

So when you go to the jury room, do put the hat of common sense on and think about what it is, having met this gentleman who is courageous, who is truthful, who has suffered for years with this sword of Damocles over his head. And he comes to trial and he takes the witness stand, and he doesn't have to do that. And I told you in opening statement he would answer every question posed to him, and he did, and you could see the cut of his jib. . . . [T]he government says don't buy what he is selling. I say buy it lock, stock, and barrel, because what he is not selling but advocating is the truth, the whole truth, the simple truth, and nothing but the truth. And imagine, imagine we are talking about an event that occurred August the 12th of 2000. Where were you? Where were we on that date? Who did we talk to a week before? What meetings did we attend? Oh, Mr. Madden, who didn't take notes and who came forth and said he had a meeting, "Well, gee, do you remember the day of the meeting." "No." Recollections do differ.

And I say this to you: When you evaluate the evidence, there is a little story that I once heard, and I think it's applicable. There was a lawyer who said to a friend of his, who was a jurist, "You know, I've got a tough case tomorrow. It's not before you. We're friends. Give me some advice. How do I proceed if the facts are against me?" The judge said, "Well, that's easy, argue the law." "Well," he said, "Suppose the law is against me." The judge said, "That's easy, argue the facts." And then the lawyer said, "Well, what if the law and the facts are against me?" And the judge said, "Well, then you pound the table." And in the closing argument we have heard [from the prosecution], it was table-pounding.

When the prosecutor stands up for closing argument, he states that the case is about the public's right to know. The defense seeks to deflate this balloon by zeroing in on the specific charge, invoking as he does so the judge's instructions. Such rephrasing of the central question is the main purpose of your introduction. As in politics, who wins or loses the argument is often a matter of who best frames it.

Also of note in the above passage is the use of sarcasm. In focusing on the question of motive, a weak point in the government's case, counsel ridicules the proposition the jurors are being asked to accept—that Rosen, who had nothing to gain by lying, nevertheless did so, placing his livelihood and reputation at risk. Counsel then segues into the other main pillar of its case: the defendant's credibility and character, as presented during direct examination. In doing so, the attorney slips into the royal "we," seeking to place himself and the jurors in the same figurative "boat" as they consider the evidence together. Encouraging this fictive partnership can be helpful, particularly in a conversational closing argument such as this one.

Note, however, that defense counsel's introduction lacks a helpful road map such as that provided by the prosecution at the close of its introduction. Letting the listeners know where you intend to take them focuses their attention and helps them mentally organize the disparate facts according to the argumentative blueprint you've designed. While the prosecution's closing argument was orderly, precise, and professional in tone, the defense's closing was effusive, emotional, associative, and colloquial. Valuable lessons can be taken from both approaches.

The Maffei Case

Let's examine how counsel in the civil case introduced their closing arguments. You will recall that this medical malpractice suit led to a complex trial involving many technicalities. The challenge facing the lawyers at closing, then, was to distill all the evidence into a persuasive argument without getting bogged down in specialized language.

Here is how the plaintiff's counsel began his closing:

MR. SANDLER: May it please the Court, ladies and gentlemen of the jury, you have been sitting here over a week, actually a full week, in which you have been in a very silent mode. You have been patiently listening, working with the schedules, taking it all in, thinking to yourself what this is all about.

And now that role will change. You will soon retire to your jury room to look at the evidence, the documents. You can talk amongst yourselves and come to a just and fair verdict. That will happen very shortly.

On behalf of the lawyers, it's important to thank you. Because the service that you perform when you sacrifice your own daily schedules to sit as judges of your fellow men and women, as jurors, it is an honor and it's a privilege; it's also one that is a unique feature of our country. So we thank you for your attention.

It's my purpose during this allotted time for closing argument to highlight for you the evidence that will support the claim of the plaintiffs. I will superimpose on the evidence some of my interpretations of what the evidence brings to bear.

And I think we should begin straightaway.

What is this case about? What were the issues? What are they?

When I came before you in opening statement, I told you that I would prove to you not that Dr. Smedley was a bad person, but that she made a mistake and the mistake cost the life of a dear fellow.

And I suggested to you that the evidence would demonstrate that but for an x-ray Mr. Maffei would be alive today. And I also proved that.

And I will explain how, so that you can be comfortable that the evidence is square.

The plaintiff's counsel here thanks the jurors in a rather somber tone, given that the case concerns the death of a patient. The introduction also anticipates an appeal from the defense regarding the doctor's character, her decency, and professionalism. By insisting that the case wasn't about whether she was "a bad person," plaintiff's counsel attempted to strip this appeal of its persuasive force.

Here is how defense counsel began his closing argument:

MR. SHAW: Thank you.

May it please the Court. Good morning, ladies and gentlemen.

This is my last chance to talk with you. As you've heard, the plaintiffs have the burden of proof in this case, so they go on first in their opening, they go first in presenting their evidence, and they go first and they have a chance to go after me in their closing.

So I want to take this opportunity, as did Mr. Sandler, to thank you very much for your service in this case. All of the attorneys and the parties are very appreciative for your service.

Mr. Sandler mentioned about the significance and the uniqueness of a jury trial in this country.

And I read a statistic somewhere that something like 90 percent of all jury trials in the world are held in the United States of America.

It's a good system. Realize, as Mr. Sandler said, you have common sense and you bring it to bear in your judgment of your peers. So we certainly thank you for your time that you devoted. One of the highest civic duties and responsibilities second to, I guess, enlisting in the military service, is to serve on a jury. So we thank you very much.

As you heard, this case is important to both sides. It's important to Mrs. Maffei but it's also very important to Dr. Smedley. There will be a lot of things that we are going to dispute that you heard from Mr. Sandler about what the evidence showed in this case. I'm not going to revisit every one of those issues, but I'm going to highlight some of which we do dispute and which we believe the judgment should be in favor of Dr. Smedley.

But one thing we don't dispute, one of the things nobody disputes is the tragic death of Mr. Maffei. We certainly recognize the compassion and sympathy that you have for her and that we have and certainly Dr. Smedley has.

You heard Dr. Smedley tell you that by that time, she'd seen hundreds of patients through the years since that time when she saw Mr. Maffei, and his presentation was not at all consistent with one who is going to leave the emergency department and die 17 hours later, that she has a clear recollection of what happened that night.

And certainly she felt sympathy and compassion and she felt the tragedy of Mr. Maffei's death and of what Mrs. Maffei has experienced.

So if your sole duty in this case was to rely on just sympathy and compassion and base your decision, then obviously we wouldn't be here. But as his Honor has instructed you, you have to treat everyone fairly and impartially.

And I'd like to briefly read to you from the jury instructions, one of the jury instructions that Judge Cahill read to you. And it's entitled "Impartiality and Consideration."

You must consider and decide this case fairly and impartially. You can't base your decision or be prejudiced by a person's race, color, religious, political, or social views, wealth or poverty. And the same is true as to prejudice for or against and sympathy for any party.

So as hard as it may be, you have to try to put aside your compassion and sympathy for Mrs. Maffei, which we all certainly have. So the critical issue then is: Was there medical malpractice in this case?

Do you find that the defendant, Angela D. Smedley, M.D., breached the standard of medical care in her care and treatment of Richard Paul Maffei?

In other words: Did Dr. Smedley fail to act as a reasonably competent medical physician in emergency medicine?

And we believe the evidence has shown that Dr. Smedley did act appropriately and she did care properly for Mr. Maffei.

And it's obvious from that definition just because there is a tragic out-come doesn't mean that there's been malpractice. And bad results can occur even with good care.

We've all heard that expression, "Bad things can happen to good peo-ple." That's what happened here. Something bad happened, a tragedy happened.

But there was no medical malpractice.

Because the plaintiffs have the burden of proof, if for some reason you can't make up your mind, if the weight is even in your mind, because plaintiff has the burden, then you must find for Dr. Smedley.

But we believe that plaintiffs have failed to meet their burden of proof and the evidence is on the side of Dr. Smedley.

Observe that the defense counsel, after thanking the jury, also attempts to defuse his adversary's emotional appeal. The jury, he says, must put aside their sympathy for the widow. This is a critical element in many emo-tionally charged disputes; one or both sides often need to remind jurors to disregard sympathies for a victim or unfortunate party.

The closing arguments in the *Oregon* case were tailored to the judge, not to a jury. The introductions were briefer and to the point. Unlike a jury trial, the judge does not interrupt with questions for the benefit of the jury. In *Oregon* the judge interrupted with comments at the inception of the argument with good news for the defendant Oregon. She was not going to order Oregon to dig up the parking lot and repave it:

THE COURT: All right.

MR. SANDLER: Thank you, Your Honor. I represent the Oregon Grille LLC.

And the evidence in this case must be focused in terms of the declaratory judgment act. It would be my request that the court adhere to the strict ruling of declaratory judgment. And if there is a declaratory judgment made, that the judgment just be a declaratory judgment and that relief be not granted because there's no proper relief requested.

Under the declaratory judgment act, if there's a particular action that is sought, then that's subject to petition. And then there are issues that relate to whether or not someone should be commanded to do something or not.

The purpose of the declaratory judgment at this stage is for declaration. That's our view. And the fact that someone asks for something and is mixed in with the "Wherefore" clause doesn't mean that that's an injunction.

And Your Honor is well familiar with the rules of injunction.

THE COURT: Well, I think I've made it clear, the plaintiffs in this, in count four, they asked only that with respect to removing the paving that the Oregon Grille do it.

I'm not persuaded there is any basis on which to order the Oregon Grille to remove the paving.

MR. SANDLER: Thank you.

THE COURT: I do not think that the "grant such other and further relief" would extend to something as substantive as a request that the county remove it.

But right now what they have before me is enter an order that Oregon shall remove all the paving.

That's injunctive relief. That is mandamus relief. That is not a declaration. And I don't think that is what the declaratory judgment contemplates.

MR. SANDLER: Yes. That's my point.

THE COURT: The declaratory judgment, all I can do is declare the rights of the parties.

MR. SANDLER: Exactly, Your Honor. Now, my next point, in four minutes, is this.

Argument

Here is the time to use the evidence and law to support your theme and request a verdict in your favor. Consider dividing each section of your argument into assertion, presentation, and conclusion. You may repeat this pattern several times within the main body of your argument.

First, assert the issues or themes of your case and then speak to the evidence and exhibits that support them. Build upon the claim, weaving together testimony and exhibits in a compelling fashion, until you reach a forceful conclusion for each assertion. When you conclude, try to engage the jurors by personally requesting that they act in accordance with the evidence you have presented.

> Consider dividing each section of your argument into assertion, presentation, and conclusion. You may repeat this pattern several times within the main body of your argument.

As you make your points, always take time to refute the evidence marshaled against you by your opponent. Explain why the contrary evidence is unpersuasive. When appropriate, pause to read passages of striking testimony. If you have the benefit of daily transcripts, you can go so far as to present testimony to the jury on a PowerPoint slide. Remember to make clear connections between your specific claims and the documents and exhibits you show to the jury. Do not present document after document without a guiding purpose. Also, avoid allowing jurors to read unnecessary text. You want their undivided attention; don't let unhelpful exhibits and visual aids steal the show.

By organizing the main body of your closing argument into repeated patterns of assertion-presentation-conclusion, you can better lead the jurors down a clear path to a firm decision in your favor. Remember, the goal of closing argument is to unify disparate information into a cohesive understanding of the facts in play. You cannot do that without a framework on which to build.

Like many criminal cases, *U.S. v. Rosen* boiled down to credibility: Whom would the jury believe? The prosecution wanted the jury to believe the testimony of its witnesses but to distrust David Rosen. Defense counsel wanted the jury to believe Rosen and to doubt the assertions of the government's witnesses. In its closing argument, the prosecution showed great facility in organizing its argument, repeating the pattern of assertion-presentation-conclusion several times. Here is an excerpt, with the elements noted:

The Assertion

There is no doubt that David Rosen knowingly caused those reports to be false in two different ways; first, he flat-out lied to Whitney Burns; second, he, himself was the concealer of numerous items he knew were required to be reported. He either witnessed these items himself or he incurred these items himself, and he knew that they never were reported.

The Presentation

And ladies and gentlemen, two ways—the direct lies and the concealing—and we'd submit that the evidence on each of these standing alone is sufficient to convict David Rosen of these crimes.

But first David Rosen lied to Whitney Burns at least three different times, each time knowingly and intentionally feeding more and more false information, each time relying on and layering and buttressing the earlier lies.

The first lie David Rosen fed to Whitney Burns is the lie known to you as Exhibit 20. Exhibit 20 is the budget that evidence establishes David Rosen created and David Rosen sent to Whitney Burns.

Of all of that, David Rosen admits discussing this budget and confirming for Whitney Burns that it is accurate, and that's a significant piece of the evidence.

The Conclusion

So just based on that conversation, when he confirmed the numbers, if you believe all the evidence that David Rosen knew the numbers were false, then that conversation alone, we would submit, is enough to find David Rosen guilty.

In response to the prosecution's assertion that the evidence pointed to Rosen's guilt, defense counsel, in its closing argument, had to galvanize the jurors' sentiments against the government's key witnesses. One of these was Reggie, the convicted felon who, before the indictment, had signed a plea bargain with the government and strapped himself with a wire before having dinner with Rosen. But the prosecution had not introduced the taped conversation into evidence, relying instead on Reggie's oral testimony, which was unfavorable to the defendant. Defense counsel's implicit assertion against Reggie, then, was that he could not be believed. The claim relied not only on his criminal past, but on the more dramatic cross-examination testimony:

The Assertion

Let's go to Mr. Ray Reggie, if we could for a minute, another star witness. Now, look, I say that probably Mr. Reggie, based on the evidence, has to be pitied more than censured. No one enjoys being humiliated and acknowledging that they have done wrong but he did: bank fraud, check kiting, lying under oath to me in front of you about his incident of putting the light on the car—

[Here an objection was entered.]

The Presentation

I recall his testimony thusly, in so many words. Question—why he put a light on top of his car if he were not pretending to be a police officer. I recall him stating to me that he had been given the light because he had some honorary officer position. I then probed a little bit further and pointed out to you that, no, indeed he did not have such a commission, but [the light] was given to him by a police officer or a sheriff because he had to guide dignitaries around. I say about Ray Reggie, beef stew. Just send him back.

And I say it's deplorable, based on the evidence in light of what's going on, that this Ray Reggie, a supposed friend of David Rosen's, calls him and says, "Let's have dinner." And he is so low, based on the evidence, that he could crawl under the belly of a snake wearing a top hat, because what he did—folks, ladies and gentlemen, what he did, if you think about it, was masquerade as a friend, come into his domain of privacy, David Rosen['s], and then he secretly recorded. Tick tock, tick tock, tick tock. Looking and probing, looking and probing. And then—and then AWOL, absent without leave. Where's the tape? Bring it forth, instead of innuendo and hyperbole.

The Conclusion

This man [Rosen], he brought it forth. I don't want to be hyperbolic either, but I suggest to you, based on the evidence, if this country looks for leaders and heroes, there is one, with the courage to take the witness stand in a case like this and to tell the truth.

Now, all of this could have been done much more briefly. The defense could have said: "Don't believe this man. He's a low-life crook, and he tricked his friend, as the evidence shows." But dramatizing a point makes it more memorable. The colorful language, the speaker's outrage, and the sense of betrayal that Rosen must have felt all come into play in illustrating the witness's character. Notice, too, that the conclusion of this segment reaches beyond the question of whether Reggie can be believed. With each claim you make and substantiate, you want to advance your argument and bolster foundational themes. For the defense, the key theme was Rosen's clean-cut credibility versus the lack of credibility among the opposing witnesses.

Peroration

The peroration of the closing argument should be the logical and emotional climax of your argument. Visual aids, the power of understatement, anecdotes, figurative analogies, and other rhetorical techniques can all enhance your emotional appeal as you speak to the jury one last time. Again, the jury remembers best what it hears first and last, so take full advantage of your last words.

Here is how the government concluded its case in *Rosen*:

So, finally, let's talk even more briefly about why all this matters, because it doesn't take a lot of explanation.

His Honor gave you an instruction on materiality, and we'd submit to you that the evidence that the defendant's lies were material to the Federal Election Commission is beyond any doubt. The question of benefit is irrelevant as to whether this crime matters or not, because as the first witness told you . . . one of the functions of the Federal Elections Commission is to be the liaison between the campaign and the public, to be the gatekeeper of the public's right to know who is giving how much to their elected officials.

It's clear from the evidence that soft money in the year 2000 had to be reported for joint fundraisers, and as we've discussed and as you've heard from Whitney Burns, it's crucial to know how much soft money is used at a joint fundraising event to know what to do with the hard money.

And this brings up a second reason that these lies matter, because besides just the public's right to know, the evidence shows clearly that it's part of the FEC's function to monitor these reports, to make decisions about who to look more closely at, what events to scrutinize more closely, what audits to do, and who to request additional information from.

In fact, even in this case, even with the numbers it did report, the FEC ended up inquiring further from the campaign about this event, and you can see that for yourself in Exhibit 43.

So it's obvious that the defendant's underreporting had the ability or potential to affect the decisions or activities of the Federal Election Commission, because, in fact, they did.

Now, getting back to the public's right to know. Let's talk about one last time the defense's constant pointing out in this trial what bad guys Peter Paul and Aaron Tonken are, and that's the best demonstration why it's so important that these reports be accurate.

Aaron Tonken is giving the first lady's national finance director gifts that equal over two months of his take-home salary, and Aaron Tonken is getting invitations to the White House.

Now, there may be nothing at all wrong with that, but our society has made a deal: people can spend big money on campaigns and thereafter gain influence and access, but the public has a right to know what price they're paying. And how does the public find out? The Federal Election Commission makes the information available.

They summarize some of the information, and they make various studies or reports to enhance the public's knowledge to how money is fed to their elected officials. And they rely on what is known as voluntary compliance; they rely on the campaigns themselves; they rely on Whitney Burns, who relies on David Rosen.

Ladies and gentlemen, the very function of the FEC is to monitor how the money is collected and spent, to be the public's guardian. The very function of the FEC is to publish accurate information to the public.

And, ladies and gentlemen, the very function was willfully and knowingly obstructed by the defendant in this case, David Rosen.

And so now I get to thank you again for your patience because this summation is at an end. The government has proven witness after witness, document after document, that David Rosen knew more, much more, than he ever told Whitney Burns; that David Rosen knew that what he did tell Whitney Burns was a lie; and finally, that David Rosen knew that Whitney Burns would use his information to file at least two specific reports of campaign activity with the Federal Election Commission. And he knew the purpose of those reports was for the FEC's review and scrutiny and more importantly to enable the public's right to know of who pays how much to elected officials.

Ladies and gentlemen, when David Rosen was in Los Angeles in the summer of 2000, he began to sell a pack of lies that is still being sold to this day.

We ask you only to examine all of the real evidence in this case, to apply only your common sense and not your sympathies or your passions, and in the end we ask you not to buy what the defendant is selling.

Ladies and gentlemen, we ask you to find David Rosen guilty beyond a reasonable doubt of the crimes charged. Thank you.

And here is how the defense concluded:

I suggest to you that when you return to the jury room you will use your common sense. You will go through the evidence. You will see for yourselves that the government has not proved its case beyond a reasonable doubt. And you will also see, to the contrary, that David

Rosen proved to you by his courageous and truthful testimony that he is innocent and that he did not intend to harm a flea, let alone the FEC.

It would be my request of all of you that when you do go to the jury room, you do one thing that I hope you remember. I cannot come back and speak to you again. I will not have that opportunity. I am prevented. . . . I would ask you to go into the jury room, and if I have missed something here or in the rebuttal the prosecutors say something that I haven't commented on, I ask you to point out to your colleagues in the jury room the evidence that contradicts what the prosecutor said; that I could not do.

Now at this time my burden ends. It goes to you. You, the members of the jury, whose task it is to render a judgment, now receive this case after the rebuttal.

And I conclude by this little tale that I learned long ago about an ancient kingdom where a wise magician was offering great counsel, but there was someone who was jealous and wanted to pull him down. And they went to the king and said, "Look, your magician for so many years has no reason to continue. He is not as smart or wise as you think." So the king said, "What do you mean?" He said, "I am going to devise a test," said the other magician, "and you take a bird in your hand, call him, and you ask him if the bird is living or dead. If he says the bird is living, you crush his little neck, open your hands, and we'll have him. If he says, however, the bird is dead, open your hands. The bird will fly and we will have him."

The day comes, the throngs are there. The drums are beating. And, sure enough, the king says to the wise man what the magician said. The magician looks, thinks very quickly, and says, I am in trouble, because if I say the bird is living and the king just presses the neck, that's it. If I say he is dead and he opens his hands, that's it. So the wise magician simply said, when the king said, "Well, tell me, is this bird living or dead?" He simply said the truth: "The answer is in your hands."

David Rosen's life and this case are now going to be in your hands. I proved based on the evidence what I said at the outset: David Rosen is the victim of other peoples' motives; that he did not intend to cheat or violate any law or rule; that he had no personal gain. He had a system. The system worked every time. It didn't work here, because people concealed or did not give him the information; and that the vagaries of what the prosecution produced with the quality of the testimony doesn't meet the burden of proof. And yet—and yet Mr. Rosen testified and told you that he did not do this; that he would never do this. And even if you want to say, "Well, anybody could say that, why wouldn't he?" Why would he testify? Only to meet you and let you meet him and see the cut of his jib.

Notice again the differences in style illustrated by these two passages. The government's peroration is smooth, meticulous, and precise as it draws a clear line between the alleged wrongdoing and the public's well-being, as embodied by the FEC. The approach is befitting of a prosecutor, who advocates for the people, for law and order, and ostensibly serves a higher purpose. The peroration for the defendant is much more emotional. The figurative analogy of the wise man and the king, familiar to many trial lawyers, leaves the jurors with a sense of profound responsibility. It implies the defendant's vulnerability and innocence.

Peroration in the *Maffei* case

As in *Rosen*, the *Maffei* trial concluded with attorneys tying their case to larger themes about public service. Plaintiff's counsel exhorted the jurors to "send a message" about the importance of taking precautionary x-rays when patients arrive in the hospital with complaints of chest pain. He also implied that any one of the jurors could find themselves in the position of the deceased one day.

All you need is courage and common sense. You have it. We can see how courteous you've been and how attentive you are. And use that common sense.

Let it work for you.

And I beseech you, when you return, return with a verdict for Mrs. Maffei. Give her the justice that she deserves.

No amount of money can bring back her husband.

No verdict in her favor can restore her. Life is precious and it flickers. And we never know—I read in the newspaper just the other day, like you did, that poor actress, she was skiing and felt fine and now she's gone. We never know.

But you're here, I'm here. We can do good. We can also send a message to the community—not an evil message, but a message that these x-rays with chest pain are crucial. It can save lives. You can save lives by telegraphing this message.

The defense counsel, on the other hand, sought to humanize the problem his client, Dr. Smedley, faced when treating the late Mr. Maffei. The analogy he offered the jurors in the peroration of closing argument effectively and memorably clarified the physician's task and so called attention away from the plaintiff's call to "send a message" to the public.

As Dr. Shank explained, there was 800 milliliters of blood found in this pericardial sac. She had the 12-ounce soda can. It was two and a third of the soda cans of blood that backed up into Mr. Maffei's heart. And Mr. Maffei died very suddenly when that happened.

That was not the presentation that Mr. Maffei had when he was in the emergency department.

I was trying to think of an analogy. It's not a great analogy, but I remember working on snow days with my mother on jigsaw puzzles and putting a puzzle together. And a lot of times with a jigsaw puzzle, you know what you are going to put together because you would see on the front cover what the puzzle looked like. Dr. Smedley didn't have even the cover of the puzzle. She had maybe one piece of the puzzle. It was only after Mr. Maffei left the emergency department that a number of the other pieces of the puzzle probably would have come into play and could have been appreciated by an emergency room physician.

It was very early in the dissection, if it was even there, for Dr. Smedley or any reasonably competent physician in the emergency department to make this diagnosis. It was only on the basis of hindsight that the plaintiffs conclude that the case could end otherwise.

Peroration in the Oregon case

The closing argument in a nonjury case that includes peroration may differ from a jury trial argument. As mentioned previously, nonjury closing arguments are characterized by less rhetorical ornaments, are often less emotional and involve, as in the Oregon case, dialogue between Judge and counsel. This give and take sometimes monopolizes the entire closing remarks. That is not to say that judges lack emotion and interest in the dramatic, but appealing to the judge in nonjury cases requires the same exercise of tailoring your argument to the listener and developing a receiver center approach as does arguing to the jury. In Oregon the last words were short and to the point:

> . . . The Point that I was going to spend most of my time on, your Honor has stated that the Court will not impose a burden on anyone, for Oregon Grille LLC to undertake the expense and burden economically of chewing up the lost and putting saw dust or I meant crusher run on that property, because truly there is not one scintilla of evidence, not one scintilla of evidence that it was not done but for the order of the landlord.

> . . . So those are the reasons why we think you should do as follows. First declare that the plaintiffs have not exhausted their remedies under

strict construction of the declaratory judgment act. And the briefs and memos, I will not get into.

Second, you should, if you do declare under count four; your declaration should be simply limited to a declaration of the rights of the parties, as opposed to giving an injunction, a mandatory injunction or order. That should be under a separate proceeding.

And why is that so? I think the declaratory judgment act makes it so because just because the Court declares the rights, it may not enforce the rights for other reasons. There may not be a balance of equity in a certain way. There may be circumstances where the Court exercises discretion because the injunction, if given, would be more deleterious than helpful. There are many reasons.

So that should be the subject of another proceeding. And I hope it's not.

I hope after you declare that Oregon does not have to assume the burden of this repaving, that whatever separate proceeding comes it doesn't involve [Oregon]. Thank you.

These excerpts help illustrate that there is no single proper way to deliver a closing argument. Every attorney is a unique individual. In closing, your persona is on full display. The jurors have closely watched you play your part for hours or days or weeks. They have come to know your quirks, your mannerisms, the tone of your voice. Closing argument is the end of your brief relationship, and you will want to connect with the jurors one last time. To do so you have to remain true not only to your client, the evidence, and the law, but also to yourself. You should not attempt to affect the style of another or pretend to be someone you are not. It is the most prosaic advice of all, but it is often forgotten at the close of a heated trial: Be yourself.

Rebuttal Argument

The government in a criminal case and the plaintiff in a civil case have the burden of proof. Failure to meet that burden spells defeat. Therefore the moving party has the opportunity to have the last word in argument—rebuttal.

This opportunity is important and must not be misconstrued. Its purpose is to confront the arguments against your case, and persuade the jury that your view of the case is correct. Its purpose is not to reargue your case outside of the context of refuting the opposing case.

The art of effective rebuttal argument is in identifying the offending point by the opposition, explaining based on the evidence why it is incorrect, and then stating why your view of the evidence is the proper interpretation.

You may find the rebuttal arguments in the *Rosen* and *Maffei* cases of interest. (Those arguments can be found in Appendixes II and IV, respectively.)

Learning Points for Chapter 9

- Logos and pathos: Logic is critical, but don't forget Cicero: "Mankind makes far more determinations by hatred, or love, or desire, or anger, or grief, or joy, or feelings . . . than from regard to truth, or any settled maxim or principle."[1] Strive to engage the jurors' reason and their emotions.

- Winning arguments is about framing them to your advantage. Use figurative analogies to vividly frame the ultimate decision in a way most helpful to your client.

- Consider in advance your nonverbal communication.

- Avoid legalese or hyperbolic language. Your diction should be clear and vivid.

- Remind yourself of all relevant rules.

- Organize your closing so that it has a clear beginning, middle, and end. Remember that you are telling a story, one that should unify disparate facts and acknowledge jurors' doubts or confusions.

---

1. CICERO, *supra* note 1.

CHAPTER 10

CLOSING ARGUMENT—A VIEW FROM THE BENCH

By the Hon. Marvin E. Aspen, United States District Judge, United States District Court for the Northern District of Illinois

In my view, a closing argument is not a science. It is an art form, an opportunity for the creative juices of the advocate to flow and shine, which need not be too overly circumscribed by an extensive laundry list of absolute "dos and don'ts." The reasons for this observation are fairly obvious: No two trials are the same. Each fact situation and applicable set of laws varies from case to case. Juries in every trial are different in composition, as are the respective credibilities of the witnesses and the nuanced degrees of persuasiveness of the evidence. Each lawyer has different and unique strengths and weaknesses of persona and presence. All of these variables must be considered by the skillful lawyer in the planning and preparation of a closing argument.

Keeping this caveat in mind, there are nevertheless certain general approaches to preparing a closing that are useful. Here are a few of these suggestions offered from the perspective of a judicial observer. They have been divided into two parts: those dealing with the organization of the closing and others relating to the lawyer's delivery. I will also illustrate some of these suggestions with examples from the effective closing arguments of the lawyers in the *Rosen* case.

ORGANIZATION—AN OPPORTUNITY OFTEN LOST

You will never have the opportunity to hold the jury in more rapt attention than you will during the opening minutes of your closing argument—especially when the argument is planned to be a relatively lengthy one. Too many lawyers squander this golden opportunity with boilerplate ritual—that is, effusive thank yous, mini-histories of and praise for the jury system, and similar offerings of truncated civics lessons. For example, consider the introductions of the government and defense in the *Rosen* case. The government thanks the judge, opposing counsel, and the jury in two short sentences and then proceeds to the substance of the case. The defense, however, espouses the role of juries in society: "The right to trial by jury is so precious to our society, it's been mentioned no less than four times in the text of the United States Constitution."

It is certainly appropriate to thank the jurors for their service and to let them know how important it is. (Especially when the judge and your opponents may have already done so, as you will not wish to appear ungracious.) But do it quickly and then get on to the substance of your argument.

An Effective Start

If you can find a way to get the jurors interested and invested during the first minutes, you will have a much better chance of retaining their attention during the full course of your closing. Use these opening minutes to whet their appetites with a concise preview of your full argument: the issues you will be discussing, your theory of the case, any key facts, and a short blueprint of how you will be organizing the full argument. The government does this effectively in the *Rosen* case by presenting a general theme of the case, "the public's right to know," and then explaining that the case boils down to three questions: "[F]irst, what did the defendant do? Second, why did he do it? Third, why does it matter?" The defense takes a different but equally useful approach, attempting to grab the jury's attention and minimize the severity of the allegations by injecting some perspective. Counsel asks the jury:

What is the issue in this case that you, the jury, will decide?

Is David Rosen charged with stealing money that belongs to others? No.

Is he charged with reaping profits to which he is not entitled? No.

Is he charged with inflicting physical harm or violence? No.

Is he charged with causing innocent people to suffer economically or lose their jobs? No.

Not only will the jurors' interest be piqued if they are given an organizational framework, but they will be better prepared to follow your argument—and eventually to review all the evidence in the context of your theory and blueprint of the case.

The Promises

Both your opening statement and that of your opponent should be viewed as promises made at the beginning of the case that the evidence will establish certain facts and inferences favorable to their respective sides. So the preparation of your closing argument should include an assessment of the opening statements to examine whether these promises have been met. Accordingly, a persuasive closing frequently will refer back to one's own opening as a promise shown by the evidence to have been kept. Defense counsel, for example, returns to a theme of its case first presented in its opening statement—Rosen's voluntary choice to testify to allow the jurors to make their own decisions about his conduct and character. Counsel points out that he fulfilled his earlier pledge that:

> David Rosen will testify. . . . He will come to the witness stand. He will tell the judge, he will tell you, the jury, exactly why he did not do this and exactly what did occur. He will tell you that he is innocent and will relate to you in his own words, answering all the questions Mr. Zeidenberg puts to him, under oath.

A compelling argument will also cast the opponent's opening as a promise that has not been fulfilled by the evidence. The government's clever twist on the defense's use of the word "concealer" in its opening illustrates the point nicely ("David Rosen is the true concealer in this case."). The government further discredits the defense's opening statement by referring to it as part of the "absolutely absurd . . . pitch" that Rosen is trying to sell. In addition, after presenting evidence of Rosen's motive to underreport and the campaign's cost concerns, the government uses a rhetorical question to imply that the evidence does not support the defense's claims in its opening statement that the campaign was complacent regarding costs. ("[B]ut do you believe for a second that Harold Ickes, Hillary Clinton, or anyone on the campaign staff was ever as complacent about their funds as the defense tried to suggest in their opening statement?").

A powerful closing can also refer to the jury's implicit promises and duties. Defense counsel in *Rosen* cleverly reminds the jury of its reciprocal promises, stating that because counsel has kept his word, the jury must acquit Rosen. In doing so, counsel encourages the jury to feel good about keeping its promise, pointing out that an acquittal should satisfy the government as well.

> I told you in opening statement—I made some promises to you, just like you implicitly made promises to me—I would demonstrate that David Rosen was innocent. If I did that, you would find him not guilty. And I also said to you, if you did that, the government still wins, because the government always wins when justice is done.

Use Demonstratives Effectively

It is extremely burdensome for any layperson to listen to and follow carefully an individual speaking nonstop for a fairly lengthy period of time. This is especially true of a lawyer's closing argument in a case rendered complex by law or fact. The subject matter is new and may be difficult for the juror. The language of the law is foreign. It is tempting and, not surprisingly, easy for ordinary citizens, who are not often required to sit still for an hour or more and listen to one person talk uninterrupted, to eventually tune out completely.

What can you do to make sure this does not happen to you? Of course, refining the style of your delivery, which is addressed later, is important.

But organization is of equal importance and you can organize your argument so that you will *not* be talking nonstop. One simple and useful way of accomplishing this is with a healthy dose of relevant demonstratives (whether high- or low-tech) to illustrate your argument and to break up the one-way dialogue. Evidence, blown-up or otherwise enhanced, an excerpt of a transcript of key testimony, an accurate summary chart (even if not in evidence and prepared especially for closing), or a legal instruction used during the course of argument will enhance the closing, give it a fresh change of pace, and help to retain the jurors' attention to its finish.

Returning to the *Rosen* example, the defense repeatedly relies on an exhibit summarizing the law at issue. Counsel uses this exhibit to refute the government's description of the law, further commenting that "the facts were not interpreted by the prosecutors either." Counsel also incorporates the jury instructions in its argument by detailing the elements of the crime ("As the judge has instructed you . . . [h]e has been charged with willfully, knowingly, and deliberately making false statements and that he had knowledge of these statements and intended to do it"), and then boiling down what these instructions mean in laymen's terms ("In other words, he sat down one day and said, 'Okay, I am 33 years old. I have a very important job. I am afraid that I could get fired and, let's see, I think I'll risk my whole career, my family, and jeopardize everything. I am going to lie. I am intentionally going to deceive people,' so for what?").

The government also frequently refers back to exhibits during its closing argument to clarify the sequence of the costs listed on the expense reports. For example, the government even uses one of the defense's own exhibits (Exhibit 548) to show how its contents (that the August 12, 2000, gala was hosted by Aaron Tonken and Peter Paul) are inconsistent with Rosen's comments to Whitney Burns (that the $366,000 was coming from Stan Lee Media).

Of course, to avoid any unwanted interruption of your argument by an objection to the use of demonstratives prepared especially for closing, show the material to the other side and get the judge's approval for its use prior to the argument. This is especially important when you intend to use summary charts not in evidence or individual jury instructions.

Remember also, when anticipating use of jury instructions during closing, to schedule the jury instruction conference before the closing argument—and you might attempt also to prevail upon the judge to give the final jury instructions before the closings.

Final Words—A Bang, Not a Whimper

End your argument at a high point. Plan on saving one of your best points, analogies, or quotes for your conclusion. And always tell the jury precisely and succinctly what the verdict should be and why. In *Rosen*, for example, the government's last statements specifically ask the jury to "not buy what the defendant is selling" and for this reason to "find David Rosen guilty beyond a reasonable doubt." Indeed, the government sums up its main argument in one attention-grabbing sentence when it says, "Ladies and gentlemen, when David Rosen was in Los Angeles in the summer of 2000, he began to sell a pack of lies that is still being sold today." Defense counsel, for its part, responds forcefully by suggesting that the jury in fact "buy it lock, stock, and barrel." While defense counsel does not specifically ask the jurors to return a "not guilty" verdict, its finale contends that the government has not met its burden of proof and manages to portray David Rosen as an honest victim by emphasizing his willingness to testify.

> End your argument at a high point. Plan on saving one of your best points, analogies, or quotes for your conclusion.

DELIVERY—BE YOURSELF

It is almost impossible to change your personality for purposes of a closing. It is far easier and more effective to analyze the strong and weak points of your persona and to utilize them in a productive manner.

By the time you are making your closing argument, the jury has carefully observed your demeanor during the course of the trial. The jurors will already have a fairly accurate impression of who you are. So do not attempt at the closing to metamorphose into something you are not. For example, if you cannot successfully pull off recounting a funny story in your day-to-day life, do not make your comedic debut before the jury. On the other hand, if you have the ability to tell a story or an anecdote that will enhance or illustrate your argument, by all means do it. For example, defense counsel's football analogy in *Rosen* in describing the burden of proof was masterful and right to the point:

> There is no question that the government has the burden of proving its case beyond a reasonable doubt. And what does that mean? In most civil cases the government has to push the ball, if you can use that, a little bit over the 50-yard line, and that's called more likely than not. But in a criminal case the government has to prove the ball—push the ball all the way up, say, to the 90-yard line, the other side's 10-yard line.

Also, defense counsel's anecdote about the cat and mouse in a box made a great point about the ability to draw inferences and was an excellent segue into discussing the holes in the government's case.

The most important qualities the jury is looking for in a lawyer are sincerity, honesty, and trustworthiness. Play up your strengths. Do the things that have already made you a successful advocate.

Respect the Jury's Intelligence

It probably is equally disastrous to argue down to the jury as it is to talk over its head. In my view the effective closing argument is a *conversation* between you and the jury—not a lecture. Do not underestimate the intelligence of your jury. The jurors will know if you have done so and will resent it. Speak to the jurors in the same style and manner as you would with an intelligent lay friend or acquaintance. For example, the government's tone during the end of its closing argument accomplishes this by appealing to the jurors' "common sense" and asking them, in informal language, "in the end . . . not to buy what the defendant is selling." The defense similarly asks the jurors to wear "the hat of common sense" when assessing Rosen's credibility and in reaching a verdict. Counsel commends the jury and hammers this point home by saying that:

> You have common sense. Sisters, brothers, parents, relatives, children, friends on surfboards, whoever it is, you know when someone is lying. You can tell that because you know how to evaluate people. All of us

as adults do. And you saw David Rosen. He looked into your eyes, and you looked into his.

And, of course, remember also that you are not arguing before a judge in a bench trial. So avoid the unnecessary use of legalese and other stilted language. If you are required during argument to use a legal term, take the time to explain it as best you can in lay language. And try not to use unnecessarily formal, multisyllabic words in your argument if you would not do so in normal intelligent conversation.

Likewise, even if comfortable to you, try to avoid complicated or obscure expressions in your argument. For example, defense counsel's statement that the legendary "sword of Damocles" was hanging over Rosen's head may not have been helpful. Not only may the jurors miss what you are trying to say, but you do not want to risk that they might perceive that you are attempting to show off your erudition at their expense.

Tell Your Story

The dullest and least persuasive marshaling of evidence during closing argument too often occurs when the attorney attempts to recap the testimony of each witness—one after another—in an effort to show how the evidence bolsters the argument. A far more useful approach is to simply tell your version of the case in story fashion—chronologically or otherwise—inserting each pertinent piece of relevant testimony or other evidence into the narrative where appropriate. Learn from the novelist and the movie or TV scriptwriter. How often would we read more than a few minutes of a novel or watch a film that tells its story in a format that presents the words of each of its characters ad seriatim? The government tells its story effectively and even begins its recap of the evidence by stating, "[L]et's talk about the story that the evidence told throughout the case." The government then generally incorporates the evidence into a story-like framework, summarizing what the witnesses stated. However, there are times during its closing argument that the government, in my opinion, offers too much detail regarding a witness's testimony that may distract the jury from the flow of its story. One example occurs when the government recaps Rick Madden's testimony. ("[L]et me take you back to Madden's testimony. And if you remember Mr. Madden, he was the general counsel at Stan Lee Media for some time. He came to court from Skadden Arps, a law firm down the street, where he works now.")

The defense exhibits a less straightforward but more colorful style by including anecdotes to help tell Rosen's story. Early into the closing argument, counsel tells the tale of an uncle who was treated to dinner by his nephew at a restaurant featuring his favorite dish: beef stew. When he realizes the meat in his stew is rancid, he has a choice of either eating what he can or sending it all back at the risk of insulting his nephew. Counsel encourages the jury, like this uncle, to send it all back—to entirely reject the testimony of a government witness. Later, when discussing a different witness, counsel need only say "beef stew" to remind the jury of this story and its moral.

Talk to the Jurors

During argument, maintain eye contact with the jurors. I have seen attorneys so enrapt in their own words that, although looking in the direction of the jury box, there is a complete failure to make meaningful eye contact with the individual jurors. Other lawyers have attempted to guess—often not very successfully—who will be the foreperson or who are the stronger personalities among jurors and to direct their arguments toward those individuals. Even if lucky enough to identify correctly the potential leaders, lavishing your total attention on those individuals during closing is a mistake. The other jurors very well may resent being ignored, and you will never be certain whether such resentment played a role during deliberation.

Both sides in the *Rosen* trial developed a good rapport with the jurors, often by using a direct but informal tone when summarizing the evidence. In discussing certain exhibits, for example, the government commented that "in the end even the defendant doesn't dispute these numbers. So don't kill yourselves about that." Defense counsel even more effectively reviewed the evidence in a collaborative fashion. When analyzing the potentially damaging testimony of Bretta Nock, he told the jury: "Let's confront it, you and I together." This is a fine example of how to move the jury to identify with counsel by defining a mutuality of purpose.

To Object or Not to Object

Some lawyers make objections during closing arguments in a transparent attempt to disrupt the flow of an opponent's argument. This is always a mistake and is usually perceived by jurors for exactly what it is. A more difficult call is whether to object if you perceive that your opponent is misstating the law or evidence or otherwise making an improper argument during closing. The answer in my view is a simple one: If the argument is *clearly* improper and prejudicial to your side, make the objection. The corollary is also correct: Don't object if the argument is borderline problematic. The following excerpt from the *Rosen* closing is illustrative:

MR. SANDLER: Let's go to Mr. Ray Reggie, if we could for a minute, another star witness. Now, look, I say that probably Mr. Reggie, based on the evidence, has to be pitied more than censured. No one enjoys being humiliated and acknowledging that they have done wrong, but he did: bank fraud, check kiting, lying under oath to me in front of you about his incident of putting the light on the car.

MR. ZEIDENBERG: Objection.

THE COURT: Overruled.

MR. SANDLER: I am going to be very specific then, sir. I asked Mr. Ray Reggie in court about an incident of impersonating a police officer and asked if he put this light on the top, and what did he say? He was a commissioner himself of police.

MR. SCHWAGER: Objection.

THE COURT: Ladies and gentlemen, the characterization of what the evidence was and what the testimony was, as I instructed you in the jury instructions, if there is a different recollection you have, yours controls. Lawyers are expected to account for the evidence in a fair-minded way and to draw reasonable inferences from that. You will be the judges of just what he said and whether he said what counsel has just referred to.

Now please proceed.

MR. SANDLER: Thank you, your Honor.

The first objection to the evidence as argued was overruled. The judge did not rule on the second objection on the disputed evidence and instead instructed the jury to follow its collective recollection of the evidence. The judge concluded: "Now please proceed."

There was no upside to the objections. The arguments were not really harmful to the objector. The downside to the objections were the dangers that the jury would perceive (1) that the objector was unfairly interrupting his opponent, (2) that the objector was attempting to keep pertinent matters from the jury, and (3) that the judge was becoming impatient with the objector.

A Concluding Thought

I have presented a few suggestions from a judge's perspective for the preparation and delivery of a successful closing argument. The arguments of the talented lawyers in the *Rosen* case have provided excellent examples of how lawyers can, at the same time, utilize the strengths of their respective personalities, be creative, and apply the general rules of organization and style to argue effectively and forcefully before the jury.

This chapter is not meant to be an exhaustive discourse on the subject. The full text of this book and the words of others who have written in this area, of course, are valuable references.

CHAPTER 11

PRESERVING AND PROTECTING THE APPEAL

There will be times when the judge or jury simply does not understand your case, and victory will not be yours. Even when justice prevails, your client should be able to appeal, and it is your job to protect that option throughout the trial.

Deep familiarity with the rules of procedure and evidence is essential for every trial lawyer. You may think you "know" the rules, but will you be able to draw upon them in the heat of trial when instantaneous decisions are demanded? You should be confident that you can. The rules govern not only your work in trial but also your client's right to appeal.

Bear in mind that appellate courts exist solely to review errors of law committed by the trial judge. It is therefore imperative to try every case with a third eye—two eyes on the trial and the third on the record that the appellate court will review. You must protect the appeal by making timely objections when appropriate, following up by a proffer when you are prevented from introducing evidence, and assuring that your request for jury instructions is adequate and, if not accepted by the court, that the record is complete with your proposed instruction. Most importantly, whenever you spot an error, obtain a ruling from the judge. Without a ruling from the court, you have not preserved the right to appeal on that matter. (Such was the fate of a lawyer who discovered what he considered to be jury misconduct. He never brought the matter to the attention of the judge. He did, however, find himself in court defending his omission.[1])

This brief chapter will examine common situations that call for objections that are critical to preserving the appeal. Before we begin, however, it is worth acknowledging that just because you can object does not mean you should. Will the objection help your case? Is it needed to preserve the appeal? If the answer to both questions is no, you will be better off saying nothing. Remember that the jury is watching everything you do. Your ethos can suffer if you make unnecessary, annoying, or losing objections. For example, there are instances in the opening statement when opposing counsel appears to be presenting the closing argument. Certainly you have the right to object, but should you? This depends on how you think the judge and jury would react. Would jurors think you were trying to hide the facts? Would they be annoyed by persistent objections? Also, if you grant wide latitude to your opposing counsel, she or he may be generous with you.

GROUNDS FOR OBJECTIONS

When rendering objections or moving to strike, you must state the specific grounds. Grounds don't have to be stated if they are apparent. Also, some jurisdictions, such as Maryland, don't require that you state the grounds unless the judge asks you for grounds. Following are several objections that may be heard in court.

Authentication

You may object on the basis of lack of authentication if opposing counsel introduces business records without establishing the proper evidentiary foundation. Today, judges usually expect counsel to agree to at least the authenticity of exhibits before trial. Given this protocol, it is a rare instance when you need to lodge an authenticity objection. Such objections can be onerous to resolve as they often demand that a third party, the custodian of the records, be hauled into court to confirm the authenticity of a particular record.

---

1. See United States v. Daugerdas, 867 F. Supp. 2d 445 (S.D.N.Y 2012).

Hearsay

Hearsay objections are frequently raised at trial. Be familiar with all the exceptions for which hearsay is allowed, lest you make a string of losing objections. Also, if you plan to introduce evidence that could give rise to a hearsay objection, plan your response in advance.

Prior Consistent Statements

Attorneys often try to use prior consistent hearsay statements to reinforce a witness's credibility. Such statements are made prior to trial, out of the context of litigation, but they are consistent with the witness's trial testimony. But a judge will prohibit the statements if whoever made them had, at the time, a self-serving motive related to the case. This came up in the *Rosen* matter.

As mentioned earlier, long before the trial, at the behest of law enforcement, Ray Reggie secretly recorded David Rosen. During the conversation, Rosen made statements that were consistent with his trial testimony. Naturally, counsel for the defense wished to present this information into evidence. But the government objected; at the time of the recorded conversation, Rosen knew he was under criminal investigation and thus, prosecutors argued, he had a motive to tell Reggie he was innocent. The judge sided with the government, ruling that the testimony was inadmissible.

Rule 404

Rule 404 deals broadly with character evidence. The rule provides that evidence of a person's character is inadmissible to prove action in conformity with that character. This policy is often referred to as the "propensity rule." Character evidence is permitted only when character is an essential issue in a charge, claim, or defense in a civil or criminal case. If, for instance, an individual has been charged with assault, evidence that underscores his or her peacefulness would be permitted for the defense.

Prosecutors frequently seek to introduce "prior bad acts" pursuant to Federal Rule of Evidence 404(b), and occasionally defense counsel may wish to impeach a government witness by citing prior bad acts. Objections can be made when the requirements of 404(b) are not fulfilled. As a result, Federal Rule 404(b) is one of the most frequently cited rules of evidence.

Notwithstanding the limitations that Rule 404 places on character evidence and "prior bad acts," Rule 608 of the Federal Rules of Evidence does allow attorneys to attack a witness's credibility using reputation or opinion and, in the context of a cross-examination, prior specific bad acts.

Lay Witness Opinion

Lay witnesses are usually prohibited from rendering an opinion. Attorneys frequently need to object when adverse witnesses stray away from the facts of the case and into the realm of lay opinion.

Data Objections

You should be ready to object to summaries or charts coming into evidence if they are not based on genuine data that you have had the opportunity to inspect, or if they misstate or mischaracterize the data.

Technicalities

There are a host of objections that often pepper the record of a trial. Compound and leading questions, calls for a narrative, and "asked and answered" queries are common. You may wish to object also on the basis that counsel assumes or misstates a fact that is not in evidence, or is argumentative or ambiguous. You should also be alert to unresponsive answers. Sometimes your opponent will ask a witness a question, and the witness, instead of answering directly, will offer an unrelated or tangential narrative. At that point, you may need to object and ask that the testimony be stricken on the basis that the answer is not responsive or is otherwise improper.

Jury Instructions

Another important opportunity for objecting arises if the judge excludes your proposed jury instructions or gives a jury instruction to which you object. The judge should give you an opportunity to make such objections at the bench. If the judge does not grant your request to give a particular instruction, it is crucial that you include the proposed instruction in the record.

CONCLUSION

As you consider these objections and others at your disposal, bear in mind that lawyers sometimes are overly aggressive in objecting to what the opposing attorney does but they may be less attentive to what the judge does. Is it proper, for instance, to object to a question that the judge interposes during trial? Generally, the answer is yes. Objecting to a question or decision from the bench can be necessary to preserve the appeal. So too can the inclusion in the record of all exhibits. Before you rest your case, review all of the exhibits to confirm that you have not left anything out. It's a sad realization if you discover, when preparing for an appeal, that the record is incomplete.

Preserving the record for appeal should not be at the forefront of your mind throughout the case, but you cannot overlook the responsibility. The ability to appeal is fundamental to our system of justice and to your duty to your client.

CHAPTER 12

WHAT JUDGES WANT FROM TRIAL LAWYERS: A VIEW FROM THE BENCH

By the Hon. W. Michel Pierson, Administrative Judge, Circuit Court for Baltimore City Maryland

This masterful book is devoted to acquainting young lawyers with techniques for persuading juries. A discussion about what judges want might seem—at first blush—to be off topic. But even when your objective is to persuade a jury, the effects of the judge's presence are obviously inescapable. The contours of the case that is presented to the jury are shaped by the judge's rulings. Furthermore, juries tend to identify with the presiding judge, and your relations with the judge will color the jury's attitude toward you. Hence, you should know what judges want from trial lawyers.

One way to pursue this inquiry is to try to see things from the judge's viewpoint. To the young lawyer, who may tend to have an elevated view of judges, this exercise may not come naturally. But as Mr. Sandler points out in his discussion of opening statements, it is important to consider the factors that influence decision makers in order to assess how they will respond to what you say and do. Let us use that approach as a foundation to envision what judges want.

I begin with the observation that, by and large, judges want to do the right thing. Consider your task in light of this axiom. Of course, you will work to convince the judge that what you want him or her to do is the right thing, which will form a theme for your arguments, whether explicit or implicit. You also have to keep in mind that you must help the judge do the right thing. You should furnish the judge with the means to perceive that ruling your way is the right thing to do, as well as the tools to enable him or her to reach the result for which you strive. In other words, help the judge out, and don't assume that the judge knows the right answer. For example, if you want to convince the judge that there is a principle that supports the admission of evidence that helps your case, be prepared to cite authority that supports your position. On a debatable point, you may have more success persuading the judge to see it your way when you supply her authority that supports your view, instead of relying on the judge to find the authority on her own.

The desire of judges to do the right thing leads us to a second important point. Judges' rulings will not be based on whether or not they like you (although they may be affected by whether or not they trust you) or whether they enjoy your style. If a judge believes that the justice of the case supports a given result, a brilliant rhetorical performance in court will probably not tip the balance the other way. It is more important for your case to look good than for you to look good. While your performance in the courtroom is important, you can never forget that thorough preparation before you enter the courtroom is also crucial to courtroom success. What you do before trial molds the facts that can be presented to the judge in court. When the facts are shaped in a way that leads the judge to conclude that the just result is compelled by them, your task of persuasion is easy. While an extended discussion of what preparation entails is beyond the scope of this comment, preparation for trial begins when the client walks into your office, and continues until the moment you enter the courtroom.

Careful advance preparation is important for another reason: judges are busy. In today's courthouses, calendars are crowded and caseloads are heavy, meaning that judges simply do not have time to waste. Therefore, you need to organize your case so that it can be presented as efficiently and succinctly as the complexities of the case will allow. You should be ready to proceed when your case is called, and your presentation must continue to move expeditiously until the end of the trial. Judges will lose patience with lawyers who have to thumb through piles of papers to find an exhibit. The same goes for a lawyer who asks for a sudden unexpected recess because he is not prepared to call another witness.

While judges want to do the right thing, it is also the case that judges must remain impartial. Not only do the canons of judicial ethics mandate impartiality, but in a jury trial the judge is required to scrupulously avoid any action that might convey to the jury an appearance of favoring either party. Therefore, you are expected to present your case without assistance from the judge. This requires intimate familiarity with the rules of court that govern trial procedure and with evidentiary principles that govern any issues that will arise during the trial. The judge cannot make objections for you or anticipate what arguments you wish to make; it is up to you to assert your position and articulate the basis for it. For example, if you make no objection to the admission of evidence, you cannot expect the judge to exclude it, even if it is inadmissible under the rules of evidence.

Judges dislike chaos. The judicial role is founded on expectations of structure and order. Judges want lawyers to behave with proper decorum and respect for the orderly conduct of court business. This begins with punctuality and compliance with court directives for timely filing. It extends to your relations with opposing counsel. Judges become impatient with lawyers who squabble and call each other names. Such conduct bespeaks a lack of professionalism. It is improper to engage in an argumentative dialogue directly with opposing counsel; your argument should always be addressed to the court. And even if opposing counsel is behaving obnoxiously, don't let yourself be drawn into descending to that level. The fact that you did not start the dispute won't excuse your participation in unseemly behavior. Interrupting the judge, opposing counsel, or witnesses is a breach of decorum, and it assails a judge's control of the courtroom. Although it can be frustrating when a witness persists in evasive or non-responsive answers, there are better ways to control such a witness than trying to talk over him. (Some of these methods are described in the chapter on cross-examination.) Likewise, interruptions when opposing counsel is arguing to the judge seldom are viewed as appropriate by the judge, even if you are trying to correct a misstatement. Instead, ask permission to respond when opposing counsel concludes.

It is important that you conform to courtroom norms. These vary from place to place. For example, judges may have different rules about whether counsel should stand when questioning witnesses, where counsel may stand when addressing the jury, or whether counsel may move around the courtroom with or without advance permission from the judge. Some judges expect counsel to await the court's permission before beginning examination of a witness. If you are unfamiliar with the practices expected in the courtroom of the judge before whom you are to appear, it may be a good idea to visit the judge's courtroom before your trial begins, or to consult with other lawyers who are familiar with the local customs or the particular judge's preferences.

In any court, a basic principle to follow is that you should regard every courtroom appearance as a formal occasion. Begin with your attire. The informality that pervades other areas of our culture does not apply in the courtroom. For any trial, it is best for lawyers of either gender to dress in a business suit. You may also be assured that the judge will notice if your tie is askew or your shirttail is out.

You should always exhibit appropriate respect for the court. This includes standing when addressing the judge, employing language that connotes respect (for example, addressing the judge as "Your Honor," or "Sir" or "Ma'am"), and otherwise speaking and behaving with deference. It is a mistake to argue with the judge once he or she has made a final ruling. That does not mean that you should not take appropriate steps to preserve the record—indeed, it is always important to protect the record no matter how overbearing the judge may be. And there may be circumstances in which it would be appropriate to remind the judge of an important consideration that may have been overlooked, such as when a hasty evidentiary ruling made in the heat of trial proceedings disregards facts of record. But remember that ultimately the judge has the last word in her or his court, and resist the temptation to continue arguing after a ruling simply because you believe that you are correct and the judge is wrong. Furthermore, avoid demonstrations of emotion when things don't go your way—whether it is losing an argument or a witness who unexpectedly hurts your case.

Conversely, respect for the judge does not mean that you should be obsequious or timid. Judges expect you to represent your client vigorously. As long as you behave courteously, a judge will not take it amiss if you assert your position firmly. Don't permit yourself to be put off stride by aggressive or close questioning from the bench; that may be the judge's way of elucidating the point in his/her mind. In the words of Frederick Bernays Weiner, "the appropriate attitude is one of respectful intellectual equality."[1]

Judges dislike falsehood. Falsity is an affront to the truth-seeking process that is the judge's world. Needless to say, you should never misrepresent a fact to the court. You should be careful not to take liberties with legal authorities that you cite to the court. You must also avoid the temptation to assert facts or law if you are not certain of their veracity. While you may find it difficult or embarrassing to admit that you don't know the answer to a judge's question, giving an answer that turns out to be false may place you in the same position as though you made a deliberate misrepresentation. Be assured that falsehood or dissembling will earn you a reputation among judges that will be hard to shake. Conversely, if a judge knows that she or he can trust your word, that reputation will also follow you.

Of course, your professional responsibility to your client will sometimes require you to assert positions that are doomed to failure. But you should try to avoid making arguments in which you do not believe. You will find that it is easier to be persuasive if you put forward propositions in which you have confidence. As judges repeatedly remind practitioners, insistence on maintaining weak arguments tends to distract the listener from focus on the advocate's strong arguments. Be selective and concentrate on your strengths.

Asserting needlessly extreme positions also detracts from your credibility. Avoid unnecessarily sharp practices and treat others with respect. A judge appreciates a lawyer who behaves with civility to her or his opponents. If you can extend a professional courtesy to your opponent without harming your client's position, consider doing so. While assertive advocacy

---

1. Weiner, Briefing and Arguing Federal Appeals, (2001).

is appropriate, your stature is enhanced when it appears that you seek a result based on substantial justice, rather than a technical point. For example, seeking to have your opponent's memorandum stricken because it was filed one day late will not be a result that the judge will be eager to countenance if no exigency requires it.

Judges empathize with jurors. They are keenly aware of the sacrifices that jury service entails, and strive to make the most efficient use of jurors' time. You need to be conscious of the time requirements of your case and you should strive to avoid unnecessary delays. The jury should not be kept waiting because at the last minute you raised an evidentiary point that has to be resolved before the jury can be brought into the courtroom; anticipate the necessity for such events, and bring them to the judge's attention well in advance. Time estimates to present a witness's testimony that are wildly at variance with the actual time required make it difficult to manage a trial and to plan its duration. It will also test the judge's patience if you take up the jury's time with unnecessary matters, such as laying foundations for exhibits that the other side does not challenge, or marking exhibits that could have been marked in advance. You should always determine before trial whether the introduction of exhibits can be streamlined. Many jurisdictions by rule or order will require you to consult with opposing counsel to determine what exhibits will require a foundation, but even where this is not the case it is a practice that you should follow.

Judges form lasting impressions of your character based on your direct and peripheral communication. The concept of ethos, referred to in Chapter 2, is important to keep in mind when dealing with judges.[2] When dealing with judges, ethos is everything. As Mr. Sandler explains, your ethos is the character that you develop with the court. Every one of your communications with the judge contributes to its formation. Unlike your interaction with the jury, which will be limited to one trial, your ethos with the judge will last beyond the trial and will color your future contacts with

---

2. The role of ethos in persuasion is explored in greater depth in WAICUKAUSKI, SANDLER & EPPS, THE 12 SECRETS OF PERSUASIVE ARGUMENT (ABA Books 2009). The reader is commended to that work, which contains many valuable specific examples of how to shape your courtroom behavior so as to enhance your ethos.

the judge, and perhaps with other judges as well. Take care to cultivate a positive character, and remember that everything that you do in court is a form of communication, whether or not intended as such.

Finally, judges admire competence in lawyers. They enjoy watching able attorneys try cases to juries. If you present and comport yourself as a prepared and professional advocate, you may rest assured that you will be giving judges what they want.

Appendix I

THE OPENING STATEMENTS IN *U.S. v. ROSEN*

Opening Statement by the Government

MR. ZEIDENBERG: Ladies and gentlemen, in August of 2000 Hillary Clinton's campaign for the United States Senate in New York was entering the stretch run. She was up against a well-financed challenger. The polls were tight. Money was tight. Running for the United States Senate in the United States is a very expensive proposition. Campaigning in a large, expensive media state like New York is particularly expensive. The responsibility for raising money for Hillary Clinton's campaign fell to this man seated at counsel table. His name is David Rosen.

David Rosen was national finance director for Hillary Clinton's Senate campaign. He also worked for an organization called New York Senate 2000. New York Senate 2000 was a joint fundraising committee made up of the Hillary Clinton campaign, the New York Democratic Party Committee, and a national committee of Democratic senatorial candidates.

It was David Rosen's job to raise the money for Hillary Clinton. But his job was more than just raising money, because as national finance director, it was his job to not only raise money but to keep track of the money that he raised and to keep track of the money that was spent in raising money. And to take that information, the amount of money raised, the expenses incurred in raising that money, and to convey that information truthfully and accurately to the compliance officer who worked for the campaign.

That compliance officer, the evidence will show, and David Rosen knew, would then convey the information that David Rosen gave her to the Federal Election Commission. Once the Federal Election Commission received that information, they would post it, make it public, so that everybody could see who was donating and how much they were donating.

Early in the summer of 2000 David Rosen met up with an eager and wealthy campaign—would-be campaign donor by the name of Peter Paul. Peter Paul approached David Rosen and told him—told David Rosen that he would like to underwrite a huge campaign event for Hillary Clinton. He proposed that he, Peter Paul, would underwrite the event.

Now, you are going to hear, ladies and gentlemen, that there are two kinds of donations that can be made to campaigns: cash donations and in-kind donations. Cash donations are pretty self-explanatory. It's when someone writes a check and gives it to the campaign. It has to be reported to the Federal Election Commission.

In-kind donations are, as you might imagine by the name, are donations made in lieu of money, typically by a vendor, so that if a vendor would like to donate to the campaign—a florist, for example, rather than giving cash, the florist may decide that they'd like to give a thousand dollars in flowers to a particular event. Perfectly legal, perfectly appropriate. But that in-kind donation needs to be reported to the FEC, Federal Election Commission, as a donation.

What Peter Paul was suggesting is that he would make a massive in-kind donation. Rather than give the money directly to Hillary Clinton's campaign, he would underwrite the event.

David Rosen and Peter Paul decided that this event would take place in Los Angeles on August 12th, 2000. It would coincide with the start of the Democratic National Convention, which was held in Los Angeles in 2000. Now, they were talking about this event for its main stages—stages in July. That left a little over five weeks to plan this entire event. Not much time.

David Rosen left his offices in New York and moved to Los Angeles for the four weeks preceding the event so that he could supervise every facet of this event.

You will hear, ladies and gentlemen, that this event was his responsibility from start to finish. He was involved in every key decision that was made. Everything from the design of the invitation to the selection of the venue, to who was sitting next to whom, he was in on the decisions.

Now, you are going to hear, ladies and gentlemen, that when David Rosen moved to Los Angeles he worked out of the offices of Stan Lee Media. Stan Lee Media was an organization, a company that was started by Peter Paul and an individual by the name of Stan Lee.

Stan Lee is a legend in the comic book industry. He created the comic book character Spider-Man, among many others.

And Stan Lee and Peter Paul came up with a company called Stan Lee Media, and for a short time, anyway, it was worth millions of dollars. It was an Internet company.

David Rosen went to work in the offices of Stan Lee Media. That was where he worked out of while he was planning the event. Also working out of those offices was an associate of Peter Paul's by the name of Aaron Tonken. Aaron Tonken was an individual who was involved in putting on celebrity-studded charity events. He had a lot of contacts in the entertainment industry, and it was going to fall on Aaron Tonken the responsibility of procuring the talent that was going to appear at this fundraising event.

The three put their heads together and came up with a concept for this event, and it was going to be billed a Hollywood tribute or goodbye to President Clinton. Its purpose, as I said, was to raise money for Hillary Clinton's Senate campaign. It was going to be a huge, star-studded event. They were going to have a cocktail reception beforehand and then a concert, and a concert to be followed by a dinner. The ticket price was going to be a thousand dollars per person for the concert; $25,000 per couple for the dinner.

Now, to justify those kind of prices, they knew they had to put on a big event, something that was star-studded, something that would attract those high-rolling donors. So they went out and they hired a Hollywood producer, a man by the name of Gary Smith.

Gary Smith is a legend in the Hollywood industry, a legendary producer who for 40 years has been in show business, and over that time has won 24 Emmys, putting on award shows like the Emmy awards, the Grammy awards, the Tony awards. He put on three presidential inaugurals, various presidential conventions. He was a pro's pro.

But one thing Gary Smith wasn't was cheap. If he was going to do this event, it was going to be done with "A-list" talent, and it was going to be done first-class all the way.

And so this was the first thing they did is they had to select a venue that was appropriate. They found a ranch in Los Angeles formerly owned by actor Robert Taylor, a 112-acre oasis in Los Angeles at the end of Mandeville Canyon. A gorgeous piece of property. The only problem is that it was isolated, and it was basically just a private residence on a beautiful piece of land. There was no stage there. There was no—nothing pre-made for an event for a thousand people and a concert. Everything that they wanted to put on had to be built on the site or brought in and trucked in: the stage, the lighting, the cameras, everything. Obviously, this added to the cost.

They decided that they were going to get, as I said, A-list talent. Cher was going to perform, Toni Braxton, Melissa Etheridge, Michael Bolton, Diana Ross. Wolfgang Puck was the caterer. John Travolta and Kelly Preston, Jennifer Aniston and Brad Pitt, Muhammad Ali were invitees.

Now, while the talent, when they were procured and came to play, said they would play for free, there were a lot of costs associated with it because although they didn't require a fee for performing, all of their expenses associated with coming and staying in Los Angeles did have to be paid.

And you are going to hear, ladies and gentlemen, that these performers didn't come to LA by bus. They required, many of them, private jets. Cher required her own particular private jet, specifying exactly the model and type she wanted.

Other performers were able to be satisfied simply by giving them first-class airfare, not only for them but for their entourage. Their hairdressers, their makeup artist, their band, and the costs associated with that began to mount.

You will hear, ladies and gentlemen, that the cost associated just with bringing in the talent was $90,000; for building a stage, over $50,000. The invitations—30,000 invitations printed, even though only 15,000 were sent out, $90,000. You will hear that there were gift bags given away for all the guests, and they had CDs of all the performers that performed at the concert. That's seven CDs, a thousand guests, 7,000 thousand [sic] CDs cost $50,000.

Someone came up with the idea to give away the chairs as souvenirs. You will hear that everyone had a director's chair with a stencil on the back commemorating the event. Why don't we give away the chairs? That will be a nice touch. They gave away $35,000 worth of chairs.

Now, as these costs began to mount, this man, David Rosen, began to panic. The purpose of this event, ladies and gentlemen, was not to throw a big party. The purpose of the event was to raise money for Hillary Clinton's Senate campaign; and the higher your costs go, the harder it is to net at the end of the day money for the campaign. And the costs began to spiral out of control.

David Rosen's event—last event prior to this that he held in New York City had been a complete flop. It had lost money. He was worried what would happen if he screwed up twice in a row. He told a friend that he thought this was going to be a career killer; that he would get fired; that this was political suicide.

You will hear that as he heard more and more bad news about the budget, he literally threw up his hands and said he didn't want to hear any more, didn't want to hear the costs, and didn't want to hear those figures repeated.

What was he going to do? The president and the first lady had already committed to attend this event. Everybody knew about it. It was coinciding with the start of the convention. He came up with what he thought was a solution. He came up with a decision to deliberately lie to the FEC by underreporting the costs associated with that event.

You will hear that budgets were created as this event progressed, and those budgets were sent to the compliance officer from Hillary Clinton's campaign. David Rosen had the—had his event coordinator send in what he knew were fraudulent budgets to the compliance officer, who then forwarded those fraudulent documents to the FEC where they were posted and made public.

Now, did he know—did David Rosen know the absolute true cost of that event? Well, ladies and gentlemen, it's hard to know the absolute true cost of anything when you literally cover your ears and run out of the room and say, I don't want to hear any more of this. It's hard to know the exact figure. But the evidence will show, beyond a reasonable doubt, that he knew the budgets that he submitted to the FEC, to the compliance officer, were complete lies.

What's that evidence going to be? Ladies and gentlemen, you are going to hear that he worked very closely with an event planner, and as she came up with these budgets and as these costs that I described to you began to mount, he told her to take off items that appeared on that budget, items that had been paid already for products that had already been delivered. He told her, take them off; the budget is too high. And she did as she was told, and those fraudulent budgets were sent in later to the FEC.

You will hear that the travel expenses that I described to you earlier for all of these celebrities, that David Rosen was involved in trying to get them jets; that he approached several friends, asking these individuals if they knew anyone with a private jet to help defray some of these costs. He knew exactly the problem with these—with getting in this talent and how expensive it was, and yet not a single dime associated with those travel costs appear on the final budgets.

You will hear that he lied directly to the compliance officer for the Hillary Clinton campaign. As this compliance officer had received preliminary budgets, she noticed that some line items, particularly for talent and entertainment, had gone down dramatically, and she asked David Rosen about it. Now, this is just prior to the event. What about this? How come it's getting cheaper? David Rosen told her it was getting cheaper because Cher had backed out; Cher was not going to perform, so she didn't have to pay any of those costs associated with bringing in Cher and her band. Well, ladies and gentlemen, you are going to see a videotape of that concert held August 12th and you are going to see Cher, in living color, did two songs that night. David Rosen knew she was going to be there. He knew she played there. But he also knew that compliance officer in Washington, D.C., wasn't likely to be at that event, and how would she ever know the truth?

You will hear, ladies and gentlemen, that David Rosen incurred over $13,000 in hotel bills in the weeks leading up to the event. It's easy to rack up $13,000 in hotel bills when you're staying in hotels like The Hermitage and the Beverly Hills Hotel that charge $300 to $350 a night. He incurred those initially on his own credit card, never reported those expenses to the FEC as he was required to do. Later he tried to get some-one, anyone, to pay them off. And you will hear he approached more than one individual trying to get them to pay off his bills. Eventually he settled on Aaron Tonken. And by pestering him for long enough, Aaron Tonken finally agreed to pay off that hotel bill.

It's legal for a donor to pay off a hotel bill, but it has to be reported to the Federal Election Commission as an in-kind donation.

You will hear that the weeks he spent at Stan Lee Media in their office space was never reported to the FEC. You will hear those thousands and thousands of CDs, 7,000 which were given away the night of the gala on August 12th, had been stored, stacked up in David Rosen's office in hundreds of boxes. He knew they were there. He knew they were given away. Not a single dime of expenses related to those CDs and gift bags pertaining to the music that was given away shows up on the budget. The only thing that shows up on the budget is a few thousand dollars for the bags in which those thousands and thousands of dollars of CDs, $50,000 worth of CDs, were given away.

Now, after—strike that. The question was, how egregious—how egre-gious was his underreporting? You will hear, ladies and gentlemen, that he reported—David Rosen had budgets report that the actual in-kind expenses were $366,000. He later amended that report, and that report was amended to read $400,000 in in-kind expenses.

The evidence will show in this case, beyond a reasonable doubt, that the true in-kind expenses was $1.1 million. He underreported by $700,000. In other words, he reported just under one-third of the true cost.

Now, after the event, ladies and gentlemen, the FBI began investigating and they began questioning people. And David Rosen had a conversation with a witness, who you will hear from, and he told this witness that he wasn't worried. He said, "It's their word against ours: Peter Paul, Aaron Tonken. They are liars. No one will believe them over me." And so he decided to ride it out.

Why did he do it? Well, the evidence will show, ladies and gentlemen, that the reason he committed this crime, the reason he underreported, was twofold. First, he knew that there was going to be outrage in the campaign, in the headquarters, over the expenses, how they'd gotten so out of control.

You will see memos that were found in David Rosen's possession written by the head of the Hillary Clinton campaign in which it was made clear that fundraisers were to keep a lid on expenses; that they weren't supposed to use their cell phones unnecessarily; that they shouldn't use messenger services when the mail would do. When you're counting pennies like that and scrutinizing budgets like that, how are you going to react when you see that you have okayed $5,000 for Patti LaBelle's hairdresser or $10,000 worth of Paul Anka CDs given away on a single night. David Rosen knew that people would be extremely alarmed and upset at those kind of expenses.

Now, it is entirely true, ladies and gentlemen, that these expenses were not being paid directly by the Hillary Clinton campaign. They were not writing checks for these items. As I told you at the outset, they were all being in-kinded, if you will, by Peter Paul. And you might rightly ask yourselves, while you are sitting there, what's the big deal if Peter Paul is paying for all this stuff? Isn't it free?

Well, to the uninformed, ladies and gentlemen, the answer to that question might sound like yes, but the evidence will show that David Rosen was anything but uninformed. You will hear, ladies and gentlemen, that there are something called soft money and hard money, and you will hear that it is much easier to raise soft money than hard money. Soft money is money that can be given without limit to a campaign from various groups, but it can't be given—strike that. It can be given to a joint fundraising committee like New York Senate 2000. That can only be used for certain purposes. It can be used for issue advertising, for instance, and for getting out the vote. It's easy to raise—relatively easy to raise soft money, because there aren't the same limits on giving it.

Hard money is what the campaign wanted and needed. Hard money is limited in how much an individual can give. At the time, it was only $1,000 per election. One thousand for the primary; $1,000 for the national—for the final election; $2,000 per cycle.

So it's much harder to raise hard money. The beauty of the hard money, though, its use is not restricted. Hillary Clinton's campaign could use it for advertising of any type they wanted. The type where a candidate can say, vote for me or vote against my opponent.

Now, getting back to those huge in-kind donations that Peter Paul was giving that sounded like free money: it's not free money, because you will hear, ladies and gentlemen, that under the law a certain percentage of money from that hard money account needs to be transferred from the hard money account to the soft money account, depending on the size and amount of that donation.

So that $1.1 million that Peter Paul was giving, a certain percentage of that David Rosen knew would have to be . . . transferred from the campaign's hard money account to the soft money account. The bigger the in-kind donation, the more money that would have to be transferred; the smaller the in-kind donation, the less money that would have to be transferred. And David Rosen knew that there was going to be a negative impact on that hard money fund by taking a massive in-kind soft money donation from Peter Paul, so he wanted that report to be smaller.

Now, ladies and gentlemen, you were asked in your questionnaire a couple questions about Senator Hillary Clinton, and, as His Honor told you, this case has nothing to do with Hillary Clinton. It is about David Rosen. You will hear no evidence that Hillary Clinton was involved in this in any way, shape, or form. In fact, it's just the opposite. The evidence will show that David Rosen was trying to keep this information from the campaign because he was afraid if they found out how much he had spent, he would be fired. So whatever your feelings about Senator Clinton—good, bad, or indifferent—they have nothing to do with this case.

This case is about one question, and one question only: Did David Rosen deliberately cause a false filing and statement to be made to the Federal Election Commission concerning the in-kind donations made to that gala on August 12th, 2000?

The evidence in this case will show the answer to that question is yes, and at the end of the case we will ask you to return a verdict that's consistent with that finding.

That would be a verdict of guilty. Thank you.

OPENING STATEMENT BY THE DEFENSE

MR. SANDLER: May it please the court, members of the jury, if I were to show you my hand and ask you if you see it, some of [you] would say, sure, I see your hand; but in reality, you don't.

You don't see my hand until I turn it all the way around. Then and only then do you see my hand.

So like this case, you have not seen this case. All we have heard is what the prosecutor says he's going to prove.

Now, as the judge said, I am Paul Sandler. I represent David Rosen. I am joined by my cousin Joe Sandler from Washington—I am from Baltimore—and my friend and cocounsel Michael R. Doyen from Los Angeles.

Together, we would like to tell you what this case is really about. It's about David Rosen's fight against the injustice of his being wrongfully accused of something he never did. I will prove to you in this case he is innocent. He is the victim, an innocent victim, of other people's motives, and I will prove this. I will prove to you that David Rosen never knew, never knew, the cost of the production and concert expenses for this Hollywood gala.

And why didn't he know it, folks? The evidence will show he did not know it, because those costs were concealed from him. They were hidden from him by two individuals: Peter Paul, who you can see on the screen, and Aaron Tonken. These individuals—representing a company known as Stan Lee Media—these individuals participated with Stan Lee Media in underwriting, paying for the costs of this event, and they had their own agenda.

David Rosen in this case was a salaried employee, the national fundraising director of the Hillary Clinton campaign. At the time he was 33 years old. The evidence will show, and I will prove this to you, he gained not one penny from this underreporting. He was not the president of an international global company where he raked in millions of dollars and caused other people, as the evidence will show, to lose their jobs. He was not an individual who profited and has great pension funds.

I will prove to you today, he has no income because of this. This case, I will prove to you, is not just a travesty but a bizarre travesty of justice, and I will ask you, and the evidence will compel you, to rectify the situation.

David Rosen never saw any of the costs that were affiliated with this larger part of the concert production. I will prove it to you. Seeing is believing. As we walk through the trial together, you will ask yourselves, because—and I will remind you where is the writing that Mr. Rosen is supposed to have seen which would educate him about the costs, in terms of the concert and the gala expenses?

Now, in terms of this event, as the prosecutor alluded, there was a concert; there was a dinner. It was separate, separate parts of the event, and during the concert there was a producer, an individual by the name of Gary Smith, who was the head producer for this concert; and I will explain, and the evidence will point to, what his role was and how he then had someone else by the name of Baumrucker take over the production.

Now, remember the dinner and the concert were separate, although it was one event. And what the government is claiming is that David Rosen failed to report hundreds of thousands of dollars that were attributed to producing this concert.

Where is the paperwork that shows he knew? He did not know. It was concealed from him.

In addition to David Rosen not making any money off of this, I will prove to you and I will say to you that the government must concede this point, folks: The Hillary Clinton campaign gained no economic benefit from this at all. And to say that the campaign was coming into a stretch and money was tight and things were desperate is to be inaccurate. I will prove that to you.

Senator Clinton, at that time and today, as well, is an individual in public life that has no trouble raising money. The coffers of that treasure chest for her Senate campaign were robust. I will prove that to you. There was no desperation. Those aren't the facts in this case.

And, yes, the FBI, as the prosecutor said, was interviewed for years. David Rosen has been trailed and played. Fourteen FBI agents surrounded his home and investigated. They come into his office and they take all his documents. He didn't destroy anything; he had nothing to hide. And, yes, the government is trying hard to prove its case.

Well, you're going to hear testimony from one of his friends, a Mr. Jim Levin. The government will call him and this individual is going to say, "David Rosen and I, we knew about this, and David told me that he was going to hide things and we'll keep it all secret." But the—you won't believe that, and I will prove to you that it's not credible. That individual, Mr. Jim Levin, just two days ago signed a plea agreement, because he has his own criminal problems. And in order to get benefit for himself, he is coming to court, and he will talk to you about what David Rosen supposedly said to him.

That's the type of evidence that you will hear from the government. But I will prove to you, through our witnesses, that David Rosen is innocent. And I will tell you this: David Rosen will testify. I am pledging that to you now. He will come to the witness stand. He will tell the judge, he will tell you, the jury, exactly why he did not do this and exactly what did occur. He will tell you that he is innocent and will relate to you in his own words, answering all the questions Mr. Zeidenberg puts to him, under oath, and explain to you that he did not do this.

So let's talk for a minute about opening statements, if I may, just for a second. As you know, in courts all across the land, prosecutors and defense attorneys, with the courtesy of the judge, present opening statements. The judge told you I didn't have to make an opening statement; we could just sit there. Mr. Rosen is presumed to be innocent. But we choose to do so.

David Rosen does not have to testify. He could sit there. We choose to present him so you can evaluate him and make your own decisions.

I should say a few words [about] what the evidence will show about David Rosen so you can get an understanding of what the testimony will be, but I will do so only briefly.

He was born in Chicago. Loving family. His folks and family are here in court. He never completed high school, but he managed with his GED to obtain the equivalency. He worked all the way through his young life. He worked at McDonald's flipping hamburgers. He sold Domino's pizzas or delivered Domino's pizzas. He sold reference textbooks, encyclopedias.

He worked in Santa Monica for the Elizabeth Glazer cancer foundation as a director of development. He has worked selling commercial real estate, and he graduated college by paying his own way. And when he was in college he became excited about political science and began to become active in Democratic Party fundraising, served as a field director raising money on job training.

Those who are familiar with the military know what that means. No one gave him a course, but he learned what the rules were and he developed systems and he developed what the responsibilities of a fundraiser was—were.

Then in 1999 an interesting phone call was received by Mr. Rosen. It was someone who was an official in the Democratic Party who wanted to know would he like to come to the White House, meet the first lady, and discuss being a fundraiser in her campaign for the United States Senate. And yes, folks, he was very excited.

He went to the White House. The evidence will show he went into the Map Room of the White House, and there he met the first lady. He was ecstatic being in that room. It was very, very exciting. But he, of course, was not a child or a youngster, and was able to contain his enthusiasm. And he had lunch with the first lady around the pool of the White House, just the two of them, and they talked politics.

And David Rosen was interested, and he was interested in helping the first lady become a United States senator; and he was very, very excited when he was offered the position of being the national fundraiser director for her campaign.

You will hear testimony that his responsibilities were to raise money throughout the United States, but not in New York. And during 1999, that summer, up through the time before we have the gala in August or, let's say, June, David Rosen was busy hopping around the country working on fundraising events.

Where did he live? The evidence will show he did not live in the White House. He lived in a little room in New York City that was no bigger than a postage stamp that someone donated to him, or a friend of a friend gave him this room. And during the time that he was working and raising funds, he will testify to what I will call parlor events, small events in people's homes.

People would come to him or he would seek out people and they would say, "Sure, we'll host an event for the senator," and they would. Then David Rosen's staff and he would work to develop the event. They had invitations to deal with. They had to explain what the rules were. And you will hear David Rosen testify, and you will learn, that the responsibilities of donors—donors are people who pay for the parties. They're the ones that have the responsibility to bring forth the costs so that David Rosen can send it to a compliance officer. He is not a CPA. He was not an accountant. He was not in charge of regulating and mastering all these expenses. People who would do the event would give those to him, and then he would send them on. That was the system, and he had a system in his office. He had a little office staff.

Could I see the—the chart that reflects the staff? Thank you.

This is a diagram, if you will, of the staff of the whole Hillary Clinton campaign and you can see where Mr. Rosen is. Here is his box, if you will. And you can see his position. And under—you can see, in that little box, interns and young people that work, and you will see the name Chris Fickes, who was his deputy. And you will see other individuals who worked on these various events.

Evidence will show that there were about over 90 events. Incidentally, none of those events caused significant problems, except an event where Mr. Aaron Tonken or Mr. Peter Paul were involved, but we will come to that.

Now, Rosen, in working on these events, appreciated and learned that it was the donor that had the responsibility to give the costs of the event. And, frequently, the times were so hectic and it took such energy to develop these events—usually about $85– to $90,000 would be a typical event, the money from the event, nothing like this gala—but Mr. Rosen and his staff would hire consultants. These consultants were political and I didn't even know this until I started becoming the lawyer for Mr. Rosen, but there is such an art to developing all these events that there are people that call themselves professional fundraisers and, indeed, Mr. Rosen became one after the campaign.

He, for example, started a company known as the Competence Group, which, of course, has no clients now, but he started becoming a professional fundraiser. And fundraisers around the country are hired as consultants, and they help David Rosen in the various jurisdictions plan the party. They know the people in the location. They get on the phone and say, "Hello, we are having an event and Jean Smith is holding it; come on over, et cetera, and it's for Hillary Clinton. Meet her and maybe you'll get enthusiastic."

And these people would work that. Terry New, for example, is the name of a consultant who worked on an event you might hear about on June 9th in 2000 in California, known as the Spago lunch or Gershman tea.

But, in any event, by the time David Rosen comes to, in June of 2000, he is pretty well grounded in what has to be accomplished in raising money for the Clinton campaign. He knows what he is supposed to do. He has prided himself, would hear others say he is doing everything right, doing things by the book, and he understood he had a system in place and the system in place for expenses were when the donor or payer would give him the costs, they would then take it to the office, put it on spreadsheets, send it into a compliance officer.

Compliance officer—you will probably meet—the government will call someone by the name of Whitney Burns. She works in Washington. She is the one that files the reports to the Federal Election Commission. Mr. Rosen doesn't.

Now, Whitney Burns would rely on people like Mr. Rosen to give the costs of an event so it could be reported, just as the treasurer, Mr. Grossman, would rely on Whitney Burns. You will meet Whitney Burns, probably one of the government's earlier witnesses in the case.

And Mr. Rosen would rely on someone—these were the people that were putting on the event—to give him the costs.

So Mr. Rosen in June, late May has a telephone call with Terry New, one of these consultants. She introduces him to this individual by the name of Aaron Tonken, and Aaron Tonken wants to get involved in fundraising. He goes to a tea I mentioned, this Gershman tea, in June.

Now mind you, he met—the evidence will show he met in 1999 at the White House, becomes the fundraising director, works all these events around the country, Iowa, Michigan, wherever. He then meets Mr. Tonken on the phone in the course of all his work.

He understands that it's a responsibility of the donor to give him the information. He then goes to the Spago lunch or tea on June 9th. Not significant, because at that tea he didn't know it. He didn't know it. His life would change forever, because he met three people for the first time in person: Peter Paul, one of the concealers; Aaron Tonken, another of the concealers; and Bretta Nock, joined at the hip with Aaron Tonken, his event planner, his person that he promoted to do dozens of charitable events, his person who was skilled in dealing with vendors and putting on these productions.

Aaron Tonken was so close to Bretta Nock that he would pay for her offices and all of her supplies and equipment. She was his person.

Now, on June 24th, another fateful day in the life of David Rosen, he receives a telephone call from his colleagues at work. One of them was Jim Levin, the person who I suggest to you will be called by the government, who will testify falsely. They—and Kelly Craighead and a few others. They said, "David"—

And I know it's improper to refer to him by first name, but I am referring to a conversation, Your Honor.

THE COURT: Go ahead.

MR. SANDLER: "David, we are going to do something very exciting," he says. "We are going to have a tremendous event in August for Senator Clinton." And he says, "What do you mean?" "Yeah, we are going to do something in Los Angeles. It's going to be a big splash. And Aaron Tonken and this guy, Peter Paul, they are going to put it all together."

And David says, "Well, when?" And they said, "During the Democratic National Convention." He'll tell you this. He will tell you this under oath. He says, "Well, wait a second. What about Gore? How can we compete with Gore? And how can we do this, what you're talking about, so quickly?" They said, "We'll work it all out."

David Rosen did not wish to go forward with this event. No, he didn't. He'll tell you that. He had reservations. He was concerned about any relationship he had with the Gore campaign, doing something during the convention at the same time; but it was all worked out and he was told, go forth, young man. Go west. Do this event. And when you meet him and he testifies, you will see his spunk, his enthusiasm, his dedication. He is a soldier, a trouper, and loyal and a leader, and he went forward. But he never knew, like that poem of Alfred Lord Tennyson, that he was walking into the valley of trouble; because when he went there, folks, he never knew what was going to come up and try to ruin him. When he went to California, he embraced this, and he was informed about how the structure of this event would work. And I'd like to show it to you. My chart, please.

I'd like to show you, if I could, what David Rosen was introduced to. He didn't own this event. This is what he was told would happen. Stan Lee Media would host the event. Stan Lee Media is a company that involves the famous Stan Lee. Indirectly, he, I learned, is the individual who created Spider-Man. The two concealers, Peter Paul and Stan Lee, they had a burning goal and desire, sinister, I suggest, the evidence will show, to promote Stan Lee Media into the public eye. And there Aaron Tonken and Peter Paul—you can see, they're the two. Mr. Stan Lee Media did not—excuse me. Mr. Stan Lee did not know that this was going on. Peter Paul and Aaron Tonken, they were the ones that Mr. Rosen was introduced to. And Bretta Nock of Wonderworks. That was her company. She was its event planner who was paid for by Stan Lee Media and worked with Aaron Tonken.

And this Bretta Nock was what was called the event planner. She was the one that hired the vendors, paid the vendor. She reported to Mr. Tonken and had great communication with not only David Rosen, but also with—also with the compliance officer, Whitney Burns, because she would have to send information to these people. What information? The cost and bills that were expended.

Then you will see what's to my left on the chart. Gary Smith, Smith-Hemion Productions. Gary Smith is also a famous person, I learned. Because being from Baltimore, I don't know all the California leaders in the industry of production, but I sure am learning. And Gary Smith, apparently, is a famous producer, and he did—he, I learned, and you will learn from the testimony—orchestrated the conventions, the Democratic

National Conventions, and is known for historically changing the tone and the mode of these conventions.

He was asked, as the evidence will show, to produce the concert part of this event and he, in certain vernacular, subbed it out, folks, to an individual by the name of Alan Baumrucker. You will meet him. The government will call him. I have a few questions for him, but not many. And Mr. Alan Baumrucker had an interesting company. Look at the name. Black Ink Productions. And Black Ink Productions did the actual work in producing, bringing forth all of the stage and the people that were going to work on the stage, the lighting, so that the concert could take place. You will notice that Mr. Baumrucker also hired vendors. So that's what David Rosen was told would be the operation of this concert and this event; and his job, his job was to raise money.

Now, he does go there. He went there on July 15th, for the first time. Even before he went there, a lot of work planning was being done. Production meetings occurred, etcetera. He comes there and he works and, yes, he did try to take seriously his role of making sure everything worked right. And he worked very hard on the invitations, on the journal—on the tribute journal that they were producing. And he worked with an individual by the name of Pat Waters, who the government will call as a witness.

He did not discuss the costs with her. He did not know what the costs were, and he, at the time, was working, making sure language was correct, that it satisfied all the different people that were in this campaign who would approve.

And you saw the chart of the campaign, and you can see how many people are on a campaign. And you have seen the television shows about how politics works, and you know how many people you've got to clear things with. And you also appreciate, as the evidence will show, which is typical, Your Honor, that when these events occur, everybody appears. Everyone has a clipboard and a pencil, and everybody is a friend of the president or wants to be a friend of the senator, and walks around saying, well, the senator said to me we've got to do this or that, and that's how—how these events are, a whirlwind. And David Rosen goes into the whirlwind and tries to get ownership of what his role is: raising the money and working through many different issues.

On the 28th of July, for example, he stays for one week, the first time, July 15th to about the 23rd, stays at a hotel, The Hermitage, and he then leaves, comes back. And when he comes back, he will tell you he had thought about staying with his sister, but when he arrives, Aaron Tonken suggests to him that, well, don't stay there. Stay at the Beverly Hills Hotel, and that's where he stayed. And Aaron Tonken said, I will pay for you. He did not—and he will tell you—run around getting people to pay for him originally, because Aaron Tonken had told him. Then Aaron Tonken backed down, and then Aaron Tonken finally paid.

Now, when David Rosen stayed at the Beverly Hills Hotel, he will tell you he did not consider that a campaign contribution at all. He considered that this—this individual he struck up this relationship with who had the money who was able to underwrite all this was going to treat him because he was working hard, and he also loaned him his Porsche to drive back and forth during his work.

He did not report this to the campaign, because he thought this was something that this individual, whom he did not know in terms of background, was doing this for him; and it was very exciting for him, and he thought it was a nice idea. It didn't make him a criminal. It doesn't make him doing something wrong. He did not consider this to be a campaign contribution to the campaign, but for him, and this is how he conducted himself and he didn't hide it and you will hear testimony many of these people at this campaign stayed at the Beverly Hills Hotel and they didn't pay.

Now, I understand that the government, the prosecutors, are going to say that they don't believe what Mr. Rosen says. This is an example of his evil mind. This is an example of his pattern and practice. Well, you won't believe that after you hear the evidence in this case. There is no reason why he is not—there is no reason for him to have reported something that he thought was a personal gift to him. There was nothing that he did wrong in that, and he did not conceal it or hide it and did not intend this to be an evil deed.

Now, David Rosen, when he is involved in the activities of planning the event, David Rosen works very closely with Bretta Nock, the event planner. And David Rosen wanted to get a budget, because he wanted to see what was going on. And at first Ms. Nock wasn't responsive to his request. But in early August she sends him a budget. This is interesting, the evidence will show, that on—there are lots of budgets. They go this way, that way, every which way, the evidence will show the planned expenses of what this gala will be. It's not written in stone. Things come off; things come on. And Bretta Nock had a number, and you will see it in evidence. The government will show it to you. And if they don't, I will. You will see a number on the budget, which shows $200,000 on the first budget for the production costs.

Now, I want to share with you what the evidence will show about costs. The most significant and, really, the heart of the case of underreporting relates to the costs for what we are going to call the concert. No one knows, to this day, what the concert costs. You will hear that some people say $2 million; some people say $1 million. I think the government now takes the position $1.2 million. You will hear Agent Smith. He will go through it all for you.

The government will call him. If they won't, I will, so we can go through it. But the point is that that's where the heart of this case is, and the charge held against David Rosen is that he hid those costs to add a little window-dressing. The government is going to attempt to show that, well, he told the event planner take this off, take that off, as if to show that David Rosen intended to hide things. And I will prove to you that's not the case at all; that he didn't intend to hide anything.

And I will also suggest to you that during the activities of the actual event itself no one could—well, I will call witnesses who were there, and they will tell you that while they were there you couldn't look around and say, "Oh, my goodness, this event cost $2 million." And I will also prove to you that David Rosen, had David Rosen known that the costs of the concert were so extraordinary—because I am going to show you budgets that he never saw just on the concert part. I will show you a letter from the concealer, Tonken, that he received from Gary Smith. The famous producer, which said, in words to this effect: Mr. Tonken, the cost of this event is going to be over $500,000. I will show that to you. The government won't introduce it to you—introduce it, but I will. And you know what? I am going to ask David Rosen, "Mr.

Rosen, did you ever see this?" I am going to ask Gary Smith, if I can persuade him to testify: "Mr. Gary Smith, did you ever give this document to David Rosen? Did you ever discuss costs with David Rosen?" I will ask Mr. Baumrucker: "Mr. Baumrucker, you agree with me, do you not, sir"—assuming the judge allows this question—"do you not, sir, do you agree with me that you never discussed directly with Mr. Rosen the production costs of this concert?" I predict he'll say, in words to the effect, "I did not. David Rosen never knew." That's the tragedy of this. Had he known, he will tell you he would have reported it. He wasn't afraid of losing his job.

I will call his super-boss to tell you that. Will call someone who will tell you who ran this whole campaign, who will tell you the campaign wasn't concerned about a dire financial situation. David Rosen's job wasn't on the line. I will prove to you, even if he had an event at the Waldorf Astoria where 300 people were supposed to come and only 80 came, that he wasn't going to lose his job.

He will tell you, by the way, when he testifies there was such an event. He will tell you, and you can see not by what he says but what he does, what he did, because an event looked like it wasn't going to be a big turnout. He ran, just like you probably would if you were running an event, to fix the problem. He would close down the larger room to make it smaller, had tables removed, and was able to generate very fine publicity for a particular ethnic group that was coming to this event. He made it look good. He took something that wasn't so good and made it look good.

So the government will say, as a result of that, he had a bad event, so he was going to lose his job. It's a bizarre tragedy, bizarre.

THE COURT: Mr. Sandler, don't worry about the time. You can characterize what the evidence has proven at the end, with the adjectives.

MR. SANDLER: I beg your pardon.

THE COURT: Just anticipate, please. What you have been doing for the most part, what the evidence will show.

MR. SANDLER: I think the evidence will show all that I have said, ladies and gentlemen.

Thank you, Your Honor.

Ladies and gentlemen. After the event occurred—after the event occurred, there were certain events that you will hear about. You will hear about Bretta Nock's role in terms of an event planner. You will hear that her role was not only to hire the vendors, pay the vendors, she was supposed to communicate with David Rosen and the compliance officer about the budgets, about the costs, and you will hear that David Rosen's responsibility was not to be Sherlock Holmes. The evidence will show that. The evidence will show he was not supposed to go in with a flashlight and root out.

Now, of course you are going to hear testimony from the government that people told David Rosen, "David, it's costing millions." We'll confront that in the context, and David Rosen will explain to you and tell you what happened and what did not happen.

I will also prove to you that David Rosen was not at all intending to harm or hurt anyone.

The government will introduce evidence that after the event there was an intention by David Rosen to obtain a false invoice for the cost of the concert. I will prove to you that's not the case at all. I will prove to you that David Rosen did not seek or ask anyone to obtain a false invoice.

I will, through the evidence, explain to you the sequence of how that occurred, and I will also prove to you that no one, except the concealers and those that were with them, knew what these costs were.

In conclusion, I will prove to you that David Rosen did not know the costs; that Mr. Rosen received no economic benefit; that no economic benefit was received by the Clinton campaign; and I will predict, based on the evidence, that your answer to Mr. Zeidenberg's question, which was the only issue in this case for you to determine, is whether David Rosen—[he pointed to David].

I hope and pray, based on the evidence, that you will embrace him when this case is over and answer Mr. Zeidenberg "no." And Mr. Zeidenberg will tell you that if that's what the evidence shows. Justice will be done. Not guilty.

Thank you.

Appendix II

THE CLOSING ARGUMENTS IN *U.S. v. ROSEN*

Closing Argument by the Government

MR. SCHWAGER: Thank you, Your Honor.

Thank you, Your Honor, counsel.

Ladies and gentlemen, let me start by thanking you all for your service. You sat through a lot to get you to this stage, and if you can believe it, my job now is to try to make things a little simpler for you.

So, ladies and gentlemen, let me just tell you that this case is about one thing: This case is about the public's right to know. The case is about the public's right to know who is paying how much to their elected officials.

The case is about the public's right to know how much Peter Paul is paying to a national campaign. The case is about the public's right to know how much Aaron Tonken is paying to a national campaign finance director.

Ladies and gentlemen, this case is about the public's right to know the truth, and the defendant, David Rosen's, continued and intentional obstruction of that public right.

And what is this case not about? Well, the case is not about sloppy or negligent record-keeping. The evidence is clear that David Rosen knew what was and what wasn't being reported to Whitney Burns, and he knew he was feeding specific lies to Whitney Burns.

The case is also not about anybody's responsibilities except the defendant's. All the attempts to blame the contributor is a transparent dodge, and the evidence shows that all of the talk of Peter Paul and Aaron Tonken and Bretta Nock concealing is without any support in the evidence.

Next, this case is not about exact numbers, because you don't have to know whether this cost $1.1 million or $1.2 million to know it was a lot more than half a million, and you don't have to know the exact number to know that any number of types of costs were left out, never reported as required.

So, finally, ladies and gentlemen, despite all the difficult testimony that you heard and that you sat very patiently through, let me relieve you and say this case is not about benefits. This case is not about whether the campaign benefited from the defendant's lies. The question of benefits in this case is only one of motive. And, ladies and gentlemen, the government doesn't have to prove motive to you.

The question of benefits is not part of the government's proof, and it's not something that you need to wrestle with to determine that David Rosen is guilty beyond a reasonable doubt of causing Whitney Burns's reports to be false.

I'll say it again: Motive is not an element of the government's case. We don't have to prove any benefit to the campaign or to anyone. But motive is helpful to understanding the big picture, and the bottom line is that the evidence shows and the defendant finally admitted on cross-examination that there were clear potential benefits to Hillary Clinton's campaign from underreporting soft money in-kind contributions. But, still, that's not what this case is about.

And so, ladies and gentlemen, since we've discussed what the case is not about, let's get back to what it is, and let's talk about the story that the evidence told throughout the case.

And we're going to do that by asking three questions: First, what did the defendant do? Second, why did he do it? Third, why does it matter?

First we'll talk about what the defendant did, what were the lies; and after that we'll talk briefly about why he did it, the motives that help you understand the bigger picture.

And, finally, we'll talk about why all of this matters. How did it affect the very function and role of the Federal Election Commission? And that's when we'll come back to the public's right to know. What did he do? Why did he do it? Why does it matter?

So first let's talk about what the defendant or how he intentionally or knowingly caused Whitney Burns's reports to be false. Let's focus on that sentence and what is not in dispute in that sentence.

The reports Whitney Burns sent to the Federal Election Commission are clearly false when they reported that Stan Lee Media made an in-kind contribution of only $366,000 approximately.

Now, the charges before you are about the amount of that in-kind contribution, but to demonstrate the full scope of the lies being told, let me take you back to Rick Madden's testimony. And if you remember Mr. Madden, he was the general counsel at Stan Lee Media for some time. He came to court from Skadden Arps, a law firm down the street, where he works now.

Rick Madden testified that he told Peter Paul and David Rosen that Stan Lee Media was not paying for this event, and Peter Paul agreed with him in front of David Rosen. And on and to corroborate Mr. Madden, you can see the checks. You can even rely on what the defense brought out from Stan Lee about personal loans to pay for the event. So you know it's true that Stan Lee Media didn't pay for this event.

And so the chart that the defendant used in the very beginning of this case, the chart that has Stan Lee Media at the top of the organizational structure of this gala, that chart continues to lie to this very day, and they brought that lie right into this courtroom.

In fact, it's contradicted by another defense exhibit and one that wasn't made specifically for this trial. Let me show you defense Exhibit 548.

Defense Exhibit 548, the defendant told you, was a chart of events that he and his assistant, Tony Chang, kept in the course of their business for— working for Hillary Clinton and New York Senate 2000.

The exhibit lists the Hollywood gala on August 12, 2004—excuse me, 2000, and it lists under the column that says, "host of event, Aaron Tonken and Peter Paul."

So when David Rosen told Whitney Burns that the $366,000 was coming from Stan Lee Media, that was just another in a series of lies.

David Rosen knew that this was Peter Paul as an individual making this payment, and if Peter Paul and David Rosen agreed to call it Stan Lee Media after the general counsel told them it wasn't going to be, then David Rosen was as much a part of that lie as Peter Paul was, and David Rosen continued that lie right into this very trial with that very chart and with his testimony.

Now, let's talk about how you evaluate the witnesses, and let's talk about Rick Madden and David Rosen. Ladies and gentlemen, as the judge instructed you, you take into account many things about witnesses when you evaluate their credibility, and you treat them all the same.

Let's start with the interests of the witnesses. Compare Rick Madden to David Rosen and ask who has the motive to lie here. I'd submit to you that the evidence shows absolutely no reason for Rick Madden to come in and take the stand and lie. And you can analyze the content of Rick Madden's testimony. He didn't just remember the conversation generally. He told you that he was called into Peter Paul's office, he told you that he remembered being called in specifically to meet someone. He remembered that Peter Paul called him up, and he remembered that when he got into the office, he was there specifically to be introduced to David Rosen.

I'd submit that between Rick Madden and David Rosen's testimony, there's no doubt which of the two is credible, which of the two is reasonable, and which of the two is true.

Now, let's get back to that first sentence we talked about and what is not disputed in the false reports, because it's clear that the $366,000 doesn't begin to cover Peter Paul's in-kind contribution.

You have evidence before you which substantiates at least $1,175,988 to begin with. And besides the testimony of Allan Baumrucker and Pat Waters, Agent Smith and others, you can skim through these receipts and the checks that are in the government Exhibits 200 through 373 to check it for yourself. You can compare those exhibits to Exhibit 74, the government's summary chart of those exhibits, and you can satisfy yourselves beyond any doubt that the number on that chart is the true ballpark of Peter Paul's or Aaron Tonken's in-kind contributions.

But in the end even the defendant doesn't dispute these numbers. So don't kill yourselves about that.

And so now let's turn to defendant's own actions, what he did. Ladies and gentlemen, we'd submit to you that what the defendant did is obvious, that the evidence, the proof is overwhelming, and that the defendant's explanations don't match the evidence in this case.

We'd submit those explanations aren't credible, they aren't reasonable, and that they aren't true.

There is no doubt that David Rosen knowingly caused those reports to be false in two different ways: First, he flat-out lied to Whitney Burns; second, he, himself, was the concealer of numerous items he knew were required to be reported. He either witnessed these items himself or he incurred these items himself, and he knew that they never were reported.

And, ladies and gentlemen, two ways—the direct lies and the concealing—and we'd submit that the evidence on each of these standing alone is sufficient to convict David Rosen of these crimes.

But first David Rosen lied to Whitney Burns at least three different times, each time knowingly and intentionally feeding more and more false information, each time relying on and layering and buttressing the earlier lies.

The first lie David Rosen fed to Whitney Burns is the lie known to you as Exhibit 20. Exhibit 20 is the budget that the evidence establishes David Rosen created and David Rosen sent to Whitney Burns.

Of all of that, David Rosen admits discussing this budget and confirming for Whitney Burns that it's accurate, and that's a significant piece of the evidence.

So just based on that conversation, when he confirmed the numbers, if you believe all the evidence that David Rosen knew the numbers were false, then that conversation alone, we would submit, is enough to find David Rosen guilty. But let's look at the evidence and examine what David Rosen's role was in creating the document.

How can you tell in his denial that he had anything to do with it is a lie? To figure that out, we're going to start with Exhibit 19-A and 19-B and Exhibit 19, the timing of these three exhibits.

You remember that 19-A—well, let's start on August 2nd, when we know that David Rosen was in Los Angeles, and remember the judge spoke to you a little bit about venue.

On August 2nd, we know that David Rosen was in Los Angeles because of his Beverly Hills Hotel bill and because Melissa Rose said she came to work for him on August 1st at Stan Lee Media's offices.

So August 2nd is the starting date that we'll consider, and let's put August 2nd in context. Let me remind you where the defendant was on July 29th. He was in New York for an event that he had told Harold Ickes would raise $250,000 for Hillary Clinton, by far the largest predicted revenue in July for David Rosen's events.

And before he left New York, those predictions of $250,000 turned into an event that raised less than $30,000 and cost almost $5,000 more than it brought in.

That event at the Waldorf was a loss; that event was a wash. So by the time the defendant came to Los Angeles, he was feeling the heat of a money-losing event, a fundraising disaster with the president in attendance.

Think about that Waldorf event; that event that cost more than it raised when you're considering whether or not there is reason for the defendant to cook the books on the August 12th Hollywood gala.

So about five days after the Waldorf event on August 2nd, back in Los Angeles, David Rosen e-mails Bretta Nock, and that e-mail is Exhibit 19-A. And if you recall, that's the e-mail that says, "Bretta, I really need a budget document." You can hear the urgency in this e-mail, and David Rosen admitted the urgency. You can tell there's a purpose to his demands to the budget document.

19-B is Bretta Nock's response. The attachment to that e-mail was the budget, Exhibit 19, and with this, Bretta Nock said, "Fill in as you deem appropriate."

What does that tell you about the relationship here? What does it tell you about the role of Bretta Nock and the role of David Rosen? Is it reasonable for David Rosen to say that he thought Bretta Nock was the one on top of every single budget item and then to claim that this e-mail is just a miscommunication? Not at all.

And look back at Exhibit 31. Exhibit 31 is the e-mail sent on July 28th, and it came with an attachment, and the attachment has the paragraph regarding the budget. Let me read that quickly. "Regarding the budget, I have the specifics for all orders I've placed for decor, etcetera. The big expenditures, such as Regal Rents, Spago catering, and Chuck's Parking, I am still waiting for their proposals.

"Regal is waiting for Spago's order, Spago is waiting for Wolfgang's menu. As for the parking, we are still waiting to hear about the use of Paul Revere High. Regarding the production/show budget, that's a question for Stan Lee Media Inc., Gary Smith."

Bretta Nock uses "I" or "we" for every item she's in charge of covering, and remember her testimony that she wasn't in charge of the concert. But the concert costs are different. She doesn't use "I" or "we." In fact, Bretta Nock, who the defendant calls a representative of Stan Lee Media Inc., Bretta Nock doesn't even know at that time the difference between Stan Lee Media and Gary Smith.

Ladies and gentlemen, this evidence shows that the defendant's explanation of the roles that he and Bretta Nock filled, well, they aren't credible, they aren't reasonable, and they aren't true.

The only reasonable reading of Exhibit 31 is that Bretta Nock is telling David Rosen, "Go ask Gary Smith yourself," and the only reasonable reading of 19-B is, "You obviously have your own numbers and your own ideas. So you make this document into whatever you need it to be."

Ladies and gentlemen, the evidence is clear that David Rosen was the driving force in this budget-creation process.

Now, you heard that the document sent with the "fill in as you deem appropriate" e-mail is Exhibit 19, and Bretta Nock said she never saw Exhibit 20, and she never included the information in Exhibit 20. Specifically, she never had a column called "New York Senate 2000," and she never had in that column a bunch of n/a's and then a $100,000 entry for "event production."

The defendant, though, tries to shift that document back onto Bretta Nock. So, ladies and gentlemen, compare the two budgets for yourself. Compare budget 19 and budget 20 and ask, "Who would have added the New York Senate 2000 column? Who would have added the $100,000 down payment in that column?"

Whitney Burns told you that David Rosen was the one who asked her for that down payment, and you know that David Rosen was the one who understood that this was a New York Senate 2000 event. And he would have accurately included that column.

And, finally, Whitney Burns told you that David Rosen sent her this budget, and that's when they spoke about it. And from that conversation she noted that the total would go up because of Cher's band expenses and someone else's band expenses.

And by the way, you just heard Agent Smith's testimony that a search of Bretta Nock's computer yielded Exhibit 19 but not Exhibit 20.

So you can take all the budgets. The budgets are Exhibits 17 through 24. Take them all back with you and see if you find all of them, except budget 20, were in one particular font. Exhibit 20 is a different font from all the rest, and it's a different format from all the rest.

So the evidence is clear Bretta Nock didn't create this, and the evidence suggests only one conclusion: that David Rosen created Exhibit 20.

So now let's talk about when it was sent to Whitney Burns and when it was discussed. Well, we have Exhibit 71, a comparison of these budgets. And from the evidence you heard, the date on Exhibit Number 20 is wrong, isn't it? The chart says that it was sent to Washington, D.C., on August 12th, the day of a $150,000 transfer. But Whitney Burns testified that this wasn't the final number she relied on for that transfer and that she got this exhibit, Exhibit 20, about a week before the August 10th transfer. A week before August 10th, ladies and gentlemen, is August 3rd. Compare budget 19 and budget 20. Budget 19 is sent from Bretta Nock to David Rosen on August 3rd. Budget 20 is sent from David Rosen to Whitney Burns around August 3rd. The numbers are nearly identical, but the new column is added in.

So what's the only conclusion to be drawn from the actual evidence? That David Rosen got Exhibit 19 from Bretta Nock, that he made the changes, that he created Exhibit 20, and then from Los Angeles, he sent or he caused to be sent Exhibit 20 to Whitney Burns on or around August 3rd.

The evidence is overwhelming that David Rosen knowingly and intentionally sent this document, and he knew exactly what it said.

So what are the specific lies on Exhibit 20? First of all, there are a lot of items that aren't on this budget, like office space, like tribute journal printing, like David Rosen's hotel and car value from Aaron Tonken, and others that aren't on the budget.

So Whitney Burns has no idea that they may be an issue at some time, but we'll talk about all the things that are left off later on.

The evidence proves beyond any doubt that David Rosen knew several of the actual numbers on that budget were false, and each one themselves, we would submit, is enough to find David Rosen guilty beyond a reasonable doubt.

Specifically, let's talk about the Black Ink Production number, the printing number, and the total in-kind number at the bottom, and let's look closely at the evidence.

But what's the earliest we know that David Rosen knew the true figures were far more than what's on Exhibit 20? Ladies and gentlemen, Pat Waters and Blossette Kitson came before you, and each independently recalled great detail about a meeting on July 16th at Peter Paul's house. It was around Peter Paul's table, and it had David Rosen sitting right next to Peter Paul.

At this meeting specific numbers were discussed in living and graphic color. You may recall what Pat Waters said about Peter Paul; that he mentioned that he had figured that the entire event would cost somewhere around $500,000, and that Gary Smith's fee alone was eating up all of that, and that he was figuring that other people were going to help him share the costs.

Again, analyze Pat Waters's testimony, analyze her reason for lying, analyze her demeanor, and we'll submit that you'll find she's an entirely credible witness.

And as for that $500,000 figure, you also heard that from Jim Levin, independently from Waters. You heard Peter Paul was upset about going past half a million, that he was irate about Gary Smith's fee, and that he was looking for another person to put up the half a million.

Ladies and gentlemen, I'd submit to you that nothing should make you more confident about the government's witnesses than when a defense exhibit corroborates what they've told you.

So let's take a look at defense Exhibit 523. The defense brought this up to show you something about the arrangements with Stan Lee. This is dated August 10th, and it shows a cosponsorship by Cynthia Gershman for $525,000. Ladies and gentlemen, this defense exhibit corroborates Pat Waters and Jim Levin on those items. Half the cost of the event was around $500,000, and Peter Paul had in mind that somebody was cosponsoring the event with him.

And Pat Waters said these items came up when Peter Paul was sitting next to David Rosen. This defense exhibit tells you how accurate and credible the amounts of the government's witnesses are.

And remember on direct exam, David Rosen didn't remember—or on cross—well, on direct David Rosen didn't even dispute the contents of this meeting; that figures were discussed, and on cross, David Rosen wants you to believe that no such figures were brought up. Well, compare David Rosen's testimony to Pat Waters's testimony.

The defense put Gary Smith on the stand, and he corroborated the government witnesses by telling you that his costs never fell below half a million dollars. They were always just over half a million dollars.

So what else was discussed at the July 16th meeting? Ms. Kitson, the talent booker, told you the meeting was about invitations, not talent. And Pat Waters gave you the numbers discussed at that meeting. Printing was to be a firm $1.50 per invitation, 55 cents for stamps, for an estimated 30,000 invitations. That's $45,000 in printing, $16,500 for postage.

Again, we can turn to independent evidence to corroborate Pat Waters, because soon after the meeting, and days before Exhibit 20 was created, 28,000 invitations were ordered at $1.50 per invitation. And you can see that in Exhibit 203, you can see that in Exhibit 203 in the binder up there, and that directly contradicts David Rosen's testimony that there were only 5– to 10,000 invitations to be printed.

Let's go back to July 16th. Pat Waters didn't say on direct or cross that there was any question at that meeting of what the costs were or any effort to conceal anything. Everyone at the table seemed to know that these numbers were firm, because they were coming down from an earlier invitation that was estimated around $88,000, and Peter Paul was irate, and Peter Paul was insistent, and Peter Paul was sitting right next to David Rosen who was echoing the concern for rising costs.

Ladies and gentlemen, is it possible that all of these witnesses remember these conversations and figures this accurately almost five years later, but David Rosen missed them completely at the time? We submit to you that it's not possible, it's not reasonable, and it's not true.

And so we submit to you that if you believe Pat Waters alone, that's enough to prove David Rosen's knowledge. And if you believe Blossette

Kitson alone, that's enough. And if you believe Jim Levin alone, that's enough. It's enough to prove David Rosen's knowledge that the figures on Exhibit 20 were false beyond a reasonable doubt. And all together, with all the other testimony, there is no doubt.

And what's the other evidence beyond July 16th? You heard numerous witnesses come in and tell you that they heard all the time constant refrains from Peter Paul from Aaron Tonken, "The costs are going up. The costs are killing me. The talent is killing me. All the costs of the entertainment of the writers."

How is it that David Rosen was the only person among all these to never hear these complaints? How is it that all these independent witnesses, most without any evidence of any bias or interest, heard all of this; but David Rosen speculates that Peter Paul concealed from him alone?

Ladies and gentlemen, again, we submit it isn't credible, it isn't reasonable, and it isn't true.

And as for David Rosen's own expressions about the cost, Jim Levin, Ray Reggie, Bretta Nock all told you they heard David Rosen himself constantly complaining about the rise in costs, and even Whitney Burns herself told you that in the several conversations she had with David Rosen prior to the gala, he expressed concerns for rising costs and said he was trying hard to keep the costs down.

Ladies and gentlemen, it's not possible for the defendant to be both watching and reducing costs when he isn't getting any information and he isn't concerned about what he's seeing all around him, is it?

And so there is no reason to doubt Ray Reggie when he told you that he sat at the L'Ermitage hotel with David Rosen and Aaron Tonken when David Rosen complained that Gary Smith was charging over a half a million dollars.

There is overwhelming reason in the evidence to find that David Rosen lied to you when he denied it. And so if David Rosen knew the concert itself was over half a million dollars and he knew the printing costs were going to be higher than suggested on that budget, then he had to know the bottom-line figure on Exhibit Number 20 was way off.

Now, the rest of the evidence you need to convict David Rosen on this particularly was admitted to by Mr. Rosen himself. He had to admit on the stand that he knew this one truth; that he knew that his conversations with Whitney Burns were meant to provide information that she would put on FEC reports. That's not at issue. It's undisputed. It's beyond any doubt. So all you need to know is what David Rosen knew.

Ladies and gentlemen, about a week later—let's move on to the second lie. On August 9th or 10th, according to Whitney Burns, the defendant fed her more information that the evidence tells you beyond any doubt was an outrageous, baseless, calculated lie, and it was, in fact, a couple of lies wrapped up in one.

Defendant told Whitney Burns on August 9th or 10th that the estimated soft money in-kind contributions for this event were $375,000, and that was down from the 468 on Exhibit 20. In fact, it came down from higher than 468 because David Rosen had told Whitney Burns there would be no actual additional expenses because Cher had dropped out.

The costs dropped to $375,000, ladies and gentlemen, on August 9th or 10th from Los Angeles, where Peter Paul was ranting and raving every day about rising costs; where Reggie told you David Rosen was complaining that the last-minute costs were crushing him, such as the chairs; where Melissa Rose recalled David Rosen and Aaron Tonken were having frustrating or tense conversations every day; where Chris Fickes, Ray Reggie, Jim Levin, Melissa Rose all recall David Rosen talking about or working on booking planes where Cher had to have a Gulfstream G4, where $35,000 worth of directors' chairs were added onto the concert budgets, hundreds of boxes of CDs in the defendant's office being put in gift bags; whereas Blossette Kitson told you there was almost daily heated, profane complaints and arguments about how much the various entertainers were costing and how much they were charging for their riders and their travels and their bands and their entourages; and where Peter Paul was complaining that he was way over his half a million dollars, and Cynthia Gershman was backing out; and finally, whereas Jim Levin told you, Peter Paul wanted the campaign to put up Cynthia Gershman's share, and Rosen and Levin told him they would cancel the event instead and the president and first lady would blame Peter Paul.

And right there in the middle of all of that, David Rosen told Whitney Burns, as she said it, that he had whittled down the costs by about

$100,000. And note that well because that's the second time you heard David Rosen acknowledge his role in controlling these costs.

The second such clear memory from Whitney Burns: David told Whitney Burns that he had whittled down the costs by about $100,000.

Ladies and gentlemen, if you believe Whitney Burns's testimony alone about that one conversation and from any one piece of the overwhelming evidence from so many other witnesses and documents that Rosen knew that that figure was a lie, we submit that you can convict David Rosen beyond a reasonable doubt on that alone.

Now, David Rosen twisted that story about Cher around for you a little bit and made it seem like he just said there were no extra costs because she didn't bring a band.

But, ladies and gentlemen, the evidence is overwhelming that David Rosen knew about and participated in the procuring of Cher's jet. And no matter whether she lives in LA or not, if that was the necessary cost that Aaron Tonken or Peter Paul had to pay to bring Cher to the event where she was a draw and she was on the invitation, then David Rosen always knew that he should have told Whitney Burns that the expenses were going up because of Cher, not down.

Two lies in that one conversation, ladies and gentlemen, and two sets of lies, Exhibit 20 and the $375,000 conversation.

And the third time period where David Rosen fed Whitney Burns a set of lies was after the event, when Whitney Burns asked David Rosen for the final information for the budget, for the invoices. David Rosen referred her to Bretta Nock. When she asked him if the $200,000 invoice—when Whitney Burns asked David Rosen if the $200,000 invoice was the final documentation for Black Ink, he said yes. And for all the information, he referred her to Bretta Nock.

And, ladies and gentlemen, that in itself was a lie, because the evidence shows it was a lie because David Rosen knew that Whitney Burns would not get all the information she needed from Bretta Nock. It was a lie because David Rosen knew that Whitney Burns needed the truth, and that in referring her to Bretta Nock, he knew that she would get nothing near the whole truth about the event. It was a lie because he knew that Bretta Nock would tell Whitney Burns the same lies that David Rosen asked Bretta to tell.

And the big part of this lie is Exhibit 24—or Exhibit 24. Excuse me.

Now, if you use government Exhibit 71, you'll see the progression—that's the comparison of the budget, and you'll see the comparison from one budget to the next, and the items from the various budgets that Bretta Nock was creating while working with David Rosen. And you can see at the end that just a number of items have disappeared.

You've heard that Bretta Nock—from Bretta Nock that David Rosen told her that the budget document was too high and that she needed to take items off the budget. And that matches Jim Levin's testimony, his independent testimony, that David Rosen said, "The cost of this event won't be the cost of this event."

So let's return to Exhibit 24-A and the evidence that defendant was the one that orchestrated this lie.

First let's discuss the defendant's alternative explanation that he was duped by some speculative conspiracy of concealers, and right from the start he betrays this theory because he tells you that he got all of his information from Bretta Nock and never got any numbers of any kind from Aaron Tonken or Peter Paul, despite the fact he was sitting at the July 16th meeting.

Yet for some reason he blames Peter Paul and Aaron Tonken while he invites Bretta Nock to his wedding.

Ladies and gentlemen, I ask you, doesn't that sound like somebody picked the most convenient targets and didn't care about the truth? The e-mail, such as Exhibit 31, and all the testimony shows that Bretta Nock was the one actively working with the vendors, collecting the invoices, creating the budgets, and sending them and discussing them with the defendant, and he knew that.

But with no evidence to make the connection, David Rosen speculates and blames Peter Paul and Aaron Tonken and over two years after learning of a federal investigation, he still invites Bretta Nock to his wedding.

Well, of course, you heard from Jim Levin that this story is nothing more than a scheme that they hatched by the defendant while he was watching the "20/20" video, and he decided what he had to work with and he decided what he could sell to anyone that would ask.

There is absolutely no evidence that Peter Paul or Aaron Tonken concealed anything about this particular event from anyone. And what really puts the lie to the repeated efforts by the defense to sell this story is that there's not even any evidence that Peter Paul concealed his convictions.

There is no evidence that anyone asked him if he had a 15- or 20-year-old record. Defendant said he got Peter Paul's information, he sent it on to the lawyers, and that they missed it.

There is no evidence that Peter Paul had an obligation to volunteer that information. He certainly had far less of an obligation than David Rosen had to report all of those hotel bills and the extra costly items he saw at the concert.

So I bring this up to point out and submit for your consideration that the defense has tried to distract you throughout this trial with lies about who was concealing what.

Again, there is absolutely no evidence whatsoever that either Peter Paul or Aaron Tonken concealed anything about this event from anyone.

But let's look at what evidence there is. All of the independent, disinterested testimony and evidence supports itself that both Peter Paul and Aaron Tonken were constantly complaining about rising costs and about the costs of bringing in entertainment, and they were doing this openly, publicly, and in front of David Rosen.

But from the time David Rosen attempted to get Jim Levin to go along with his plan to blame Tonken and Paul, to the very opening statement by the defense in this case, and to the defendant's own testimony, David Rosen, the record-breaking salesman, who told the *Business Magazine* that he could sell anything to anyone, has been trying to sell the same baseless and transparent dodge called "the concealers."

Ladies and gentlemen, when you realize how absolutely absurd that pitch is, you can apply that absurdity to everything that David Rosen has tried to sell you.

So between Bretta Nock, who is supported by Exhibits 19-B and 31 and numerous witnesses, between Bretta Nock acknowledging to you that she followed David Rosen's direction and she took costs of her budget and she obtained and collected and sent a fake invoice—between—and David

Rosen's baseless sales pitch that Bretta Nock was part of the concealers conspiracy, there is no doubt which explanation is supported by evidence.

And so—no doubt which explanation is credible, and no doubt which explanation is reasonable, and no doubt which explanation is true.

And just consider the evidence in the context of the lies that David Rosen told to Whitney Burns back in August, and you know that he needed Bretta Nock to back him up and help support the lies that he set in motion.

That's three lies, ladies and gentlemen, Exhibit 20, the 300—and the conversation about it. The $375,000 conversation and the fall referral to Bretta Nock and vouching for the $200,000 invoice.

But there is a little bit more than that here, because the evidence is overwhelming that David Rosen hid any number of in-kind costs or contributions that he knew had to be reported. And we only need to deal with a few of them. And let's start by dispelling some more of the defendant's blame games and dodges. We already addressed the blame he tried to lay on Peter Paul and Aaron Tonken and Bretta Nock, but you also heard from the first cross-examination all the way throughout this trial the defendant's pitch, that it's the contributor's responsibility to report their costs and in-kind contributions.

The evidence shows there is nothing but a transparent dodge. Sure, they have a responsibility to report honestly, but that's not the end of [the] question.

Every witness, prosecution or defense, who talked about the contributor's responsibility also agreed that the fundraiser had to report to the compliance officer any cost or in-kind contribution that the fundraiser was aware of, even if he hasn't gotten the final receipt yet. And it's absurd to think otherwise.

The defendant wants you to believe that if a contributor doesn't tell you how much it costs, if they don't stick a bill in your pocket before they walk in the door, then that in-kind contributions doesn't exist for the purposes of the FEC and the public's right to know.

Again, ladies and gentlemen, we argue that's an attempt to evade responsibility by the defendant, and it proves you shouldn't take any of his claims seriously.

The evidence and the common sense show beyond any doubt that the defendant, the fundraiser in charge of this event, the man Blossette

Kitson and Pat Waters were introduced to as managing the finances for the gala event, David Rosen, had an absolute obligation to let Whitney Burns know if there were in-kind contributions made at the event, even if he didn't know the final figure. It's clear he had the obligation.

Let's talk specifically how David Rosen willfully and intentionally ignored that obligation in a way he knew would make Whitney Burns' reports false. We'll go through some of the items that the evidence proves beyond any doubt that the defendant knew about and which never made it to Exhibit 24-a.

Let's talk about the costs the defendant personally incurred. The evidence showed that the office space he used was an in-kind contribution that had to be reported. The FEC guide, which the defendant entered into evidence, also shows that David Rosen should have known that the phones, the supplies, and that office space should have been reported. There's absolutely no legitimate reason why those items were never reported, except that David Rosen didn't want her to know. The defendant had Bretta Nock create the budgets he was using with Whitney Burns, but how would Bretta Nock know to put such items on her budgets unless David Rosen had told her to?

Now, a lot has been made about the hotel bills and the car that Aaron Tonken made available for David Rosen while he was working on the gala. Ladies and gentlemen, we'd submit to you that there is no doubt why Aaron Tonken paid for either David Rosen's $3,500 L'Ermitage bill or $9,300 Beverly Hills Hotel bill and lent him his $80,000 Porsche for several weeks.

Ladies and gentlemen, we'd submit to you that David Rosen knew all too well that Aaron Tonken's friendship was part of the game that was made completely in connection with David Rosen's role and in connection with the work that they were doing together on the gala fundraiser.

And, again, the FEC guide that the defendant entered into evidence shows any cost or contribution for the campaign made in connection with one of these events is an in-kind contribution, and David Rosen knew that.

Ladies and gentlemen, again, look at the defense Exhibit 548. Aaron Tonken is listed as the host on four different events on this exhibit.

David Rosen knew that Aaron Tonken was getting invitations to the White House. The defendant's own witness, Jane Hedgepeth, had to admit that those two facts would have raised her eyebrows had she known that, but the defendant never provided any opportunity for Whitney Burns's eyebrows to be raised. He just kept it to himself, and he told at least two people to keep it to themselves.

And, once again, the mere fact that defendant asks you to believe that he thought Aaron Tonken's motives were unrelated to his role in a federal campaign, of the campaign of the first lady of the United States, that's beyond any doubt another lie.

Again, we'd ask you to apply your own good sense. The defendant met Tonken in June. In July he's moving into one of the swankiest hotels in L.A. and driving around an $80,000 sports car. Ask yourself how many one-month-old business associates become such good friends that, with no other motive at all, they give you nearly $15,000 in gifts. Well, you heard and saw Blossette Kitson's reaction when asked if she thought Aaron's payment for her hotel was a gift, "Oh, absolutely not." She nearly fell back in her chair. She thought it was a ridiculous suggestion, and she had known Aaron Tonken a lot longer than David Rosen has. Ladies and gentlemen, the campaign itself saw the inherent danger in accepting such contributions, and the evidence—from the evidence you can infer that that is why they prohibited accepting such gifts from donors.

And what about the L'Ermitage? Even if the defendant did pay the L'Ermitage bills himself, his explanations why he had to report it weren't the least bit believable.

You heard him go back and forth about whether his trip was personal or business. You heard Mr. Zeidenberg ask him if he thought a dinner with a friend made a business trip a personal one, and you heard him twist the language of Exhibit 61, one of Harold Ickes's memos.

Ladies and gentlemen, take a glance through the defense Exhibit 510, the campaign guide, and on page 9 it makes clear that a paid campaign staffer's use of his own money are contributions, unless they're under $1,000 or reimbursed.

Of course, that's what the Ickes's memo meant, and so when the national finance director of Hillary Rodham Clinton's campaign tells you that he doesn't think spending his own money on his job is a reportable in-kind contribution, I'd submit to you, don't believe it.

And while the defendant tried to dance around the requirement for the office space, his protégé, Chris Fickes, understood that requirement perfectly well. He pursued and reported that information on numerous occasions, and he learned the ropes from David Rosen.

So, ladies and gentlemen, the evidence is clear he did say that there are things he doesn't want to hear about, and he's not afraid to say it. And that makes David Rosen the true concealer.

Ladies and gentlemen, David Rosen knew from any number of sources that there were costs that were concealed from Whitney Burns, and David Rosen intentionally avoided finding out the details, and the evidence suggests only one inference: that he intentionally avoided getting the readily available receipts, that he avoided letting Whitney Burns know there were additional costs that needed to be followed up on. Those are the facts of a true concealer.

Just like David Rosen concealed Olivia Newton-John and David Benoit's travel expenses in June of 2000, just like he attempted to conceal from you that Olivia Newton-John was something more than a guest at the event, just like he concealed the L'Ermitage bill one way or another from Whitney Burns, just like he concealed his office space and supplies and expenses for his time at Stan Lee Media, just like he concealed Aaron Tonken's gifts of the hotels and the Porsche, just like he concealed then and now that Peter Paul as an individual was the true underwriter and not Stan Lee Media, and just like he concealed what he plainly heard at the July 16th meeting, that the costs were rocketing over half a million dollars; and just like he has concealed his knowing and intentional underreporting from Whitney Burns, Alan Grossman, from Hillary Clinton's campaign, and now he's attempted to conceal it from you.

Ladies and gentlemen, the evidence is overwhelming. David Rosen is the true concealer in this case, and that's just the last of the many independent ways you can find David Rosen guilty beyond a reasonable doubt of causing Whitney Burns's reports to be false.

And so it seems like we've discussed this forever now, what the defendant did; so briefly now let's talk about why he did it, and let's talk about motive. And to start, remember this doesn't need to be proven to you. We offer this evidence only to help you put the larger picture of what he did in context.

We've all sat patiently through a lot of talk about actual potential benefits, but the bottom line is this: As Jim Levin, Ray Reggie, Bretta Nock all independently told you, David Rosen was terrified at how costs were spiraling out of control.

Even Whitney Burns told you that David Rosen said he was concerned about the in-kind costs rising and was trying to keep them down. Again, why in the world would David Rosen have told Whitney Burns he was concerned about them if rising soft money in-kinds didn't matter to David Rosen or the campaign?

And so, again, I'd submit there is no doubt whatsoever which witnesses appeared more credible between Whitney Burns and David Rosen; and that David Rosen did, in fact, express such concern to Whitney Burns.

If David Rosen had truthfully estimated a million dollars in soft money in-kind contributions on August 9th or 10th, when, as he told you, hard money was getting even harder, then a lot of things would have changed.

David Rosen testified himself here this morning that if he knew such and such a cost were higher, he would have canceled that. If he knew such and such a cost were rising out of control, he would have canceled that part of the event. So that's what he was facing: This huge Hollywood gala that he was putting on, the biggest of his career, he said, if I had reported the million dollars, then maybe they would have canceled that event.

And David Rosen was scared for his job because he was losing control of a second event in a row. The Waldorf event was projected by David Rosen to be the largest revenue-maker for July. The gala had the same amount projected for Hillary Clinton's campaign.

Is it reasonable to think that David Rosen wouldn't be worried about what the campaign thought about the Waldorf event? Is it reasonable to think he wouldn't have been worried that the campaign would find out about all the waste at the gala?

Remember Harold Ickes's memos found at David Rosen's office. Those are Exhibits 61 through 69, and read through those. The evidence is clear, of course, the defendant was worried. David Rosen was worried about the campaign finding out about giving away $35,000 worth of chairs and $50,000 worth of CDs. He was worried that they would find out about paying $30,000 for Cher to fly in for two songs and $30,000 for Muhammad Ali to fly in for a quick toast.

Of course, the members of the campaign at the event saw the chairs, the CDs, saw Cher up there, but they never saw the costs of these things, and that's what David Rosen concealed.

In fact, look at the evidence about Kelly Craighead at the walk-through the night before the event. Melissa Rose, who didn't remember much, remembered intense conversation between Craighead and Rosen. Ray Reggie independently told you what that conversation was about.

Kelly Craighead, Hillary Clinton's assistant, was demanding to know how much the event was going to raise, angry at the extravagance, at what she saw, and David Rosen refused to answer her, repeating only that he's the fundraiser and he's in control.

Of course, you know from the evidence that he had no control whatsoever of anything except what he told Whitney Burns and the campaign.

Obviously David Rosen and the campaign were concerned. And the reason for that [as] Andy Grossman, the treasurer for New York Senate 2000, pointed out, each one of those soft money in-kind items cost money. He pointed out if you had a choice between $10,000 worth of flowers and $1,000 worth of flowers donated in soft money in-kinds, then you take the $1,000. Because the higher the soft money in-kind, the more hard money you have to transfer.

The CDs would have cost some of those precious hard dollars. The $30,000 jet for Cher would have cost some of those precious hard dollars. The $17,000 video screen would have cost some of those precious hard dollars.

And on direct examination David Rosen tried to sell you that there was no reason why he might underreport, but do you believe for a second that Harold Ickes, Hillary Clinton, or anyone on the campaign staff was ever as complacent about their funds as the defense tried to suggest in their opening statement?

Remember when they tried to describe that the campaign was in perfectly fine straits and there was no concern over money that would have been a motive for David Rosen?

It's not credible, it's not reasonable, and so we'd submit it's not true.

The common sense and the evidence shows that wasting money was never acceptable in Hillary Clinton's campaign.

The bottom line is this, and it's indisputable according to the evidence: that David Rosen would have believed at the time he was lying to Whitney Burns that by underreporting the soft money in kinds, he was potentially benefiting the hard money accounts of New York Senate 2000 and Hillary Clinton's campaign and possibly preventing a second hard money-losing event in a row.

So, finally, let's talk even more briefly about why this all matters, because it doesn't take a lot of explanation.

His Honor gave you an instruction on materiality, and we'd submit to you that the evidence that the defendant's lies were material to the Federal Election Commission is beyond any doubt. The question of benefit is irrelevant as to whether this crime matters or not, because as the first 18 witnesses told you and as the defendant's own witness Jane Hedgepeth told you, one of the functions of the Federal Election Commission is to be the liaison between the campaign and the public, to be the gatekeeper of the public's right to know who is giving how much to their elected officials.

It's clear from the evidence that soft money in the year 2000 had to be reported for joint fundraisers, and as we've discussed and as you've heard from Whitney Burns, it's crucial to know how much soft money is used at a joint fundraising event to know what to do with the hard money.

And this brings up a second reason that these lies matter, because besides just the public's right to know, the evidence shows clearly that it's part of the FEC's function to monitor these reports, to make decisions about who to look more closely at, what events to scrutinize more closely, what audits to do, and who to request additional information from. In fact, even in this case, even with the numbers it did report, the FEC ended up inquiring further from the campaign about this event, and you can see that for yourself in Exhibit 43.

So it's obvious that the defendant's underreporting had the ability or potential to affect the decisions or activities of the Federal Election Commission, because, in fact, they did.

Now, getting back to the public's right to know. Let's talk about one last time the defense's constant pointing out in this trial what bad guys Peter Paul and Aaron Tonken are, and that's the best demonstration why it's so important that these reports be accurate.

Aaron Tonken is giving the first lady's national finance director gifts that equal over two months of his take-home salary, and Aaron Tonken is getting invitations to the White House.

That Whitney Burns would use his information to file at least two specific reports of campaign activity with the Federal Election Commission. And he knew the purpose of those reports was for the FEC's review and scrutiny and more importantly to enable the public's right to know of who pays how much to elected officials.

Ladies and gentlemen, when David Rosen was in Los Angeles in the summer of 2000, he began to sell a pack of lies that is still being sold to this day.

We ask you only to examine all of the real evidence in this case, to apply only your common sense and not your sympathies or your passions, and in the end we ask you not to buy what the defendant is selling.

Ladies and gentlemen, we ask you to find David Rosen guilty beyond a reasonable doubt of the crimes charged. Thank you.

Closing Argument by the Defense

MR. SANDLER: Thank you, Your Honor. May it please the court, members of the jury, good afternoon. As you know, I am Paul Sandler, and I represent David Rosen, and I want to echo the words of Judge Matz and the prosecutor about thanking you for your patience. Serving on a jury is one of the most important public services any citizen can give. The right to trial by jury is so precious to our society, it's been mentioned no less than four times in the text of the United States Constitution. We have a jury of citizens in criminal trials to prevent oppression by government officials and because we have citizens, such as you, serving on juries as the last check and balance in government, the government cannot be unrestrained in its power over all of us. It's very, very vital that we preserve trial by jury, and that's why everyone thanks you and that's why we stand when you come and you go, out of respect for you and the vital role that the citizen plays in cases just like this.

Now, in a short time you will take this case with you to the jury room. You have been sitting here for about three weeks in what, up until now, has been a silent role in a somewhat unique criminal trial. Soon you will render a verdict which will be fair, just, and equitable, and it's my purpose at this time, to the extent the court allows me, to proceed to review with you the salient materials of evidence superimposed by the instructions that the judge has given.

And I first ask you this: What is the issue in this case that you, the jury, will decide?

Is David Rosen charged with stealing money that belongs to others? No.

Is he charged with reaping profits to which he is not entitled? No.

Is he charged with inflicting physical harm or violence?

No.

Is he charged with causing innocent people to suffer economically or lose their jobs? No.

As the judge has instructed you, he is charged with causing false information to be filed before the Federal Election Commission. He has been charged with willfully, knowingly, and deliberately making false statements and that he had knowledge of these statements and intended to do it. In other words, he sat down one day and said, "Okay, I am 33 years old. I have a very important job. I am afraid that I could get fired and, let's see, I think I'll risk my whole career, my family, and jeopardize everything. I'm going to lie. I am intentionally going to deceive people," so for what? He's scared for his job?

First of all, Mr. Ickes came from Washington to tell you he had no reason to be. Secondly, even if he were, many people sometimes are concerned about this or that. There is no evidence here that he had such a concern. So when you go to the jury room, do put the hat of common sense on and think about what it is, having met this gentleman who is courageous, who is truthful, who has suffered for years with this sword of Damocles over his head. And he comes to trial and he takes the witness stand, and he doesn't have to do that. And I told you in opening statement he would answer every question posed to him, and he did, and you could see the cut of his jib. And I will review with you some of the other witnesses in a bit. I will say this to you: The government says don't buy what he is selling. I say buy it lock, stock, and barrel, because what he is not selling but advocating is the truth, the whole truth, the simple truth, and nothing but the truth. And imagine, imagine we are talking about an event that occurred August the 12th of 2000. Where were you? Where were we on that date? Who did we talk to a week before? What meetings did we attend? Oh, Mr. Madden, who didn't take notes and who came forth and said he had a meeting, well, gee, do you remember the day of the meeting? No. Recollections do differ.

And I say this to you: When you evaluate the evidence, there is a little story that I once heard, and I think it's applicable. There was a lawyer who said to a friend of his, who was a jurist, "You know, I've got a tough case tomorrow. It's not before you. We're friends. Give me some advice. How do I proceed if the facts are against me?" The judge said, "Well, that's easy: Argue the law."

"Well," he said, "suppose the law is against me." The judge said, "That's easy: Argue the facts."

And then the lawyer said, "Well, what if the law and the facts are against me?"

And the judge said, "Well, then you pound the table."

And in the closing argument we have heard, it was table-pounding; and I will explain to you in a minute, and then I will proceed.

First of all, the law. We saw in evidence Exhibit 510. Just an example: "Notifying the recipient: the donor needs to notify the recipient candidate committee of the value of an in-kind contribution. The recipient needs this information in order to monitor the donor's aggregate contributions and to report the correct amount."

That's the law. That is, in fact, the evidence, and I will explain how it relates to the facts.

Now, the prosecutor has also said, "Well, just take any one of our witnesses"—and I am going to take them one at a time, and we are going
to talk about them—but just take any. "Take Whitney Burns. Just on her
testimony, you should convict."

Well, I would suggest that a fair-minded jury, when the government
has a burden, a burden beyond a reasonable doubt, that a vague conversation ought not to be the basis of proof beyond a reasonable doubt. And
I want to quote. I don't want to use hyperbole, because I believe what I
heard was hyperbole, taking a fact and stretching it.

For example, this case is not about the public's right to know. Of course
the public has a right to know. Well, pulling that noble theory and weaving it into a case where it doesn't necessarily apply does not convey to you
an accurate picture of what the facts in this case are. This case is about
what the judge said it was. You have his instructions. You look at those
instructions when you go into the jury room. You will find what the case
is about. Did David Rosen intend—sit down, plan to scheme, and hatch
a plan and then cover it up? Of what? Of what? Underreporting the cost
of an event when you heard the overwhelming evidence that he never
received or knew what those costs were?

And then you have to ask yourself, wearing the hat of common sense,
well, maybe he made a mistake. Maybe he was rushing around. Maybe it
happened. But does it look, from the evidence or the facts there, that he
intended to do it?

Use your common sense: Does a young man—young from my perspective—go on the witness stand, look at people that are judging him, swear
under oath that he didn't intend it? No. They don't testify. Those type
of people don't step up to the plate. They let their lawyers go through a
whole dialogue of reasonable doubt, which I will explain to you and show
you why there is in this case. But first we are going to set forth from the
evidence what the facts are.

Let me read to you the—this one statement—this—this witness that
you should alone—and I want to take the one that—don't want to be glib
and pick something that's so obvious that favors the defense. I want to show
you one of their prime examples where allegedly David is conspiring with
Whitney Burns and telling her in sinister terms that he is working and

whittling down costs, and that, you know, the costs were really $100,000 less. And I know this—I mean, you have to be in the room. He is on the cell phone and he says, "Now is my time to tell her to cheat and she'll never suspect it. I will be slick and quick about it, and I will hide."

Here's the conversation: Can you describe that conversation for the jury? Basically—and I am quoting. I am quoting facts, ladies and gentlemen, not hyperbole. Showed you the law was not what the government said it was when I showed you that exhibit. I am going to show you the facts were not interpreted by the prosecutors either, the facts you and I heard.

Basically, I mean, David had said that he had been trying to keep—to whittle the costs down, and to keep the costs down was one of the things he had been working on at the event. And he said that he thought that the expenses had dropped. The—I think we discussed—my recollection of the conversation is very vague in terms of the details about why.

You know, David Rosen took the witness stand, and he explained that conversation to you. He said that the Exhibit 20 that was referred to had a different amount than he had understood from Bretta Nock. What was the different amount? Well, you remember it. We saw it. We see it. Exhibit 20. Excuse me. And you see the 300 and then the 100. And that was different than he had received from Exhibit 19 and explained to Whitney Burns that as a result of his understanding of what was going on, there was $100,000 high from her, and it should be the amount that he thought, and he told her that. And that is the conversation as David Rosen testified, and it does not in the slightest contradict Whitney Burns. It simply states what he remembered saying to her. She indicated that she was vague. And what—remember when the government earlier in the argument said, "Well, this Exhibit 20, David Rosen said it was prepared by Whitney Burns and he explained why this matched up." The fact that the government takes the hard drive of Whitney Burns and doesn't find that exhibit doesn't mean Whitney Burns didn't prepare the—

MR. ZEIDENBERG: Objection.

THE COURT: Okay; I think you are inadvertently referring to Whitney Burns when you mean to say Bretta Nock.

MR. SANDLER: Yes, I thank you. Thank you, counsel.

Just because the government searches the hard drive of Bretta Nock and doesn't find the exhibit doesn't mean that Bretta Nock didn't prepare it. You could see David Rosen, you heard his schedule. You saw how he operated in terms of his schedule, and you can understand when he says he didn't prepare any budgets. He didn't. He had no basis or knowledge to prepare any budgets. In fact, he had asked Bretta Nock for the budget, and you saw the budget.

The point that I make here is that when the government says David Rosen sent this budget to Whitney Burns and then has a conversation with her and then tries to back out of the budget, it doesn't make sense. You don't send a budget, for example, of $400,000, then back out of it, if that's what the government is saying. This exhibit, Exhibit 20, is a document that David Rosen briefly spoke to with Bretta Nock, and he did not, as he testified, intend to cheat or deceive her at all. He was going on his good faith and basic understanding of what occurred.

And I say to you as follows based on this one example: There are so many examples, when you go back and recount the evidence of how the government by hyperbole switched and shaped the witnesses to come up with particular answers that would fit into the groove of what they dreamed occurred in this case.

I will give you another example. An example would be with this idea of a false invoice. Remember in the trial, ladies and gentlemen, the government wanted to demonstrate that David Rosen perpetrated a fraud by obtaining a false invoice? Remember that invoice, government Exhibit 9? There it is. Okay. I think you can remember it, and you will see it in evidence.

That's the invoice that was the subject of testimony, and the government wants you to believe that David Rosen procured a false invoice as an example of his evil mind. And let's look at the circumstances. Let's look at the circumstances, what happened, in fact. On January 9th Bretta Nock met with Agent Smith. She had said that she testified three—I'm sorry, that she had met with him three times, four times, five times. When she met with him on January 9th, I asked her—not on January 9th of '02 but in court—"Is it true that you could not recall when you spoke to Agent Smith on January 9th, '02 if Rosen had asked to get the invoice from Black Ink Productions?" Her answer: "Yes."

Now, why is that significant? It's significant because two years after the event, the agent, you'll remember, spent thousands of hours on the case, met with many different witnesses time after time. When the agent confronts her at that time, she says she has no recollection if David asked her.

Then follow with me, follow the evidence, not the hyperbole. Come down to earth and look at the facts, because on the 30th of January '03, she has another meeting with the agent. Same agent, more hours. Remember, the indictment is under seal that they keep going. "Is your" my question—"is your recollection refreshed about whether you told the government agent on the date that I referenced that you could not be sure if it was either David Rosen or Whitney Burns that asked for the invoice?"

She answered, "David Rosen, yes, or New York Senate 2000."

And then I said to her, "What do you mean 'New York 2000'? Is that what you mean?"

By Bretta Nock, answer: "Yes."

Okay; so here is another example. January 9th, '02, Ms. Nock doesn't know who it was that told her to get this so-called false invoice. January 30th, little shift, could be David, could be Whitney.

And then you heard the trial testimony. I'm going to read it to you, because I don't want you to think we are walking away from any fact. At the trial just several days ago I said, "So what was your conversation? Speaking about the invoice. What do you recall about your conversation with Mr. Rosen about that invoice?" Answer, "Again that any line item that was going to be on my budget without any direct knowledge I needed substantiation for."

Okay. That's what she says he said. Did he make any suggestions? Not did he give you any instructions even, but at least she—they are getting out from her the answer they want. Oh, yeah, absolutely, to call Black Ink Productions and obtain that invoice.

Of course we have uncontradicted testimony that when she called Mr. Baumrucker, she said Jim Levin wanted the invoice, and that's uncontradicted.

And you heard Mr. Levin—and I will come to him soon. When you heard Mr. Levin testify, he said, of course the president wanted a video. And how it is—but you will see, for archival television production.

So this is another example of where when you pay attention to the facts, you can see the government has no alternative but to pound the table.

And what I would like to do now is to take you through briefly—because I know you are saturated with lawyers and facts, and I don't want to burden you or impose on you—but I want to take the opportunity to do two things. I want to talk to you about—refresh your recollection about David Rosen's testimony, what he is about, what he did. And then I want to talk to you, in particular terms, about proof, whether the government has met its proof beyond a reasonable doubt.

Remember, David Rosen, who worked his way through school, who had many, many jobs, took the GEDs, becomes a graduate of college, goes into politics, goes into fundraising, and has a wonderful opportunity to become the national fundraising director of the senatorial campaign. And he had stated to you, clearly, that in the time period of his office, he had done over 90 events, and they were all over the country, and he hopped and he skipped and he jumped to do these events. He had systems for setting up the events. He had systems for obtaining from hosts in writing their invoices. He talked to you about what he meant by sometimes expenses were rolled in, catering, lump sum. He did not have to put himself to the exposure of cross-examination, to the humiliation and the concern, the nerves, all of that, but he is courageous and he told the truth, and you can see that by watching him, by looking at him and observing his demeanor. Because I think that's very important.

You have common sense. Sisters, brothers, parents, relatives, children, friends on surfboards, whoever it is, you know when someone is lying. You can tell that, because you know how to evaluate people. All of us as adults do. And you saw David Rosen. He looked into your eyes, and you looked into his.

He had a system where, as Ms. Dobbs said—remember, she was one of the hired consultants—that a donor would or a host would frequently want you to go to a representative—that's right, go to a representative—of the host, and Mr. Rosen would do that or his aide would do that. And, you know, in all of those events, the only problem with events that he had was when Aaron Tonken was involved. And this idea of hiding Olivia Newton-John, this idea of underreporting in the Spago tea, and the gala, he had no other problems. This—and this business about, well, the Waldorf event was so frightening to him that as a result of that it precipitated him to lie and cheat and jeopardize all he had worked for, dishonor himself and his family to commit a crime of what? No personal benefit to him. No harm even to the campaign. It doesn't make common sense, and that is the one point I agree with. Even though I say it's table-pounding, common sense is what really should help you resolve this case.

Now, he told you that when he went—he was not in favor of the gala. I think it's interesting to pause here for a minute on this, this road to the truth, as I'd like to call it. The first stop is the Tullman event. Remember the Tullman event in Chicago? And remember how the government—I told you in opening statement—I made some promises to you, just like you implicitly made promises to me—I would demonstrate that David Rosen was innocent. If I did that, you would find him not guilty. And I also said to you, if you did that, the government still wins, because the government always wins when justice is done.

And I told you that David Rosen was not enthusiastic about—I would prove to you, not enthusiastic about the idea of this event. The government went to great lengths to disprove that. They had their Jim Levin come to court, among other things, and painstakingly take you through—take you through this conversation at a bar after the event where Aaron Tonken is proposing the event and David—excuse me—is so excited and receptive, which was the opposite of what I said. He wasn't excited and receptive.

And I want to say to you I am going—ladies and gentlemen of the jury— I am going to use a little term, and maybe you can follow it. And the term is going to be BS, and it's not what you think it is. It's about—and I will to tell you the reference, because you heard what Jim Levin—Mr. Levin, sorry, Your Honor—said to me when I pointed out to him he might have told me that the allegations against Mr. Rosen were false at the wedding. He said another word: BS.

There was a fellow, every week he took his great-uncle to a restaurant. His uncle loved beef stew, and it was his favorite meal, and it was the nephew's favorite night. And they'd go to a wonderful new restaurant, advertised the best beef stew in the world. And they go into the restaurant, the great-uncle puts his fork into the—you know, the beef stew when it's served. He tastes it, and the meat is rancid. Now what is he required to do? Poke around and find some beef that's really good, credible, tasteful, or send it all back? And that's what he did: He sent it back.

And as far as Jim Levin is concerned—I'm not trying to be cute; I am trying to illustrate a point—he should be sent all the way back. You should believe nothing of what he said.

And instead of saying BS for what he said it stood—of what he stood it for, I say BS to you, beef stew, as far as Mr. Levin is concerned, because his testimony totally lacked credibility. Not only did he have, admittedly, cheated the school system in Chicago, defrauded them, inflated bills, but he lied blatantly on the witness stand. He lied about everything he said David said.

He admitted to you—it's like he came here and said, "Hello, I am one of the biggest liars and frauds and cheats in my community I duped everyone, and now I am going to tell you something so believe me." It's not because he pled guilty and had a criminal deal with the government that should cause you to be suspicious. It's because, we use the term, the cut of his jib: how he acted and conducted himself on the witness stand and what he said to you about himself. "I am a fraud. I am a—don't believe me." And that's how you differ in terms of evaluating the credibility of witnesses.

Sure, everyone has a motive. I have a motive to talk to you about the evidence. I am an advocate who believes in my cause. You have beliefs. That doesn't make you a salesperson who disowns the truth.

When you look at David Rosen and you saw how he testified and conducted himself and you compare that to Mr. Levin, you see and understand what I am talking about.

Mr. Levin said that he had met with David Rosen after the Tullman event and that he had planned—you know, was receptive to this idea. Mr.

Rosen said it didn't happen. All the way from Chicago come Mr. and Mrs. Ebeling. They told you where he went directly after that event.

Jim Levin said he went to see Gary Smith and had Gary Smith reduce his fees. What did Gary Smith tell you? It didn't happen. Never happened.

As far as Jim Levin is concerned: BS, send him back, because there is nothing you can believe about what he testified. It's incongruous when you think about it. Pacts and secrets and at the walk-through when there is excitement and hullabaloo and enthusiasm that David is going to say to him, "We are not going to report these costs." Ludicrous. And David denied it, and you can believe it.

Now, after the Tullman event—specifically, by the way, the point I was trying to raise with Mr. Levin was that his statements that David Rosen met with him to conceal and plan to hide have no basis and credibility. You cannot, should not, accept his word over the word of anyone.

He also had a little discussion about taxes, if you remember. I wanted to know about his tax returns. He told the prosecutor one thing two minutes ago and comes back and tells the court something else. You remember that. He told the prosecutor he didn't make any money, so he didn't file taxes. And then he tells me, well, it's because it's on extension. Well, if you don't make money, don't file taxes, you know, you don't get extensions. He knew that.

So I would just discount everything he says, ladies and gentlemen, on that evidence.

Then David Rosen goes to his first trip to California, and he works on the invitations, and he told you exactly what he did. There is no credible evidence that he was given specific facts about concert production and costs. It was so early, probably all he had to work on was the information he had received from Bretta Nock. And I will discuss that in a minute.

But when he comes back the second time—oh, paying the bill, by the way, paying his own bill at the Hermitage that the prosecutors want to blow out of proportion to show that he had an evil mind doesn't match up to the facts. He paid his own money. What reason would he have not to disclose it if he thought he had to? It's ridiculous.

And then coming in and having Mr. Tonken let him borrow the Porsche and drive the Porsche. And then the prosecutor is suggesting that he hid the costs of the hotel. Well, it was open, notorious, to use a term. He wasn't trying to hide that from anyone. He simply received the benefit that Mr. Tonken gave to—gave him.

He worked in the office. And remember where the office was? There was so much testimony about the—Mr. Rosen being in the room or hearing. You saw where his office was. Aaron Tonken. And you see where Peter Paul's office is way over there. And you have that Document 552. The government made it look like every minute David Rosen is in the room with Peter Paul, who is telling him, "I'm paying this, I'm paying that."

The only person, by the way, who gave a definite number was the beef stew man Jim Levin who said, "I was in the room with Peter Paul, and he said there was a million dollars that he had been paying." Interesting, isn't it? Where is Peter Paul? Where is Aaron Tonken? Why aren't they here? Why are they absent without leave? AWOL, as we call it. The government has the burden in this case. Why didn't they call them? Why didn't Peter Paul come and talk to you and say, "Yes, I was there. I spoke to him, and I told him that specifically." Where is Aaron Tonken, who Mr. Baumrucker called the ultimate producer? Where is Mr. Tonken, who Mr. Baumrucker called the ultimate producer, who Bretta Nock said she relied on? Where are those witnesses? Why aren't they here? The government will tell you we didn't need them. We had some other people. They had the burden of proof.

Let's go to Mr. Ray Reggie, if we could for a minute, another star witness. Now, look, I say that probably Mr. Reggie, based on the evidence, has to be pitied more than censured. No one enjoys being humiliated and acknowledging that they have done wrong, but he did: bank fraud, check kiting, lying under oath to me in front of you about his incident of putting the light on the car—

MR. ZEIDENBERG: Objection.

THE COURT: Overruled.

MR. SANDLER: I am going to be very specific then, sir. I asked Mr. Ray Reggie in court about an incident of impersonating a police officer and asked if he put this light on the top, and what did he say? He was a commissioner himself of police.

MR. SCHWAGER: Objection.

THE COURT: Ladies and gentlemen, the characterization of what the evidence was and what the testimony was, as I instructed you in the jury instructions, if there is a different recollection you have, yours controls. Lawyers are expected to account for the evidence in a fair-minded way and to draw reasonable inferences from that. You will be the judges of just what he said and whether he said what counsel has just referred to.

Now please proceed.

MR. SANDLER: Thank you, Your Honor.

I recall his testimony thusly, in so many words. Question: Why he put a light on the top of his car if he were not pretending to be a police officer. I recall him stating to me that he had been given the light because he had some honorary officer position. I then probed a little bit further and pointed out to you that, no, indeed he did not have such a commission, but it was given to him by a police officer or a sheriff because he had to guide dignitaries around. I say about Ray Reggie, beef stew. Just send him back. And I say it's deplorable, based on the evidence in light of what's going on, that this Ray Reggie, a supposed friend of David Rosen's, calls him and says, "Let's have dinner." And is so low, in my opinion, he could crawl under the belly of a snake wearing a top hat, because what he did—folks, ladies and gentlemen—what he did, if you think about it, was masquerade as a friend, come in to his domain of privacy, David Rosen, and then he secretly recorded. Tick tock, tick tock, tick tock. Looking and probing, looking and probing. And then and then AWOL, absent without leave. Where's the tape? Bring it forth, instead of innuendo and hyperbole. This man, he brought it forth. I don't want to be hyperbolic either, but I suggest to you, based on the evidence, if this country looks for leaders and heroes, there is one, with the courage to take the witness stand in a case like this and to tell the truth.

Now, as we move forward and we go forth in terms of what Mr. Rosen did, when he goes to this event, he asked—he had interaction with Bretta Nock. And when he spoke to Bretta Nock, he did receive information in July, just as the government, the prosecutor, said, regarding the budget. And you will see—you will be able to see this Exhibit 31.

Is that right? Exhibit 31: "Regarding the budget, I have specifics for all the orders I have placed for decor, etcetera." I—I won't read it to you. "Regal was waiting for Spago" and then, "Regarding the production show budget, that's a question for Stan Lee Media Inc. (Gary Smith)."

Go look at Exhibit 24a. 24. All of them. I will tell you this much, every one of these items is reported on these budgets, including the production costs, because Bretta Nock sent him the exhibit. $200,000. And you will see it when it says event production.

And David Rosen told you that he understood from the get-go the budget was $300,000: the $100,000 paid for by his committee, and the $200,000 that he understood Bretta Nock gave to him.

Now, when I—when I examined the evidence in the case, and I looked through the transcript to be helpful to you, I read and I will read to you in a few minutes—some of the comments that individuals said about David Rosen who were called by the government, who were actually called by the government.

I say to you that Mr. Rosen in his approach to this matter acted reasonably and properly and had no intention of harming anyone. He took the information from Bretta Nock. He used that as the budget. He worked with that. He continued to maintain that position.

Whenever Whitney Burns called him, what did he do? He referred her to Bretta Nock. And what did Whitney Burns say about Bretta Nock? I am going to read it to you in a minute, but I am going to tell you what it's going to say. Refer—he referred me to Bretta Nock. "I had more calls with Bretta Nock than I did with David Rosen, because she had the details." And that's because David Rosen understood Stan Lee Media was indeed the individual company and entity that was running the show.

This business with Madden and all of that, David—every single person who testified understood Stan Lee Media was the underwriter. Baumrucker, Smith, even Bretta Nock, who testified she worked for Stan Lee Media and she was the representative of Stan Lee Media. So who would David Rosen go to? Stan Lee Media. He never thought that anyone else was doing that.

That exhibit of Tonken and Paul, it's synonymous with Stan Lee Media. You know in business when someone is in a company, you can refer to them or the company synonymously. And you know based on what you have heard, that's how David Rosen approached it.

I want to take a few minutes, now that I have given you, again, a—or repeated again in tying in some of the information, what happened actually. How David approached this; how he was not Sherlock Holmes when he went to the event looking at trusses and writing things down; how it was very reasonable to expect he'd get the numbers, he'd pass it on, or he'd refer the caller, Whitney Burns, to Bretta because he was on the road for other events.

But my job—my job is not to prove to you David's innocence, although the evidence cries out for that. I want to invite your attention to another instruction of the judge's, and that is about reasonable doubt. There is no question that the government has the burden of proving its case beyond a reasonable doubt.

And what does that mean? In most civil cases the government has to push the ball, if you can use that, a little bit over the 50-yard line, and that's called more likely than not.

But in a criminal case the government has to prove the ball push the ball all the way up, say, to the 90-yard line, the other side's 10-yard line.

In other words, on a scale, if it's a civil case, the scale tips ever so slightly, but in a criminal case, the government has to put so much evidence against Mr. Rosen, it has to weigh it down. That may be theoretical. I will give you a little practical example.

Let's assume you go home tonight and you have a box, and you put a cat in the box and a mouse. You close the lid. You come back an hour later, the mouse is gone. One could firmly believe that the cat ate the mouse. What if you come back later and you put the same—it has to be the same cat this time. You put the cat in a box and the mouse, close the lid, come back an hour later again, and there are holes in the box. No longer would you firmly believe the cat ate the mouse.

And I want to talk to you now about some of the holes in the government's case, the burden that they failed to meet.

There's not a single piece of paper demonstrating that David Rosen was provided the cost of the gala, other than what he received from Bretta Nock.

I said to you at the beginning, seeing is believing. Where is the evidence? General, oral statements, the costs are high. They are going over my budget, assuming that happened. Where is Peter Paul to put on the evidence? Where is Aaron Tonken to put on the evidence? Not there, not there at all.

Bretta Nock hired the vendors. Bretta Nock was the hub of the event. It's undisputed that she provided him that Exhibit 19, which was the first budget after David—he wasn't desperate for a budget. He said, "Bretta, I really need a budget; get on it with it," because he had asked her before. That's where the production costs came from. He is not a concertmaster. He doesn't know what it was. I mean, to take us through a movie to look at trusses and lights and all of that, that's not his job. He is not Sherlock Holmes. He had a specific system in place, as you heard.

I did show witness's Exhibit 503, which was the letter there from Gary Smith to Aaron Tonken, to demonstrate from the evidence that Mr. Rosen never saw it. And you know what? You know what? I suppose if David Rosen did call Gary Smith or Baumrucker and could get through, maybe they would have responded to him, but he didn't, and that's not a crime. He went to Bretta Nock, who had the details, and he thought everything was in line. And that's a question of credibility. That's a question of belief and confidence in what someone says.

And you, yourself, know from your own experience in life you could have made a mistake, but it wasn't intentional. You could have had a situation which was truly innocent, and it was a mistake. You didn't catch something. It doesn't mean you cheated and planned a scheme. It just doesn't.

Reasonable doubt. No specific evidence that Tonken, Paul, or Nock told Rosen of the costs, other than what he reported.

The only evidence of costs given to Mr. Rosen was from Bretta Nock. She was the representative of the host. Mr. Rosen followed his system. And the ultimate producer, Mr. Tonken, as Mr. Baumrucker said, ran that show. Mr. Baumrucker said very clearly, when I asked him, what was your understanding of the role of mister—that Mr. Tonken played in this event? Folks, I am not summarizing. I am reading. "He was the client. He was the ultimate producer."

Ms. Nock, further testimony, my question, "Do you agree with me that Mr. Rosen would rely on you to obtain and provide invoices to him and costs to him?"

Imagine, this is the heart of the case. This is the government's witness. By the way, the government's witness who said that Mr. Rosen was ethical, honest, tried to do things right. This is a government's witness.

They call him a liar, a pack of lies, deceiver. Their own witness, he said—two of them, Fickes, they give him credit for trying to keep things by the book.

People are not superhuman. People can—although in this instance you may not say so, people can make mistakes or miss a number. They are not superhuman. But this is a man of integrity, and he—he testified before you. You heard him answer the questions.

Here's the question: "Do you agree with me Mr. Rosen would rely on you to obtain and provide invoices to him and costs to him?" Wow, what did she say? Do you remember? "Yes. Yes. I am the government's witness. I am here to tell you yes. He relied on me. But I was working through Aaron Tonken and Stan Lee Media in regards to all my approval of expenses and invoices."

That's the testimony. This is an innocent man. And he has told you, and the government's witnesses agree, oppressed and compressed, worked over time after time, they come forth by subpoena and they give answers, but they are not specific. They are vague. And they first say that David Rosen tries to do things by the book and he is an honest person.

Reasonable doubt. No meaningful evidence that Rosen told Bretta Nock to take items off the book.

I am going to read from you—to you. I'm not going to be hyperbolic. First she says—this is my question.

Question: "In your work with David Rosen, were you satisfied at the time, the year 2000, that he wanted to make sure that everything was done ethically and properly?"

What does she say? Do you remember the answer? Answer: "Yes."

"And would it be your testimony before the jury, that you, that he was always concerned about following the correct campaign finance protocol?"

This is the government's witness, the prosecutor's witness. "Yes." She says, "Yes."

And I read—I read some of this to you, because I do not want you to think that I am selling you anything but the truth. I do not want to hide what the government says is their best evidence. I want you to see that David Rosen confronts it, and he says it's wrong. They have got the wrong person.

I don't know why this case has been going on or what they are doing, based on the evidence. I don't know if Jim Levin, what he says is politically motivated. I don't go there. I only go on what the evidence is and what was said. And I say to you that—"Mr. Fickes, would you agree with me that his custom and practice was to observe the highest standards within his work?" "I would. I think so." "Would you agree with me they'd always teach you and would have—that you would have observed his custom and practice to be playing it straight by the book?" "Yes." "Did he ever tell you in the years that you worked for him to do something that you considered to be illegal?" "No."

"Did he ever tell you during the years you worked with him to do something that was in your view unethical?" "No."

So here's Bretta Nock. I mean, let's confront it, you and I together. Because I am sure on rebuttal when the government has its turn looking over all I say and focusing, they'll want you to hear this too. Did he—simply, it's talking about taking items off the budget.

Answer: "I don't really—I don't recall exactly which items he discussed and he wanted to take off."

That's the testimony. It's vague, inconclusive. And you heard what David Rosen said. Items were added on to the budget as well. He didn't tell her to add or subtract. She had testified the budgets kept emerging and changing.

I showed you earlier, just for the purpose of refreshing, that there was no—no meaningful evidence that David Rosen procured a false invoice. I walked us through that episode. I also walked you through the episode with Whitney Burns that David Rosen—there is reasonable doubt that David Rosen told Whitney Burns to improperly lower the costs. I explained, I reviewed his testimony about that with you.

I commented about the role of Peter Paul and Aaron Tonken, and I told you they aren't here, and you know that as well as I do. You saw the video. You have heard the evidence about where they live now, what they are, and you know that these are the individuals that everybody from the government—the government was asking other people, what did they say? What did they say? I wonder why they didn't call them.

The same thing with the tape, as far as motive is concerned, intent, what could his motive be? Think about this: A 33-year-old individual who saw life not from the easy road. I told you, you know, he's financially insecure. What's he going to do? Why would he do this? What evidence is there that he would benefit from this? Because he had a failed event. You think a person like Mr. Ickes comes all the way from Washington; you think he is hedging when he says to you that he valued Mr. Rosen, that his job was never in jeopardy?

One point, another argument of the government is that because a *Washington Post* article revealed that Mr. Paul had a prior background, Mr. Rosen shuddered for his job. He didn't have any role in the vetting of that. He was a decent person. He is. His concern would be for his candidate. That's natural. That's loyalty. That's the kind of person you want.

We looked through the issues with what we call—I will call funny money, for lack of a better term, where Mr. Tonken and Mr. Peter Paul would have had all kinds of different checks from different companies. Awful strange. You saw Stan Lee himself hurt by the conduct of the company going under. You heard the lawyer say why: stock fraud, manipulation. I mean, come on now, how—what is David Rosen supposed to do? Get out a searchlight and become a supersleuth? He went to Bretta Nock. That's it. And Bretta Nock doesn't contradict it, and Whitney Burns said she went to Bretta Nock. Why did she go to Bretta Nock? She went to Bretta Nock because she had the details and she had the knowledge, and she spoke to Bretta Nock more often than David Rosen, because Bretta had the information.

And interestingly, after the event in October—after the event in October, Whitney called Bretta, she used the term fishing. She wanted information. What did Bretta do? Nothing. Gave her the same old invoices, except I think she said at one point she gave her a bill for her services. David Rosen didn't tell her to take the bill off any budget, but there it appeared. How come Bretta Nock didn't say, "Oh, wait a second, the concert is more, or there is more information? Because David told me to cheat and lie, and I'd better come clean." Nothing, not nothing.

Do you think that when the agents visited Bretta Nock she had any concerns about herself? Do you think that based on the evidence Bretta Nock had any issues to deal with? She was here. Mr. Baumrucker was here. He knew that he gave a false document. Mr. Rosen didn't.

Do you know, ladies and gentlemen, the situation here as I see it based on the evidence, as the evidence reflects, that the government—the prosecutors look at the world through dirty windows, and they see everything wrong. I ask you when you go to the jury room to look at the world through clean windows and determine what is wrong and what is right. Because based on the evidence in this case, the government has failed to meet its burden, but Mr. Rosen has proven his innocence.

It's not laughable to see the sequence of events. You can see how long this case proceeded. You can see what the evidence—what the chart revealed from the indictment, from the Ray Reggie call through the meeting, the search warrant, the indictment under seal, and then now thank goodness for Mr. Rosen, the trial. And it's no laughing matter either to examine the chart, the understanding that Mr. Rosen had of the events, which the prosecutors mock, respectfully, that Mr. Rosen is creating another fraud unto the court. That is so far from the truth. This is what he understood how the organization was. This is how he examined it. And it's not anything different than the testimony in the court.

All the people say that Stan Lee Media, they understood was running, or Aaron Tonken or Peter Paul.

Bretta Nock herself—excuse me—as I just pointed out to you and read to you her testimony, she acknowledged it's not a dream. She was the representative, and that's who she worked through right there. She said that. And that's who David Rosen looked to, and that's the sum and total of the evidence.

I suggest to you that when you return to the jury room you will use your common sense. You will go through the evidence. You will see for yourselves that the government has not proved its case beyond a reasonable doubt. And you will also see, to the contrary, that David Rosen proved to you by his courageous and truthful testimony that he is innocent and that he did not intend to harm a flea, let alone the FEC.

It would be my request of all of you that when you do go to the jury room, you do one thing that I hope you remember. I cannot come back and speak to you again. I will not have that opportunity. I am prevented. I—the rules do that. I would have liked to introduce the wire tape to you, but it was prohibited by the rules of evidence.

MR. ZEIDENBERG: Objection.

MR. SANDLER: I cannot—

THE COURT: Mr. Sandler, don't comment on any evidentiary rulings.

MR. SANDLER: Yes, sir.

THE COURT: Disregard that last statement.

MR. SANDLER: I beg your pardon. I would ask you to go into the jury room, and if I have missed something here or in the rebuttal the prosecutors say something that I haven't commented on, I ask you to point out to your colleagues in the jury room the evidence that contradicts what the prosecutor said that I could not do.

Now at this time my burden ends. It goes to you. You, the members of the jury, whose task it is to render a judgment, now receive this case after the rebuttal.

And I conclude by this little tale that I learned long ago about an ancient kingdom where a wise magician was offering great counsel, but there was someone who was jealous and wanted to pull him down. And they went to the king and said, "Look, your magician for so many years has no reason to continue. He is not as smart or wise as you think." So the king said, "What do you mean?" He said, "I am going to devise a test," said the other magician, "and you take a bird in your hand, call him, and then you ask him if the bird is living or dead. If he says the bird is living, you crush his little neck, open your hands, and we'll have him. If he says, however, the bird is dead, open your hands. The bird will fly, and we have him."

The day comes, the throngs are there. The drums are beating. And, sure enough, the king says to the wise man what the magician said. The magician looks, thinks very quickly, and says, "I am in trouble, because if I say the bird is living and the king just presses the neck, that's it. If I say he is dead and opens his hands, that's it." So the wise magician simply said when the king said, "Well, tell me, is this bird living or dead?" He simply said the truth: "The answer is in your hands."

David Rosen's life and this case are now soon going to be in your hands. I proved based on the evidence what I said at the outset: David Rosen is the victim of other people's motives; that he did not intend to cheat or violate any law or rule; that he had no personal gain. He had a system. The system worked every time. It didn't work here, because people concealed or did not give him the information; and that the vagaries of what the prosecution produced with the quality of the testimony doesn't meet the burden of proof. And yet—and yet Mr. Rosen testified and told you that he did not do this; that he would never do this. And even if you want to say, well, anybody could say that, why wouldn't he? Why would he testify? Only to meet you and let you meet him to see the cut of his jib.

Thank you for your patience. I also, since I will not be seeing you again, want to publicly take the opportunity to thank Judge Matz, who in an impartial fashion guided us to this point.

Thank you.

Rebuttal Argument by the Government

MR. ZEIDENBERG: Ladies and gentlemen, I just want to take a couple more minutes. I promise it's not going to take long. I don't have any funny stories for you. I don't have any good analogies. I just want to stick for a couple minutes on the facts.

Mr. Sandler had a—had a little diagram up there that says reasonable doubt. And the way I wrote it down, it said no specific evidence that Tonken, Paul, or Nock told Rosen the costs other than what he reported. No evidence, he says. Would that be true for Mr. Rosen's sake? But, in fact, ladies and gentlemen, you know there was evidence. It's overwhelming, and Mr. Sandler didn't deal with any of it.

Who told him about the costs? Peter Paul told him about the costs on July 16th at Peter Paul's house. Peter Paul had a conversation and told David Rosen and everyone else present that his budget was already blown. They were one week into the event. It's July 16th, one weekend, and his budget was blown. He said he is already over a half a million dollars that's all eaten up by Gary Smith's fees.

How do you know that conversation happened? Ladies and gentlemen, you have overwhelming, unrefuted evidence. Pat Waters was there. Remember, she was the woman who came in who did the invitations. She was the one who was getting chewed out by Peter Paul in very blue language. She remembered it vividly. $88,000. He was furious. He says his budget was through the roof. David Rosen was sitting right next to him when he said it.

Pat Waters told you that she had a budget for her printing. Ladies and gentlemen, think about it. Peter Paul is saying $88,000. That's way too much. David Rosen says, "I heard that part." Well, have you ever heard a conversation with someone who starts a sentence by "That's too much," and doesn't finish it with "My bottom line is x"? And, in fact, that's exactly what he said. He said, "$88,000, that's too much. My bottom line is $1.50 per invitation." They were talking about 30,000 invitations. That's $45,000 just for the printing costs for invitations. How does Pat Waters remember that so vividly? And David Rosen, that's direct evidence that he knew the costs were way over $500,000 on July 16th. It's corroborated by Blossette Kitson, who was also there. Remember her? The talent promoter from New Jersey. She was there for the same conversation, remembered the same thing.

Now ask yourselves, why would Pat Waters lie? Why would Blossette Kitson lie? What possible motive would they have to lie? Zero.

What motive would David Rosen have to continue his lie? Isn't that self-evident? He says, "No evidence that Tonken or Paul or Nock told Rosen the cost."

Well, what about Bretta Nock's testimony? She told you point blank, point blank, David Rosen told me to take the costs off the budget. Mr. Sandler says, "Well, she was vague about it."

I will just take you back. Your memory controls.

I asked her: "Okay, now, did these—the items that you just listed, did they represent goods and services that were actually provided to the gala."

"Yes."

"Were these vendors actually paid?"

"Yes."

"None of those costs showed up on the final budget; is that correct?"

"That's correct."

"And can you tell us, Mrs. Nock—Ms. Nock, why that is?"

Answer, "I was instructed to take certain expenses off." "Who instructed you to do . . . take them off?"

"David Rosen."

"What did he tell you?"

"Simply the overall figure needed to project a lower cost, so we adjusted the items accordingly."

Does that sound vague to you, ladies and gentlemen? Is there something unclear about that testimony about what Ms. Nock testified?

No other evidence that anyone knew. What about the testimony from Ray Reggie? He testified, yeah, he had a plea agreement. Ray Reggie pled guilty, took responsibility for the crimes he committed in Louisiana, came in here, took an oath, and showed you his plea agreement that if he lies or if he fabricates evidence, his plea agreement will be ripped up and he will be prosecuted to the maximum extent.

You have to think about that, of course you do, but doesn't his testimony mesh perfectly with David Rosen's—strike that, with the testimony you heard from these other witnesses?

Jim Levin, same thing. Jim Levin told you that there was—that Peter Paul was complaining because only his budget was blown, and he said someone else had initially promised, according to Peter Paul, to kick in the money. And now you see from a defense exhibit that that second person who is going to kick in a half a million dollars was Cynthia Gershman. It's corroborated.

A name that Mr. Sandler never mentioned, either on David Rosen's direct testimony or in his closing argument, Rick Madden, the general counsel of Stan Lee Media. Why would he lie? Why would he lie when he comes in here and tells you, "I had a meeting, I had a meeting with David Rosen, I had a meeting with Peter Paul, and I made it clear to both of them that Stan Lee Media is not contributing to this event?" What did David Rosen tell you about that conversation? I don't remember.

So let's just review. It's not a question that there is no evidence. It's a question that they will not face the evidence. Pat Waters, her testimony, apparently it never happened. That conversation at the kitchen table in Peter Paul's house never happened. Blossette Kitson, never happened. Jim Levin, never happened. Ray Reggie, never happened. Bretta Nock, never happened. Rick Madden, never happened. Whitney Burns, Whitney Burns is confused. That's seven witnesses, ladies and gentlemen, any one of which, if you believe them—

THE COURT: Excuse me. I don't want those individuals being brought in now, not now.

MR. ZEIDENBERG: That's seven witnesses, ladies and gentlemen, any one of which, if you believe, provide you evidence beyond a reasonable doubt, taken together, taken cumulatively, it's beyond any doubt, any doubt the defendant's guilt that he knew those costs.

I want to just point to one specific set of questions we were talking about earlier today with the defendant up there on cross-examination. Mr. Sandler makes much about how courageous he is and what a hero he is for being willing to take the stand, and how credible he was. Well, that's for you to decide, ladies and gentlemen. And ask yourselves how credible it was that story he told you about that $3,500 bill he picked up at the Hermitage hotel that he said he paid out of his own pocket. And he would have you believe that Aaron Tonken didn't pay, he just decided to spend half a month's salary on his own rather than stay at his sister's for free, or, even better yet, stay at a hotel in town that the campaign would have paid for. Instead, this man, who admits he is not independently wealthy, would prefer to pay $3,500.

I'd suggest to you, ladies and gentlemen, he is not being truthful; that the fact is that Aaron Tonken picked up that bill as well, and he didn't want you to know the truth. And if you use your common sense, I think you'll come to the same conclusion. Nobody making the kind of money this man is making can afford to pay $3,500 for nine days in a hotel when he can stay in a perfectly nice hotel for free.

And I suggest to you even further that his testimony he presents that he had no inkling that Aaron Tonken might want something in return for that $10,000 hotel bill that he picked up at the Beverly Hills Hotel—this man is not a babe in the woods. He is an experienced finance director spending years in politics, working with donors and working with politicians.

"Sir, did it ever occur to you that maybe Aaron Tonken would want something for all that money?" "No, it never occurred to me." Do you believe that, ladies and gentlemen?

Mr. Sandler also made a big point out of "Where's the tape? Where's the tape?" Well, what do you know about when that tape was made? It took a little bit to get David Rosen to admit it, but he finally did, that by the time that tape was made he knew he was under investigation by the FBI and by the grand jury, and so he wasn't going to say anything incriminating on that tape.

The more interesting question you might ask yourselves, ladies and gentlemen, is where is Kelly Craighead, the woman that was with David Rosen and Jim Levin the night they met Aaron Tonken? And as for Peter Paul and Aaron Tonken and that line of argument, where are they? Where are they?

Well, I am going to ask you to ask yourselves something, ladies and gentlemen. I have already ticked off for you seven witnesses, any one of whom's testimony, if believed, proves guilt, evidence of guilt beyond a reasonable doubt of the defendant. Do you, for a second, think that if Aaron Tonken or Peter Paul took the stand, David Rosen would put his cards on the table and say, "Okay, you got me," if they said that David Rosen knew about these expenses? Or do you think he would say, it was all you guys. It was you, Peter Paul. It was you, Aaron Tonken. That's been his dodge from the beginning.

Ask yourselves, when you're considering this evidence, ladies and gentlemen, about the motives. The motives of the witnesses and the motives of the defendant. And you are going to come to a conclusion that there is no reason for all of these people to come in and testify falsely against David Rosen.

And Mr. Sandler says he can't be Sherlock Holmes. He can't be going out ferreting out all these expenses. Ladies and gentlemen, Sherlock Holmes, is he Mr. Magoo? Is he blind? Is he deaf? Here he is, an experienced fundraiser on the scene for one reason: to supervise this event, the biggest event of his career. And he would have you believe he never asked a question. He never heard a conversation. He never heard a snippet that suggested this budget was out of control and that he is the only person, notwithstanding the fact that he was working at those offices and he never heard a thing? I suggest that testimony is not heroic. It's desperate. It's desperate, and there is no reason for you to believe it when you weigh it against the evidence.

Ladies and gentlemen, consider the evidence. Consider the motives. And when you do that, you are going to come to one conclusion, and that is David Rosen knew those expenses were far, far in excess of what he reported to the Federal Election Commission.

There is no conspiracy surrounding David Rosen. The only conspiracy is the one he tried to enter into with Jim Levin to keep this secret so that no one would know, but now we do.

Thank you, ladies and gentlemen.

Appendix III

OPENING STATEMENTS IN THE *MAFFEI* CASE

OPENING STATEMENT BY THE PLAINTIFF

MR. SANDLER: Plaintiffs are ready for the opening statement, Your Honor. May it please the Court, members of the jury, on March 8th, 2006, Dr. Angela Smedley misdiagnosed the medical condition of the late Richard Maffei. He was 52 years old He had registered at the emergency room of the hospital around 3:00 o'clock in the morning. He complained of a sudden feeling of closure at his throat, chest pain, and low back pain, as the medical records will so state. He was seen by Dr. Smedley and discharged around 7:00 o'clock in the morning. He didn't know it, but he was experiencing a medical emergency because he had a tear in the largest vessel of his heart, the aorta. The diagnosis of the doctor: ear infection, sore throat, allergic reaction; the prescription: steroids, antibiotics; head home, it will take a while to kick in. But it didn't have to happen. It didn't have to happen, because all the doctor had to do was take a simple x-ray and from that x-ray the diagnosis could have been made.

Now, before I tell you exactly what we are going to prove in this case, I want to comment about the nature of this lawsuit. This suit is one that I would call professional negligence. Often we hear the term, malpractice, medical malpractice. I don't like the word, "mal." It's ancient Latin word meaning evil. We didn't bring this case to punish anybody or bring this case to say someone was bad. But this is medical negligence. We are required to live in our lives. We drive cars. We go through a stop sign without stopping, someone gets hurt, we have a responsibility. This is a case of negligence. In essence, we have a lawsuit that deals with a wrongful death of the late Mr. Maffei, brought by Mrs. Maffei against the doctor for an adequate award, if there could ever be for this type of loss.

My name, as the judge told you, is Paul Sandler. With me is Eric Harlan. We represent Ms. Maffei. She brings the case against the doctor and her employer, the Physicians Emergency Group, Charles Physician Emergency Group, for negligence. It's a wrongful death case and right of survivorship case. What does that mean? Wrongful death, in a sense, it's a fancy word to say Mrs. Maffei, because she lost her husband, has a right to sue for the loss of income he would have brought to her, [for] pain and suffering, and [for loss of] companionship. Also Mr. Maffei isn't here, so he can't speak, but his estate in law speaks for him. It's called a right of survivorship where he sues for his pain and suffering. That's the nature of the lawsuit. And under the circumstances of this case, when you go back to the jury room at the end of case, you will find and I'll prove to you the negligence that brought about this horrible result.

This brief introduction should be such to suggest to you the awful solemnity of the occasion—that causes you and me to be face-to-face. There's no two ways to look at it. This is a human tragedy. Let's examine what I am going to prove to you under the circumstances.

Well, if you could go back in time, if any of us could go back in time, like sometimes we think about maybe a vacation ten years ago, three years ago, you could go back to March 8, 2006, and go to the area of the home of Mr. and Mrs. Richard Maffei, and if you with me could peer into the window legitimately of their home, you would have seen two of the happiest people on earth. They had only been married eight and a half years at that time. It was his first marriage and her second. She'll tell you when I call her to the witness stand how wonderful her relationship [was]. They had so much together; they were lovers, they were friends, they were companions. They would socialize with family, very big family people. And they would share each other's family. Mrs. Maffei had two little nieces then and Rick Maffei would play games with them, hide and seek, take them shopping. She liked to garden. He'd help her in the garden, he would do things around the house, paint, fix up, cook, all of that. Never did they dream that this would happen.

He was a very, very wonderful person, as the evidence will show. He had a broad smile, friendly disposition. He loved people. He was a very handsome man. He was over six feet tall, weighed over 240 pounds. What did he do for work? The evidence will show he was a heavy lift operator at Sparrows Point. He worked double shifts, leave five in the morning, come home 10 at night, 12 at night. Mrs. Maffei worked. When they weren't working, they were together, the yin and the yang.

Mr. Maffei surprised in a very sad or startling way, I should say, Mrs. Maffei around 10 o'clock on March 8th, 2006. He came home unexpectedly early from work. He came home because he had pain that brought him to his knees is what he told her, in the chest, closing of the throat, low back pain, and the pain did not go away. So at 3 o'clock or thereabouts in the morning, Mrs. Maffei drove him to the hospital and there, the triage nurse, the triage nurse is the head nurse who interviews people. Probably you know if you have been to the hospital, [the nurse will] assess your issue so you can be placed in line to be seen. So the triage nurse met with him. It's documented in the hospital records that he had reported closing of the throat, chest pain, and back pain. It's interesting because the chest pain was recorded, as health care providers do, they measure, Your Honor, they measure, as you know, the intensity of the pain on a scale of 1 to 10. So they had a measuring of a scale of 1 to 10 and they registered his chest pain as about a 3 out of 10. About an hour later, he had an additional measurement of chest pain, 5 out of 10. Here the chest pain was radiating to the neck. I have a little summary that we'll put into evidence to show you what the hospital records reflect in terms of his chest. Can we clarify that a bit?

Three out of 10, then about an hour later you can see additional chest pain. Do you have that? Can we get that more focused, please? Three out of 10, 5 out of 10, 2 out of the 10, 30 minutes later, an hour later, and an hour later. You will see the actual records. The actual record will show what his symptoms were. I am emphasizing that, chest pain is crucial to understand the x-ray issue in this case. As a result of the chest pain, he was worked up for an EKG, where they put all those sticky things on your chest, you lie down, they come down and they report. His EKG was abnormal. It was abnormal in this record. He had a propensity for left ventricular hypertrophy. But what was unique about this abnormal finding is when his blood pressure was taken, it was low blood pressure. Someone should have gone, "Uh-oh, this doesn't look right, this could be a problem."

He was seen by the doctor. When he's seen by the doctor, she tells Mrs. Maffei, "Good news, your husband is not having a heart attack." The reason the evidence will show she said that was because Mrs. Maffei expressed great concern because not too far behind in time, her dad had chest pain and had a heart attack. Naturally, she was concerned that Rick, or Mr. Maffei, was going to have a heart attack. The doctor said no. The doctor then discharged him with the diagnosis of an allergic reaction, sore throat and an ear infection. He goes home; she gets the medicine.

That day neither of them go to work, which is unusual. They are home. He's uncomfortable. They are waiting for the medicine to kick in. They have no concern that there is anything wrong because they were told, they were given the diagnosis. And about 11:00 that evening, 11:15, he comes upstairs and gets a sweater because he wasn't feeling well and he was cold. Then Mrs. Maffei, unsettled because she didn't hear something or it was too quiet down there, she goes downstairs and that's when she finds him. He was on the floor, his legs, his feet under the couch. I'm not going to go into the details except to say Mrs. Maffei became hysterical, called 911 in a panic. Listen to what they say. She tried to do what she could, went to the neighbor's, found someone to help her and then the medics came and he was gone.

So what happened? We are going to prove to you what happened. We'll prove to you that the doctor should have understood to take an x-ray because what he died from was a dissection of the aorta. The aorta, which you are going to learn about maybe more than you want as the next couple days unwind, is that large vessel from the heart, the heart vessel, carries the blood, and what happened to Mr. Maffei was happening when he was in the hospital, his aorta was dissected, it tore, and blood, instead of going through the channel of the vessel, went to another channel, two channels, and caused a widening of the entire vessel.

So, let me start to explain what the evidence will show. Let's assume this little common paper towel setup is the aorta. My fist is the heart. This is the aorta. The lumen of the tube is where the blood goes through. In terms of the tear or dissection, the aorta has walls, the intima, the media, and the adventitia, three walls. What happened is when there is a tear, the blood goes not only in the lumen but another channel through the vessel, and that's not good because it's not supposed to happen. When it gets very powerful and pulls apart, it bursts or ruptures and then lots of blood pours in.

What happened to Mr. Maffei that evening is it burst and the blood then went around the heart into the sac that carries the heart, which we call the pericardium and the blood coming in stopped the heart from pumping. It smothered it, crushed it, stopped it. And life ended; he died.

It all could have been prevented, as we'll prove, by an x-ray. Why? Because an x-ray would have revealed an irregularity in that area and a doctor looking at that irregularity would have ordered a CAT scan and the CAT scan would have showed the dissection. And I am going to call Mr. Shadoff, a cardiologist, who will explain all of this to you. He will explain to you the workings of the aorta. He will show you, for example, what the aorta looks like, which I am showing you now, one of our exhibits. I want you to see, for example, remember my talking about the tube or the lumen? This is what we call the true lumen, this is the root of the aorta, and here is the false lumen, where the tear is, and then the blood flows all the way up to the ear, the carotid artery, iliac artery down the back, and goes everywhere. When it's in that false channel, it's causing problems and damage. The wall's coming apart and flowing that way. That is in all of our bodies. That is part of our circulatory system. And this dissected or tear of the aorta is exactly what was going on with Mr. Maffei and it's exactly the diagnosis that could have and should have been made.

So, you will hear evidence that, well, while the dissection was happening while he was in the hospital, it was so small and itty bitty, it would not have shown up on an x-ray because it's not, this is really what is important, the tear doesn't show up on the x-ray. What shows up on the x-ray is a change in the structure of the center of the chest. It's an area called the mediastinum. It's a widening. The mediastinum is widened.

Do we have an example to show? See if we can cut the light and get this better for the jury here. Okay. Here you have the area where you will see is the mediastinum. And that would be the example of a normal chest x-ray. And let's show the example of the widening of the mediastinum. You can see the dark parts, the chest area, you can see how it curves out. Dr. Shadoff will explicitly show that to you. Trained medical personnel can see the difference in this the same way a gardener can see when a small plant is ready to bloom where the average person might not see it. It may look subtle to you, but it isn't. You will see it clearly displayed by Dr. Shadoff, a cardiologist, with that widening of the mediastinum. The CAT scan would have automatically been ordered and the dissection or tear would have been seen.

Even the autopsy report is the report you will learn reports the cause of death. The cause of death was recorded as cardiac tamponade, rushing of the blood in the cardiac sac, caused by the rupture from the tear of the dissection of the aorta. You will see the autopsy report suggest and reveal that the tear was about one centimeter. Might seem small, but it's 25 percent of the diameter of the aorta, which is four centimeters, which is big. And because the doctor did not take the chest x-ray, this wasn't discovered.

You will hear evidence that when Mr. Maffei was in the hospital being interviewed by Dr. Smedley, he told her, according to her notes, on page 23 and 24 of the medical records, which you will have to look at, that he didn't have chest pain. That can't be because when he was in the hospital, Mrs. Maffei will tell you, it was because of chest pain. They worked him up for the EKG because of chest pain. You will see his chief complaint in the medical record, page 39. His chief complaint in the hospital was chest pain. Okay. Chest pain. You will have a clear view of that when you have the actual hospital [record].

She also will, by the way I want to point out to you, Dr. Smedley will and has testified that had she believed, let me actually read to you what the question will be.

"If you believed that Mr. Maffei had been experiencing chest pain, would you have ordered a chest x-ray?"

Answer: "If I believed he was having chest pain, I would have ordered a chest x-ray."

Question: "It's not difficult to obtain a chest x-ray of a patient," I am skipping, "in the emergency room in March of 2006, correct?"

Answer: "Correct."

So there is no question that with chest pain comes an x-ray. There is no question this poor fella was complaining of chest pain.

What I am saying to you, I hope, is of interest. What counsel is saying to you, I hope, is of interest. But what the medical records say are cold, hard facts that have no bias or spin. Those medical records show chest pain all through. And the obligation was to take the chest x-ray.

You will also hear testimony that Mr. Maffei told Dr. Smedley, she'll say, that he denied ever having chest pain. How could that be? It must be a mistake on her part, the negligence I am talking about, because he had chest pain all through the notes. In addition to that, she never documented that he denied ever having chest pain. If a patient, Dr. Shadoff will tell you as an expert witness, if a patient goes to the hospital and complains of chest pain, tells the doctor, "I don't have chest pain," the doctor is required to probe and say, "Well, what about all these notes? What about the EKG for chest pain?" Dr. Smedley didn't do that. In fact, she'll tell you, she'll tell you she never looked at the nurses' notes. Except for the one triage note, she didn't look at the nurses' notes. Dr. Shadoff will tell you it's his opinion that that's wrong. A doctor in an emergency room at all times when confronted with issues, even if they are not classic issues, is almost like a Sherlock Holmes to detect, get all the facts, put the facts together, and weed out what it isn't. It's called a differential diagnosis. Clearly, all the facts had to be known. When the doctor doesn't look at the full record, you will hear that that is just a mistake.

You will hear also testimony to the effect that, well, even if the x-ray were taken, even if it were taken, no big deal, because that little tear in the aorta when he was in the medical office of the hospital was so itty bitty, he couldn't have been having a dissection, that no one could find it because it's in the root. You will learn from Dr. Shadoff, that root is submerged in the pericardium. You wouldn't see it anyway. Why would the mediastinum be widened? Because remember when I showed you the second channel, that second channel is widening when it's going forward. He complained about neck pain, ear pain, because the widening of the mediastinum would be there because the second channel was going to the carotid artery in his neck and the back pain was in the iliac artery. That section makes it imperatively true that it showed as it would have shown on the x-ray because of his symptoms.

Now, when you hear evidence about the neck pain and the low back pain, think of them like when we were kids and heard somebody read *Robinson Crusoe*. He was on the sand, no one was there. Then he found a footprint. Each of those symptoms is a footprint in the sand telling you, telling you, of those symptoms, crying out, telling you there is something here. What is it? What is it?

You will hear the emergency room was so busy they were on a special code not to take on other new patients. You will also hear testimony that when Dr. Smedley discharged Mr. Maffei, it was toward the end of a long shift, a night shift.

Mistakes happen. This is not to punish. This is to prove to you, I am going to prove to you everything I just said. You will also hear that the low blood pressure was a symptom and a sign. All this time the poor fellow was in the hospital with his wife, signs and sounds were ringing, they just weren't heard. They just weren't heard.

So, when the case ends, you will have all the evidence and you will understand this particular case did not have to happen. I'll ask you then for an adequate award. Thank you very much for your patience.

OPENING STATEMENT BY THE DEFENSE

MR. SHAW: Good morning, ladies and gentlemen of the jury. My name is Ron Shaw. Together with Mr. Morrow, we represent Ms. Smedley. Obviously, if we agreed [with] the evidence that Mr. Sandler discussed, we wouldn't be here. There are two sides to the story. We strongly believe the evidence will show you, will convince you Dr. Smedley acted appropriately and did not commit medical malpractice. As you heard, this is a medical malpractice case and Dr. Smedley, we believe the evidence will show, treated Mr. Maffei appropriately and did not commit medical malpractice.

Now, this is an important case to Mrs. Maffei, but it's also a very important case to Dr. Smedley. Mr. Sandler went first in his opening. He will go first in presenting the witnesses. We go second because the burden of proof is on Mr. Sandler and Mrs. Maffei. You will hear the plaintiff's side of the story first and then our side. We ask you to please wait until you have heard all the evidence and keep an open mind before you make a decision in this case. But we strongly believe that what the evidence will show in this case is that the plaintiff's case is based on hindsight, because at the time that Mr. Maffei was in the emergency department, he did not have the full-blown dissection that ultimately showed up. In fact, it wasn't until after he died and there was still mystery as to what had caused his death, that an autopsy was ordered and it was only at the autopsy, only at the autopsy that the diagnosis of aortic dissection was made.

The evidence will show the symptoms Mr. Maffei had while he was in the emergency department on March 8, 2006, were not typical of aortic dissection. He had throat complaints, he had an earache, and a brief episode of low blood pressure We'll see the low blood pressure only lasted ten minutes of the over four hours he was in the emergency department.

The nurses did report at various times complaints of chest pain, but I am going to show you in a few moments the nurses' notes about the chest pain and the throat pain. I'll show you those all came before Dr. Smedley saw Mr. Maffei and when Dr. Smedley saw Mr. Maffei, he explicitly denied having chest pain. I'll also show you the nurses' notes and you have to decide whether Dr. Smedley acted appropriately in trusting the nurses' notes.

You will see the symptoms Mr. [Maffei] had in the emergency department were very common. People come in the emergency department all the time with sore throats, earache, blood pressure may be up and down while in the emergency department. But these symptoms are not caused by aortic dissection. In hindsight, we know Mr. Maffei, if he did have an aortic dissection at that time, it was very small and likely could not have been picked up by a chest x-ray. Therefore you will see he didn't have, I will show you in a moment, the symptoms that you would expect in a patient that had aortic dissection that extended from the top of his heart all the way down to below his waist and all the way up to above his neck, which was in the autopsy. If he was having that type of dissection when he was in the emergency department, he would have had much more profound and distinct symptoms. What happened—this was a very small if even present dissection that could not be picked up by a chest x-ray. In hindsight, we know in looking at the autopsy that the dissection worsened after discharge and, finally, about 17 or 18 hours later, ruptured all the way from a very small tear up and down all the way down below his waist.

Mr. Sandler told you that Mr. Maffei's death was tragic and we certainly agree that his death was tragic. Everyone in this room can agree his death was tragic. And all of us, Dr. Smedley, her legal team, everybody in the jury, everybody is obviously concerned about the tragedy. It would obviously be natural to have sympathy and compassion for Mrs. Maffei. But as His Honor will instruct you at the end of the case, you have to try as hard as you can to put the sympathy and compassion for Mrs. Maffei aside. That can't be the guiding rule for your decision in this case. Your decision in this case, as hard as it is, is going to have to be based on whether Dr. Smedley acted appropriately and whether she committed medical malpractice.

So, what is medical malpractice? At the end of the case, His Honor will likely instruct you that it's the failure to act as a reasonably competent health care provider. What does that mean? That sounds like a long legal term, failure to act as a reasonably competent health care provider. Well, it means that Dr. Smedley is held to act as other physicians in her field would act. Unfortunately, like everything else and in life, medicine is not perfect. So just because there is a tragic outcome does not mean that there has been medical negligence in the case. The physician needs to act based on what is known to her and make decisions based on those symptoms and as in this case, she had, didn't have a picture, a clear picture at all of an aortic dissection because the symptoms were not there. Merely because a bad result occurs does not mean there's been medical negligence. You will hear from the plaintiff's experts but you will also hear from defense experts, Dr. Shank and Dr. Goldstein, who will testify that Dr. Smedley, based on information available to her, based on everything known to her at the time, acted with the accepted standards of care.

The plaintiff alleges in this case given Mr. Maffei's symptoms of throat/chest pain—we'll go over the nurses' notes in a minute, see what the confusion is—and the blood pressure, low blood pressure [that] Dr. Smedley should have checked the pulse and blood pressure in both arms. You will see from her testimony that she did check pulse in both arms. And she should have ordered a chest x-ray—rayed. The plaintiffs do not allege Dr. Smedley should have made the diagnosis of aortic dissection based on Mr. Maffei's symptoms because the symptoms did not point to aortic dissection. Rather, the plaintiff contends, based upon the one complaint the nurse wrote down, the chest pain, that Dr. Smedley should have ordered a chest x-ray. You saw and we'll show you in a moment a chest x-ray. The chest x-ray would not have made the diagnosis of aortic dissection. The plaintiff contends that a chest x-ray would have been abnormal, however, and further studies would have been done. We'd strongly dispute that. We'll show you in a few moments why that chest x-ray would have been normal.

Plaintiffs allege the chest x-ray would have been abnormal and, therefore, one of these other studies should have been done that would have made the diagnosis. Again, we believe the plaintiff's case is based on hindsight based on the autopsy that was done.

We believe, well, the evidence will show you, and we'll show you the medical records, I'll show you in a moment; Dr. Smedley did report that Mr. Maffei told her that he had no chest pain. He told her that rather he had throat tightening and throat pain and he denied that he had ever had chest pain or he was having chest pain at the time. Dr. Smedley did, in fact, take pulses in both arms that were normal. He had an episode for a little over ten minutes of a lower blood pressure, but by the time he saw Dr. Smedley, that blood pressure had normalized and it was normal throughout the rest of his emergency room stay and, in fact, when he was discharged, it was well within normal limits.

The evidence is going to show there was no medical reason for Dr. Smedley to order a chest x-ray and that had the chest x-ray been ordered, it would have been normal because the dissection was very small.

If Mr. Maffei had had an aortic dissection that was anything other than tiny, he would expect to see more symptoms. These are some of the symptoms that are often seen with aortic dissection. A sudden ripping, tearing chest pain. That's absent. A sense of doom. That was absent. Sweating. There is no evidence of that. No nausea, no vomiting, no episode of stroke-like symptoms because the blood is not going to the brain, arm pain or weakness because the blood is not going out to the arm, a heart murmur because the blood is backing up into the heart. No shortness of breath because the heart is not going back in the lungs, he can't breathe appropriately. Other abnormal lung conditions including funny-sounding breath sounds, [rattles], or bronchitis when he's breathing. He would have abdominal pain because the blood is not going outside. If the dissection has gone outside the normal channel of the aorta and the blood going out of the aorta supplies all the body, if there is a big enough tear and the blood is going down that other channel, if it's big enough to be seen on chest x-ray, he's going to have some, maybe not all, but at least some of these symptoms. He may even have an autopsy [showing] that the dissection went all the way down to below his waist and he would not have gotten sufficient blood to his legs. The evidence will show while Mr. Maffei was in the emergency department his blood pressure promptly got better, his throat pain went away and he was discharged in good condition.

I am going to spend a couple minutes now talking to you about Dr. Smedley. Dr. Smedley graduated from Loyola College locally in 1992, attended University of Maryland Medical School, graduating in 1996, and then spent three years of training at the University of Maryland Medical School, after medical school in emergency medicine and at the University of Maryland Shock Trauma. She became board certified in Emergency Medicine in the year 2000, which lasts until ten years' certification (she'll have to repeat that next year) and began employment at the University of Maryland in the Emergency Medicine Department and then actually worked on the volunteer faculty at the University of Maryland three years after that. Before she started at Charles Emergency Physicians in August of 1999. And she was employed at Charles Emergency Physicians and you will hear that Charles Emergency Physicians provides emergency room services at GBMC. It's not technically an employee of GBMC but provides emergency services at CBMC. Dr. Smedley worked there until September of 2006, when she decided to go back to the University of Maryland because she enjoyed teaching and working with residents and people in training. Dr. Smedley is now back at the University of Maryland in the Emergency Department there as an assistant professor of medicine at that institution where she assists in training residents after they have completed medical school.

I do want to spend a few moments to show you the medical records you are going to see. These medical records will come into evidence by agreement of counsel pertaining to that emergency room visit on March 8, 2006. You will see Mrs. Maffei brought Mr. Maffei to the emergency department at GBMC at 3:39 on March 8, 2006. It says "brought by C," that means brought by car. So if anybody has been to the emergency department, they know the first thing [that] generally happens is they walk in, see someone [at the] front desk, and they sit you down and ask you questions: "What brought you to the emergency department? What are your symptoms?" That's called triage. Triage was done by Nurse Rittenhouse. You will see triage was done almost simultaneously. Registration says it was 3:39; triage says 3:38. The chief complaints the nurse writes down: "Sudden onset last PN of sensation of lump in throat, intermit CP," short for intermittent chest pain. "Denies shortness of breath, nausea, diaphoresis." Diaphoresis is sweating. Also low back pain. History of chronic back pain, disc degeneration. Immediately his pulse was taken. Pulse was 67. That was normal. It was taken on the left side. Radial means it's taken from this artery here and pulse is normal. In fact, if he was having a full-blown dissection at that time, his pulse would not have been normal and would not have been normal strength. His blood pressure was taken initially, as you will see on this side, it was 91 over 44, that's at 3:38. It was repeated seven minutes later, it was 71 over 43, which is still low. But then it was repeated ten minutes later on the right and the left side and now it had returned to normal. So the only abnormal blood pressure or lower blood pressure were from 3:38 to 3:45 and by 3:55, his blood pressure was normal the rest of the emergency room visit.

He was also asked and they actually looked at his breathing, Mr. Maffei's breathing, he was breathing 17 breaths per minute, which is normal, and his pulse oxymetry, how much oxygen was he getting in his bloodstream, that was 98 percent, which is also normal. He described his pain as throat/chest. These are things of change in the emergency department. Now they do things by computer and they enter things in, so rather than writing down complaints, they have to go to the computer to write down things. That may be a possible explanation to what we'll see as some confusion by the nurses as to what kind of pain he's having. You will see the intensity level is 0 to 10, 0 being no pain, 10 being the most pain one can have. I guess if you bang your shin real hard on something or somebody hits your shin with a hammer, for a few seconds that will be 10 out of 10 pain. He described the pain, or the nurses wrote it down as 3 out of the 10. You will see the skin color was normal, skin moisture was normal. He wasn't sweating, he was awake, alert, appropriate. He was oriented. He knew what was going on. His mood was very calm and [he] walked into the emergency department. Not a picture of someone who is very ill or about to die in 20 hours of an aortic dissection. And you will hear testimony that aortic dissections can move very rapidly, move very fast. Aortic dissection can start, it can stop, it can be a very small tear if it stops and then progresses hours and hours and hours later, which we believe is what the evidence in this case will show.

After Mr. Maffei is triaged at around 3:40—and you will hear testimony that Mr. Maffei was taken immediately back to the examining room. While he's back in the examining room waiting for Dr. Smedley to see him, the nurses come in periodically to check on him. So, they check on him at 4:56, which is a little over an hour later. At that time they write chest pain, yes, chest pain, intermittent, chest pain radiation location, into the neck, chest pain has been going on one to three hours. That's already inconsistent with what he told the triage nurse. He told the triage nurse it started hours before. This nurse writes that the pain intensity level was 5 out of 10. And you will see that in fact that was true and really seen in a few moments why something more should have been done at that time if that was a realistic complaint.

You will see the nurses came back, another nurse came back, or the same nurse came back—JI is the nurse—came back at 5:41. So, about 45 minutes later, his blood pressure is 104 over 64, which is normal, and now the nurse writes he's having throat and chest pain and the intensity level is 2 out of 10.

What is confusing and inconsistent and doesn't make sense in this case is that there are emergency room protocols for what happens when a patient comes in with chest pain. It's undisputed in this case Dr. Smedley doesn't even learn of Mr. Maffei's presence for over two hours after he arrives. But the nursing triage protocol provides if in fact the patient is having chest pain, the triage nurse or primary nurse, that would include the triage nurse and then the nurse who wrote two other times there was chest pain, should notify the physician that he is having chest pain or systolic blood pressure under a hundred, which is what happened initially. When that blood pressure rose back up to normal after ten minutes, 15 minutes, the nurses obviously felt it wasn't necessary to notify the physician. If the nurses felt this was worrisome, significant chest pain, they were obligated to notify Dr. Smedley and they did not.

The triage guidelines, emergency department guidelines, also provide that if the reported pain is greater than 4 out of 10, the nurse must notify the emergency department physician of the patient's pain, document the patient's pain score, and document any intervention. As you saw at 4:56 a.m. on March 8th, the nurse writes that Mr. Maffei is having 5 out of 10 throat and chest pain and Dr. Smedley was not notified. This protocol also provides if the patient is more than 35 years old, and Mr. Maffei was, that with this chest pain, a portable chest x-ray, CXR should be ordered. That was never ordered by the nurse. So the nurses noted throat or chest pain, one or two or combination of them at three a.m., 3:30 a.m., 4:56 a.m., and 5:41 a.m. Dr. Smedley still does not know about the existence of Mr. Maffei in the emergency department. You will have to decide for yourself why the nurses didn't notify Dr. Smedley, but we submit that's because they felt that this was actually throat pain and not—

MR. SANDLER: I am going to object, Your Honor.

THE COURT: Overruled.

MR. SHAW: Not significant enough to notify Dr. Smedley. The nurses did not follow the chest guidelines. They didn't notify Dr. Smedley and didn't see Mr. Maffei immediately. Anybody knows when someone comes in with chest pain, one of the important things to do is move promptly and have the patient evaluated. But Mr. Maffei is triaged at 3:38 a.m., Dr. Smedley sees him in the ordinary course of her rounding and seeing patients more than two hours later at 5:55 a.m. And you will see in a moment when Dr. Smedley saw Mr. Maffei, Dr. Smedley had seen the triage nurse where Mr. Maffei had complained of throat and chest pain. She had seen that. So immediately Dr. Smedley, her antennae go up, bells and whistles go off in her mind, why is this patient described as having throat and chest pain? I haven't seen him yet, they haven't done a chest x-ray. She asked Mr. Maffei, are you having chest pain? Are you having, did you have chest pain? What kind of chest pain. What is it? And you will hear from Dr. Smedley in this regard. You will hear from Dr. Smedley and you will see as documented in Dr. Smedley's record that Mr. Maffei denied he was having any type of chest pain or tightness. In fact, he advised that the pain and the tightness was in his throat.

This is Dr. Maffei's [sic] handwritten record. She's not limited by what she can enter in a computer, of what she found that day. You will see that Dr. Smedley writes the date and the time, 5:55 a.m. And then Dr. Smedley took a history and I'll have to interpret some of this, some of the abbreviations, but you will hear from Dr. Smedley.

"Fifty-two [year old] white male comes in complains of onset 9:00 p.m. of sense of throat closing. Sore. Rapid onset over about ten minutes."

You will see the 0 with a line drawn through it. That's doctor's shorthand for none or absent. Diaphoresis, which is the sweating, no diaphoresis, 0 with a line through it, no nausea, 0 with a line through it, that's actually SO, Dr. Smedley didn't complete her O, B. No shortness of breath. Next entry, 0 with a line through it, CP, no chest pain. Mr. Sandler said Dr. Smedley did not document the finding of no chest pain. There it is, no chest pain. Pain, nonexertion. Upon further history, Dr. Smedley said Mr. Maffei had a niece visiting, C, line over it with strep one W, week, ago. That's the history Dr. Smedley took. Then Dr. Smedley went through these preprinted elements of a patient's anatomy and constitution, including whether he's having, Mr. Maffei is having any fever or chills. If you draw a line through it, it means not present. If you circle it, it means present. Mr. Maffei had no favor, no chills, eyes were not red. Originally, Mr. Maffei told Dr.

Smedley he wasn't having an earache. You will hear from the doctor, after she looked in his ears and saw redness, he said, well, maybe I do have a mild earache from time to time. ENT stands for ear, nose and throat. RESP stands for respiration or breathing. He had no shortness of breath or cough. CV stands for cardiovascular. And again, Dr. Smedley drew a line through it that he was having no chest pain. GI stands for gastrointestinal. He was having no abdominal pain, no nausea, no vomiting. And then as far as his, what does PS stand for? Psychosocial means no abnormalities of mood or affect. His memory was grossly intact, alert, and oriented times three. Not a patient who looks like he's critically ill or doing poorly. Dr. Smedley also wrote, L, TM means tympanic membrane, that's inside the ear, erythema means redness inside the left ear. She wrote mild OP, oral pharynx, that's the throat, erythema. Dr. Smedley on physical examination looked at Mr. Maffei's throat and ears; they were red consistent with a sore throat. His respirations were normal and no abnormal breaths sounds. The doctor puts the stethoscope on your chest, listens to the back and lungs to see if there is any abnormal breath sounds. Dr. Smedley did not find any, which the evidence will show if Mr. Maffei was experiencing a dissection other than that was incredibly small, too small to diagnose by chest x-ray, he would have had symptoms. Dr. Smedley signed the report at that time. She made this report contemporaneous with her examination. And then Dr. Smedley also made other records, this other second page of records, and in fact an EKG had been done and Dr. Smedley wrote that there was normal sinus rhythm, meaning that the heart was normal rate, not an irregular beat. There was some evidence of left ventricular hypertrophy, which means the left side of the heart was enlarged, but that could be for any number of reasons. She wrote no acute ST changes. If you look at EKG, there are certain waves that are very consistent with myocardial infarction. He did not have those, so Mr. Maffei was not having a heart attack. So Dr. Smedley checked off she discussed the treatment, that's TX, diagnosis, DX. The x-ray, the prescription RX, and follow up with patient and family and her diagnosis was ALL, allergic, RXN, reaction, ear INFXN, infection, and Dr. Smedley signed it.

After Dr. Smedley saw Mr. Maffei, the nurses still came back periodically to check on Mr. Maffei and you will see that they came back at 7:18, which is over an hour later. He's still breathing normally, his chest shape and chest expansion were normal and symmetric. They did another cardiovascular assessment. You will see 7:20, this is a different nurse. This nurse writes no chest pain complaint. What's the chest pain intensity, 0 out of 10. Chest complaint, none. Chest complaint intensity, 0 out of 10. Ten minutes later, 7:30, another assessment is done of vital signs and pulse in the left arm is still normal and blood pressure, Mr. Maffei's blood pressure is 124 over 72, absolutely normal. If this was a dissection that was big and growing, Dr. Smedley would have seen a totally different picture.

And then here's some confusion in the nurse's notes. So, at 7:20, the nurse writes no chest pain. At 7:30, let's go back, you will see this record here, 7:30, and what I am going to show you now is the carry-over to the next page but it's also an entry made at 7:30, 7:20, no chest pain, 7:30, throat and chest pain intensity rating, 2, and then another note at 7:30, are you having chest pain now? No. Chest pain reassessment, the reassessment apparently was done exactly at the same time. Pain location, throat, chest, pain intensity, 0. Are you having chest pain now? No. Pain intensity rating, 0. Two absolutely inconsistent entries made at the same time.

So you will hear from Dr. Smedley that when she met and examined and talked with Mr. Maffei, she, as the physician, relies on her own assessment. She was aware of the triage notes complaint of chest pain and throat, throat/chest pain. But the nurses' notes as we see were confusing and inconsistent. The nurse plus Dr. Smedley knew part of the chest pain and protocol would include seeing her immediately. She was not consulted immediately. Therefore, we submit, nurses must not have felt this pain, whatever it was, was not a significant issue. In fact, when Mr. Maffei is discharged at 7:40, he denied any pain at present, no respiratory difficulties noted, talking in full sentences, condition is stable at the time of discharge.

We are not going to go back, but I forgot to mention one thing. If you look at the nurses' notes closely, they have a time as far as when symptoms occurred and another time as far as when they entered them.

You see for a couple of entries, they were not made until two days later. Mr. Sandler stood up and said Dr. Smedley didn't look at some of the nurses' notes. Some of the nurses' notes are not made contemporaneously, they are made later. The last couple entries were made two days after Mr. Maffei left the emergency department. That's another reason why Dr. Smedley relies on her own assessment of the patient and not the nurses' notes as the patient goes through the hospital staff. At the time of discharge, Mr. Maffei had no pain. His blood pressure was normal. He had no breathing problems. He was calm and he was alert. This is the discharge instructions that were given, the diagnosis of sore throat and swelling and ear pain and he was asked to take antibiotics and steroid dose pack. Mr. Maffei signed this.

We believe our evidence is going to show Dr. Smedley's care was appropriate because she took a history of Mr. Maffei's complaints, he denied he was having chest pain despite what the nurses wrote and there was no reason to order a chest x-ray. Had a chest x-ray been ordered, the evidence will show the dissection was so small as evidenced by the lack of symptoms that it would not have been picked up on a chest x-ray. When you are performing a physical examination, Dr. Smedley also had no reason to order a chest x-ray.

So, you have heard and Mr. Sandler showed you the demonstration [of] what an aortic dissection is with a roll of paper towels; I'll agree with that except that the aorta is not as big in relation to the opening as a paper towel. I would take a lot of those paper towels off because the width of the aorta is not that big in comparison to the opening that's called a lumen. There are three layers to the aorta. There is a tear on the intima layer that causes blood to go down along the length, not only the opening but down through the tear. Aortic dissection of this type can be very sudden and many patients died before they even get to the hospital. This is the heart down here, the aorta coming up. There's an inside lining called the tunica intima. There's the middle layer, the muscle layer, the tunica media, and then the outside layer. What happens is there is a small tear right here and because the blood is going this way, the blood can get in here, not only goes through the opening like the hole in the pipe, but also can go down the lining of the blood vessel. And even at autopsy, this tear was small, it was less than a centimeter, which is less than a third of an inch. When it originally happened, it was about a third of an inch.

Mr. Maffei did not have symptoms of aortic dissections when he was at GBMC. These are some of the symptoms I showed you before. He had none of them. Sudden chest pain, he didn't have it. Excruciating chest pain, no. Ripping, chest pain, shortness of breath, pale skin, sense of impending doom, extreme anxiety, sweating, heart murmur, nausea, vomiting, upper extremity pain, lower extremity pain, upper extremity weakness and paralysis, lower extremity weakness and paralysis, abdominal pain, and stroke. Not every patient will have every one of these symptoms. When a patient is having an aortic dissection and can be diagnosed by a widening mediastinum [the patient] will have many of these symptoms. What he had was sensation of throat close, throat redness, sore throat, ear infection, eardrum redness, and a family member with recent strep throat. That's very consistent with Dr. Smedley's diagnosis of allergic reaction, ear infection, and sore throat. We believe in hindsight, [Mr. Maffei's] dissection was likely very small at GBMC because there was a lack of symptoms, lack of all those symptoms. Also looking at the autopsy reports that we now have. This is a copy of the autopsy report. And you will see at the time Mr. Maffei died there's a sac around the heart called the pericardium. The blood came out into that sac and outside the heart and back up into essentially the aorta and essentially smothered the heart. That happens in a matter of moments after this dissection progressed suddenly and dramatically. The autopsy also showed the medial dissection false lumen, that's when the blood goes down between the lining of the aorta, extended the entire length of the aorta, and involved the right common iliac artery. That's the artery down here. Also involved the left common carotid artery, which is up into the neck. If Mr. Maffei had a dissection of that type of that extent at the time he was in the emergency room, he would have had symptoms.

You can see that we believe based on the autopsy and based on the lack of symptoms and you will hear expert testimony, the dissection began there but there were no symptoms. At this stage of the dissection, it's not detectable by chest x-ray. The blood begins to go down here but [is] not detectable by chest x-ray. Here's the heart. As you saw from

Mr. Sandler's x-ray, the x-ray doesn't make the diagnosis of aortic dissection. It shows a widened structure that [if] enough blood had gone outside the normal channel of [the] aorta, it would have widened Mr. Maffei's mediastinum. Evidence will show at the time Mr. Maffei was in the emergency department, he had a very small tear, but there was a lack of symptoms. Therefore, it would not have been a wide mediastinum. It was only after, and this is the aorta, this is the normal channel, and this is the blood outside the aorta, it would actually surround, once the blood goes out, it goes around the whole aorta, outside and inside, and widens the mediastinum. That our evidence would show was not what would have been seen had Dr. Smedley ordered a chest x-ray. So, these symptoms, impending sense of doom, shortness of breath, aortic insufficiency, chest pain, pale skin, sweating, nausea and vomiting, those would have began to appear once the aorta became more dissected and blood came out. But there was an absence of that when Mr. Maffei was in the emergency department. There was no reason for Dr. Smedley to take blood pressure in both arms. Had she done that, it would have been normal because the dissection had not extended. We believe the evidence will then show Mr. Maffei's dissection enlarged after he left the emergency room and he died when suddenly this dissection progressed from a small tear all the way down below his waist and all the way up into his neck. You can see from this diagram, this is where the dissection has extended. This is the inside of the aorta, but the red much larger opening is in the outside of the normal channel and the blood, the dissection is extended all the way down below his waist, Mr. Maffei's waist, and all the way around the outside of the heart, which caused the condition called cardiac tamponade. The heart is beating but the blood gets inside the pericardial sac; it essentially keeps the heart from beating. That's what caused Mr. Maffei's sudden death when this dissection extended all the way down.

So, as I mentioned before, Mr. Sandler has the burden of proof in this case. If you believe, they have to prove by abundance of evidence that there was medical negligence and damages and because he has the burden of proof, Mr. Sandler gets to go first. We ask that you keep an open mind until you have heard all of the evidence. When you have heard all the evidence, including from our experts, Dr. David Shank, emergency medicine physician, you are only going to hear from one emergency medicine physician, same specialty as Dr. Smedley. That's the defense side. The plaintiffs do not have emergency medical physicians to testify in this case. You will hear from the Elliott Goldstein, intensive care physician, who deals with these types of sudden emergencies.

We believe at the end of the case, our evidence will show Dr. Smedley treated Mr. Maffei appropriately, did not commit medical malpractice, and with all due respect would ask for a verdict in favor of Dr. Smedley in this case.

Thank you so much for your attention. We attorneys will try to move this case along. Judge Cahill is good about moving cases along. We'll finish this case quickly as possible but both sides have a story to tell and both sides want to make sure that justice is done for their clients. Thank you so much.

Appendix IV

CLOSING ARGUMENTS IN THE *MAFFEI* CASE

Closing Argument by the Plaintiff

MR. SANDLER: May it please the Court, ladies and gentlemen of the jury, you have been sitting here over a week, actually a full week, in which you have been in a very silent mode. You have been patiently listening, working with the schedules, taking it all in, thinking to yourself, "What is this all about?"

And now that role will change. You will soon retire to your jury room to look at the evidence, the documents. You can talk amongst yourselves and come to a just and fair verdict.

That will happen very shortly.

On behalf of the lawyers, it's important to thank you. Because the service that you give when you sacrifice your own daily schedules to sit as judges of your fellow men and women, as juries do, is an honor and it's a privilege. It's also one that is a unique quality of our country.

We have juries every day sitting in judgment of their peers, making decisions. And it's not taken lightly.

We thank you for your attention.

It's my purpose during this allotted time for closing argument to highlight for you the evidence that will support the claim of the plaintiffs. I will superimpose on the evidence some of my interpretations of what the evidence brings to bear.

And I think we should begin straightaway.

What is this case about? What were the issues? What are they?

When I came before you in opening statement, I told you that we would prove to you not that Dr. Smedley was a bad person, but that she made a mistake and the mistake cost the life of a dear fellow.

And I suggested to you that the evidence would demonstrate that but for an x-ray Mr. Maffei would be alive today. And I also proved that.

And I will explain how, so that you can be comfortable that the evidence is square.

I also proved, and you will consider as another issue, about whether the x-ray should have been undertaken, whether if the x-ray were taken of Mr. Maffei whether it would have shown what I said to you in opening statement it would show, an abnormality. And that from the abnormal x-ray, a further test known as a CAT scan or some other tests would have then been required to reveal the heart problem that he had.

We never intended to prove or never suggested to you from the x-ray someone would see a dissection of the aorta. That is not medically feasible. But an x-ray would have revealed a widening of the mediastinum or an abnormality, which would have required the CAT scan.

And then once the issue was resolved that the x-ray should have been taken and, yes, more likely than not it would have shown an abnormality, we then produce evidence to you that the treatment would have been surgery, and the surgery would have saved his life; and he would have been able to work for at least ten years and live another 15 years.

That is the crucial theme, the central force of our case.

So the question that you ask and must ask: Did Mr. Sandler prove his case more likely than not?

And to answer that question, you will be, of course, eager to review and talk among yourselves [about] the quality of the evidence. Because, as you know, and I'll review with you again, the defense raises certain counterarguments to Mrs. Maffei's claim.

So I would like to take you through and present to you basically what some of the witnesses said and how those witnesses contributed to the theme.

Now, we have to go back. Remember the first witness we called in this case was a cardiologist by the name of Dr. Shadoff. And Dr. Shadoff, that was Tuesday morning. He came before Dr. Shank and before the defense put their case on.

And I think if I try to refresh your recollection, it may come back to you as to the significance of Dr. Shadoff.

First who he is. He's a prominent and respected cardiologist, very knowledgeable about issues of the heart.

And he was very explicit and demonstrative in terms of what he suggested to you in terms of his testimony, which was that the nature of the symptoms presented by Mr. Maffei were such that it required a chest x-ray. And he explained exactly what would be seen on the chest x-ray.

And because he testified on Monday and this is now Friday, and we have heard a lot of testimony since Dr. Shadoff testified, I would like to review with you in a little detail the testimony of Dr. Shadoff. Because he, I think, sets forth clearly what I promised in opening statement I would prove to you.

So I have taken the liberty—now, I have a transcript of the pertinent testimony of Dr. Shadoff so you can hear his exact words, not wonder have I been quoting him right or am I exaggerating, because I don't want to do that.

So some of the questions are as follows:

"Did you hear counsel state to the jury [in his opening statement], at the [time] Mr. Maffei was in the hospital that the dissection was so slight it would never have shown up on an x-ray, meaning there would not be any type of irregularity on the x-ray?"

You can follow if you wish.

"Yes, I heard that."

"Is that correct? Do you agree with that?"

"Absolutely not."

Just briefly, we will get into why not.

Answer: "Because the symptoms they described could only come from the fact that the dissection already involved the artery going up into the neck, or else he wouldn't have had neck pain and ear discomfort, and already involving the artery going down through the back toward the right leg, or else he wouldn't have had back discomfort."

So what Dr. Shadoff is explaining was in his view, his opinion, the dissected aorta, dissected aorta of Mr. Maffei, the dissected aorta had progressed so that it was in the artery from the neck, the carotid artery, and then progressed down to where the back was so that he would have had back pain. [Jury is viewing a diagram as counsel points to it.]

As you recall, his symptoms in the hospital included pain in the neck and pain in the back and chest pain, closing of the throat.

So Dr. Shadoff said that if you did take the x-ray, you would see the widening of the mediastinum because, as he pointed out, the symptoms reflected on the nurse's notes indicate that.

So Dr. Shadoff explained what the widening of the mediastinum is. That this [counsel pointing to the diagram] would be the aorta, this is the tear, this is the root, and that the walls separated and that blood would come here. And as blood went around in the second channel, there would be a widening. And that would show up on the x-ray, a peculiarity of the x-ray. And as a result there would be a need to go forward with a CAT scan.

Now, it's crucial. Because when you look at the symptoms, which you saw—you saw that in the nurses' notes—the triage note to be specific—Mr. Maffei is reported to have among other complaints the complaint of chest pain. The note reflected that on a scale of 1 to 10 the chest pain was 5 out of 10 radiating to the neck, and you know that the back pain was there. You also know that Dr. Smedley didn't see the nurses' notes.

And I'll talk about that in a minute.

But those were his symptoms. It doesn't involve what Dr. Smedley saw or not.

The question I'm addressing now is, assuming you agree that the x-ray could have been and should have been taken, the defense takes the position, "Well, it doesn't matter because you wouldn't have seen anything on the x-ray anyway and certainly not a widening of the mediastinum." And I'm suggesting that you conclude that based on the evidence, based on just what Dr. Shadoff testified to that the doctor would have seen something, yes the widening of the mediastinum, which would then call for the x-ray. Ladies and gentlemen, remember another defense raised is that that the nurses did not take a chest x-ray and thus the doctor did not have the responsibility.

Now let's see what Dr. Shadoff says about this defense as I posed questions to him during his testimony.

"Do you agree that if the nurses do not take an x-ray, the doctor does not have a responsibility to take the x-ray?"

"No."

"Why?"

"The ultimate responsibility is the physician's to order the test."

So one of the defenses about the x-ray was the nurses had the responsibility. That's why they put in, I suggest, the nursing protocol, because it—and Dr. Smedley said, "Well, I rely on my nurses."

But the point that I want to bring to your attention through evidence, and I do so now, is simply this: The nursing protocol may have called for taking an x-ray. Dr. Smedley, when I questioned her, acknowledged that certainly 5 out of 10 would have called for an x-ray. But the fact that her nurses that she relied on didn't come to her doesn't take away her awesome responsibility to do what is right under the circumstances, which is to take the x-ray.

Then I went further. And I asked Dr. Shadoff: "Tell us whether you have an opinion to a reasonable degree of certainty whether or not if the nurse fails to take a particular test or administer a certain procedure and those same conditions exist at a later time when the doctor is examining the patient, that the fact that the nurses didn't do a test or procedure, the doctor doesn't have the responsibility to do so?"

"I do have an opinion."

"What is your opinion?"

"The opinion is that's still ultimately the doctor's responsibility."

Remember also that the defense argues that even if there were a tear in the aorta when Dr. Smedley saw Mr. Maffei in the hospital that fateful day, the tear was so slight there couldn't be any kind of showing on an x-ray Do you remember that?

But Dr. Shadoff testified that the defense is not correct, because the tear would have been a size to create this false channel which I just pointed out to you. Dr. Shadoff then testified that the cause of death, which we all know, was cardiac tamponade, and that explained how the poor fellow's heart stopped beating and why it did.

He also testified that a surgical procedure would have saved his life. And he then is asked as follows: "Could the dissecting aorta have been diagnosed? How could it have been diagnosed or would have been diagnosed?"

He says the first step would have been a chest x-ray. Why a chest x-ray? Because with aortic dissection, if a chest x-ray shows an abnormality of the silhouette of the heart and vascular structures, then you have a very high level of suspicion that aortic dissection has occurred and leads you to do further testing.

What type of further testing? It could come into three categories. The easiest test is to order a CAT scan test with injection of dye to outline the aorta. A very simple test that takes maybe five, ten minutes to do.

What would have been revealed with the CAT scan? A CAT scan would have shown if the aorta had a tear, and a tear extending up into the left carotid artery and left arm artery and around down into the abdomen and the belly, tracking the right leg.

Now, as we know, another argument of Dr. Smedley is that the patient told her something different than what triage note had said. That is that Mr. Maffei told her that he had not complained of chest pain and was not experiencing chest pain at the time he was being seen by the doctor.

Remember what Dr. Shadoff said about what the doctor should do when there is a conflict between the nurse's notes and what the patient later tells the doctor: "All right. Question: What do you believe? Do you believe the patient when you talk to the patient, or do you believe the nurse based on hearsay? Do you [read] the note and not worry about the note because you have the patient in front of you?" And Dr. Shadoff says, answer: "You know, I reconcile it right on the spot. Usually if the note—I always bring the nurse back and say to the patient that, 'You told the nurse, or three different nurses, that you had chest pain and now you're telling me you don't. Tell me which of these it is.' It's an important issue; you have to reconcile this."

Another question: So in order for your opinion—in order for your opinion in this case to be valid and that a chest x-ray should be ordered, you have to accept what? That Dr. Smedley got it wrong, she wasn't the final decision-maker, and she should not have trusted the patient when he—when she questioned him. And you'll hear from Dr. Smedley. And he told her that he did not have chest pain and had not had chest pain, what he had was throat tightening. You can't accept that testimony in order to offer that opinion in this case; isn't that true? This is Mr. Shaw questioning the plaintiff's expert. The answer: No, that's not true. And in point of fact, it's well known that discomfort in the throat and neck is one of the equivalents of chest discomfort in patients who present with heart dissection. And, incidentally, Dr. Smedley acknowledged that too. Anyone would acknowledge that.

So when Ms. Maffei is on the witness stand and describing where the pain is, she points above the collarbone. So if it's not chest pain, it's throat pain. But certainly when I question Dr. Smedley, the reason she immediately said no at first—and I remember well. What I asked her was, "Weren't we more concerned about the tightening of his chest?" And she said "no" at first. But then I reminded her she had stated that she had been, because that was the truth. And, remember, coming to see Dr. Smedley is not a doctor, but a hard-working lady who loves her husband who was scared to death that he was having a heart attack because of her father.

So then Mr. Shaw asked: Could Mr. Maffei, who was walking around with all this dissection all the way down to here, the left, the common iliac artery up into the common carotid artery, have survived for another 18 hours?

Answer: "Yes."

So you would dispute another health care provider that comes into this courtroom and disagrees with that?

And she says, "Obviously."

"And Mr. Maffei was leaking blood outside the artery. This artery also—the aorta also supplied blood to the rest of the body, correct?" Answer: "Yes."

Question: "All the blood comes from other portions of the body through that aorta, does it not?" Answer: "Yes, sir."

"And if the dissection was all the way down the right common iliac artery, wouldn't you expect the patient to have other symptoms, including stomach pain, shortness of breath, including heart murmur, including arm weakness or leg weakness? If he got a dissection into his left common carotid artery would there also have been stroke-like symptoms? Do you agree?"

Answer: "It's not just—no. It's absolutely not. And the reason that I don't agree with that is that there was clearly adequate blood flow going into the left arm and the left side of the brain to prevent a stroke from occurring. But not adequate blood flow that pain was appreciated."

Question: And the pathologist—that is the person who does autopsies. The pathologist described this dissection, that this tear extends into the right common iliac artery but clearly—strike that. It didn't involve any outside branches of the artery which would have caused other symptoms. And that's the key, that's why that the defense's position that the man would have been a walking dead person during all this time is not valid, because the autopsy does not show the issue involving other side branches of the artery. It was just straight up and around.

And that's the key to resolving the defense. So when you go back into the jury room and you discuss this issue, please remember what Dr. Shadoff said, "Yes, he would have had that, he did have that." And he didn't have other symptoms because of the flow of the blood. Blood flow straight around into the lumen and around. It did not go to the side branches of the artery, which would have caused those other symptoms.

And, by the way, let's face it, there are several experts; we called Dr. Shadoff and we called Dr. Carey. And, of course, the defense, we heard just their expert, Dr. Shank. These are individuals who have various specialties and various credentials.

But one point is for sure, Dr. Shadoff truly understands and specializes in cardiac issues. He understands what happens and how patients should be examined and diagnosed and what the symptoms mean.

And when you saw on that chart the nurse's note that I showed you earlier that pain was going into the neck, that's crucial. And when Dr. Smedley, trying her best—and, by the way, as I say, this, of course, is a terribly sad and tragic case. Everyone is upset about it. And I understand their compassion and her terrible angst.

But to say that when—if she had seen those nursing notes her concern would not have been heightened just defies common sense.

By the way, she said she didn't need to see the nurse's notes because she depended on her nurse. And Dr. Shank agreed, just looking from the triage note if the patient says something different, you don't just say okay and move on, you got to bring the nurse in. That's what their own experts say.

He also said, by the way, and I will point that out, that he admits that there would have been some abnormality [on] the x-ray. That's crucial. Because that really takes the ax to the defense as it should, an admission of abnormality.

Now, of course he's defendant's doctor, so he is not going to jump up and say, "Yes, Mr. Sandler, you're right." We're not on television. It doesn't work that way. But what he did concede—that the x-ray would be abnormal. That's all that we've said about the x-ray, the purpose of the x-ray.

Then he's asked on examination, "So if I understand your testimony, you're saying that the size of the tear almost didn't change from the time that the patient came to GBMC?" And he said, "That's right."

So, in essence, what I would like you to consider is the credibility of Dr. Shadoff. Think about his testimony as you deliberate and review his resume. This is the heart doctor's heart doctor. This is the real McCoy.

This guy, this poor guy came in this hospital with a dissection, he came in with chest pain and throat pain. It was constant throughout. And for a reason that we don't know, this doctor just missed it. And that's the problem in this case.

Now let me move forward, just to remind you what Mrs. Maffei's testimony was. She testified her husband comes home from work—now, think about this. Fifty-two-year-old Richard Maffei, six feet tall, over 240 pounds, heavy lift operator at Sparrow's Point. Is he going to the emergency room of a hospital at 3:30 in the morning for a little sore throat and earache? It's preposterous. And the records don't even support that. He was having some problems, big-time problems. And he was trying to find out about it.

Now, Dr. Smedley, of course, she has testified in her differential diagnosis she had [the] aorta in mind. But what happened was she was thinking myocardial. She got an enzyme test. She assured Mrs. Maffei that there was no heart attack and went on and didn't follow through with ruling out the other issue, the other symptom. And, hence, we have this problem.

Now, just to emphasize, because this case is so important and I don't want you to think that I'm misconstruing testimony last week or three days ago. I wanted to—I told you I'd read from Dr. Shank. And I don't have to show it, but I'm reading from his testimony where he says—where I said, I'll ask the question differently.

Question: "Had his x-ray been taken at all for any reason, would you agree that his x-ray would have been minimally abnormal?" Interesting. And he answers, "Yes, sir I told Mr. Harlan in my deposition that it could have been."

So I'm not just saying that. That's what he said. You would have seen it. I think you can conclude based on the evidence of Dr. Shadoff and based on the evidence of Dr. Carey that the widening of the mediastinum would have been the abnormality.

Like I said, this gentleman, he's honest, but he's not going to jump over the witness stand and shake my hand and say, "You're right." But he did acknowledge what was truthful, there would have been an abnormality in that x-ray.

So I wanted to turn to you now and to remind you that Dr. Carey testified that Mr. Maffei was an excellent candidate for surgery. That's because the nature of the dissection when caught at that time allowed for normal, regular surgical repair.

Now, Dr. Carey is a very competent heart surgeon. And a heart surgery is one of the most difficult surgeries other than brain surgery. And he's done hundreds of surgeries. He is not going to go on this witness stand and tell you a tall tale. He told you that he believed exactly what I asked you to believe, that had the dissection been uncovered, this man would be here today and we would not.

And I think that you can accept that for a number of reasons. First, his inherent credibility and authenticity and, second, it's not really opposed by the defense. Nor is the fact that he would live for 15 years or have worked for ten years.

Now, I cannot go back in time and tell you all that happened in that emergency room. No one can.

But I have brought the records to you and I have brought the witnesses to tell you, to share with you. Now, remember, no way is it possible to go back. But I do want to share something with you. I want to pretend we could. And I want to go back, because I want to examine the nature of some of the defenses. Because I've summarized our evidence in terms of what our case is. Namely, that he comes to the hospital with the complaints documented, that the x-ray should have been taken. It wasn't. Had it been taken, the abnormally would have been uncovered; a CAT scan would have been taken and the proper diagnosis made.

All of you heard this. It's been a week. So, I don't want to keep you thinking that you don't understand the English words. It's very plain. And I do want to share with you, however, some of the defenses and help you come to grips when you are in the jury deliberating room; I certainly am not invited, and nor should I be.

Maybe some of the ideas I impart to you from my observation of the evidence will help you understand. The first issue I wanted to talk about is the defense, which is simply that, "Well, I could have, if I believed he had chest pain, taken an x-ray. But he said he didn't have chest pain." Then the testimony is he also said he never had chest pain. And this is why it gets difficult, just as it got difficult when I asked her, "Well, wouldn't you have a heightened concern if you saw that?" Her answer was, "No. Because my concern was so heightened to begin with."

If her concern was so heightened to begin with, she would have followed up with it, as Dr. Shadoff said, at that stage and getting that nurse in, going through it. But she doesn't do that, Dr. Smedley doesn't do that. Instead she said she documented that, she resolved it with him and documented it.

But she didn't document it. I want to review that with you. Remember, their own expert, Dr. Shank, explained what his procedure was in terms of resolving this difference. And we are talking about that she said no chest pain. Now, of course, the sensation of the throat closing, which is acknowledged by Dr. Smedley, is a symptom of a heart problem. She didn't deny that. And when you saw Mrs. Maffei, I don't know, chest, throat. And what can a patient know?

All of us people who have issues with health can know that sometimes there can be pain and you don't exactly know where it is or what the etiology is, as they call it. You just know it hurts and it's there. It wasn't a sore throat. He was more concerned with his throat closing. But she does—oh, at one point in opening statements, as I remember, Mr. Shaw suggested that when she struck "CP" here in this line, which says "Circle if present," that was her documentation Then the doctor picked up on that and said it's inferred. That doesn't infer that there was a healthy, proper discussion about reconciling these inconsistencies, if there were. So I just point that out to you.

So when the answer comes that I didn't have to take the chest x-rays because he said he didn't have any, of course it doesn't sound relevant. So I relied more on the patient telling me this than the notes. Well, because that is a way to get out of this jam.

And the point is, her own doctor wouldn't, her own expert wouldn't let her out.

Remember, he said to her, and when—I'm going to read from some of the cross-examination.

She said she had worked that night the evening night shift, overnight shift, that's 11 at night to 7 in the morning.

"And at that time that Mr. Maffei was seen by you, you agree that there was only one doctor available at that time."

And she says, "At the time that I saw him, yes." She adds, "But, to be complete, when I arrived, there was still that other physician. And then he wasn't back at the time I saw him."

"So your answer is yes, you were the only doctor at that time?"

And she says, "At that time I saw him, yes."

Then I said—and I wanted to ask this question because I want to be able to have a conversation with, one-way conversation with you at this time to point out to you that this throat closing is not your allergy, sore throat or your little red throat. Probably everyone's throat is a little red. But I am talking that this was different.

I want to emphasize that. And I emphasize that that again goes against the defense's theory of the case.

So I asked her: "And when you did see him, did you agree he was worried about the sense of closing in his throat, which he felt was more than just a sore throat? Isn't that true?"

"No, that's not true."

Well—and I said to her: "I would just like to refresh your recollection, because that was three years ago. But in your deposition you said yes. And I went through that. You remember?"

And then she said yes to the question.

"Does that refresh your recollection? Do you say that you agree that that's what you testified to?"

"Yes."

"So when he felt he was more worried about the sense of closing in his throat, his wife was also present, isn't that true?"

And the answer: "His wife was present."

"And she was worried about her husband?"

"Yes."

Question: "She was particularly worried about heart conditions, isn't that true?"

"Yes, she was."

And then I had some more dialogue with her and she said: "I reassured him that his symptoms and results are reassuring and it didn't look like he was having a heart attack."

Then I asked her further: "When you see triage notes with chest pain 3 out of 10, you were concerned about an aortic problem; isn't that true?"

"Yes."

Now, again "yes" the answer was.

"That's one of many things that can cause chest pain."

"Is it 'yes,' though, that you were concerned about an aortic problem at that time you saw the triage note?"

Answer: "That was not my major concern, but, yes, I believe. Yes."

And then I went into further discussion with her about the issue of the—had she seen those other notes which she had available to her would that have been of more concern?

But she says no, which defies common sense.

So I've summarized for you the evidence I have discussed with you, the theme of our case of how the evidence fits in, where the defense does not answer us in terms of where we go in terms of this case.

And now I want to talk to you about the standard of care that was required, so you can understand exactly what our position is.

And it's as follows: Dr. Smedley was required to appropriately evaluate and interpret Mr. Maffei's medical history to determine the potential for life-threatening diseases. That is the standard of care.

And the medical history, I suggest to you, was not properly attained. She did not examine the full record. And as a result, she missed something very important.

Now, of course, it is true that a dissected aorta is rare. And it's not your everyday common cold. But that is irrelevant to the standards of a doctor, because it is on her checklist.

She herself acknowledged it went through her mind, just went out.

And that's the mistake.

She also should have performed a physical examination, sufficient and adequate to diagnose or exclude potential life-threatening disease processes.

She didn't do that properly.

She is supposed to obtain diagnostic studies to diagnose or exclude potential life-threatening disease processes.

She should have considered not only a myocardial infarction, heart attack, but the pulmonary embolism, which is blockage at the lung.

We mentioned aortic dissection. And it just didn't happen. As a result, we have the case before us.

I want to say a word about now the pain and suffering, the damages, and what we are seeking.

The judge talked about it on the verdict sheet, which I'm going to show you with some suggestions and talk about how you might go forward with that.

But there's something that deserves a certain conversation, and that is Ms. Maffei's heartache and her feelings.

This is not fun. She is not doing this for fun. And it is extremely personal to her. And she did go to see a psychiatrist to get help at Sheppard Pratt, and she does still seek counseling. And I haven't even told her I was going to say this. But she—when she went to her doctor, she had mentioned to him and described how she was feeling. And she told him that she couldn't sleep, she was so upset she can't be alone, and that she has to—she has repetition of nightmares and is miserable.

And I have to say this to you. After they gave you the evidence, who wouldn't be? Who would not cry out and say, Why me? Why my husband, Richard?

It is so bad that she said she is angry. Isn't it just what human nature is? And does it not show the depths of her love for her husband?

I think you can look at her and see that this is not someone looking for jackpot justice or coming to courts for any reason other than the love of her husband and to seek an adequate award.

And I want to show you, if I could, the verdict sheet that the judge mentioned. This is the first page.

Thank you, Stephanie.

And it says: "Do you find that defendant, Angela D. Smedley, M.D., breached the standard of medical care in her care and treatment of Richard Paul Maffei?"

And I'm going to ask you, based on the evidence in the case that we've proved, that we brought to you, to check the box yes.

And then it says "If your answer to Question 1 is yes, please answer Question 2. If your answer to Question 1 is no, do not answer any further questions."

I ask you on behalf of Mrs. Maffei to go further, go the extra step that she deserves.

"Do you find that the breach of the standard of care by Dr. Smedley was a proximate cause of the plaintiff's injuries?"

And I would ask you, based on the evidence and based on this case, to say yes.

"If your answer is yes, please proceed to Question 3. If your answer is no. . . ." Now, here I took, "How much money do you award, if any, for economic damages?"—and that's based on the testimony that you heard from the economist. Future loss of earnings, that number, $510,384 is what you heard from the economist, which takes into consideration the future earnings and pension and health benefit. And then I ask you to consider loss of household services, which calculated to $167,923. And funeral expenses of $5,000.

. . . So I ask you to consider the total of $684,382 as the compensatory damages for Mrs. Maffei based upon what happened to her husband.

There's another category of damages which we call noneconomic damages. And you have within your discretion to award for emotional distress, pain, and suffering.

And you can and should consider Mrs. Maffei's mental anguish, emotional pain and suffering, loss of society, loss of companionship, loss of marital care, loss of attention, loss of advice or counsel.

That number can be as high as a trillion, which would be ridiculous, or it can be low as a zero, which I suggest to you would also be ridiculous. Somewhere in between is the proper amount.

I am not going to suggest to you a particular figure. That is within your discretion. Because in your role as a jury you, in a sense, wear an invisible robe because you're the judge of this case.

However, I'm going to suggest to you as follows, that if you were to examine her pain and suffering every day and consider, if some people go to a dentist for root canal work, they may pay seventy five-dollars for a day to be free of pain. Everyone is different.

But you can understand that if one would pay seventy-five dollars a day to be free from pain and Mrs. Maffei's mental anguish continues day by day by day, week by week by week, that you might want to consider the example I just presented to you as a frame of reference for rendering to her an adequate award for her pain and suffering. And you should also consider that Ms. Maffei said to you very candidly, she feels she is on the upswing. And that's good.

So in terms of a specific dollar amount that you should give for her emotional suffering, use your discretion wisely to render a fair award. You are the judges, you are the jury. And I respectfully suggest to do what is right and what's fair, to give Mrs. Maffei an adequate award for the loss of her husband.

Also I also remind you that Mr. Maffei himself cannot speak to you. But his wife is here to speak for him. He suffered as well, pain and suffering. And he is entitled too. He had a horrible day; he's no longer here. And we're talking about someone's life, someone who deserved your full and careful attention, as you are giving it.

So I want to conclude now. I've spoken probably too long. But I wanted to be forthright: astronomical damages would be disgraceful. But to have the wisdom to appreciate that we are here to compensate someone for a loss that is deserved to be compensated. You need to have to bring your sense of justice to do what is right.

And sometimes it's hard to do what's right. It's important to adhere to the judge's jury instructions. And it's also important to do what's right and to understand, by the way, that if a lawyer such as myself may misspeak or do something that you thought wasn't proper, appreciate that we are all human beings all doing the best we can.

All you need is courage and common sense. You have it. We can see how courteous you've been and how attentive you are. And use that common sense. Let it work for you. And I beseech you, when you return, return with a verdict for Mrs. Maffei. Give her the justice that she deserves.

No amount of money can bring back her husband. No verdict in her favor can restore her. Life is precious and it flickers. And we never know. But you're here, I'm here. We can do good.

We can also send a message to the community—not an evil message, but a message that these x-rays with chest pain are crucial. It can save lives. You can save lives by telegraphing this message. Do your duty. I tried to do mine. Now it's up to you. Thank you very much for your attention.

THE COURT: Thank you, Mr. Sandler.

Closing Argument by the Defense

THE COURT: Mr. Shaw.

MR. SHAW: Thank you.

May it please the Court.
Good morning, ladies and gentlemen.
This is my last chance to talk with you. As you've heard, the plaintiffs have the burden of proof in this case, so they go on first in their opening, they go first in presenting their evidence, and they go first and they have a chance to go after me in their closing.

So I want to take this opportunity, as did Mr. Sandler, to thank you very much for your service in this case. All of the attorneys and the parties are very appreciative for your service.

Mr. Sandler mentioned about the significance and the uniqueness of a jury trial in this country. And I read a statistic somewhere that something like 90 percent of all jury trials in the world are held in the United States of America.

It's a good system.

Realize, as Mr. Sandler said, you have common sense and you bring it to bear in your judgment of your peers. So we certainly thank you for your time that you devoted. One of the highest civic duties and responsibilities second to, I guess, enlisting in the military service, is to serve on a jury. So we thank you very much.

As you heard, this case is important to both sides. It's important to Mrs. Maffei but it's also very important to Dr. Smedley.

There will be a lot of things that we are going to dispute that you heard from Mr. Sandler about what the evidence showed in this case. I'm not going to revisit every one of those issues, but I'm going to highlight some of which we do dispute and which we believe the judgment should be in favor of Dr. Smedley.

But one thing we don't dispute, one of the things nobody disputes is the tragic death of Mr. Maffei. We certainly recognize the compassion and sympathy that you have for her and that we have and certainly Dr. Smedley has.

You heard Dr. Smedley tell you that by that time, she'd seen hundreds of patients through the years since that time when she saw Mr. Maffei, and his presentation was not at all consistent with one who is going to leave the emergency department and die 17 hours later, that she has a clear recollection of what happened that night.

And certainly she felt sympathy and compassion and she felt the tragedy of Mr. Maffei's death and of what Mrs. Maffei has experienced.

So if your sole duty in this case was to rely on just sympathy and compassion and base your decision, then obviously we wouldn't be here.

But as His Honor has instructed you, you have to treat everyone fairly and impartially.

And I'd like to briefly read to you from the jury instructions, one of the jury instructions that Judge Cahill read to you. And it's entitled "Impartiality and Consideration."

You must consider and decide this case fairly and impartially. You can't base your decision or be prejudiced by a person's race, color, religious, political or social views, wealth or poverty. And the same is true as to prejudice for or against and sympathy for any party.

So as hard as it may be, you have to try to put aside your compassion and sympathy for Mrs. Maffei, which we all certainly have.

So the critical issue then is: Was there medical malpractice in this case?

And the definition I showed you in my opening statement and His Honor has read to you, the legal definition of "medical malpractice" is the failure to act as a reasonably competent doctor.

Your decision, that will be the first question that you see on verdict sheet:

"Do you find that the defendant, Angela D. Smedley, M.D., breached the standard of medical care in her care and treatment of Richard Paul Maffei?"

In other words: Did Dr. Smedley fail to act as a reasonably competent medical physician in emergency medicine?

And we believe the evidence has shown that Dr. Smedley did act appropriately and she did care properly for Mr. Maffei.

And it's obvious from that definition just because there is a tragic outcome doesn't mean that there's been malpractice. And bad results can occur even with good care.

We've all heard that expression, "Bad things can happen to good people." That's what happened here. Something bad happened, a tragedy happened. But there was no medical malpractice.

Because the plaintiffs have the burden of proof, if for some reason you can't make up your mind, if the weight is even in your mind, because plaintiff has the burden then you must find for Dr. Smedley.

But we believe that plaintiffs have failed to meet their burden of proof and the evidence is on the side of Dr. Smedley.

So March 8th, 2006, at 3:39 a.m., Mr. Maffei comes to the emergency room.

In retrospect and hindsight—I've used that phrase a number of times in this case. In hindsight, did Mr. Maffei have an aortic dissection in place? Yes, he did. A big dissection that should have been picked up.

And—you've heard from Dr. Shank.

And we believe in retrospect there was a dissection there, that it all had just started and it was—it was so small that it could not have been diagnosed.

We strongly dispute—and I will talk to you about that in a few moments—that had a chest x-ray, had it been ordered for whatever reason, that would have demonstrated enough evidence to move on to the next step.

Now, you have to understand—or I'm sure you understand plaintiffs' allegations in this case. It's not that Dr. Smedley somehow, from the symptoms that Mr. Maffei had, should have made a decision of that rare condition, aortic dissection. They have not gone that far. But they do say that had Mr. Maffei—had Dr. Smedley considered chest pain and felt that was real, that she should have ordered a chest x-ray, that chest x-ray would have been abnormal, and because the chest was not just abnormal but would have caused a widened mediastinum and this chest x-ray with the widened mediastinum, then Dr. Smedley would have gone and ordered yet another test, and that other test, whether CAT scan or MRI, somehow would have made the diagnosis of an aortic dissection.

As Dr. Shank explained—and I will talk to you in a moment with some diagrams. He said the chest x-ray may have been mildly abnormal only because the left side of the heart was mildly enlarged and maybe because there was some tortuous type of blood vessel there. But it would not have demonstrated a widened mediastinum that would have called for a follow-up CAT scan.

So the plaintiffs are basing their case on hindsight based on now what we know as is the autopsy, from the autopsy.

They contend that this single complaint, the primary complaint—now since on cross-examination Dr. Shadoff tried to extend it to other symptoms. But the chief complaint the plaintiffs contend should have led to this chest x-ray was chest pain.

And at the risk of sheer—of too much repetition, I do want to go over with you very briefly about the chest pain complaints.

Now, from the registration note at 3:39 under "Reason for Visit," there is no mention of any chest pain. Only back pain and throat closing up.

Then at four—excuse me. At 3:39 in the triage note there is a note of sudden onset last p.m. of lump in throat, intermittent chest pain, also low back pain, history of chronic low back pain and disc degeneration. That's their note at 4:56. And whereas at 3:39 the complaint was throat, chest pain, at 4:56, or 4:51 rather—I'm sorry—4:56, the complaint is now just chest pain, 5 out of 10. And then again at 5:41, now the description is moved back to throat and chest pain.

I have to admit, I looked through all of these records. I've lived with this record for a couple years. I still have a hard time finding things through these records.

And the purpose of that record, as Dr. Smedley told you, is for the nurses to maintain the record of the vital signs and the condition of Mr. Maffei for record purposes.

But if there's a symptom or is a problem or a condition that causes those nurses concern, they are required to not just put those symptoms down on this chart, they are required to contact the physician.

And so you may question, Why is Mr. Shaw repeatedly referring to that?

We're trying to understand how the nurses could write "chest pain" and yet not follow protocol.

You saw the protocol or the chest triage guidelines. If there's chest pain, the physician should be notified. You notify the physician if the patient is really having chest pain. You document it on a scale of 1 to 10.

The registration clerk doesn't write any pain in the chest. The triage nurse writes, Throat, slash, chest. Maybe she's not sure.

But certainly at 5:46 a.m., when the nurse writes chest pain 5 out of 10, paragraph five here says, If reported pain is greater than 4 out of 10, the nurse must notify the ER physician of the patient's pain.

Why didn't that happen? Again, at 5:56—or—I'm sorry—5:41 there's throat and chest pain that is a character of 2 out of 10. And still Dr. Smedley is not notified.

So Mr. Sandler and his expert want the doctor—want to hold Dr. Smedley accountable for not seeing the second two reported complaints of pain.

You heard Dr. Smedley. I thought she was rather adamant about it and very believable. As soon as she saw the triage note and saw that there was chest pain, her concern was high, very high.

And Mr. Sandler asked her, had the second report of chest—rather, the third report of chest pain [made] her concern even higher. Dr. Smedley said, "My concern was already high. If I'd seen those two other reports of chest pain, it would not have changed my concern." So that, I submit, is not a relevant consideration in this case that Dr. Smedley didn't see this nurse's note. First of all, they are inconsistent and they are confusing And Dr. Smedley is the physician in this case. She's the one some of you—I read a book about Harry Truman. I was born after, shortly after he was president. But he always said, "The buck stopped here," or the buck—well, the buck stopped with Dr. Smedley. It was her decision as to what to do with this complaint of chest pain.

Even Dr. Shadoff admitted that. Dr. Shadoff admitted that. And you heard from Dr. Shank, it's not atypical for some reason for a nurse to record a complaint that is not told by that patient to the physician when she—when the physician sees the patient. Apparently it happens with more regularity than you and I would normally believe.

And Dr. Shadoff acknowledged that it's his responsibility as the physician to make that decision: Is it real or is it not real?

And Dr. Smedley did that in this case.

Now, Dr. Shank and Dr. Shadoff said occasionally or sometimes they will go approach the nurse about—to try to clear up the dispute. Dr. Smedley—they always do that. Dr. Smedley didn't do that in this case.

But you heard from Dr. Smedley that she was satisfied. She was heightened, her concern heightened because of this chest pain, but she was satisfied after talking to Mr. Maffei that Mr. Maffei didn't have chest pain. He described a throat type of tightening. He put his hand up around his throat like this.

And that may be part of the reason why the nurse was saying—one of the couple of nurses says throat, slash, chest, because he was putting his hand up to his throat.

So the plaintiffs contend also that back pain, there should have been some significance made of Mr. Maffei's back pain.

Back pain is described two places. That's described in the registration note which I just showed you, where there was no chest pain of any kind. And you see these places where it's described, this triage note, and it was described in Dr. Smedley's note.

It's not described at all by the nurses when they go to check Mr. Maffei between triage and the time Dr. Smedley sees Mr. Maffei.

And you heard from Dr. Smedley that she talked with Mr. Maffei, that Mr. Maffei told her he had had chronic or long-standing back pain for a number of years.

Mrs. Maffei acknowledged that Mr. Maffei had had a disc degeneration and had seen a physician earlier in their marriage.

And Dr. Smedley was convinced that this back pain was not something new, not something of sudden onset, but it was something that had been plaguing him for years.

Mrs. Maffei asked Dr. Smedley, can we get an MRI for the back pain? And Dr. Smedley said the back pain for the disc, for the problem in your back, it's from not an urgent situation, it's been long-lasting, that doesn't need to be done tonight.

It's very telling, despite the inaccuracies and inconsistencies of the nursing note, as far as seeing Mr. Maffei between triage and the time Dr. Maffei—Dr. Smedley sees the patient, that the nurses ask the patient, "Do you have any pain?" and he never tells them he's having ongoing back pain.

The chest pain or the term "chest pain" or words "chest pain," when someone walks into the emergency department these days—and it's been that way for a number of years, a long time actually—bells and whistles go off, red flags go up. Chest pain, this can be something really significant—this could be life-threatening.

It doesn't make sense in this case if Mr. Maffei was truly having significant back pain or chest pain that Dr. Smedley was not consulted from 3:39 a.m. until she saw the triage note at 5:55 a.m.

Plaintiffs also want to rely on the EKG that was done. And you saw the EKG was abnormal.

That EKG didn't make a diagnosis of heart attack. In fact, they said there was no heart attack. The only thing the EKG showed was the left side of the heart was slightly enlarged.

That—and there's this testimony that the EKG should have led to the diagnosis of aortic dissection.

Plaintiffs look at the EKG, plaintiffs look at this issue of chest pain, this issue of back pain. But what they don't—what you didn't hear them talk about—and Mr. Sandler showed you my questioning of Dr. Shadoff where Dr. Shadoff denied that showed the accent of his other symptoms was significant.

I do want to go over with you this chart that you've seen at that time that I introduced as Defense Exhibit Number 6.

And you saw also Defense Exhibit Number 9, which shows the heart and the aorta, which is the muscle that's dissected.

It's the largest blood vessel in the body. It comes out of the heart. And after each breath we take, we breathe in oxygen. And the oxygen from the heart, from the right side of the heart pumps the blood down to our lungs, in the lungs. The blood picks up oxygen from our lungs, it comes back into the left side of our heart. And then with each beat of the left side of our heart it sends out oxygenated red blood through this major artery, the aorta.

All of the blood everywhere in the body, that comes from that aorta that when—after it gets oxygen from the lungs.

And the aorta starts out about three, three and a half centimeters across, as Dr. Shank told us, and comes all the way down to here. And there are branches off of that, Dr. Shadoff said.

And Dr. Carey said they believe this dissection had extended and was moving down this way.

Well, if the dissection had extended, it's going to cause symptoms other than just chest pain or even back pain. It's going to cause problems in going up into the brain.

We know in the autopsy the dissection had extended up the carotid to the brain.

If the dissection is extended, the blood is going outside the blood vessel, the normal amount of blood is not getting through to the, to those portions of the body.

So if you take a hose and you are going down the middle of the hose and operate, create a similar dissection, a lot of water or some of that water is going to go off course and it's not going to go to its intended site.

If that was happening while Mr. Maffei was in the emergency department, it would cause stroke-like symptoms. He would feel poorly. He would have extreme anxiety and a sense of impending doom.

If the blood is not going where it should be, that the normal volume of blood—even, say, only three-quarters of the blood is going where that should be, with that quarter of blood not going where it should be, he's—it's going to back up into the lungs. He's going to have shortness of breath. His heart is not going to work appropriately. He's going to have aortic valve insufficiencies. He's going to have severe chest pain that comes and is tearing and stays the entire time.

His skin is going to be pale. He's going to be sweating. He's going to be nauseous and vomiting. And the patient would have extreme pain in his arms and his extremity.

None of those symptoms were present.

You had heard from Dr. Shank. He looked at the autopsy. And the autopsy showed—he even had the page memorized—which I do not—the page number.

But it showed a 10-millimeter-long transfer that was about 12 millimeters before the noncoronary cusp, which as I recall would be about here. Dr. Shank's term, you heard the dissection may have extended a little bit at this point but stopped for whatever reason.

So that the entire time that Mr. Maffei was in the emergency department, he wasn't experiencing the symptoms that would have given a good indication to or a strong clue to Dr. Smedley that he was having an aortic dissection or about to have an extension.

It was only after Mr. Maffei left the emergency department and went home that this dissection extended.

And when it did extend ultimately, it extended all the way down to the common iliac artery, which is down below the waist, it extends up into the neck and it—and the blood backed up to the pericardial sac surrounding the heart.

As Dr. Shank explained, there was 800 milliliters of blood found in this pericardial sac. She had the 12-ounce soda can. It was two and a third of the soda cans of blood that backed up into Mr. Maffei's heart. And Mr. Maffei died very suddenly when that happened.

That was not the presentation that Mr. Maffei had when he was in the emergency department.

I was trying to think of an analogy. It's not a great analogy, but I remember working on snow days with my mother on jigsaw puzzles and putting a puzzle together. And a lot of times with a jigsaw puzzle, you know what you're going to put together because you would see on the front cover what the puzzle looked like.

Dr. Smedley didn't have even the cover of the puzzle. She had maybe one piece of the puzzle. It was only after Mr. Maffei left the emergency department that a number of the other pieces of the puzzle probably would have come into play and could have been appreciated by an emergency room physician.

It was very early in the dissection, if it was even there, for Dr. Smedley or any reasonably competent physician in the emergency department to make this diagnosis. It was only on the basis of hindsight that the plaintiffs conclude that the case could end otherwise.

You also saw in the autopsy report—if I remember where I put it—that the proximal aortic root was dilated to four centimeters in diameter. You heard Dr. Shank tell you that the normal size of the aorta is three to three and a quarter.

So even after that catastrophic dissection, with 800 milliliters or cc's of blood into the pericardiurn, the aorta was only three-quarters to one centimeter larger.

That would not be something, Dr. Shank told you, that would have shown up as a widened mediastinum.

The plaintiffs showed you at one point in time—I believe did show you the difference between a normal x-ray and a widened mediastinum. It was a huge difference, not a difference of about that much, three-quarters of a centimeter.

And the chest x-ray, as everyone acknowledged, would not have made the diagnosis. It would not have been—if it would have been abnormal, as Dr. Shank said, it would be only abnormal because of the enlarged left side of the heart, it would not have been abnormal because it wasn't—wasn't even abnormal, wasn't abnormal at the time of autopsy. Because the aorta was only minimally larger than it would have been before the dissection occurred.

So Dr. Shank showed you what was Defense Exhibit Number 7, showing the normal width of the mediastinum.

Had Dr. Smedley, for whatever reason, ordered, hypothetically, a chest x-ray on March 8th, the dissection was so small and had stopped, it would not have shown up. A enlarged mediastinum would not have been visible on any x-ray.

In fact, I'll jump ahead to that. You may ask yourself what is the second question in this jury verdict sheet.

We submit that to the question: "Do you find that defendant, Angela D. Smedley, M.D., had breached the standard of medical care in her care and treatment of Richard Paul Maffei?," we believe the evidence to that strongly suggests no.

But the second question says, if you do go on: "Do you find that the breach of the standard of care by Dr. Smedley was a proximate cause of the plaintiff's injuries?" The answer to that question has to be no.

Because the plaintiff contends only that Dr. Smedley should have done the chest x-ray.

Had she done the chest x-ray, the mediastinum would have been of a normal width and it would not have produced or suggested any further inquiry or any further testing.

It was only after, as in other cases where the other dissections, where the blood gets into the aorta, the aorta dissects out like an aneurysm, like the old rubber inner tubes where the wall comes out, would that have caused a widened mediastinum. And that was not present in this case, as Dr. Shank told you, even at autopsy.

Now, we heard from Dr. Shadoff. He came here from New Mexico. He's been in Maryland 25 times to testify. He travels, apparently, over a lot of this country. He's been in 20 different states to testify. In any given year he's made as much as $100,000.

But what's really telling in this case is Dr. Shadoff is a cardiologist. We didn't hear from a single emergency room physician as an expert for the plaintiff. That's the specialty that Dr. Smedley practices.

So Dr. Shadoff, who is a cardiologist, he deals only with the heart. And he said—and I'm sure it's true—he did get in the emergency room sometimes to treat patients. But he gets to the emergency room only after, only after the emergency room doctor has examined a patient and sorted out any number of a host of different problems.

He acknowledged, unlike Dr. Smedley, he doesn't have to consider patients with skin problems or bone problems or lung problems or brain problems or eye problems or ear problems or throat problems or any host of other problems. He's focused on the heart and the cardiac condition. And, we acknowledged, [he] has better expertise in that than Dr. Smedley.

But cardiologists aren't health care providers who see patients in the emergency department.

And I submit, as Dr. Shadoff conceded at the end of his testimony, that he would not have ordered a chest x-ray had he been in Dr. Smedley's shoes.

Do you recall when I was asking him questions and asking about the chest pain, and he said, "Mr. Shaw, you can't take these things individually, you have to look at the entire picture?"

And I said, "Let's look at the entire picture."

Let's assume, as Dr. Smedley has testified or will testify at deposition, let's assume based on the medical record that Mr. Maffei didn't have chest pain, that he had low back pain and his low back pain was chronic and not new and was not radiating up into his back. That was caused by his disc problem.

Let's also assume that Mr. Maffei had redness in his throat and [an] earache. Let's also assume that Mr. Maffei had pulses that were equal in both arms.

If you assume those—and I don't know you don't. But assume they're true because that is what Dr. Smedley testified to and that's what the medical record supports from Dr. Smedley, you would agree that there was no reason to order a chest x-ray?

And he said, "I do agree with that."

I said for you to come from New Mexico to Baltimore County, Maryland, and testify against Dr. Smedley, you can't believe what she said, you can't believe the medical record and you can't believe her testimony.

And he denied that.

But that's exactly the case.

I'm not going to go on. You've heard the testimony. We rely on your common sense. I want to thank you very much again for your participation in this process.

At the end Mr. Harlan is going to—I pulled a muscle in my back yesterday and it wasn't bothering me until I just moved. I will stand still.

We ask respectfully you find in Dr. Smedley's favor in this case by voting unanimously "no" on question number one.

Thank you so much.

REBUTTAL ARGUMENT BY THE PLAINTIFF

THE COURT: Mr. Harlan.

MR. HARLAN: Thank you, Your Honor. Members of the jury, good afternoon. I want to address just a couple of points that Mr. Shaw made and suggest to you why the evidence doesn't support them.

With respect to the issue of causation, would the x-ray have been relevant? What would it show?

I believe and I suggest the evidence shows the x-ray would in fact have been abnormal and that because, as you heard the testimony, Mr. Maffei's dissection was indeed or had indeed propagated to his carotid artery and all the way down the descending aorta by virtue of the fact he complained of neck pain, ear pain, and low back pain, which Dr. Smedley testified to was different from the kidney stone pain he had. And it was different, it was something new.

Dr. Shadoff testified that this type of dissection can happen rapidly, that you can have a tear and a dissection can occur, and that indeed you can walk around with something like, say, for 17 hours. But what eventually killed Mr. Maffei was not the dissection itself, but when the aorta finally at the site of the tear burst and blood poured into the pericardium.

Mr. Shaw suggested, based on Dr. Shank's testimony, that Mr. Maffei would have to have a whole host of symptoms if in fact his dissection had extended that far. He showed you the diagram.

I don't know. It's here.

He showed you the diagram that Dr. Shank was talking about yesterday about all of the important arteries and the blood supply, the branches of the aorta.

But what Dr. Shadoff testified to and what is absolutely uncontradicted by virtue of the autopsy report is that absolutely none of these vessels, other than the iliac artery way down here, were compromised or none of these vessels. This dissection spread. It was simply the carotid into the subclavian and all the way down.

That explained the back pain. That explained the throat and neck pain on the left side and the ear pain.

Dr. Shadoff indicated, based on his testimony or his opinion as a cardiologist dealing with cardiac issues, that Mr. Maffei would not be having stroke-like symptoms, would not have had all these conglomerative symptoms that Dr. Shank testified to because none of those other arteries had dissected.

Mr. Shaw pointed out that because of the tear, because it was ten centimeters and it was a small tear—excuse me—one centimeter and because the dilation of the aorta shown on x-ray was only four centimeters, only just a little bit bigger than it normally would have been, that that wouldn't have shown up on x-rays because it's too small to show up.

And [Dr.] Shadoff agrees and plaintiffs agreed that the four centimeters wouldn't have shown up on the x-ray because, as Dr. Shadoff testified to, that is at the aortic root, it's down on the lower, what is the side of the aortic root on autopsy.

And what shows up on x-ray is not the actual initial tear, not the side of the aortic root, but the widening of the aorta when it comes up, because blood has gotten into a small tear.

When the tear is small, as Dr. Shank suggested, but big enough to allow blood to get in, it widens the blood vessel. So it would have shown up on x-ray because it did go up and it did so far as to involve the carotid and did go down and involve the descending aorta.

That is what would have shown up, not the four centimeters.

And the plaintiff never nor did Dr. Shadoff opine that four centimeters was what would show up on x-ray.

There's nothing in the autopsy report—and you'll have an opportunity to look at it in the jury room that gives an indication of how wide the rest of the aorta was. But we know from [the] autopsy it had dissected and we know from Dr. Shadoff's testimony that it had widened. Because that's what happens when blood gets into the vessel.

Why there's nothing mentioned in the autopsy is, as Dr. Shank testified, when it finally ruptured, when it finally burst by the tear 17 hours after Mr. Maffei left the emergency room, all of the blood from the aorta and the blood from the heart poured into the pericardial sac causing death.

So I believe the evidence does show, and I would submit to you that it is true that had an x-ray been taken while Mr. Maffei was in the ER before he left the ER, that you would have an abnormality, a sufficient abnormality to prompt Dr. Smedley to order a CAT scan, whereupon the dissection would have been conclusively diagnosed, Mr. Maffei would have been taken to surgery, he would have survived, and would be with you here today.

Ultimately, there is absolutely no way to know a hundred percent what the actual x-ray would have shown because that simply wasn't taken. Which leads to the ultimate question as Mr. Shaw said: Should an x-ray have been taken?

Dr. Smedley acknowledged that she believes if she had a chest x-ray, if she would have taken a x-ray, the x-ray probably would be irrelevant. We heard that a million times.

Dr. Shank suggested to you, "Well, there's all these signs and symptoms of aortic dissection."

I don't have to put a chart up showing a bunch of signs, all of the signs that you would expect. Because you recall Dr. Shadoff's testimony is that one major sign, the one common sign of aortic dissection in almost every case is chest pain.

Dr. Shank spoke about that too. If you recall from his testimony yesterday, he said migratory chest pain, chest pain that moved around. If you recall from the notes, when Mr. Maffei reports to the triage nurse he had chest pain, chest and throat, 3 out of 10, 3:43 in the morning. Then to a different nurse at about 4:50, if I recall, the pain was 5 out of 10 and was chest radiating to the neck. Then further indication of chest pain.

Then by the time Dr. Smedley saw Mr. Maffei, he was talking about his throat closing up, migratory pain.

So should Dr. Smedley have ordered a chest x-ray based on this? I will suggest you find that she should have.

It was documented in the nurses' notes. Dr. Smedley had a suspicion of it.

But you recall that even before Dr. Smedley set foot in the treatment room, she reviewed an EKG that was normal for heart attack, didn't show signs of myocardial infarction. And she had received and reviewed cardiac enzymes that were negative. And based upon that, she immediately assured—reassured Mrs. Maffei and her husband that he wasn't having a heart attack.

So I would suggest to you that when Mr. Maffei was talking about his throat closing up and pressure in his throat, whether he called it "chest pain" or whether it was in this part of his chest or this part of his chest or this other part, it's cardiac pain, it's an equivalent of a cardiac issue.

And with the clean cardiac enzymes and the clean EKG, Dr. Smedley wasn't focusing on this anymore. She focused on other things and ultimately diagnosed Mr. Maffei with earache, sore throat, allergic reaction, which according to Dr. Shadoff and in Mr. Shaw's final comment about how Dr. Shadoff had agreed with Dr. Smedley's diagnosis, so he says, that in order for Mr. Maffei to have that as a correct diagnosis I think Dr. Shadoff said, "I would have to assume that the throat discomfort and the neck discomfort and the ear discomfort were from a coincidental, totally separate illness, that it was coincidental it affected the same side of the body where we know this dissection occurred.

And I don't believe in coincidence in things like this in medicine."

I would respectfully suggest, ladies and gentlemen, that this is not a case based on hindsight. It's a case based on oversight.

Dr. Smedley didn't appreciate that a throat closing up was a cardiac sign and required that a chest x-ray be taken. Had that been done, we would not be here today. For that reason, I respectfully request when you retire to the jury room you consider all of the evidence and you return a verdict in favor of Ms. Maffei. Thank you.

THE COURT: Thank you, Mr. Harlan.

Appendix V

OPENING STATEMENTS IN THE *OREGON* CASE

OPENING STATEMENT FOR THE PLAINTIFFS

THE COURT: Mr. McCann, you may call your first witness.

MR. McCANN: Actually I was going to give a brief opening statement, your Honor. I think it's necessary in this case because of—

THE COURT: All right. You go ahead and do opening. Then they will respond.

And I will make a point of listening closely when we begin with the testimony, since opening statements are not evidence.
So go ahead.

MR. McCANN: Absolutely. Thank you, your Honor.

First let me introduce my clients who are here today, Dennis Sutton and Kathleen House.

Both of those individuals, your Honor, live in close proximity to the subject property. Mr. Sutton in particular. He is also a director of the Falls Road Community Association, which is also a plaintiff in the case, which you may or may not know, your Honor, a community association whose geographical boundaries encompass this property and which has actually been in existence some fifty years now as a community group.

The property itself, your Honor, is 2.63 acres approximately. It's owned by Baltimore County. It sits at the southwest corner of Shawan Road and Beaver Dam Road. It's occupied presently by the Oregon Grille, a fine restaurant owned and operated by the Defendant, Oregon LLC, which leases the property from Baltimore County.

The property itself is undoubtedly unique. It's part of the federally listed historic district. It's an RC 4 zone, which is resource conservation zone, under the zoning regulations and which is designated for the protection of watersheds in the county. And a tributary actually runs right through this property, your Honor, which is classified as a Use Three Stream, meaning that's a stream for naturally producing trout. The building itself is also a historic building. It's on the Baltimore County Landmarks list of historic buildings.

For all of this, Oregon LLC pays rent to Baltimore County, your Honor, of approximately $415 per month, and has done this for many years.

What is here before you today, your Honor, essentially, is to enforce certain legal restrictions that have been imposed upon Baltimore County and Oregon LLC. And the history of those legal restrictions, your Honor, some are convoluted, but it's my job to make that as simple and clear as possible. And that's what I'll do now.

It really begins in 1994. At that time the building which is now the Oregon Grille was a dilapidated old general store that had been in existence since the mid 1800's.

Before Oregon had, the grill had even been constructed, before it even leased the property, your Honor, Baltimore County on behalf of Oregon LLC filed petitions with the zoning commissioner in Baltimore County. And these petitions, among other things, sought to convert this historic building into a restaurant and also sought a ruling from the zoning commissioner that the County, as the petitioner, was exempt from the zoning regulations and other laws as it relates to this building because it is the County.

In June of 1994, deputy zoning commissioner Timothy Kotroco, who is now the head of the Department of Permits and Development Management, and who will testify in this case, your Honor, he ruled as zoning commissioner, number one, that this building could be converted as a restaurant, but, number two, the County was not absolved the responsibility of complying with the zoning regulations by virtue of the fact that they owned the property, but rather since this property was going to be used by a private corporation, a private individual, it should and would be subject to the zoning regulations.

However, in order to insure that property which, after all, is a part of the Oregon Ridge park, your Honor, was kept small scale, low key, Mr. Kotroco imposed certain restrictions on improvements that he gave.

Among those are part two of the five legal restrictions that at the end of the day we'll be asking to your Honor rule on. The first two of these five was in Mr. Kotroco's ruling in June of 1994. Number one, Mr. Kotroco held that Oregon LLC is prohibited from, in essence, any catering, no hosting of weddings, outdoor events at this restaurant and, number two, no tents, canopies, or similar overhead coverings on the outside rear patio portion of the restaurant. Mr. Kotroco allowed table umbrellas but not tents, canopies, or similar overhead coverings.

Both parties in that zoning case, your Honor, appealed to the Board of Appeals, which is the next level of administrative appeal. The parties being the community and the County.

On appeal while specifically pending, the parties actually entered into a agreement, a restrictive covenant agreement, which will be in evidence, came to an agreement, and the Board accommodated that agreement and incorporated the terms of that agreement between the parties into its order it entered in February of 1995.

In the Board of Appeals' order in February 1995, the Board imposed the restrictions of, again, one, no catering, two, no tents or similar overhead coverings, and then a new one, your Honor, the parties had agreed upon, and that is that the parking area at the restaurant, a large parking area, would remain a nonpaved surface such as stone or a similar permeable surface unless otherwise required by law.

And importantly, your Honor, neither—none of the parties appealed that Board decision back in 1995.

The next step of things, your Honor, occurred in 1996 where after the County undertook responsibility of filing this petition and see it through the end of the Board of Appeals' order, the County eventually entered a lease agreement with Oregon LLC and it—in March of 1996. They entered a specifically, both an assignment of the previous lease that the store, the general store had, and also what is called a supplemental lease agreement.

And in that supplemental lease agreement, your Honor, the parties agreed that the County and Oregon LLC to impose the same restrictions that were imposed by Mr. Kotroco and the Board of Appeals, namely, what I'll refer to as restrictions one, two and three, the no hosting of parties or catering, two, no tents or canopies, and, three, that the parking area would remain nonpaved unless as required by law.

Fast forward, your Honor, to 2004, when Oregon LLC, this time on their own behalf—the County was not a party to those petitions—this seven years after the lease agreement and the Board of Appeals' order, Oregon LLC sought to eradicate certain restrictions in those orders and in the, in the lease agreement and expand the parking lot into an additional .47 acres located on the west side of the property and allow fifty-five additional spaces.

The Board of Appeals, your Honor, in July 2004 denied what it called the second bite of the apple and chastised the—

MR. SANDLER: Object, your Honor. This is not evidence that is going to be proven.

THE COURT: What he says—

MR. SANDLER: It's argument.

THE COURT:—you know, obviously it's not evidence. It's something that he has some desire to say. We are just trying to get through it as quickly as we can.

The objection is overruled.

MR. McCANN: Thank you, your Honor.
The Board denied the relief sought by Oregon LLC after a five-day hearing. And it did characterize the petition filed by Oregon LLC as a

second bite of the apple to do exactly what it agreed not to do back in 1995, and that those petitions were barred by the doctrine of res judicata.

With respect to the parking lot, your Honor, the Board went a step further in 2004 and denied Oregon's request to resurface this additional part of the parking lot, this .47 acre, and denied its request to have fifty-five additional parking spaces on the grounds that there is a provision in the zoning regulations, your Honor, that requires in the RC 4 zone only ten percent of any lot can be covered with an impervious surface. And the Board found that this additional parking area, in fact, the existing parking area, had already well exceeded that ten percent limit.

So that's the fifth restriction, your Honor. Just sort of a recap.

And I'm sorry if I'm being repetitive. But the five restrictions we seek to enforce are no catering or outdoor events and, summarizing them, no tents, canopies or similar overhead coverings. The parking lot shall remain unpaved, ninety-four parking spaces and no more. And, lastly, this ten percent limitation on the amount of impervious surface. Those are the five restrictions, your Honor, that I think you'll find could not be any clearer.

But what has happened since July 2004 is remarkable to say the least.

In November 2006, two years later, without notice to the public, without putting a bid out to any, to contractors, the County hired a contractor to pave the parking lot. Not only pave what existed but to pave more of it with an impervious blacktop surface that we contend was in direct violation of the Board's order, the supplemental lease agreement, and the zoning regulations, specifically the ten percent impervious surface limitations.

Now, undoubtedly, your Honor, the County and Oregon LLC will point the finger at each other—think they have already done that in this case. Oregon will say, The County made us do it. The County will say, we had to do it because the ADA, Americans with Disabilities Act, required us to do it.

We believe, your Honor, the evidence will show that the paving of this parking lot was not required by the ADA and that in fact was a joint effort by the County and Oregon LLC to get around what the law provided in the form of the Board's order, its own lease agreement, and the zoning regulations. Not only that, your Honor, but aside from the parking, the paving of the parking lot, the paving of the parking lot far exceeds the ninety-four spots that the Board clearly permitted.

We will have testimony, your Honor, that there are at least 138 parking spaces today as a result of the paving that took place back in 2006.

In addition, in violation of the restriction limiting the outdoor coverings to table umbrellas, what they have installed on the rear patio of the restaurant are large overhead permanent canopies covering multiple tables on the rear patio.

And then lastly, by virtue of the increased paving on the parking lot, the ten percent limitation that the Board found had already been violated is even more so in violation of the zoning regulations today.

I was going to give you a little bit of procedural background, but it sounds like you're up-to-date on that, your Honor, in terms of the counts we filed and Judge Cox's ruling. And with that I'll sit down.

Thank you.

THE COURT: All right. Who wants to go next?

Opening Statement for Oregon, LLC

MR. SANDLER: May it please the Court.

As you know, I'm Paul Sandler. I represent Oregon Grille. And in these brief remarks I'm going to present to the Court what I intend to prove in this case.

And first I'm going to prove to you that this case should not be in this Court because the Plaintiff did not exhaust their administrative remedies.

I will call a witness as an expert in zoning that will testify that there's a clear remedy administratively available to the Plaintiffs, which is Baltimore County zoning regulation 500.7.

What does that say? That says—I'll summarize it, neighbors have complaints about one another in terms of use of the property, they have a remedy, the zoning commissioner. And they can petition, not just write a letter but to have a petition and hearing.

Why is that significant? I'll prove to you in the case that under the declaratory judgment act statutory Courts and Judicial Proceedings Article 3–409, that if there is available remedy for an aggrieved party that the court is prohibited from issuing a declaratory judgment. It's a axiomatic rule. That failure to exhaust remedies is not only a glaring defect that I will prove, but it also has an approved implication as to how this matter could be resolved.

So that's the first major point. Although because we call testimony from witnesses, it may not be the first point of testimony.

We will also prove that the Oregon Grille Limited, the LLC, who is represented by Ted Bauer, who I introduced to your Honor, received a command from the landlord to pay for the County repaving of the parking lot. And under the order that Mr. McCann—and he did say this, and I want to just emphasize this. A key aspect of this case is this repaving of the parking lot. But the parking lot is not prohibited from being repaved. It's only if—it has to be according to provision in a certain condition unless otherwise required by law.

And I'm going to prove to you the County also—that there was a necessity for the landlord to take action to solve a glaring problem with the parking lot. The parking lot, as you'll hear evidence, was in deplorable condition, stone and sand that were a hazard to the guests, particularly to guests that are handicapped. There were rocks, ruts, there were potholes. The winter it couldn't be cleaned or shoveled because—or plowed because of the nature of the parking lot. It was a danger, a hazard, a danger, and people complained, people tripped, people were upset.

The County as the landlord as well as the tenant had responsibility under law, it's not just the ADA that required, I will prove to you, the parking lot to be repaved but, your Honor, under existing laws, premises liability law is another example of what was required to maintain safety.

In essence, you will conclude at the end of the case that the Plaintiff really wants to set back progress by fifty years. In other words, no longer is it desirable to have a safe, sound, attractive looking parking lot, but rather unpaved. For what? So people can break their necks or so that a small business can't thrive?

I will also prove to you that in terms of while the rest of the world is starving and they're almost at war, this Court is now going to have to hear evidence from an expert that an umbrella is an umbrella, because the Plaintiffs are upset about that.

I'll prove to you they have no personal standing to even make these claims. It becomes, as I'll prove to you, beyond reason.

The other point that I will prove to you is that Mr. Bauer and the restaurant are the wrong party to be named in this case. It was the County, the landlord. And I'll put, you'll see, letters to Mr. Bauer that say, You must do that or else. And he did that.

You will also hear testimony that clearly will point out from an expert that the repaving, the only intent of having a pervious parking lot was to be courteous and fair to the environment. Because water would essentially seep through and not run off. But you'll hear testimony from the experts that have examined this parking lot that will satisfy you that the repaving has done no damage to the environment. There is a storm runoff system and there is absolutely no difference in terms of the effect of the environment as a result of the paving. And that will be significant.

You will also hear that in terms of the number of parking spaces that the County law requires -we'll have experts on this—County law requires 145 spaces. The prior exceptions allowed the restaurant to use less spaces because they didn't need those spaces. But now the County apparently wanted to have parking spaces properly lined and complying with the law.

You will hear testimony that the requirement of the 145 spaces is satisfied, appropriate, and in order for this particular case.

You will also hear testimony that the ADA requires this parking lot to have been upgraded to the point where it is.

So, in conclusion, you will find, first, that the proper forum for this case is the zoning commissioner. You will also conclude, based on the testimony, that under existing law, premises liability, ADA, local, state laws, that it was very much within reason and at the discretion of the landlord to order the tenant to pay for the repairs because that was the obligation under the lease.

You'll also hear testimony that if you were to declare that the regulations or the ordinances were not complied with, that there is no remedy that is presented in this case for you to exercise any affirmative granting of relief because the mandamus claims were denied.

And under the declaratory judgment act, if there is a declaration, there should be a separate count for particular relief, and that would be equitable relief. And we argue that comes in another time, so discretionary reasons—why even if you make a declaration you should not exercise discretion to require certainly Mr. Bauer to repave the lot.

We'll have testimony that will show you and demonstrate to you undertaking that would be a product of close to half a million dollars. And the small business could not afford that. It would be totally draining on them to make such a finding, I suggest.

So that's the sum and substance, your Honor, of what this case is about. And I would look forward to presenting the evidence at the appropriate time.

OPENING STATEMENT FOR BALTIMORE COUNTY

THE COURT: All right. Mr. Nolan.

MR. NOLAN: Your Honor, I intend to call four witnesses. I think Mr. McCann is going to call three of them in his case.

The first is Mr. Robert Barrett, who is the Director of Baltimore County Department of Recreation and Parks. He was the individual who's charged with the responsibility of overseeing the parks and including Oregon, the property on which Oregon Grille sits. And he had received information that there were problems with the parking lot, potential danger to customers because of the potholes, and not ADA compliance.

He contacted Mr. Timothy Kotroco, who is here in the courtroom sitting next to Mr. Barrett on the right, the Director of the Department of Permits and Development Management.

Mr. Kotroco contacted Hunter Rowe, who is the individual in the black shirt to our left. And he has experience and he's on the Commission for Disabilities. He went on and he conducts an inspection. He reported back to Mr. Kotroco and reported back to Mr. Barrett, and he said there were safety issues with respect to the customers using the parking lot and the parking lot is not compliant with ADA.

Mr. Barrett in turn sent a letter to Mr. Bauer, there are problems, your Honor, under the triple net lease, we must remedy them at your own expense, pave the parking lot.

Mr. Bauer then, Mr. Bauer didn't know who to get as a paver apparently. Mr. Barrett knew Mr. Cowman, who is in Reisterstown. Mr. Cowman's firm paved the parking lot and Mr. Bauer paid $85,000 for that paving.

This was all done because the law, as Mr. Sandler indicated, says that: Number one, the ADA preempts anything else under state law and you must be compliant with it; number two, the law of premises liability says if you're the landlord and you are having people come on your property and invitees and someone falls in a pothole, breaks their leg, you have liability. So that what is required is compel Mr. Barrett to take the action that he did.

There will also be testimony from Mr. David Carroll, who was the former head of Maryland Department of Environment and the former head of Baltimore County Department of Environmental Protection and Resource Management, who will testify that really there is no harm here because under state law the crushed stone surface that was allowed as an exception to the bituminous paving way back before the Deputy Zoning Commissioner and Board of Appeals is not a surface that is impervious and, therefore, the surface was impervious from the time it was first installed, and paving it asphalt has made absolutely no change and has had no effect on the environment. Mr. Carroll will say that in fact the crushed stone surface that was on that lot is worse for the environment and the asphalt paving is better.

And that would be the testimony, your Honor. don't know how it's going to play out because Mr. McCann is going to call these witnesses. I'll just simply cross-examine them and probably not have to call three of them in my case.

Thank you, your Honor.

Appendix VI

CLOSING ARGUMENTS IN THE *OREGON* CASE

CLOSING ARGUMENT FOR THE PLAINTIFFS

MR. McCANN: Your Honor, in my opening statement what I said to you was that in this case the Defendants would point the finger at each other. And I think, your Honor, that its fair to say that's exactly what happened.

What the County witnesses have told this Court is that they did not select or hire Mr. Cowman, they did not contract with him, in fact, they never saw his invoice which constitutes effectively the contract in this case. They never received any plans and specifications. They were not there on site when the paving was performed. They did not direct Mr. Cowman how much or where the paving was to be.

Oregon, for its part—

THE COURT: But the County says, We required the paving, we didn't hire the paver but we required the paving. That's what the County says.

MR. McCANN: I understand—

THE COURT: Required, right.

MR. McCANN:—they say that. That's what they say.

THE COURT: Right. As the landlord, we require you to do this.

Is there any contention that the County has to issue an order to tell a tenant what to do with a property?

MR. McCANN: Well—

THE COURT: Can't a landlord tell a tenant by letter, You must do this?

MR. McCANN: My point is beyond that, your Honor, is that the County, again, either by active participation or by active omission, was complicit in this.

THE COURT: Complicit. They ordered it.

MR. McCANN: Ordered or and turned their head.

They did not—the alleged reason—and I'll get to the ADA in a moment. If the alleged reason for paving it was the ADA, they did nothing, nothing to insure that that was—that ADA problem, if there was one, was fixed. They did nothing to insure that the liability problem, if there was one, was fixed.
They—at the moment, your Honor—

THE COURT: What do you mean they did nothing to insure that the ADA problem was fixed?

Apparently they sent Mr. Rowe out and he looked at it and said it's fixed.

MR. McCANN: Well, I agree with your Honor. But—

THE COURT: Nobody looked at the ADA. But Mr. Rowe—I mean, Mr. Barrett didn't look at it. But he and Mr. Kotroco rely on Mr. Rowe.

MR. McCANN: I was speaking more specifically to what the ADA does or does not require and what the County did. I think it's clear -

THE COURT: I don't think the ADA required that whole parking lot to be paved.

MR. McCANN: I agree with you completely, your Honor. In fact, I think it sounds like you looked at the regulations.

Not only does in not require paving of the parking lot, it requires—it doesn't even require paving of the four parking spaces. All it requires is an accessible route that is not paved but is clean surface, you know, those things that are mentioned in the regulations. That accessible route is a defined term in the regulations. It's defined as an unobstructed path—which is exactly what this path is—from the parking lot to the restaurant. So not one foot of the parking lot should have been paved under any interpretation of ADA, your Honor.

And just think about it as a matter of common sense. Why would you need to pave the four corners, the middle, the closest corners of the parking lot for a person in a wheelchair? Why do you need to do that when you have handicapped spaces?

If more handicapped spaces are needed, that's one thing. But the law only requires four. That is what was provided.

So Mr. Barrett and Mr. Kotroco were truthful, your Honor, about what—they relied upon Mr. Rowe and Mr. Rowe exclusively. Mr. Kotroco called him, That's my go-to guy, that that's who they send these type of things to. They relied entirely on his memo.

And I think if you look at his memorandum, your Honor, which is in evidence, you'll find that—

THE COURT: Where does it say that anybody needs to pave this parking lot? It doesn't say that.

MR. McCANN: Correct.

THE COURT: I understand.

MR. McCANN: Correct.

THE COURT: But I guess it seems to me that the obstacle the Plaintiffs face here is that according to the Board of Appeals' opinion, your Exhibit 16, this parking lot—maybe not the whole thing that got paved in '06, but it did have bituminous concrete in the past and one other— Mr. Hoffman was arguing that it had tar and chip—which is consistent with Mr. Sutton's testimony—and a stone base and macadam.

So it has been paved before, not to this extent. But clearly at least in '04 there had been—some sort of paving existed.

The requirement that's imposed by the Board's order, the supplemental lease agreement here is that it be nonpaved surface and that it be permeable.

If your Honor is suggesting—

THE COURT: But the Board of Appeals is saying in '04 that this bituminous concrete, which is what's there, is impervious, and this tar and chip stone base, macadam, that's impervious. They're saying italready has an impervious surface.

MR. McCANN: Absolutely. And the Board expressed concern about it.

But to me, your Honor—and, you know, we may disagree on this—it sounds like we do—but I see that testimony, even Mr. Carroll's testimony, as completely irrelevant. It really is.

What difference does it make? Let's assume—and there is a disputed fact. Let's assume it was paved the way it was today back in 2006. All that tells your Honor is that they violated back then, they violated every day since then, and still violated today.

THE COURT: Wait a minute.

It was in violation, you're saying, in '04? Before they ever paved in '06 it was in violation?

MR. McCANN: I'm not saying that, your Honor. I'm speaking hypothetically.

I'm saying let's assume it was. All that tells us is that they violated the orders the whole time, they violated the lease agreement the whole time. You know, that two wrongs cause five hundred wrongs for every day past. But two wrongs don't make a right.

I don't understand Mr. Carroll's testimony at all, your Honor, it's relevance.

The bottom line is he admitted in cross-examination, and your Honor I think has agreed, that there's no dispute in this case that that parking lot is presently paved, it's paved in violation of the supplemental lease agreement and the Board's order.

What's ironic, your Honor—and there's a lot of irony in this case. But in the Defendants' summary judgment papers, their story was that the County went beyond what the ADA required and paved the whole thing. That was it. That's their big story. This is all discretionary, they asked Judge Cox for summary judgment on that basis. What the evidence is actually told—number one, your Honor, my point I made below and my point again is that's a implicit concession that the ADA does not require the entire parking lot.

Not only that, but there's no evidence of any, of such decision ever being made, I mean, whether it's discretionary or nondiscretionary, whatever you want to call it, administerial. I call it administerial. But there's no evidence of any decision.

The County did not make the determination as to what part of the parking lot should or should not be paved. At most, what Mr. Rowe found was that this parking lot needed, the accessible route needed to be fixed and these four parking spaces must be provided.

The County wasn't involved in the paving anyway, as your Honor already pointed out, wasn't there, didn't contract with Cowman, didn't tell him where to pave. So I find all of that, the evidence has not born that out at all, your Honor, that there even was a decision that the County could call discretionary. And even if we had some evidence—

THE COURT: The discretionary decision is telling the Oregon Grille to pave it. That's the decision.

MR. McCANN: You're correct.

That's where I was headed exactly next, your Honor.

If there ever was an arbitrary or a decision that was unfounded, a decision that was unfounded by a County official, there is no basis for the entire parking lot to be paved. And that's what was done.

There was no basis under the ADA for them to require it. There was no basis—and I think your Honor has already hinted at this—for tort liability fears or accident fears rather. There's been no accidents, there's been no injuries, there's been no lawsuits.

THE COURT: Well, they don't have to wait for an injury or an accident or a lawsuit to be concerned about liability.

MR. McCANN: That is true.

THE COURT: What I said is that you can fill in your potholes if you're worried about it. Worrying about people slipping and falling doesn't mean you have to pave.

MR. McCANN: Correct, your Honor.

But what they did do, what they did do in this case was they waited for an accident to happen. They waited for March 2006, when Mr. Rowe apparently told them to do something about it, and November 2006.

If the tort liability was really such a concern, why didn't they do something about it early? There's not a shred of evidence of the County doing anything before it left it up to Mr. Bauer to take care of.

If it was so important—in fact, I think what Mr. Rowe said is that there is a thing called a priority matrix in Baltimore County that prioritizes what government property should or should not be taken care of first.

This property wasn't even in the priority matrix, according to him. We also have no evidence, your Honor, of any remedial measures, no filling in the potholes between

March of 2006 and November of 2006.

So what I'd like to—the chart, I think, your Honor, is helpful. But— that's Exhibit 39. Because I think it identifies the source of the legal restrictions.

Beginning first with the paving. I think it is undisputed, as a matter of fact, that the parking lot was paved in violation of things that I've identified in this chart. I think it's undisputed as well—

THE COURT: But I hear you saying that the landlord directs the tenant that the parking—in the supplemental lease agreement the landlord says the parking area shall be nonpaved. And then the landlord says to the tenant, Go pave it.

So, I'm not sure when the landlord changes its mind about what it required, that that is a restriction.

It certainly is a restriction on Oregon Grille. Oregon Grille could not make that decision by itself. Baltimore County is the landlord which had said you may not pave and then changed its mind in 2006 and said you must pave.

MR. McCANN: The problem with that, your Honor, there's no evidence that they changed their mind at all. In fact, what Mr. Barrett said, Mr. Barrett wasn't even aware there was a Board of Appeals order, wasn't aware there was a restriction in the lease agreement—

THE COURT: Mr. Barrett did not look at any of that.

MR. McCANN: So they made no decision again, is my point. There's no evidence of any decision being made by the County, Listen, this would be better off if it was paved for whatever reason.

I think that the reasons that were proffered were illegitimate. The ADA, there's not any evidence. And tort liability. There's not even any evidence of a decision.

So—plus, your Honor, I don't think—and I hope the ruling of this Court is not that the County on any day it wants can violate a provision in its own lease because it wants to. And I just can't imagine that's the case.

These are agreements. They mean something.

Ultimately they are entered into for the public benefit. That is what the County is here for.

So I don't think that the County, without amending the lease somehow, can do what it did. And even if it amended the lease, the Board of Appeals' order still stands. And that should—is separately enforceable on the issue of the pavement.

On the other issue of ninety-four parking spaces, again, your Honor I do not believe there's a dispute that there are more than ninety-four parking spaces presently in this parking lot.

Mrs. House, her testimony is uncontradicted. She counted them. She said there's at least 138. We have an aerial in evidence which your Honor can certainly look at. You may need that magnifying glass. That's Exhibit 27. You can literally count the spots from the aerial post-paving and determine that there's way more than ninety-four spots.

By the way, there is no reason, there's been no evidence offered as to why the County let more than ninety-four spots be paved. They haven't even offered an ADA or tort liability reason for that.

There's been no reason whatsoever. In fact, I think that the state of the evidence is that Mr. Cowman made a mistake and paved too much, that he paved beyond what should have been accounts for that difference in spaces.

I doubt it. But that's what the state of evidence is.

On the "canopy versus umbrella" issue, your Honor, I won't say a lot about that other than to point out that as I think I did in cross-examination, that we are talking about table umbrellas. That is the term used. Not umbrellas, table umbrellas.

And we all know that table umbrellas—we probably all have them around our house on our deck. It's an umbrella that sets above the table and provides shade and protection to those seated at that table.

THE COURT: This language "table umbrellas" is not on Plaintiffs Exhibit 39. You just have this "no tented canopies or similar overhead covering."

MR. McCANN: Yeah. I have identifying legal restrictions. That a permissive—that language—and we don't dispute that, your Honor. But that language was added after the restrictive language that I've identified on this chart.

That was my purpose in preparing this chart.

THE COURT: And what document?

MR. McCANN: It's in wherever that language appears. "No tents, canopies or similar overhead coverings" your Honor, is—

THE COURT: You mean the supplemental lease agreement?

MR. McCANN: I believe it is, your Honor. I believe it is. And I can confirm that.

THE COURT: Supplemental lease agreement, Plaintiffs Exhibit 12, that I have, somebody's highlighted it. Not me. And it does not have "umbrellas" language.

MR. McCANN: What it does, your Honor, if you recall, the supplemental lease agreement, which is Plaintiffs Exhibit 12—and it's stamped as Exhibit A of the Zoning Commissioner's decision and that's part of our exhibits.

If you will, the Zoning Commissioner's decision—

THE COURT: Exhibit 6?

MR. McCANN: Exhibit 12 of Plaintiffs.

THE COURT: Zoning Commissioner's Exhibit 6.

MR. McCANN: It is. But the supplemental lease agreement, it is attached—

THE COURT: Oh, okay. You're saying it's attached.

MR. McCANN: It's in that language. It's page 12 of the attached Exhibit A which is the order of the Zoning Commissioner, which is why I prepared the chart. Because I agree with your Honor, it's—

THE COURT: It says, Petitioners shall be permitted to have table umbrellas—

MR. McCANN: Correct.

THE COURT:—on the patio.

MR. McCANN: Correct.

THE COURT: It doesn't say on the tables. All right.

MR. McCANN: Just a couple more points about the "canopies versus umbrella" issues, your Honor. The photographs sufficiently show there are only six of these, not one for every table. There are multiple tables. They are large, obviously. They are permanent structures. They're electrical, they have lighting. And they were installed with cranes.

How many table umbrellas that you're aware of are installed with cranes? According to the testimony of Mr. Sutton.

The other thing, if you look at the invoice that Defendant submitted, they call these structures "umbrellas." I don't think that means much.

But what I would like to do, I think the invoice, your Honor—those invoices reflect that the so-called umbrellas are capable of being interconnected. If you look at the photographs, they are essentially a single tent or canopy. think collectively these six large structures collectively violate the letter if not the spirit of the Board's order, the Board's order in the supplemental lease agreement.

And recall, your Honor, the plan that was approved which is in evidence—I think it's 11-A. It's the plan that showed the ninety-four parking spaces, shows the extent of the leased area.

There's been no reason offered why that plan has not been followed today. In fact, I think what Mr. Sutton's talking about is how this plan has been thrown out of the window and the parking lot has over the years since 1991 been increasingly expanded to the point where it is today, paved at least to its western border.

These pursuits were exhausted, your Honor. I'm not sure if you are exhausted by that argument or not.

THE COURT: You may address it if you say something you've never said before in this hearing.

MR. McCANN: I will say something. I've said it briefly this morning. But I think the key—and I'll limit it to this, because I think, your Honor, you're either going to agree with us or not agree with us.

But 500.7, whether you agree with us or not agree with us, deals with code enforcement, which all deal with enforcement of the zoning regulations. But the key in my mind, your Honor, is the section that was not cited until this morning in Defendant's memorandum. They didn't raise it in any motion for summary judgment, didn't raise it in their motion to dismiss. So this Article 32—I'm sorry—Section 32-3-601, which talks about—it does talk about the Board's order.

THE COURT: You addressed that in your partial response to Defendant's motion for judgment.

MR. McCANN: Correct.

THE COURT: Okay. Do you have anything to add aside from what you submitted this morning?

MR. McCANN: Only to emphasize if I could, your Honor, that 32.3–607 provides for the proceeding for which we're here today, that is, an action by any person whose property is affected by any violation, including abutting and adjacent property owners, whether specially damaged or not, may maintain a action in an appropriate court.

THE COURT: That's for injunctive proceedings.

MR. McCANN: For reason of injunction. Requiring the return of the property to the extent possible to its condition before the violation. That's exactly what we've asked for in this case, your Honor.

THE COURT: Well, I have only before me, I have only count four, the declaratory judgment.

MR. McCANN: Part of that count is seeking the removal of the paving in this parking lot.

THE COURT: Right. You ask that Oregon remove it.

MR. McCANN: Correct.

THE COURT: All right.

MR. McCANN: Thank you very much, your Honor.

CLOSING ARGUMENT FOR OREGON, LLC

MR. SANDLER: May it please the Court.

I would like to take, if I can, at least five minutes for my closing argument.

THE COURT: All right.

MR. SANDLER: Thank you, your Honor. I represent the Oregon Grille LLC.

And the evidence in this case must be focused in terms of the declaratory judgment act.

It would be my request that the Court adhere to the strict ruling of declaratory judgment. And if there is a declaratory judgment made, that the judgment just be a declaratory judgment and that relief be not granted because there's no proper relief requested.

Under the declaratory judgment act, if there's a particular action that is sought, then that's subject to petition. And then there are issues that relate to whether or not someone should be commanded to do something or not.

The purpose of the declaratory judgment act this stage is for declaration. That's our view. And the fact that someone asks for something and is mixed in with the "Wherefore" clause doesn't mean that that's an injunction.

And your Honor is well familiar with the rules of injunction.

THE COURT: Well, I think I've made it clear, the Plaintiffs in this, in count four, they asked only that with respect to removing the paving that the Oregon Grille do it.

I'm not persuaded there is any basis on which to order the Oregon Grille to remove the paving.

MR. SANDLER: Thank you.

THE COURT: I do not think that the "grant such other and further relief" would extend to something as substantive as a request that the County remove it.

But right now what they have before me is enter an order that Oregon shall remove all the paving.

That's injunctive relief. That is mandamus relief. That is not a declaration. And I don't think that is what the declaratory judgment contemplates.

MR. SANDLER: Yes. That's my point.

THE COURT: The declaratory judgment, all I can do is declare the rights of the parties.

MR. SANDLER: Exactly, your Honor. Now, my next point, in four minutes, is this.

When you look at—and under, I guess, a thread, a thread that runs through courts' decisions and the purpose of upholding the rule of law, we always have to think in terms of what public policy means, not what is going on in the community generally dealing with elections and public officials. That's not what public policy is.

Public policy underlies decisions of courts, particularly (inaudible) at the trial court level. And I'm asking the Court to consider the other aspects of the case. I'm not going to touch on the paving because I'm moving on.

But if what the Plaintiff wants to take a decision that good County officials testified that they make for the benefit of safety and to revert back to the stone age where all that's going on in the neighborhood is certainly contemporaneous with what's going on at the Oregon restaurant.

Now let's talk about the umbrellas. I'm not going to mention anything more than we have an expert, an architect. You have the bill that shows what it was. You have a picture. And you have no testimony that there's a tent.

The only testimony you have from the Plaintiffs is they don't like it, it's big, it's bold, and it shouldn't be there. And they went to all these technical points of how a crane put them in.

It is what it is. And the pictures that we showed you and experts testimony I think you should give credibility to that and rule that the umbrellas are umbrellas.

But I can't spend anymore time on it. I think it's something that your Honor, with experience and judicial appropriateness will make the proper ruling.

In terms of the "exhaustion of remedies" issue, I smiled because I—and this is a compliment to Mr. McCann.

I knew when I put the injunctive proceedings issue as an officer of the Court in that memorandum that something would follow. And indeed it did. Because he wants you to believe in the exhaustion issue that that is his panacea or proves that there's no remedy.

I want to make two comments about that.

First, when the law says "a remedy," it means a remedy. Whether the aggrieved party doesn't like the remedy is irrelevant. Whether the remedy is something that is not as effective, it's irrelevant.

But the second point that I want to make is that this injunctive proceeding is a technical rule that relates to a person whose property is affected by the violation. And that's a term of art.

Because there's an entire procedure that the law enunciates when an aggrieved party makes the complaint. There has to be a hearing. Of course there's a fine of $200, that's a penalty. And everyone knows, and you can take judicial notice, that when there's a fine and the taxpayer doesn't pay, the property can be put up for tax lien auction, there can be other proceedings.

But there is no basis, I respectfully submit, that there's not an avenue for the Plaintiffs to have taken in this case. And there would be a proper procedure for appeal through that process.

So that's the finishing touch that I give on the issue of exhaustion of remedies.

I want to then move on to the other issue dealing with the requirement of paving because of the provision that it's a subdivision. And Mr. Kaplow gave his opinion there's so many acres involved that that particular statute doesn't apply.

Finally with regard to the parking lot, the parking spaces. I tried to point out, and when you look at the opinions of the court, you will see that it wasn't so much an order preventing additional parking, it was the restaurant coming in and saying we'll take less, we don't need as much. And when— that's very clear in the order where the parking—

THE COURT: That was true initially.

MR. SANDLER: Yes.

THE COURT: Then in the later—when they were seeking to have permission to have outdoor events they didn't want more parking then.

MR. SANDLER: They did, they did. But then when that was granted there was no reason to go forward. The testimony was that—

THE COURT: Well, it wasn't granted. It was not granted. They did not get permission to do outdoor events.

MR. SANDLER: That's correct.

THE COURT: So the parking spaces stayed limited.

MR. SANDLER: Correct.

But the parking spaces originally stayed limited as a variance from the standard. And that was the testimony. That's the point in that.

So, in conclusion, I believe that when you look at the testimony of Mr. Bauer through his affidavit dealing with the condition of the parking lot, you listen to the experts, to the opinion of the County officials who inspected, they had legitimate concerns.

And when you think about it, to say that the parking lot should go back to dirt and crusher run is to ignore the business and the needs of a small business, who has eighty-five employees and has vendors, to thrive. This is hurting the business.

And the Court can take judicial notice that in this day and age, for a matter of public policy, for what purpose? What does it accomplish?

Let's assume that you granted this, you said okay, dig it up, County, okay, take away your umbrellas, okay, you can't have parking. For what goal? What purpose? None.

It's contrary to what public policy is all about. It's contrary to the evidence in the case. And it doesn't fit the term of propriety in the legal context. And finally—

THE COURT: Ninety-four parking spaces only.

MR. SANDLER: I beg your pardon?

THE COURT: Ninety-four spaces only, you haven't addressed that.

MR. SANDLER: I addressed the ninety-four parking spaces. You heard testimony that the standard is 145. And that the—the reason it's limited to ninety-four spaces was because it was a variance.

In other words, it's twisted around in this sense. 145 is evidence of what the parking spaces should be. But when the original plans were developing years ago, there was no need for 145, so a request was granted to have less than 145.

And I started to get into that, that you can take judicial notice that the reason parking spaces, the regulations for parking spaces is because in the context of zoning, your Honor, in order to develop or grow in a business or to build a commercial establishment, there must be a certain number of parking spaces for the square footage of a building.

So in this particular context, the number of 145 was what was required for parking spaces. But the restaurant at that time in the stone age, if you will, didn't need 145. So they come in and say, Okay, let us have an excuse that you recognize so we don't have to meet the County requirement. And they got it through.

Then, that's right, they came back, they wanted to expand, and they were beaten back. So there was no need to go from the ninety-four up.

Now it's that way, and there's no testimony as to how it got there or why.

But the point is, the law is 145, and they asked for less and now they comply with the law.

So once again I say, as matter of public policy, it makes no sense when a establishment complies with the regulations, to take away almost half

of the spaces to reduce the number of people that can go to the lot or—
and you can imply or infer from that the safety issues.

Because there was testimony that people were parking on that busy road,
and that's not good. Why should the community or people that attend
that business of the restaurant be jeopardized to that effect?

Someday, somehow, it's not unreasonable to think there could be a
problem, a serious problem as a result of trying to take the restaurant and
reduce it to a difficult place to visit and making it difficult for people to
park or enjoy their dinners and for the employees that work there.

So what can you infer could happen? Okay, employees, you park somewhere else and let these spaces be for guests.

And that has a very deleterious impact on the community. And for
what purpose?

The lot is handsome, neat, dustfree, complying with the rules of the
County, and serves as a very safe, appropriate place for people to park.

So the point that I was going to spend most of my time on, your Honor
has stated that the Court will not impose a burden, if it does impose a burden on anyone, for Oregon Grille LLC to undertake the expense and the
burden economically of chewing up the lot and putting the sawdust—or,
I meant, the crusher run on that property, because truly there's not one
scintilla of evidence, not one scintilla of evidence that this was not done
but for the order of the landlord.

And I think the Court recognizes that it's not just the landlord, it's the
County. And the testimony is clear about that.

So those are the reasons why we think that you should do as follows.
First, declare that the Plaintiffs have not exhausted their remedies under
strict construction of the declaratory judgment act. And the briefs and
memos, I won't get into it.

Second, you should, if you do declare under count four, your declaration should be simply limited to a declaration of the rights of the parties,
as opposed to giving an injunction, a mandatory injunction or an order.
Because that, if it does come, should be a separate proceeding.

And why is that so? I think the declaratory judgment act makes it so
because just because the Court declares the rights, it may not enforce the
rights for other reasons. There may not be a balance of equity in a certain

way. There may be circumstances where the Court exercises discretion because the injunction, if given, would be more deleterious than helpful. There are many reasons.

So that should be the subject of another proceeding. And I hope it's not.

I hope after you declare that Oregon does not have to assume the burden of this repaving, that whatever separate proceeding comes it doesn't involve [Oregon]. Thank you.

CLOSING ARGUMENT FOR BALTIMORE COUNTY

THE COURT: Mr. Nolan.

MR. NOLAN: Thank you, your Honor.

First I want to thank you for taking this case. And I also want to thank you for the obvious effort you've put into understanding the record.

If I understood what you said and if this in fact is going to be your ruling, that Baltimore County will not have to tear up the parking lot and replace it with crusher run because there was no request for that relief, and that there's no other ancillary relief, you would not give that as ancillary relief under the circumstances—

THE COURT: I'm not going to order Baltimore County to tear up the parking lot.

MR. NOLAN: Then I don't need to talk very much longer.

Just to preserve the record, I will incorporate my prior arguments that I made at the conclusion of the Plaintiffs' case.

I only have one comment on the umbrellas. As I said, I think it looks like an umbrella. But I think there was some reference by Mr. McCann to the fact that they are somehow connected. And I don't believe that the evidence supports that. They are not connected.

And I would simply say that I think it's important for the Court to declare in this case that the Plaintiffs have no standing or no right to try to enforce the terms of a lease to which they are not a party.

I think that's a very—the County has a lot of leases. And to think that someone who is not a party to the lease can come along and say, Okay, you have to do this or you have to do that, you didn't do this or you didn't do that, it would be very—it would create a very chaotic situation.

So that would be a declaration that we would request the Court to make if the Court agrees with us.

And, of course, the declaration that the fact that the relief requested in subparagraphs B, C, and D in the Plaintiffs' complaint is not supportable by the evidence, that the County cannot be forced to do something that is, in fact, discretionary as determined by Judge Cox.

And I would even ask the Court to take a look at the section they have cited for their relief. Because I don't really think it supports what they're asking this Court to do.

And with that, I will conclude. And, again, thank you for your attention in the case.

THE COURT: Mr. McCann.

MR. McCANN: Briefly, your Honor.

On the issue of pleading, I would just ask your Honor not simply take a look at the count it is, look at the factual allegations throughout the amended complaint, which clearly went to point the finger to the County and Oregon for failing to do what they were supposed to do, specifically, paragraph eleven, paragraph twelve which says as sort of a summation: Accordingly—and I apologize for reading, your Honor, but only one sentence—Plaintiff brings this action asking the Court to compel Oregon and the County to comply with their plain and unambiguous obligations under the law and under their contract.

And there are allegations like that throughout the complaint, paragraph fifteen included, which I will not read to you.

But I heard Mr. Sandler use the words "strict construction of the acts". And think he knows as well as you know, your Honor, that the declaratory judgment act is not an act that requires strict construction.

THE COURT: The law is clear it's to be construed liberally and in accordance with its remedial purpose.

MR. McCANN: Right. So I will not repeat that law to you.

But the other thing that I think is not entirely accurate and what Defendants have said to the Court, that it's not necessary for us to have no other remedy, that this be our last shot. That is not what the declaratory judgment act says or contemplates.

But I think if you look at all of it—and I know you have that all in front of you. I'm not going to repeat the arguments. But the administrative proceedings that they've been raising willy-nilly throughout this case and raising for the first time this morning—this is the County raising these—don't you think the County should know what procedures we should or should not have followed.

The reason they're raising this last minute this morning, this new section 32, if you look closely at those, your Honor, we believe they do not address the case we have with us today. And even if they did, I can't imagine a case where futility is more appropriate, more relevant, the futility exception is more appropriate.

The issue of 145 spaces, the law is not 145 as Mr. Sandler says. I think you hit the nail on the head when you indicated, your Honor, that they requested more than ninety-four, they were denied more than ninety-four. Any supposition about reasons why Mr. Bauer in his mind wanted less space or more space doesn't matter. But it's clear that the plan called for more. The plan was disapproved, and the law as that stands today is ninety-four parking spaces and no more.

Finally—and Mr. Sandler has repeated this throughout his case—what does all this accomplish? What's the goal? Why should the Court be involved?

He speaks of public policy. Apparently the public policy that Defendants are most concerned with is having handsome parking lots. No mention whatsoever over the reasons why we're here today, that this building is historic, that the property is historic. These limitations were imposed for a reason, to protect the stream, to protect the watershed.

So to simply throw all of those out the window as they do in one fell swoop, that there's no reason to do any of this, I think is inaccurate and just wrong.

So with that, I also thank you, your Honor. This is not an easy case. We appreciate, my clients certainly do. I think it's fair to say that they think they got a fair shot whether we win or lose. And we appreciate that.

INDEX

About the Author

Paul Mark Sandler is a partner in the law firm of Shapiro Sher Guinot & Sandler, P.A., and is an active trial lawyer. He is the author of the first edition of *Anatomy of a Trial* and *Raising the Bar: Practice Tips and Trial Technique for Young Maryland Lawyers*. He is the co-editor of *Appellate Practice for the Maryland Lawyer: State and Federal*, and co-author of *Model Witness Examinations*; *Pattern Examinations of Witnesses for the Maryland Lawyer*; *Pleading Causes of Action for the Maryland Lawyer*; *The Winning Argument*; *12 Secrets of Persuasive Argument*; and, with Grimm and Fax, *Maryland*

Discovery Problems and Solutions. Sandler is a frequent lecturer on trial and appellate practice, founder and former chair of the Litigation Section of the Maryland State Bar Association, and past secretary of the Litigation Section of the American Bar Association. He is a fellow of the American College of Trial Lawyers.